Windows Phone 7 XNA Cookbook

Over 70 recipes for making your own
Windows Phone 7 game

Zheng Yang

BIRMINGHAM - MUMBAI

Windows Phone 7 XNA Cookbook

First published: February 2012

Production Reference: 1090212

Published by Packt Publishing Ltd.
Livery Place
35 Livery Street
Birmingham B3 2PB, UK.

ISBN 978-1-84969-120-8

www.packtpub.com

Cover Image by John M. Quick (john.m.quick@gmail.com)

Credits

Author
Zheng Yang

Reviewers
Ioannis Panagopoulos
Elbert Perez
Gareth Williams

Acquisition Editor
Steven Wilding

Lead Technical Editor
Chris Rodrigues

Technical Editors
Joyslita D'Souza
Arun Nadar
Azharuddin Sheikh

Copy Editor
Laxmi Subramanian

Project Coordinator
Leena Purkait

Proofreader
Bernadette Watkins

Indexer
Monica Ajmera Mehta

Graphics
Manu Joseph
Valentina D'Silva

Production Coordinator
Melwyn D'sa

Cover Work
Melwyn D'sa

About the Author

Zheng Yang is a hands-on Technical Leader with five years combined professional experience providing core development engineering for global Microsoft Consumer-Facing Applications and as an independent Game Developer. He is a dynamic, results-oriented developer with a proven history of providing innovative solutions to complex technical problems. When he was a student, he achieved recognition from Microsoft Research Asia and Microsoft Imagine Cup Team. Zheng Yang has advanced technical knowledge of key development technologies including C#, the .NET framework, C++, Visual Studio, DirectX, and SQL Server. He has solid expertise across the full life cycles of both Software Development and Game Production.

About the Reviewers

Ioannis Panagopoulos is a Computer Engineer with a PhD in Computer Systems Design specializing in software development for commercial as well as scientific applications. Since 2010, he has also been an MVP for Microsoft. He has participated in many software development projects targeting a vast variety of application domains in collaboration with companies and research facilities. He is also offering consulting services regarding software design and implementation in .NET technologies. He has given lectures in higher education in areas including of operating systems software development and hardware design. He is also an invited speaker in several Microsoft development events. His current software development passions are WPF, ASP.NET MVC, the Entity Framework, XNA in WP7 and HTML5. He lives in Athens, Greece.

Elbert Perez is a full-time independent Game Developer working exclusively on Windows Phone using XNA and Silverlight. Elbert has created over 13 games on these frameworks with the majority of them breaking the top 20 downloaded games.

www.PacktPub.com

Support files, eBooks, discount offers, and more

You might want to visit www.PacktPub.com for support files and downloads related to your book.

Did you know that Packt offers eBook versions of every book published, with PDF and ePub files available? You can upgrade to the eBook version at www.PacktPub.com and as a print book customer, you are entitled to a discount on the eBook copy. Get in touch with us at service@packtpub.com for more details.

At www.PacktPub.com, you can also read a collection of free technical articles, sign up for a range of free newsletters, and receive exclusive discounts and offers on Packt books and eBooks.

http://PacktLib.PacktPub.com

Do you need instant solutions to your IT questions? PacktLib is Packt's online digital book library. Here, you can access, read, and search across Packt's entire library of books.

Why Subscribe?

- ▶ Fully searchable across every book published by Packt
- ▶ Copy and paste, print, and bookmark content
- ▶ On demand and accessible via web browser

Free Access for Packt account holders

If you have an account with Packt at www.PacktPub.com, you can use this to access PacktLib today and view nine entirely free books. Simply use your login credentials for immediate access.

This book is dedicated to:

My parents, Decheng Yang and Guangxiu Shen, for giving me the spirit and belief to pursue my dream.

Thanks for always encouraging me to do what I love to do.

Table of Contents

Preface

Windows Phone certainly held the hot spot at the world-class consumer electronics event, the International CES in January 2012. Microsoft CEO Steve Ballmer said, "The past year has really been about the whole push to build what can clearly be the strong third ecosystem in the smartphone market, with a very differentiated point of view."

In fact, Windows Phone has many strong and compelling specialties in mobile markets—People Hub, Live Tiles, Marketplace, and Xbox Live. We believe 2012–2013 will be a remarkable year for Microsoft and Windows Phone.

As a developer, everyone hopes to rock the world by using their creativity. How do we do it? We could write an application, but what kind of application? Games? Why? Well, games are the most dazzling way to grab the attention of, and also to entertain people. Why Windows Phone? Windows Phone provides seamless access to your Xbox Live space and is equipped with handy development tool set to make your game global. How? Read this book!

Windows Phone 7 XNA Cookbook is a unique choice covering everything you need to know to develop games on the Windows Phone. It explains all the core areas of XNA game development for Windows Phone, such as controlling sensors, gestures, and different kinds of cameras. The 2D game development recipes will introduce you to the techniques of sprite animation, texture rendering, and graphical user interface creation. After that, the book moves on to more cutting edge topics, with recipes covering 3D graphic rendering, animation and collision detection, and key methods of improving loading efficiency. As a game development book, you will also find throughout discussions and hands-on examples about performance optimization to make your games run faster. Finally, the book presents all of the steps you need to take to make your games show up in the Marketplace—the world stage of game development. It's your time!

What this book covers

Chapter 1, Jump into Windows Phone Developer Tools and XNA Game Studio 4.0, tells you the background of Windows Phone and how to set up the development environment for building your first Windows Phone game.

Chapter 2, Playing with Windows Phone Touch and Sensors, shows you how to use the basic gestures including tapping, swiping, and dragging. You will also learn the techniques for using the accelerometer.

Chapter 3, Coordinates and View—Your First Step into XNA Game Development on Windows Phone 7, explains how 2D and 3D coordinates work in Windows Phone XNA development and how different types of cameras can be used as view.

Chapter 4, Heads Up Display (HUD)—Your Phone Game User Interface, explains how to work with 2D graphics rendering and demonstrates the essential techniques to make GUI controls, such as buttons, list controls, and so on.

Chapter 5, Content Processing, explains Content Pipeline, which is a very unique technology in XNA. It preprocesses the assets including images, 3D models, audios, and so on; also, you can customize different formats for pre-loading. Content Pipeline accelerates the game asset loading speed and gives you flexibility to define your own content model.

Chapter 6, Entering the Exciting World of 3D Models dives into the mystery 3D world in Windows Phone XNA. You will learn a lot of interesting topics on 3D with examples from model viewing to animation.

Chapter 7, Collision Detection, explains an eternal topic in game development. In this chapter, you will get the core ideas of collision detection for 2D and 3D objects, a little harder but useful, the corresponding examples will make your life easier.

Chapter 8, Embedding Audio in your Game, shows you the methods for adding the audio, music, and sound effects into your game. It also demonstrates how to use the XNA framework to add stereo sound to your game.

Chapter 9, Special Effects, teaches you how to work on the built-in effects such as dual-texture effects and environment mapping. Moreover, you will discover how to render the current screen display onto a texture and use it to make screen transition.

Chapter 10, Performance Optimization—Fast! Faster!, specifically shows you how to make your Windows Phone game run faster. It provides you with hands-on examples and tips you can employ to make sure your game gives the user a seamless experience.

Chapter 11, Launching to the Marketplace, focuses on the process of submitting your application to the Microsoft Marketplace, so that everybody using Windows Phone can download your work. It covers all of the steps required, from preparation to submission.

What you need for this book

▸ Microsoft Visual Studio 2010 Professional or Express

▸ Windows Phone Developer Tools

▸ Microsoft DirectX SDK (June 2010)

Who this book is for

If you are an aspiring programmer with some basic concepts in C# and object-oriented knowledge who wants to create games for Windows Phone, this book is for you. It is also for experienced programmers who want to transfer from Windows or Xbox to the Windows Phone 7 platform. Only basic knowledge of C#, .NET, and Computer Graphics is required.

Conventions

In this book, you will find a number of styles of text that distinguish between different kinds of information. Here are some examples of these styles, and an explanation of their meaning.

Code words in text are shown as follows: "Put the code into the `LoadContent()` method:"

A block of code is set as follows:

```
// Stop the accelerometer if it's active.
if (accelActive)
{
    try
    {
        accelSensor.Stop();
    }
    catch (AccelerometerFailedException e)
    {
        // the accelerometer couldn't be stopped now.
    }
}
```

New terms and **important words** are shown in bold. Words that you see on the screen, in menus or dialog boxes for example, appear in the text like this: "Choose **Visual Studio 2010 Express for Windows Phone**, and the main page for downloading the tool will show up."

 Warnings or important notes appear in a box like this.

 Tips and tricks appear like this.

Reader feedback

Feedback from our readers is always welcome. Let us know what you think about this book—what you liked or may have disliked. Reader feedback is important for us to develop titles that you really get the most out of.

To send us general feedback, simply send an e-mail to feedback@packtpub.com, and mention the book title through the subject of your message.

If there is a topic that you have expertise in and you are interested in either writing or contributing to a book, see our author guide on www.packtpub.com/authors.

Customer support

Now that you are the proud owner of a Packt book, we have a number of things to help you to get the most from your purchase.

Downloading the example code

You can download the example code files for all Packt books you have purchased from your account at http://www.packtpub.com. If you purchased this book elsewhere, you can visit http://www.packtpub.com/support and register to have the files e-mailed directly to you.

Errata

Although we have taken every care to ensure the accuracy of our content, mistakes do happen. If you find a mistake in one of our books—maybe a mistake in the text or the code—we would be grateful if you would report this to us. By doing so, you can save other readers from frustration and help us improve subsequent versions of this book. If you find any errata, please report them by visiting http://www.packtpub.com/support, selecting your book, clicking on the **errata submission form** link, and entering the details of your errata. Once your errata are verified, your submission will be accepted and the errata will be uploaded to our website, or added to any list of existing errata, under the Errata section of that title.

Piracy

Piracy of copyright material on the Internet is an ongoing problem across all media. At Packt, we take the protection of our copyright and licenses very seriously. If you come across any illegal copies of our works, in any form, on the Internet, please provide us with the location address or website name immediately so that we can pursue a remedy.

Please contact us at copyright@packtpub.com with a link to the suspected pirated material.

We appreciate your help in protecting our authors, and our ability to bring you valuable content.

Questions

You can contact us at questions@packtpub.com if you are having a problem with any aspect of the book, and we will do our best to address it.

1

Jump into Windows Phone Developer Tools and XNA Game Studio 4.0

In this chapter, we will cover:

- ▶ Installing Windows Phone Developer Tools
- ▶ Creating your first Windows Phone XNA application
- ▶ Deploying your game on an emulator or device
- ▶ Getting familiar with orientation
- ▶ Using DrawableComponent and GameServices

Introduction

Windows Phone 7 is a new platform from Microsoft. It succeeds the Windows Mobile and combines the UI features of Microsoft Zune. Windows Phone is a consumer-oriented platform while Windows Mobile is more about business. On Windows Phone 7, or the latest release of Mango, you have more flexibility to develop with the hardware using the user design tool Microsoft Expression Blend and Design. Besides the approach to develop regular applications, Windows Phone also provides the capability to make amazing mobile games around Xbox Live based on XNA Game Studio 4.0. Unlike the previous version, XNA 4.0 is included in a tool collection called Windows Phone Developer Tools utilized for producing Windows Phone games. With the tools and Visual Studio 2010, it will be easy to have and employ the Windows

Phone application to the device. As a bonus, if you were a marketing-oriented developer, the App Hub would be an attractive place for promoting your applications and making income. In this chapter, you will discover the most useful and common features of XNA 4.0 for Windows Phone. Even if you are relatively new to Windows Phone 7 and XNA 4.0, this chapter should get you up and running. Can't wait to begin Windows Phone 7? Let's begin.

Installing Windows Phone Developer Tools

Microsoft XNA Game Studio 4.0 is included as part of the Windows Phone Development Tools. It is a set of software tools that can be used by developers to create games for Windows Phone 7, Xbox LIVE Indie Games, and Windows. The entire tool package contains:

- Visual Studio 2010 Express for Windows Phone
- Windows Phone Emulator Resources
- Silverlight 4 Tools For Visual Studio
- XNA Game Studio 4.0
- Microsoft Expression Blend for Windows Phone

Installing the toolset is the first step of your Windows Phone XNA game programming journey. In this recipe, you will learn how to set up the handy programming environment.

How to do it...

The following steps show you how to install the Windows Phone Developer Tools.

Visual Studio 2010 is a required tool for XNA game development. If you do not have it:

1. You can download it from `http://www.microsoft.com/express/downloads/`.
2. Choose **Visual Studio 2010 Express for Windows Phone**, and the main page for downloading the tool will show up. Then follow the on-screen guidance to finish the downloading and installing process.
3. Once web installation begins, your computer must connect to the Internet to completely download the installer.

The following are the steps for installing XNA Game Studio 4.0 with Windows Phone Developer Tools:

1. Navigate to `http://create.msdn.com/en-us/resources/downloads` to download XNA Game Studio 4.0.
2. Click on the link to download XNA Game Studio 4.0 you will see a new download page.
3. Follow the on-screen guidance to finish the downloading and installing process.

Now, all the preliminary work of XNA game development is done.

Creating your first Windows Phone XNA application

After installing the Visual Studio 2010 and Windows Phone Developer Tools, I am sure you cannot wait to begin your first Windows Phone XNA application. In this section, you will start the charming journey, learn about the basic and important code of XNA, and how this code works. It is easy to get started.

How to do it...

1. Once the XNA Game Studio 4.0 is successfully installed, click the top-left menu item **File | New | Project**. The XNA and Windows Phone Game Project Template will show up in the **New Project** window, as shown in the following screenshot:

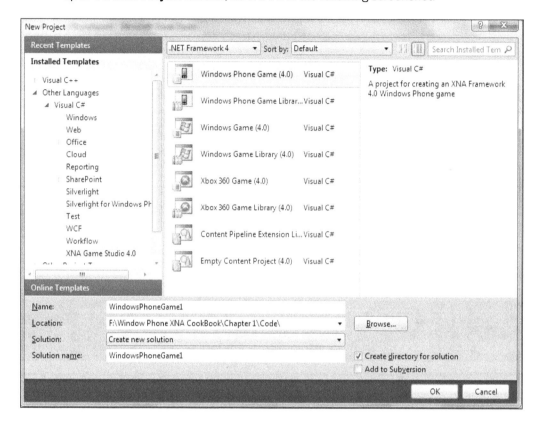

2. In the **New Project** pop-up window, select **Visual C#** from the left-hand side pane, and then choose the **Window Phone Game** project template.

3. Next, give a **Name**, **Location**, and **Solution name** to the project. **Solution name** will be the same as your project name by default.

4. Finally, click **OK** to let Visual Studio 2010 automatically create the Windows Phone Game project for you.

5. The generated Windows Phone Game project **WindowPhoneGame1** automatically has the main game functionalities; the other generated associate project **WindowsPhoneGame1Content** is responsible for the game content:

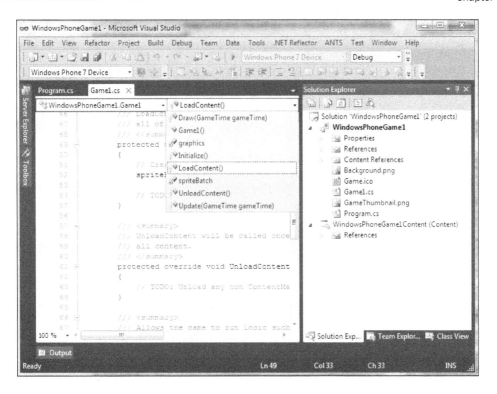

How it works...

The basic methods in `Game1` class residing in `Game1.cs` of your first Windows Phone Game project **WindowsPhoneGame1** are very useful. They are clear and easy to understand according to the method name and comments. This template is your first gift, and you will find new ways here to speed up your development. The complete game skeleton presents several significant methods:

> • `Game1()` constructor method: The constructor, called before the `Initialize` method, is a typical one found in any class and, therefore, has the same meaning used to set default values to required elements. For example, instantiating the graphics device manager, define the game frame rate, and so on.

> • `Initialize()` method: Sets default and preliminary values to your game, queries and initializes user-based information, such as starting positions and frame updating rate.

> • `LoadContent()` method: Loading all game content may include images, sprite sheet, sounds, models, and so on. In XNA game development, all artwork loading should be done in the `LoadContent()` method before the `Update()` and `Draw()` methods.

- ▸ `UnloadContent()` method: Unloads all game content and content managers, a controller of all contents with loading and unloading when the objects used in your game need specific disposing or unloading.

- ▸ `Update()` method: This method is very important when your game is running. It performs ongoing game logic such as calculating current positions, physics, collisions, and states; collecting the input information from various input devices; updating animations. Note that at this stage you only decide upon the current frame to display. Drawing is not performed because all drawing should be done by the `Draw()` method. It updates the camera, refers to the update animation note, plays audios, and so on. The `Update()` method updates the game logic, which will make your game more fun depending on the interaction with the game data, such as player life, experience value, and score.

- ▸ `Draw()` method: As the method name implies, in this method your work is to render all the graphics, including 2D and 3D views, onto the screen to make the game data visible, so that players can experience the real game world.

For the recipes in the following chapters, we will be revising this code many times from different perspectives. When you build the project and run it, you will see an emulator window with a solid blue background by default. Your first XNA Windows Phone Game is done, although it is just a blank screen as shown in the following screenshot. Isn't it easy?

Deploying your game on an emulator or device

In the previous recipe, you completed your first XNA Windows Phone Game. In this recipe, you will learn more details on how you can deploy your Windows Phone application on the emulator or device.

Getting ready

When you build the Windows Phone 7 project, in the **Output** window, you will see the building messages similar to the following screenshot:

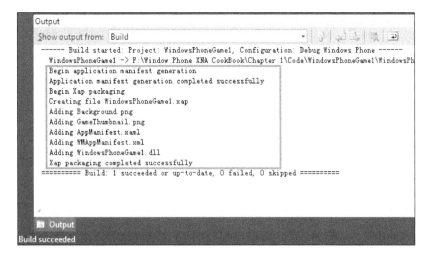

Here, you may be curious about Xap packaging. A `.xap` is a simple file similar to a `.zip` file, renamed to `.xap`. It contains the app and all relevant dependencies. There are a number of possible `.xml` files that could be included inside `.xap`, such as required security access level.

For better understanding, you could change the extension from .xap to `.zip` and use WinZip to extract the `.zip` file. Several necessary information will be presented such as the content directory with `.xnbl` binary files, dependency files with `.dll` extension, configuration xml files, an `xml` file named `AppManifest`, and so on. The xaml file is very important for Windows Phone 7 applications. This file provides the emulator or device with the application start-up information, the entry point, and the dependency.

How to do it...

After project building, the next step is to deploy your Windows Phone 7 XNA application to the device or emulator. The direct method is by using Visual Studio Deploy Options, as shown in the following screenshot:

In the drop-down list, you could choose **Windows Phone 7 Emulator** or **Windows Phone 7 Device**. If you are a member of App Hub, which is free for students and is charged at $99 for regular users, you can successfully deploy to the real device or the emulator. Otherwise, you can choose the emulator as the test platform.

If using an emulator, Visual Studio 2010 will boot the emulator first, and then initialize (this may take a long time if the user's PC does not have hardware virtualization enabled.) The next step is to copy the `.xap` file to the emulator and execute it.

If using the device for the first time, the preparation work is a little complex (I promise this is only once), as follows:

1. The first step is to check if the Zune software is installed on your computer. (If the Zune software has not been installed, you can download it from `http://www.zune.net/en-US/products/software/download/default.htm`).

   Besides this, you need to make sure that your phone has loaded the proper device drivers. At this point, you are now ready to start publishing your custom app to the phone.

2. Next, you will need to click **Start** | **All Programs** | **Windows Phone Developer Tools** | **Windows Phone Developer Registration**. You will see a screen as shown in the following screenshot. You can use the **Windows Live ID** that you linked to. You can also unregister the device.

Wow! All the preparation work is over now. It is now time for the final step, that is deploy. Open **Visual Studio 2010** and choose **Windows Phone 7 Device** in the drop-down list.

[If you deploy the application to your phone device and not the emulator, the phone must be turned on and unlocked (displaying the start/home tiles screen). To debug on the phone you just need to hit Run (**F5**).]

3. Run the application.

4. When you have done this, on your Windows Phone, you will need to slide over to the **Application list** page with a right direction button at the top-right, and search for the application you named before. Touch it and run the application.

Getting familiar with orientation

The orientation for Windows Phone 7 stands for different directions, landscape or portrait. By default, XNA programs for Windows Phone 7 run in landscape mode. This recipe discusses how to transcend those defaults and explores other issues involving screen size and events.

Getting ready

The following two screenshots demonstrate the different modes of Windows Phone 7. The image on the left indicates the landscape mode with a resolution of 800 * 480 and the screenshot to the right shows the portrait mode with a resolution of 480 * 800. By default, XNA for Windows Phone is set up for a landscape orientation. If you prefer designing your game for a portrait display, it's easy to do.

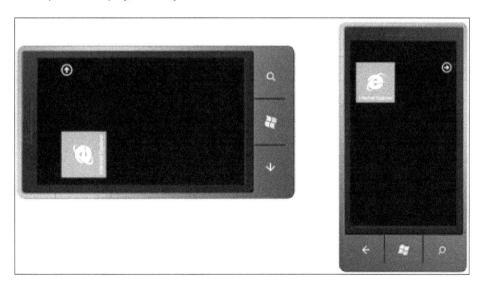

How to do it...

Now, let's create a new Windows Phone Project named **WindowsPhoneOrientation**. Find the class `Game1` in `Game1.cs`. You can also rename the filename and class name to any other name you like:

1. Add the following line in the class field:

   ```
   Texture2D arrows;
   ```

2. Next, find the `Game1()` constructor and insert the following lines:

   ```
   graphics.SupportedOrientations =
       DisplayOrientation.Portrait |
       DisplayOrientation.LandscapeLeft|
       DisplayOrientation.LandscapeRight;

   // Switch to full screen mode
   graphics.IsFullScreen = true;
   ```

Downloading the example code

You can download the example code files for all Packt books you have purchased from your account at `http://www.packtpub.com`. If you purchased this book elsewhere, you can visit `http://www.packtpub.com/support` and register to have the files e-mailed directly to you.

3. Load the following content in the `LoadContent()` method:

   ```
   // Load the arrow content.
   arrows = Content.Load<Texture2D>("Windows Phone Arrow");
   ```

4. In the next step, add the following lines to the `Update()` method:

   ```
   graphics.SupportedOrientations = DisplayOrientation.Portrait |
       DisplayOrientation.LandscapeLeft|
       DisplayOrientation.LandscapeRight;
   ```

5. Find the `Draw()` method and insert the following code:

   ```
   spriteBatch.Begin();

   // Draw the directions texture centered on the screen
   Vector2 position = new Vector2(
       GraphicsDevice.Viewport.Width / 2 - arrows.Width / 2,
       GraphicsDevice.Viewport.Height / 2 - arrows.Height / 2);
   spriteBatch.Draw(arrows, position, Color.White);

   spriteBatch.End();
   ```

6. All done! Build the project and run it in the emulator. Change the orientation by clicking on the change buttons located at the top-right of the emulator. If the application runs well, you will see three different presentations, as shown in the following screenshots:

How it works...

In step 1, `Texture2D` represents the images, `SpriteFont` represents text, showing the different directions.

In step 2, in class constructor, set the `SupportedOrientations` attribute of `GraphicsDeviceManager` (here is `graphics`) to `DisplayOrientation` options: `Portrait`, `LandscapeLeft`, and `LandscapeRight` enables the Windows Phone to adjust the resolution according to the different orientations.

In step 4, you may be curious about the code. Why do we have to set `SupportedOrientation` in a similar way as we have in step 2? The reason is that the responsibility of the `Update()` method is to update the game status, game logic, input, and so on. Here, for Windows Phone Orientation, the `Update()` method needs to listen to the changes in the device orientation. The method should react to any change between `Landscape` or `Portrait` mode. Once the orientation meets the settings of the `DisplayOrientation`, the `GraphicsDeviceManager(graphics)` will apply the change to the default device. Again, when the `Update()` method completes its work in every cycle, by default, the XNA will call the `Draw()` method to render the new face of the game.

In step 5, the snippet provides a way for placing the image or texture in the middle of the screen. Half of the viewport just makes the top-left of the image locate at the center of the screen. We need the center of the image to replace the image top-left point, therefore, we should subtract half of the width and length of the image. Then the `SpriteBatch.Draw()` method renders the image on the Windows Phone screen. Notice that all the position manipulations and sprite drawing methods must be placed between the `SpriteBatch.Begin()` and `SpriteBatch.End()` methods.

Using DrawableComponent and GameServices

In XNA game programming, a lot of built-in or customized objects exist in the game data container. When the quantity increases and it becomes onerous for you to manage, you will need a service to make your XNA programming life easier; this recipe will give you the necessary guidance.

Getting ready

In an XNA application, some parts or objects of your game need to be separately updated or drawn, such as radar, player, or monster. Within your XNA game, you need to create separate defined classes for the substances, then build an instance of one of them, initialize it, update it, and finally, render it to the screen within the `Draw()` method reserved for game loop calling. Hence, you need to define these kind of classes, which have their own `Initialize()`, `Load/UnloadContent()`, `Update()`, and `Draw()` methods, so that you can easily call them in the XNA game loop.

Again, it is better to inherit these classes from `GameComponent`, which promises your classes are added to the Component List, `Game.Component` — a global objects manager in XNA application. It simplifies the management of the game shared objects to the delight of the XNA programmer

Furthermore, if you are sure your separated class has the rendering ability, `DrawableGameComponent` could be the best choice for you because the overridden `Draw()` method will be called automatically from `DrawableGameComponent`.

How to do it...

1. As an example, define a `Radar` class inherited from `DrawableGameComponent`:

```
public class Radar : DrawableGameComponent
{

    . . .
```

```
Rectangle destRec;
Rectangle playerPositionRec;
Vector2 playerVector;
List<Vector2> enemiesPosition;

Texture2D texture;
SpriteBatch spriteBatch;
Texture2D texPlayerPosition;

public Radar(Texture2D texture, Rectangle rectangle,
    SpriteBatch spriteBatch, Game game) : base(game)
{

    // Initialize the radar member variables
    . . .
}

protected override void Draw(GameTime gameTime)
{
    spriteBatch.Draw(texture, destRec, Color.White);
    spriteBatch.Draw(texPlayerPosition, playerVector,
        Color.Red);
    foreach (Vector2 vec in this.enemiesPosition)
    {
        spriteBatch.Draw(texPlayerPosition, vec,
            Color.Yellow);
    }
    base.Draw(gameTime);
}

protected override void Initialize()
{

    // Initialize the device
    . . .
    base.Initialize();
}

protected override void LoadContent()
{

    // Load radar and player texture content
    . . .
    base.LoadContent();
}

protected override void UnloadContent()
{
    base.UnloadContent();
}
```

```
public override void Update(GameTime gameTime)
{
    // Update the player position
    . . .
    base.Update(gameTime);
}
}
```

2. Now, that you have defined your GameComponent, the next step is to insert the Component to the GameComponent list of the Game class. Once added, the overridden method will be called automatically:

```
public Game1()
{

    . . .

    Components.Add(new Radar(this));
}
```

3. Another way is to initiate the instance first and then pass it to the Add() method. The second approach provides the door. Sometimes, you might need to update some public variables of the component. For the Radar class, you can update the player's position:

```
Radar radar;

public Game1()
{

    . . .
    Components.Add(radar);
}
```

4. The Draw() method in the Game class is a very simple ascribe to the GameComponent list. The Draw() method of DrawableComponent belongs to the GameComponent list and will be called automatically. The code snippet is similar to the following code:

```
protected override void Draw(GameTime gameTime)
{
    GraphicsDevice.Clear(Color.CornflowerBlue);

    base.Draw(gameTime);
}
```

How it works...

In step 1, the code presents a brief code snippet of the `Radar` class inherited from `DrawableGameComponet`. So far, your focus is on how to override the `Initialize()`, `Update()`, `LoadContent()`, `UnloadContent()`, and `Draw()` methods.

2

Playing with Windows Phone Touch and Sensors

In this chapter, we will cover:

- ▶ Creating your first touch application/game
- ▶ Taking your touch application to the next level
- ▶ Creating a Touch Directional Pad(D-Pad)
- ▶ Dragging and swiping objects
- ▶ Controlling images with Multi-Touch control
- ▶ Using accelerometer to make a ball move on your phone

Introduction

Input is the essential part of a game; without it, even with the extremely cool graphical effects, it is not a real game. Input gives players the opportunity to interact with the game world and it delights them. You will find Windows Phone 7 games completely different from traditional desktop games, as they do not have a keyboard and a mouse. You might wonder what can we do for input?

The touchscreen and a new amazing piece of hardware, accelerometer, bring you a brand new experience in playing Windows Phone 7 games. By just tapping the touchscreen and moving or twisting your hands, you can play a whole game on a Windows Phone 7. Isn't it fabulous? In this chapter, you will discover how great these features are and learn to use them in your XNA game programming.

Creating your first touch application/game

For Windows Phone 7, touchscreen is the most convenient way of allowing the user to interact with your game. The screen, where all actions and gestures take place, is 800 * 480 for landscape mode and 480 * 800 for portrait mode. Based on the hardware, Windows Phone 7 will give the player a hand to actually touch the game as it unfolds, bringing it to life. In this recipe, you will discover how Windows Phone 7 touchscreen works and see how to get the benefits of using this functionality.

Getting ready

For Windows Phone touchscreen interactions, the most common behavior is **Tap**. When your finger touches the touchscreen, the `tap` event will be triggered. In XNA, the touchscreen input is referred to as a `TouchPanel` class and the method is referred to as `GetState()`. This static class provides the input and gesture information. We will begin with the basic concepts and properties.

The most Important methods for the `TouchPanel` class are: `TouchPanel.GetState()` and `TouchPanel.TryGetPreviousLocation()`.

The GetState() method

The `GetState()` method will return `TouchCollection`, a list-based data structure. The element `TouchLocationState` actually represents the touch tap position. The code for it is as follows:

```
public enum TouchLocationState
{
    Invalid = 0,
    Released = 1,
    Pressed = 2,
    Moved = 3,
}
```

The frequently used state is `TouchLocationState.Pressed`. For a `TouchCollection` object, you can use an integer as the index to look up a special finger and a `TouchLocation`, when `Pressed` or `Released`. If there is no finger touching the screen, `TouchCollection.Count` will be `zero`. When a finger first touches the screen, touch collection contains only one `TouchLocation` object with the `State` set to `Pressed`. Subsequently, if the finger has moved, `TouchLocation.State` will change to `TouchLocationState.Moved`. When the finger is lifted from the screen, `TouchLocation.State` will change to `TouchLocationState.Released`. After that, the `TouchCollection` will be empty if no screen operations take place. The following table is generated when a finger taps the screen:

Frame	Touch Collection ([item1], [item2], ...)
0	*([Id = 1, State = Pressed])*
1	*([Id = 1, State = Released])*
2	*N/A*

The following table is generated when a finger touches the screen, moves across the screen, and is then lifted:

Frame	Touch Collection ([item1], [item2], ...)
0	([Id = 1, State = Pressed])
1	([Id = 1, State = Moved])
2	([Id = 1, State = Moved])
...	([Id = 1, State = Moved])
n	([Id = 1, State = Released])
n + 1	N/A

The previous description is about how one finger can interact with touchscreen, but how about using more fingers? When Multi-Touch happens, fingers will be touching, moving, and lifting from the screen independent of each other. You can track the particular finger using the `Id` Property, where the `Id` will be the same for the Pressed, Moved, and Released State. The following table is generated when two fingers simultaneously touch the screen, move across the screen, and then each finger is lifted individually:

Frame	Touch Collection ([item1], [item2], ...)
0	*([Id = 1, State = Pressed], [Id = 2, State = Pressed])*
1	*([Id = 1, State = Moved], [Id = 2, State = Moved])*
2	*([Id = 1, State = Moved], [Id = 2, State = Moved])*
3	*([Id = 1, State = Released], [Id = 2, State = Moved])*
4	*([Id = 2, State = Moved])*
5	*([Id = 2, State = Released])*
6	*N/A*

Dictionary objects with keys based on ID are very common for getting the designated finger information.

The TryGetPreviousLocation() method

This method allows you to calculate the difference between the positions under the Moved state. If the state is `TouchLocationState.Pressed`, this method will return `false`, and the previous state tried to get will be invalid.

The GetCapabilities() method

This method returns a data structure, `TouchPanelCapabilities`, which provides access to information about the capabilities of the input:

```
public struct TouchPanelCapabilities
{
    public bool IsConnected { get; }
    public int MaximumTouchCount { get; }
}
```

The `IsConnected` attribute indicates the availability of the touch panel for use; it is always true. The `MaximumTouchCount` attribute gets the maximum number of touch locations that can be tracked by the touch pad device; for Windows Phone 7 the number is not less than 4.

Although this was a little theoretical, these materials are very useful for your future Windows Phone XNA game programming. Now, let's begin with an example which is simple, but clear. It will help you understand the main concepts of the XNA Touch Technique.

How to do it...

This application presents a white ball in the center of the landscape mode screen. When your finger taps it, the ball color will change to red:

1. First, you will have to create a new Windows Phone 7 Game Project: go to **File | New Project | Windows Phone Game** and name it `TouchEventTap`. Then, add the following lines in the `TouchTap` class field:

   ```
   Texture2D texRound;
   Rectangle HitRegion;
   bool isSelected = false;
   ```

2. The next step is to insert the code to the `LoadContent()` method:

   ```
   texRound = Content.Load<Texture2D>("Round");
   HitRegion = new Rectangle(400 - texRound.Width / 2, 240 -
       texRound.Height / 2, texRound.Width, texRound.Height);
   ```

3. Create an `UpdateInput()` method. This is the most important method in this example. Your application could actually interact with your fingers with the help of this method:

   ```
   private void UpdateInput()
   {
   ```

```
// Get the touch panel state as a TouchCollection
TouchCollection touches = TouchPanel.GetState();

// Check the first finger touches on screen
if (touches.Count > 0 && touches[0].State ==
  TouchLocationState.Pressed)
{
    // Examine whether the tapped position is in the
    // HitRegion
    Point touchPoint = new
        Point((int)touches[0].Position.X,
        (int)touches[0].Position.Y);
    if (HitRegion.Contains(touchPoint))
    {
        isSelected = true;
    }
    else
    {
        isSelected = false;
    }
}
}
```

4. When you have finished creating the `UpdateInput()` method, you should call `UpdateInput()` in `Update()`:

```
protected override void Update(GameTime gameTime)
{
    . . .

    UpdateInput();

    . . .
}
```

5. The final step is drawing, so add the following code to `Draw()` before `base.Draw(gameTime)`. It will look similar to the following code:

```
spriteBatch.Begin();
if (isSelected)
{
    spriteBatch.Draw(texRound, HitRegion, Color.Red);
}
else
{
    spriteBatch.Draw(texRound, HitRegion, Color.White);
}
spriteBatch.End();
```

6. Build and run the application. The game will run as shown in the screenshot to the left. When you tap the ball, the ball color will be changed to red. Once you tap the outside region of the ball, the color will go back to white:

How it works...

In step 1, you used the `Texture2D` object for the ball image, the `Rectangle` for the `HitRegion`, and a bool value `isSelected` for ball hitting status.

In step 2, you must make sure the `Round.png` file is added to your referred content project before technically loading the round image in code. The initialization for the rectangle object `HitRegion` is to define the center of the screen in landscape mode; 400 is half of the screen width, and 240 is half of the screen height.

In step 3, as a typical Windows Phone XNA program, `TouchPanel.GetState()` should be the first line for Touch operations. Then check that `touches.Count` is over `0` and `TouchLocationState` is `Pressed` to make sure your finger has tapped on the screen. Subsequently, we shall examine the tapped position to check whether it is in the `HitRegion`. `HitRegion.Contains()` does the job for us. `HitRegion` is a rectangular object, the `Rectangle.Contains()` method computes the four-sided area of a rectangle to check whether it includes the position. If yes, the bool value `isSelected` will be set to `true`. Otherwise, it will be `false`. `Update()` and `Draw()` use the `isSelected` value to do the corresponding work.

In step 5, with `isSelected` value, we determine whether to draw a red ball or a white ball. When your finger taps inside the ball, its color will be red; otherwise, it restores to white. That's all. You can review the complete project in our book code files.

Taking your touch application to the next level

Now, we have done the first sample of touch tap, very easy, huh? Maybe you feel it's not exciting enough yet. The next example will be more interesting. The ball will randomly show up in every possible place within the touchscreen, and your job is to click the ball as soon as possible; every valid click will be counted and shown as scores at the top-left of the screen. The new sample's name is `TouchTapRandomBall`.

How to do it...

Create a new Windows Phone 7 Game project in Visual Studio 2010 named `TouchTapRandomBall`. Change the name from `Game1.cs` to `TouchTapRandomBallGame.cs`. Then add the `Round.jpg` and `gamefont.spritefont` to the associated content project:

1. The first operation is to add the lines as field variables:

```
GraphicsDeviceManager graphics;
SpriteBatch spriteBatch;
Texture2D texRound;
Rectangle HitRegion;
bool isSelected = false;

//start position of round, in the center of screen
int positionX = 400;
int positionY = 240;

//random number Axis X and Y
Random randomX;
Random randomY;

//the range for random number of start and end of X, Y
int startX, endX;
int startY, endY;

//total time
float milliseconds = 0f;

//score count
int count = 0;

//game font
SpriteFont font;
```

2. Based on the variables, the next step is to add the lines into the `LoadContent()` method:

```
spriteBatch = new SpriteBatch(GraphicsDevice);
texRound = Content.Load<Texture2D>("Round");

randomX = new Random();
randomY = new Random();

// The X axis bound range of touch for ball
startX = texRound.Width ;
endX = GraphicsDevice.Viewport.Width - texRound.Width;

// The X axis bound range of touch for ball
startY = texRound.Height;
endY = GraphicsDevice.Viewport.Height - texRound.Height;

// Define the HitRegion of ball in the middle of touchscreen
HitRegion = new Rectangle(positionX - texRound.Width / 2,
    positionY -      texRound.Height / 2, texRound.Width,
    texRound.Height);

// Load the font definition file
font = Content.Load<SpriteFont>("gamefont");
```

3. The next block of code is for the `Update()` method:

```
// Accumulate the elapsed milliseconds every frame
milliseconds +=
    (float)gameTime.ElapsedGameTime.TotalMilliseconds;

if (milliseconds > 1000)
{
    // When the milliseconds greater than 1000 milliseconds,
    // randomly locate a new position for the ball
    HitRegion.X = randomX.Next(startX, endX + 1);
    HitRegion.Y = randomY.Next(startY, endY + 1);

    // Reset the milliseconds to zero for new milliseconds
    // count
    // make the ball not been selected
    milliseconds = 0f;
    if (isSelected)
      isSelected = false;
}
```

4. Besides the previous code, we still want to count how many times we tapped the ball. The following code would reach the point. Insert the highlighted line to `UpdateInput()`:

```
Point touchPoint = new Point((int)touches[0].Position.X,
    (int)touches[0].Position.Y);
if (HitRegion.Contains(touchPoint))
{
    isSelected = true;
    count++;
}
else
{
    isSelected = false;
}
```

5. Add the following lines to the `Draw()` method:

```
spriteBatch.Begin();
if (isSelected)
{
    spriteBatch.Draw(texRound, HitRegion, Color.Red);
}
else
{
    spriteBatch.Draw(texRound, HitRegion, Color.White);
}

spriteBatch.DrawString(font, "Score:" + count.ToString(),
    new Vector2(0f, 0f), Color.White);
spriteBatch.End();
```

6. Now you've done all the necessary code work, let's build and run the application. You will discover a jumping ball in the touchscreen. Each time you tap the ball successfully, the score on the top-left will increase by one, as shown in the following screenshots:

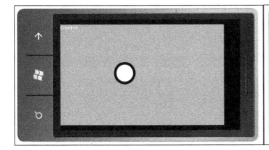

How it works...

In step 2, the `randomX` and `randomY` objects indicate the random location of the ball. `startX` and `endX` are the range in the *X* axis for `randomX` and `startY` and `endY` are the range for `randomY`. The time will be calculated in milliseconds and the count variable will be responsible for the score.

In step 3, the calculation for `startX`, `endX`, `startY`, and `endY` stand for controlling the ball moving inside the screen because the ball position is randomly generated. Then we make the `HitRegion` locate in the middle of the screen. The last line is for loading and initializing the font.

In step 4, `ElapsedGameTime`—a `Timespan` object—represents the amount of elapsed game time since the last update or last frame. In every `Update`, we add the elapsed time to the `milliseconds` variable. Once the value is greater than `1000 milliseconds`, the code will generate two random numbers for X and Y of the `HitRegion` position that will be used in the `Draw()` method in the same frame. After the new values are generated, we reset the `milliseconds` variable to `0` and deselect the ball.

In step 5, when your finger taps on the ball, the `UpdateInput()` method will handle it and add one to the `count` variable; this number will appear on the top-left of the touchscreen.

Creating a Touch Directional Pad (D-pad)

In a Windows game, we have arrow keys to control directions. In Xbox, we have the gamepad controller to set different orientations. In Windows Phone 7, we only have the touchscreen for the same work, so we need another tool to accomplish this aim. The solution is the Touch Directional Pad. Touch Directional Pad gives you comfortable controlling experiences in game playing when adjusting the directions. In this recipe, you will learn how to create your own Touch Directional Pad on Windows Phone 7.

How to do it...

1. The first step is to create a new Windows Phone 7 Game project named `WindowsPhoneDpad`, and change `Game1.cs` to `DpadGame.cs`. Then add field variables in the `DpadGame` class, as follows:

    ```
    //Font for direction status display
    SpriteFont font;

    //Texture Image for Thumbstick
    Texture2D texDpad;

    //4 direction rectangles
    Rectangle recUp;
    ```

```
Rectangle recDown;
Rectangle recLeft;
Rectangle recRight;

//Bounding Rectangle for the 4 direction rectangles
Rectangle recBounding;

//Corner Margin, 1/4 of Width or Height of square
int cornerWidth;
int cornerHeight;

//Direction String
string directionString;
```

2. The next step is to add the following lines to the `LoadContent()` method:

```
//Load the Texture image from content
texDpad = Content.Load<Texture2D>("Dpad");
    recBounding = new Rectangle(0,
    this.GraphicsDevice.Viewport.Height -
    texDpad.Height, texDpad.Width,
    texDpad.Height);

//Load the game font file
font = Content.Load<SpriteFont>("gamefont");

//Calculate the corner height and width
cornerWidth = texDpad.Width / 4;
cornerHeight = texDpad.Height / 4

//Calculate the Up rectangle
recUp = new Rectangle(recBounding.X + cornerWidth,
    recBounding.Y,
    cornerWidth * 2, cornerHeight);

//Calculate the Down rectangle
recDown = new Rectangle(recBounding.X + cornerWidth,
    recBounding.Y + recBounding.Height - cornerHeight,
    cornerWidth * 2, cornerHeight);

//Calculate the Left rectangle
recLeft = new Rectangle(recBounding.X,
    recBounding.Y + cornerHeight, cornerWidth,
    cornerHeight * 2);
```

```
//Calculate the Right rectangle
recRight = new Rectangle(recBounding.X + recBounding.
    Width - cornerWidth, recBounding.Y + cornerHeight,
    cornerWidth, cornerHeight * 2);
```

3. The third step is to insert the code to the `Update()` method:

```
// Check the Tap point whether in the region of the 4
// direction rectangle
TouchCollection touches = TouchPanel.GetState();
if (touches.Count > 0 && touches[0].State ==
    TouchLocationState.Pressed)
{
    Point point = new Point((int)touches[0].Position.X,
    (int)touches[0].Position.Y);

    // Check the Tap point whether in the 4 direction
    // rectangle
    if (recUp.Contains(point))
    {
        directionString = "Up";
    }
    else if (recDown.Contains(point))
    {
        directionString = "Down";
    }
    else if (recLeft.Contains(point))
    {
        directionString = "Left";
    }
    else if (recRight.Contains(point))
    {
        directionString = "Right";
    }
}
```

4. In the `Draw()` method, we add the following lines:

```
//Draw the font and Touch Directional Pad texture
spriteBatch.Begin();
spriteBatch.DrawString(font, "Direction : " + directionString,
    new Vector2(0, 0), Color.White);
spriteBatch.Draw(texDpad, recBounding, Color.White);
spriteBatch.End();
```

5. Finally, build and run the application. Click the Right and the Up part on the thumbstick, and you will see something similar to the following screenshots:

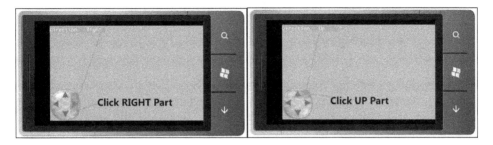

How it works...

In step 1, the four rectangle objects: `recUp`, `recDown`, `recLeft`, and `recRight` individually represent the **Up**, **Down**, **Left**, and **Right** directions. The `recBounding` is a rectangle that surrounds the D-pad image. It is convenient for you to control the position of a D-pad and locate the relative positions of the four direction rectangles. The `cornerWidth` and `cornerHeight` variables are used for calculating the square gap to corners. Actually, for a square thumbstick, the two variables have the same value. The last variable `directionString` shows the direction when you tap on the different parts of the thumbsticks.

In step 2, the code is mainly responsible for loading the D-pad image, calculating, and defining the four clickable direction rectangles. The main idea is easy. You can understand the logic and layout from the following figure:

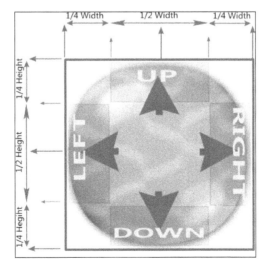

The initialization of `recBounding` gives the bounding rectangle position, at the bottom-left of the screen. Since the thumbstick image is a square, the `cornerWidth` and `cornerHeight` is a quarter of the side. You can see in the previous screenshot that the width of `recUp` and `recDown` is half of the length and the height is a quarter. For `recLeft` and `recRight`, the width is a quarter of the side and the height is half. For every direction rectangle, the shorter side should be at a distance of `cornerWidth` or `cornerHeight` to the thumbstick bounding rectangle side.

In step 3, when you get the tapped position, you should check whether the position is within one of the four direction rectangles. If yes, then according to the rectangle, the direction will receive the appropriate value, that is: Up, Down, Left, or Right. Once the updating is done, the last step will present the image and string on the screen.

In step 4, the method renders the direction string on the top-left of the screen and the thumbstick image at the bottom-left.

Dragging and swiping objects

For Windows Phone 7, XNA 4.0 provides two main ways to get touchscreen input. Basically, one is based on tap. With the `TouchPanel.GetState()` method, you can look up the particular finger by the ID for the raw access to touch point. The Gesture System is another advanced input approach, which provides a number of pre-defined touch gestures, so that you don't have to work out how to read the common touch gestures using raw data. The `TouchPanel.ReadGesture()` method offers you a chance to interact with the touch screen in another way. In this recipe, you will get close to two of the most exciting gestures of touchscreen: dragging and swiping.

Getting ready

For Windows Phone XNA programming, the `TouchPanel` class has an important subclass `GestureSample` and a corresponding method `ReadGesture()`. Based on `GestureType` enum to interact with your gestures, Windows Phone 7 supports the following:

- **Tap**: You touch the screen and move away one time, a single point.
- **DoubleTap**: You touch on the screen two times in a short time.
- **Hold**: You touch and hold the screen at one point for more than one second.
- **FreeDrag**: Touch and freely move your finger on the screen.
- **HorizontalDrag**: Move your finger around the *X* axis of the screen, either in landscape mode or portrait mode.
- **VerticalDrag**: Move your finger along the *Y* axis of the screen, either in landscape mode or portrait mode.

- ▶ **DragComplete**: Lift your finger from the screen.
- ▶ **Flick**: A quick swipe on the screen. The velocity of flick can be retrieved by reading the Delta member of `GestureSample`.
- ▶ **Pinch**: Pinch behaves like a two-finger drag. Two fingers concurrently moving towards each other or apart.
- ▶ **PinchComplete**: Lift your fingers from the screen.

If you want to use some of the gestures in your Windows Phone 7 XNA game, the best way is to enable them in the `Initialize()` method as follows:

```
TouchPanel.EnabledGestures =
    GestureType.Tap |
    GestureType.FreeDrag |
    GestureType.Flick;
```

Then in the `Update()` method, you could interact with the gestures as follows:

```
while (TouchPanel.IsGestureAvailable)
{
    GestureSample gesture = TouchPanel.ReadGesture();
    switch (gesture.GestureType)
    {
        case GestureType.Tap:

            . . .
            break;

        case GestureType.FreeDrag:

            . . .
            break;

        case GestureType.Flick:

            . . .
            break;
    }
}
```

The `while` loop is used to check whether the `gesture` property is enabled. If you have set the `TouchPanel.EnableGestures` in the `Initialize()` method, then at least one gesture, the `IsGestureAvailable` will be `true`. The `TouchPanel.ReadGesture()` method will then retrieve the gesture taking place on the screen and you can write your own logic to react to the different gesture types.

Now, you know the basic skeleton code for manipulating the Windows Phone 7 gestures. Moreover, I will explain the `GestureSample` class, which defines the four properties of type Vector2:

- **Delta**: Holds delta information about the first touchpoint in a multitouch gesture
- **Delta2**: Holds delta information about the second touchpoint in a multitouch gesture
- **Position**: Holds the current position of the first touchpoint in this gesture sample
- **Position2**: Holds the current position of the second touchpoint in this gesture sample

The `Position` property indicates the current position of the finger relative to the screen. The `Delta` property presents the finger movements since the last position. The `Delta` is `zero` when the finger touches on the screen and remains there.

Furthermore, we should thank Charles Petzold's who reminds us of the following:

- *Position* is valid for all gestures except *Flick*. *Flick* is positionless, only the *Delta* value could be tracked.
- *Delta* is valid for all *Drag* gestures, *Pinch* and *Flick*.
- *Position2* and *Delta2* are valid only for *Pinch*.
- None of these properties are valid for the *DragComplete* and *PinchComplete* types.

Now that we've covered the basic ideas of gestures, let's look at a simple example in which you can drag the ball to the middle of the screen. If you swipe it, the ball will fly away and will come back when it collides with the screen bounds.

How to do it...

1. In Visual Studio 2010, click **File | New | Project | Windows Phone Game** and create a Windows Phone Game project named `DragSwipe`. Change `Game1.cs` to `DragSwipe.cs` and then add the following lines as fields:

```
GraphicsDeviceManager graphics;
SpriteBatch spriteBatch;
Texture2D texBall;
Rectangle HitRegion;

// Ball position
Vector2 positionBall;
bool isSelected;

// Ball velocity
Vector2 velocity;

// This is the percentage of velocity lost each second as
```

```
// the sprite moves around.
const float Friction = 0.9f;

// Margin for screen bound
const int Margin = 5;

// Viewport bound for ball
float boundLeft = 0f;
float boundRight = 0f;
float boundTop = 0f;
float boundBottom = 0f;
```

2. The second step is to add the following lines in the `Initialize()` method:

```
// Enable gestures
TouchPanel.EnabledGestures =
    GestureType.Tap |
    GestureType.FreeDrag |
    GestureType.Flick;
```

3. After the gestures are enabled, you need to insert the following code to `LoadContent()`:

```
spriteBatch = new SpriteBatch(GraphicsDevice);
texBall = Content.Load<Texture2D>("Round");

// Set the HitRegion of ball in the center
HitRegion = new Rectangle(
    GraphicsDevice.Viewport.Width / 2 - texBall.Width / 2,
    GraphicsDevice.Viewport.Height / 2 - texBall.Height / 2,
    texBall.Width, texBall.Height);

// Set the ball position to the center
positionBall = new Vector2(
    GraphicsDevice.Viewport.Width / 2 - texBall.Width / 2,
    GraphicsDevice.Viewport.Height / 2 - texBall.Height / 2);

// Define the bound for ball moving
boundLeft = 0;
boundRight = GraphicsDevice.Viewport.Width - texBall.Width;
boundTop = 0;
boundBottom = GraphicsDevice.Viewport.Height - texBall.Height;
```

4. Add the following code to the `Update()` method:

```
TouchCollection touches = TouchPanel.GetState();

// Check the first finger touches on screen
if (touches.Count > 0 && touches[0].State ==
```

```
            TouchLocationState.Pressed
        {
            // Examine the tapped position is in the HitRegion
            Point point = new Point((int)touches[0].Position.X,
                (int)touches[0].Position.Y);
            if (HitRegion.Contains(point))
            {
                isSelected = true;
            }
            else
            {
                isSelected = false;
            }
        }
        // Check the available gestures
        while (TouchPanel.IsGestureAvailable)
        {
            // Read the on-going gestures
            GestureSample gesture = TouchPanel.ReadGesture();

            //Process different gestures
            switch (gesture.GestureType)
            {
                case GestureType.FreeDrag:
                if (isSelected)
                {
                    // When the ball is being dragged, update
                    // the position of ball and HitRegion
                    positionBall += gesture.Delta;
                    HitRegion.X += (int)gesture.Delta.X;
                    HitRegion.Y += (int)gesture.Delta.Y;
                }
                break;
                case GestureType.Flick:
                {
                    if (isSelected)
                    {
                        // When the ball is swiped, update its
                        // velocity
                        velocity =  gesture.Delta *
                            (float)gameTime.ElapsedGameTime.
                            TotalSeconds;
                    }
                }
                break;
            }
```

```
    }

    // Accumulate the velocity of every frame
    positionBall += velocity;

    // Reduce the velocity of every frame
    velocity *= 1f - (Friction *
        (float)gameTime.ElapsedGameTime.TotalSeconds);

    // Check Bound, once the ball collides with the bound, change
    // its direction to the opposite.
    if (positionBall.X < boundLeft)
    {
        positionBall.X = boundLeft + Margin;
        velocity.X *= -1;
    }
    else if (positionBall.X > boundRight)
    {
        positionBall.X = boundRight - Margin;
        velocity.X *= -1;
    }
    else if (positionBall.Y < boundTop)
    {
        positionBall.Y = boundTop + Margin;
        velocity.Y *= -1;
    }
    else if (positionBall.Y > boundBottom)
    {
        positionBall.Y = boundBottom - Margin;
        velocity.Y *= -1;
    }

    // Update the position of HitRegion
    HitRegion.X = (int)positionBall.X;
    HitRegion.Y = (int)positionBall.Y;
```

5. The final `Draw()` method is very simple:

```
protected override void Draw(GameTime gameTime)
{
    GraphicsDevice.Clear(Color.CornflowerBlue);

    spriteBatch.Begin();
    spriteBatch.Draw(texBall, positionBall, Color.White);
    spriteBatch.End();
```

```
        base.Draw(gameTime);
    }
```

6. Build and run the project. The application will look similar to the following screenshot:

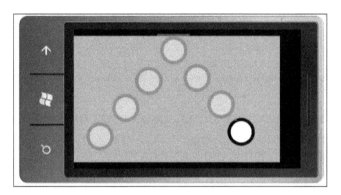

How it works...

In step 1, the first four variables are the necessary objects for rendering texture and string on the screen. `positionBall` indicates the ball position. The `Friction` variable is used for calculating the ball velocity that changes in every frame. The `Margin` variable defines the distance between the active limited bound for ball and viewport. The four integers `boundLeft`, `boundRight`, `boundTop`, and `boundBottom` are the active bound values for controlling the ball movement inside the screen.

In step 2, the code enables the `Tap`, `FreeDrag`, and `Flick` gestures in this application. This means that you could track these actions and perform the corresponding logic.

In step 3, we set the `HitRegion` and `positionBall` to the center of the screen. This makes the ball moving-bound have a distance away from the ball texture width to the screen right side and from the screen bottom to the height of the ball texture.

In step 4, the first section of the code is used to check whether the tapped point is inside the ball. If yes, `isSelected` will be true. The code in the `while` loop is used for reading and processing the different gestures. While the `GestureType` is `FreeDrag`, we update the ball position by `Gesture.Delta`, the same as the `HitRegion`. When the `GestureType` is equal to `Flick`, it means you are swiping the ball very fast. We use the `Delta` value to update the ball velocity along the game elapsed time. After the `while` loop, you can use the latest value to perform your own logic. Here, we update the velocity following the inertia law with the game elapsed time in every frame. The next section is the bounding checks for the moving ball, as long as the ball collides with the bound, the ongoing ball direction will be changed to the opposite.

Controlling images with Multi-Touch control

Windows Phone 7 supports Multi-Touch Control. With this technique, developers can do any creative operation using their fingers such as to control car steel in a racing game, to rotate and zoom in/out images, to hit balls that come up from different positions concurrently, and so on. In this recipe, you will know how to control images using the Multi-Touch technology in Windows Phone 7.

Getting ready

In the movie *Minority Report*, Tom Cruise wears gloves with flashing lights on every finger, grasping and zooming the images on the glass wall without touching them. I am sure the incredible actions and effects impressed you at that time. Actually, I am not Tom Cruise, I am not the director Steven Spielberg, and the glass wall is not in front of me. However, I have Windows Phone 7, and although the effect can be as cool as the movie, I still want to present you with the amazing Multi-Touch on image controlling. Now, let's begin our journey.

How to do it...

1. The first step is to create a Windows Phone Game project named `MultiTouchImage`. Change `Game1.cs` to `ImageControl.cs` and then add a new class file `Mountain.cs` to the project. The complete class will be as follows:

```
public class Mountain
{
    // The minimum and maximum scale values for the sprite
    public const float MinScale = 0.5f;
    public const float MaxScale = 3f;

    // The texture object
    private Texture2D texture;

    // The scale factor for pinch
    private float scale = 1f;

    // The center position of object
    public Vector2 Center;

    // The Scale property of object
    public float Scale
    {
        get { return scale; }

        // Control the scale value within min and max
```

```
            set
            {
                scale = MathHelper.Clamp(value, MinScale,
                    MaxScale);
            }
        }

        // The HitRegion Property
        public Rectangle HitRegion
        {
            get
            {
                // Create a rectangle based on the texture center
                // and scale
                Rectangle r = new Rectangle(
                    (int)(Center.X - (texture.Width /2 * Scale)),
                    (int)(Center.Y - (texture.Height /2 *Scale)),
                    (int)(texture.Width * Scale),
                    (int)(texture.Height * Scale));

                return r;
            }

        }

        public Mountain(Texture2D texture)
        {
            this.texture = texture;
        }


        public void Draw(SpriteBatch spriteBatch)
        {
            spriteBatch.Draw(
                texture,
                Center,
                null,
                Color.White,
                0,
                new Vector2(texture.Width / 2,
                texture.Height / 2),
                Scale,
                SpriteEffects.None,
                0);
```

```
        }
    }
```

2. Now you have completed the `Mountain` class. The second step is to add the fields to your `ImageControl` main game class for interacting with the mountain texture:

```
GraphicsDeviceManager graphics;
SpriteBatch spriteBatch;


// Texture file for mountain
Texture2D texMountain;

// Mountain object
Mountain mountain;

// Bool value tracks the mountain object selection
bool isSelected;
```

3. The next step is to insert the code in to the `LoadContent()` method:

```
// Create a new SpriteBatch, which can be used to draw
textures.
spriteBatch = new SpriteBatch(GraphicsDevice);
texMountain = Content.Load<Texture2D>("Mountain");

// Initialize the mountain object
mountain = new Mountain(texMountain);

// Define the center of mountain
mountain.Center = new Vector2(
    GraphicsDevice.Viewport.Width / 2,
    GraphicsDevice.Viewport.Height / 2);
```

4. Next, you should enable the `Pinch` and `Drag` gestures in the `Initialize` method:

```
TouchPanel.EnabledGestures =
    GestureType.Pinch | GestureType.FreeDrag;
```

5. Then add the following core logic code for Multi-Touch in Windows Phone 7 to the `Update()` method:

```
// Allows the game to exit
if (GamePad.GetState(PlayerIndex.One).Buttons.Back ==
    ButtonState.Pressed)
    this.Exit();

// Get the touch position and check whether it is in HitRegion
TouchCollection touches = TouchPanel.GetState();
```

```
if (touches.Count > 0 && touches[0].State ==
TouchLocationState.Pressed)
{
    Point point = new Point((int)touches[0].Position.X,
        (int)touches[0].Position.Y);
    if (mountain.HitRegion.Contains(point))
    {
        isSelected = true;
    }
    else
    {
        isSelected = false;
    }
}

// Check the Gestures available or not
while (TouchPanel.IsGestureAvailable)
{
    //Read the gestures
    GestureSample gestures = TouchPanel.ReadGesture();

    // Determine which gesture takes place
    switch (gestures.GestureType)
    {
        // When gesture type is Pinch
        case GestureType.Pinch:

        // When the mountain texture is selected
        if (isSelected)
        {
            // Get the current touch position
            // and calculate their previous position
            // according to the Delta value from gesture.
            Vector2 vec1 = gestures.Position;
            Vector2 oldvec1 =
                gestures.Position - gestures.Delta;

            Vector2 vec2 = gestures.Position2;
            Vector2 oldvec2 =
                gestures.Position2 - gestures.Delta2;

            // Figure out the distance between the current
            // and previous locations
            float distance = Vector2.Distance(vec1, vec2);
            float oldDistance = Vector2.Distance(oldvec1,
                oldvec2);
```

```
        // Calculate the difference between the two
        // and use that to alter the scale
        float scaleChanged =
            (distance - oldDistance) * 0.01f;

        mountain.Scale += scaleChanged;
    }

    break;

    // When gesture is FreeDrag
    case GestureType.FreeDrag:

    // When the mountain texture is selected
    if (isSelected)
    {
        mountain.Center += gestures.Delta;
    }
    break;
    }
}
```

6. In the `Draw()` method the code is easy:

```
spriteBatch.Begin();
mountain.Draw(spriteBatch);
spriteBatch.End();
```

7. Now, build and run the project. Then start the Multi-Touch simulator, if you do not have Windows Phone 7. When the application runs well, you can experience the amazing Multi-Touch feeling, as shown in the following screenshots. When your fingers move outwards, the application runs similar to the screenshot to the right:

How it works...

In step 1, in the `Mountain` class, we have defined the `MinScale` and `MaxScale` to limit the scale value variation range. In the `set` operation of `Scale` property, the `MathHelp.Clamp()` method is used to perform the value limitation work of scale. The `HitRegion` property is responsible for returning the start point and size of the texture bounding box based on the texture center and size. In the `Draw()` method, we use another overload method of `SpriteBatch.Draw()` because we want to change the scale value of the texture. The complete parameter specification is as follows:

```
public void Draw (
    Texture2D texture,
    Vector2 position,
    Nullable<Rectangle> sourceRectangle,
    Color color,
    float rotation,
    Vector2 origin,
    Vector2 scale,
    SpriteEffects effects,
    float layerDepth
)
```

The `texture`, `position`, and `color` parameters are easy to understand. The `sourceRectangle` is used to determine which part of the texture needs to be rendered. In this example, we set it to `null` to draw the entire texture. The `rotation` parameter will rotate the texture with the actual passing value. The `origin` parameter defines the position around which rotation and scale can take place. The `effects` parameter applies `SpriteEffects` to texture; here, we set `SpriteEffects` to `None`. The last parameter `layerDepth` gives the layer order for drawing.

In step 3, the code snippet loads the Mountain image and initializes the mountain position to the center of the screen.

In step 5, the code tests the touch point to check whether it is inside the mountain region. Then in the `while` loop, when `TouchPanel.IsGestureAvailable` is `true`, you get into the core code of Multi-Touch Pinch gesture. In this case, once two of your fingers tap on the Windows Phone 7 touchscreen, the code will read these two positions and calculate the previous position after you move the two fingers. It then calculates the distance between the current positions and the previous position. Based on the subtraction value of the two distances, you will get the scale change factor to change the size of the mountain texture and render it in `Draw()`.

Using accelerometer to make a ball move on your phone

Accelerometers, which are useful for game programming, are becoming more common nowadays. An accelerometer is a device, a kind of a sensor, contained in the Windows Phone 7 that can report the device's current axis or orientation. In other words, it can tell if the device is lying on the horizontal plain or rotated to the vertical position. This data from accelerometer presents the Windows Phone 7 game programmers with the opportunity to work with gravity, orientations, and so on. Instead of using the touchscreen, or pressing a button to move objects on the screen, the accelerometer makes it possible for players to shake or adjust the Windows Phone 7 device in whichever direction they want. The game play will take the corresponding actions. This feature of Windows Phone 7 creates a lot of possibilities for a game programmer. In this chapter, you will learn how to use this feature.

Getting ready

When you have a Windows Phone 7 in your hand, you will enjoy the accelerometer in the device. Just imagine playing a racing game, such as *Need for Speed* or *GTA* without any controller or keyboard, instead only using your hands. It is very exciting! As a Windows Phone programmer, understanding and mastering the accelerometer technique will make your game more attractive and creative. The two most common usages of accelerometer are:

▶ Orientation adjustment
▶ Movement track from initial position

The accelerometer sensor in Windows Phone 7 will tell you the direction of the earth relative to the phone because when the phone is still, the accelerometer will react to the force of gravity. Besides this, corresponding to a sudden action, such as a shake of the device, is also a very special function for inspiring your creativity.

Representing the output of Windows Phone 7 accelerometer in 3D vector is straightforward for its developers. Vector has direction and length, the (x, y, z) for 3D vector means the direction from the origin point (0, 0, 0) to the (x, y, z) point. We could learn the basic concepts and calculation from some computer graphics or linear algebra books.

While programming on a Windows Phone 7, you should be clear on the 3D coordinate system, no matter how the phone orients. The 3D coordinate system is completely different from the 2D coordinate system, in which the origin point is located at the top-left of the screen of Window Phone 7. The 3D coordinate system in the phone is a right-hand system. Here, you just need to know that the positive Z axis always points to the front as shown in the following screenshots. The screenshot to the left is for the landscape mode and the one to the right is for the portrait mode:

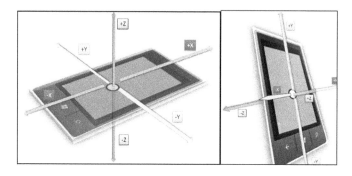

In landscape mode, the increasing Y towards the top side is parallel to the control pad and the increasing X is perpendicular to the control pad towards the right side. In portrait mode, the increasing Y towards the top side is perpendicular to the control pad and the increasing X towards the right side is parallel to the control pad. In addition, the 3D coordinate system remains fixed relative to the phone regardless of how you hold the phone or whatever the orientation is. The accelerometer is the reason to change the Windows Phone 7 orientation. In the next section, I will introduce you to the basic programming skeleton for the Windows Phone 7 accelerometer.

For a typical Windows Phone 7 XNA accelerometer application, the first step is to add a `Microsoft.Devices.Sensors` reference to your project and then add data members to the game to hold the accelerometer data:

```
Accelerometer accelSensor;
YourClass substance;
bool accelActive;
Vector3 accelReading = new Vector3();
const float ACCELFACTOR = 2.0f;
```

The Vector3 variable `accelReading` will be used to read the position data from `AccelerometerReadingEventArgs`. The second step is to add an event handler for the `ReadingChanged` event Accelerometer object:

```
public void AccelerometerReadingChanged(object sender,
    AccelerometerReadingEventArgs e)
{
    accelReading.X = (float)e.X;
```

```
    accelReading.Y = (float)e.Y;
    accelReading.Z = (float)e.Z;
}
```

This method returns `void`, and passes two parameters; one is the sender, another is the `AccelerometerReadingEventArgs` to get the accelerometer reading. After this, you should add a reference in the `Initialize()` method:

```
accelSensor = new Accelerometer();
substance = new YourClass();

// Add the accelerometer event handler to the accelerometer
// sensor.
accelSensor.ReadingChanged += new EventHandler
    <AccelerometerReadingEventArgs>(AccelerometerReadingChanged);
```

When you are done with the preparation, you need to start the accelerometer:

```
// Start the accelerometer
try
{
    accelSensor.Start();
    accelActive = true;
}
catch (AccelerometerFailedException e)
{
    // the accelerometer couldn't be started.  No fun!
    accelActive = false;
}
catch (UnauthorizedAccessException e)
{
    // This exception is thrown in the emulator - which doesn't
    // support an accelerometer.
    accelActive = false;
}
```

After it is started, the accelerometer calls your event handler when the `ReadingChanged` event is raised. Update your stored `AccelerometerReadingEventArgs` class (previously shown in the event handler code), and then use its data in your `Update()` method:

```
if (accelActive)
{
    // accelerate the substance speed depending on
    // accelerometer
    // action.
    substance.speed.X += accelReading.X * ACCELFACTOR;
    substance.speed.Y += -accelReading.Y * ACCELFACTOR;
}
```

The final code is a skeleton snippet used to stop the accelerometer sensor. To avoid having your event handler being called repeatedly when your game is not actually using the accelerometer data, you can stop the accelerometer when the game is paused, when menus are being shown, or at any other time by calling the `Stop()` method. Like the `Start()` method, this method can throw an exception, so allow your code to handle the `AccelerometerFailedException`:

```
// Stop the accelerometer if it's active.
if (accelActive)
{
    try
    {
        accelSensor.Stop();
    }
    catch (AccelerometerFailedException e)
    {
        // the accelerometer couldn't be stopped now.
    }
}
```

The complete accelerometer skeleton snippet will be as follows:

```
using Microsoft.Devices.Sensors;
. . .

public class Game : Microsoft.Xna.Framework.Game
{
    Accelerometer accelSensor;
    YourClass substance;
    bool accelActive;
    Vector3 accelReading = new Vector3();
    const float ACCELFACTOR = 2.0f;

    protected override void Initialize()
    {
        base.Initialize();
        accelSensor = new Accelerometer();
        substance = new YourClass();

        // Add the accelerometer event handler to the
        // accelerometer sensor.
        accelSensor.ReadingChanged += new EventHandler
            <AccelerometerReadingEventArgs>
            (AccelerometerReadingChanged);
```

```
        // Start the accelerometer
        try
        {
            accelSensor.Start();
            accelActive = true;
        }
        catch (AccelerometerFailedException e)
        {
            // the accelerometer couldn't be started.  No fun!
            accelActive = false;
        }
        catch (UnauthorizedAccessException e)
        {
            // This exception is thrown in the emulator - which
            // doesn't support an accelerometer.
            accelActive = false;
        }

    }

    protected override void LoadContent()
    {
        . . .;
    }

    protected override void Update(GameTime gameTime)
    {
        if (accelActive)
        {
            // accelerate the substance speed depending on
            // accelerometer action.
            substance.speed.X += accelReading.X * ACCELFACTOR;
            substance.speed.Y += -accelReading.Y * ACCELFACTOR;
        }
    }

    protected override void UnloadContent()
    {
        // Unload any non ContentManager content here
        // Stop the accelerometer if it's active.
        if (accelActive)
        {
            try
            {
```

```
                    accelSensor.Stop();
                }
                catch (AccelerometerFailedException e)
                {
                    // the accelerometer couldn't be stopped now.
                }
            }
        }
    }
```

So far, I suppose you are familiar with the basic code of Windows Phone 7 accelerometer. Now, let's make a new accelerometer project: a white ball will move around within the Windows Phone screen depending on your hand movement.

How to do it...

1. First, create a Windows Phone Game project in Visual Studio 2010, named `AccelerometerFallingBall` and then change `Game1.cs` to `FallingBallGame.cs`. For accelerometer, you should add a `Microsoft.Devices.Sensors` reference to the project's reference. Then, add `Ball.cs`.

2. After the preparation work, you should insert the following lines to the `FallingBallGame` class field:

```
GraphicsDeviceManager graphics;
SpriteBatch spriteBatch;

// Ball object
Ball ball;
Texture2D texBall;
Rectangle recBound;
Vector2 position;

//Accelerometer object
Accelerometer accelSensor;

// The accelActive bool value indicates whether the accelerometer
// is turned on or off.
bool accelActive;

// Demonstrate the direction of accelerometer
Vector3 accelReading = new Vector3();

// Amplify the variegation of ball velocity
const float ACCELFACTOR = 2.0f;
```

```
// Viewport bound
int boundLeft = 0;
int boundRight = 0;
int boundTop = 0;
int boundBottom = 0;
```

3. Add the following lines to the `Initialize()` method of the `FallingBallGame` class:

```
accelSensor = new Accelerometer();
accelSensor.ReadingChanged += new EventHandler
    <AccelerometerReadingEventArgs>
    (AccelerometerReadingChanged);

// Start the accelerometer
try
{
    accelSensor.Start();
    accelActive = true;
}
catch (AccelerometerFailedException e)
{
    // the accelerometer couldn't be started.  No fun!
    accelActive = false;
}
catch (UnauthorizedAccessException e)
{
    // This exception is thrown in the emulator - which
    // doesn't support an accelerometer.
    accelActive = false;
}
```

4. Then, add the `AccelerometerReadingChanged()` method in the `FallingBallGame` class:

```
public void AccelerometerReadingChanged(object sender,
    AccelerometerReadingEventArgs e)
{
    accelReading.X = (float)e.X;
    accelReading.Y = (float)e.Y;
    accelReading.Z = (float)e.Z;
}
```

5. The fifth step is to insert the code into the `LoadContent()` method of the `FallingBallGame` class:

```
// Create a new SpriteBatch, which can be used to draw
```

```
// textures.
spriteBatch = new SpriteBatch(GraphicsDevice);
texBall = Content.Load<Texture2D>("Round");
recBound = new Rectangle(GraphicsDevice.Viewport.Width / 2 -
    texBall.Width / 2,
    GraphicsDevice.Viewport.Height / 2 - texBall.Height / 2,
    texBall.Width, texBall.Height);

// The center position
position = new Vector2(GraphicsDevice.Viewport.Width / 2 -
    texBall.Width / 2,
    GraphicsDevice.Viewport.Height / 2 - texBall.Height / 2);

//Bound Calculation
boundLeft = 0;
boundRight = GraphicsDevice.Viewport.Width - texBall.Width;
boundTop = 0;
boundBottom = GraphicsDevice.Viewport.Height - texBall.Height;

//Initialize ViewPortBound
ViewPortBound viewPortBound = new ViewPortBound(boundTop,
    boundLeft, boundRight, boundBottom);
// Initialize Ball
ball = new Ball(this, spriteBatch, texBall, recBound,
    position,viewPortBound);
```

6. This step makes the ball interact with the accelerometer's latest value. Add the following lines to the `Update()` method of the `FallingBallGame` class:

```
if (Microsoft.Devices.Environment.DeviceType ==
    DeviceType.Device)
{
    if (accelActive)
    {
        // Accelerate the substance speed depending on
        // accelerometer action.
        ball.Velocity.X += accelReading.X * ACCELFACTOR;
        ball.Velocity.Y += -accelReading.Y * ACCELFACTOR;
    }
}
else if (Microsoft.Devices.Environment.DeviceType ==
    DeviceType.Emulator)
{
    // Simulate the Keyboard when running on emulator
    KeyboardState keyboardCurrentState = Keyboard.GetState();

    if (keyboardCurrentState.IsKeyDown(Keys.Left))
```

```
        ball.Velocity.X -= 5f;
    if (keyboardCurrentState.IsKeyDown(Keys.Right))
        ball.Velocity.X += 5f;
    if (keyboardCurrentState.IsKeyDown(Keys.Up))
        ball.Velocity.Y -= 5f;
    if (keyboardCurrentState.IsKeyDown(Keys.Down))
        ball.Velocity.Y += 5f;
    }

    ball.Update(gameTime);
```

7. Build and run the project. The ball will move with the shake of your hand, as application is shown in the next screenshot:

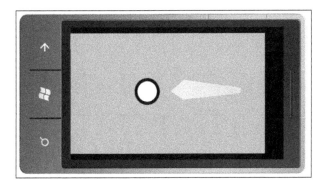

How it works...

In step 2, in the first section, we declare the `Ball` object, the texture, bound, and position of the ball. Then we declare the `Accelerometer` object. The bool value is used for indicating whether the accelerometer is active or not. The `Vector3` variable `accelReading` stands for the direction of the accelerometer. `ACCELFACTOR` will make the accelerometer change more obvious. The next section covers the variables used for bound check.

In step 3, the code initializes the `accelSensor` object and associates the `EventHandler` with the `ReadingChanged` event for the accelerometer object. It then enables the accelerometer.

In step 4, the `AccelerometerReadingChanged` method is responsible for updating `accelReading` with every accelerometer direction change.

In step 6, notice that with the `Microsoft.Devices.DeviceType`, we do a check on the device type for Windows Phone 7 development. It is a challenge when using the emulator that you want to work with the accelerometer having specific hardware. You can even simulate it through the keyboard. When your application is running on a real Windows Phone 7 device, the code will read the actual data from the accelerometer in the device to update the ball velocity. Otherwise, you should enable your ball to simulate the information to change the ball velocity by 5 units per valid keyboard press.

It's important to note that before using the keyboard to simulate, you have to press the *PageUp* key to enable the keyboard and the *PageDown* key to deactivate it.

3
Coordinates and View—Your First Step into XNA Game Development on Windows Phone 7

In this chapter, we will cover:

- ▶ Drawing the axes for a 2D game
- ▶ Setting up the position, direction, and field of view of a fixed camera
- ▶ Drawing the axes for a 3D game
- ▶ Implementing a First-person shooter (FPS) camera in your game
- ▶ Implementing a round rotating camera in a 3D game
- ▶ Implementing a chase camera
- ▶ Using culling to remove the unseen parts and texture mapping

Introduction

In the real world, how do people recognize a particular scene, know the weather, or differentiate between colors? Yes, through vision. We can see the world around us with our eyes. To the simulation of eyes, scientists first invented the camera and then the video camera. We now have the chance to see pictures and video just as we would with our eyes. For modern video games, especially in 3D, the virtual camera plays the same role as the eyes. It helps you to explore the virtual game world. You can move, jump, climb, and so on, just as you would in real life. You may have played real-time strategy games such as *StarCraft II* or *Warcraft* 3. In these games, you are in complete control of the world, like God. Or, you have probably played some first-person games such as *Quake* or *Half-life* as a warrior. Sounds like magic? Do you hope to be the magician? Do you want to perform the magic? Would you like to make your game look similar to a movie?. If so, this chapter is for you. You will learn how to set and use the camera in Windows Phone 7 XNA Games.

Drawing the axes for a 2D game

In 2D or 3D game programming, the axes are the basis for the position of objects. With the coordinate system, it is convenient for you to place or locate the objects. In 2D games the coordinate system is made up of two axes, *X* and *Y*. In 3D games, there is another axis, that is the *Z* axis. Usually, drawing the axes on your screen is a handy tool for your game debugging. In this recipe, you will learn how to render the axes in 2D in Windows Phone 7.

How to do it...

Follow the given steps to draw the 2D axis:

1. Create a Windows Phone Game project in Visual Studio 2010, change the name from `Game1.cs` to `Draw2DAxesGame.cs`. Then add a new class named `Axes2D.cs`. This class is responsible for drawing the 2D line on screen. We declare the field variables in the `Axes2D` class:

   ```
   // Pixel Texture
   Texture2D pixel;

   public int Thickness = 5;

   // Render depth of the primitive line object (0 = front, 1 =
   // back)
   public float Depth;
   ```

2. Then, we define the overload constructor of the `Axes2D` class:

```
//Creates a new primitive line object.
public Axes2D(GraphicsDevice graphicsDevice, Color color)
{
    // create pixels
    pixel = new Texture2D(graphicsDevice, 1, 1);

    Color[] pixels = new Color[1];
    pixels[0] = color;
    pixel.SetData<Color>(pixels);

    Depth = 0;
}
```

3. When the `pixel` data size and `color` are ready, the following code will draw the line object:

```
public void DrawLine(SpriteBatch spriteBatch, Vector2 start,
    Vector2 end)
{
    // calculate the distance between the two vectors
    float distance = Vector2.Distance(start, end);

    // calculate the angle between the two vectors
    float angle = (float)Math.Atan2((double)(end.Y - start.Y),
        (double)(end.X - start.X));

    // stretch the pixel between the two vectors
    spriteBatch.Draw(pixel,
        start,
        null,
        Color.White,
        angle,
        Vector2.Zero,
        new Vector2(distance, Thickness),
        SpriteEffects.None,
        Depth);
}
```

4. Use the `Axes2D` class in the main game class and insert the following code at the top of the class:

```
// The axis X line object
Axes2D axisX;

// The axis Y line object
```

```
Axes2D axisY;

// The start and end of axis X line object
Vector2 vectorAxisXStart;
Vector2 vectorAxisXEnd;

// The start and end of axis Y line object
Vector2 vectorAxisYStart;
Vector2 vectorAxisYEnd;
```

5. Initialize the axes objects and their start and end positions, add the following code to the `Initialize()` method:

```
// Set the color of axis X to red
axisX = new Axes2D(GraphicsDevice, Color.Red);

// Set the color of axis Y to green
axisY = new Axes2D(GraphicsDevice, Color.Green);

// Set the start and end positions of axis X
vectorAxisXStart = new Vector2(100,
    GraphicsDevice.Viewport.Height / 2);

vectorAxisXEnd = new Vector2(700,
    GraphicsDevice.Viewport.Height / 2);

// Set the start and end positions of axis Y
vectorAxisYStart = new Vector2(
    GraphicsDevice.Viewport.Width / 2, 50);
vectorAxisYEnd = new Vector2(
    GraphicsDevice.Viewport.Width /2, 450);
```

6. Draw the two line objects on the screen and insert the following code in to the `Draw()` method:

```
spriteBatch.Begin();
axisX.DrawLine(spriteBatch, vectorAxisXStart, vectorAxisXEnd);
axisY.DrawLine(spriteBatch, vectorAxisYStart, vectorAxisYEnd);
spriteBatch.End();
```

7. Now, build and run the application, and it will run similar to the following screenshot. Please make sure that the Windows Phone screen has been rotated to landscape mode:

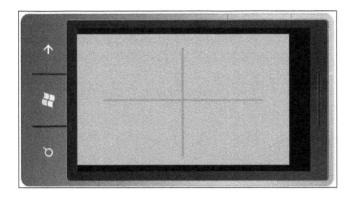

How it works...

In step 1, in the 2D line drawing for Windows Phone 7, we use pixel texture to present the line point by point; the `Thickness` variable will be used to change the pixel size of the line object; the `Depth` value will be used to define the drawing order.

In step 2, the constructor receives a `GraphicDevice` parameter and a `Color` parameter. We use them to create the pixel texture, which is of one unit width and height, and set the `color` to the `pixel` texture through the `SetData()` method; this is another way of creating a texture in code.

In step 3, the `SpriteBatch` is the main object for drawing the line objects on the screen. The `start` parameter represents the start position of the line object; the `end` parameter indicates the end position. In the method body, the first line will compute the distance between the start and end points, the second line will compute the slope between the two positions; the third line will draw the pixels one by one from the start position along the line slope to the end along the angle. This is a more generic method of drawing every line.

In step 5, the *X* axis is located in the middle of screen height, the *Y* axis is located in the middle of screen width.

In step 6, within the `SpriteBatch` rendering code, we call the `axisX.DrawLine()` and `axisY.DrawLine()` to draw the lines.

Setting up the position, direction, and field of view of a fixed camera

In the 2D world of Windows Phone 7 game programming, the presentation of images or animations with *X* and *Y* axes is straightforward. You just need to know that the original point (0, 0) is located at the top left of the touchscreen, and the screen width and height. Now, in a 3D world, things are different, as there are now *X*, *Y*, and *Z* axes and the original point is not simply sitting at the top left of the touchscreen. In this recipe, you will learn how to deal with the new coordinate system.

Getting ready

In 3D programming, especially for Windows Phone 7, the first thing we must make sure of is the coordinate system, which is on either the right hand or the left hand. In Windows Phone 7 XNA 3D programming, the coordinate system is on the right-hand, which means the increasing *Z* axis points towards you when you are playing a Windows Phone 7 game.

The next step is to set the camera, like the eye, to make the objects in the 3D world visible. During the process, we save the position and direction in a matrix, which is called the View matrix. To create the View matrix, XNA uses the `CreateLookAt()` method. It needs `Position`, `Target`, and `Up` vectors of the camera:

```
public static Matrix CreateLookAt (
    Vector3 Position,
    Vector3 Target,
    Vector3 Up
)
```

The `Position` indicates the position of the camera in the 3D world; the `Target` defines where you want to face the camera; the `Up` variable is very important because it represents the rotation of your camera. If it is positive, everything goes well, otherwise, it will be inverted. In XNA, the `Vector3.UP` is equal to (0, 1, 0); `Vector3.Forward` stands for (0, 0, -1); `Vector3.Right` is the same as (1, 0, 0); `Vector3.Down` stands for (0,-1,0). These predefined vectors are easy for you to apply in your game. Once you have understood the View matrix, the next important matrix for the camera is called Projection. In the 3D world, every object has its own 3D position. If we want to render the 3D objects on the screen, which is a 2D plain, how do we do it? The Project matrix gives us a hand.

Before rendering the objects from the 3D environment to the 2D screen, we must know how many of them need to be rendered and the range. From the computer graphics perspective, the range is called Frustum, as shown in the following figure:

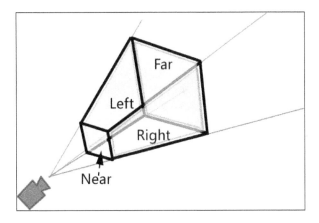

The **Near**, **Right**, **Left**, and **Far** planes compose the Frustum to determine whether the objects are inside it. In Windows Phone 7, you can use the `Matrix.CreatePerspectiveFieldofView()` to create the Projection matrix:

```
public static Matrix CreatePerspectiveFieldOfView (
    float fieldOfView,
    float aspectRatio,
    float nearPlaneDistance,
    float farPlaneDistance
)
```

The first parameter here is the field of view angle around the *Y* axis which, similar to the human eye's view, has a value of 45 degrees. Also, you can use `MathHelper.PiOver4`, which means ¼ of Pi which is the radian value of 45 degrees; the `aspectRatio` parameter specifies the view width divided by height, and this value corresponds to the ratio of the back buffer. The last two parameters individually represent the near plane and far plane for the frustum. The value for the near plane defines the beginning of the frustum. It means any object nearer than the plane will not be rendered, and for the far plane it is vice versa.

In your Windows Phone 7 game, you can update the View matrix, similar to the FPS game, and the value depends on the screen input. In the drawing phase of your 3D game, it is required to pass the View and Projection matrices to the effect when you are rendering certain objects to let the rendering hardware know how to transform the 3D objects to proper positions on the screen.

Now that, you have learned the essential ideas for the camera, it's time for programming your own application.

How to do it...

1. First, you need to create a Windows Phone Game project in Visual Studio 2010. Then change the name from `Game1.cs` to `FixedCameraGame.cs` and add `Tree.fbx` from the code bundle to your content project. For the 3D model creation, you can use commercial tools, such as AutoDesk 3DS MAX, MAYA, or the free alternative named Blender. Then, in the field of the `FixedCameraGame` class, insert the following lines:

   ```
   Matrix view;
   Matrix projection;
   Model model;
   ```

2. Then, in the `Initialize()` method, we will add the following lines:

   ```
   Vector3 position = new Vector3(0, 40, 50);
   Vector3 target = new Vector3(0, 0, 0);

   view = Matrix.CreateLookAt(position, target, Vector3.Up);
   projection =
       Matrix.CreatePerspectiveFieldOfView(MathHelper.PiOver4,
           GraphicsDevice.Viewport.AspectRatio,
           1, 1000.0f);
   ```

3. Next, we load and initialize the `Tree.fbx` 3D model located at the associate content project, into our game. Add the following code to the `LoadContent()` method:

   ```
   model = Content.Load<Model>("Tree");
   ```

4. The last step for our game is to draw the model on the screen. Insert the following lines into the `Draw()` method:

   ```
   // Define and copy the transforms of model
   Matrix[] transforms = new Matrix[this.model.Bones.Count];
   this.model.CopyAbsoluteBoneTransformsTo(transforms);

   // Draw the model. A model can have multiple meshes, so loop.
   foreach (ModelMesh mesh in this.model.Meshes)
   {
       foreach (BasicEffect effect in mesh.Effects)
       {
           effect.EnableDefaultLighting();


           // Get the transform information from its parent
           effect.World = transforms[mesh.ParentBone.Index];

           // Pass the View and Projection matrix to effect
           // make the rendering hardware how to transform the
   ```

```
            // model
            effect.View = view;
            effect.Projection = projection;
        }

        mesh.Draw();
    }
```

5. Now, build and run the application. It will run similar to the following screenshot:

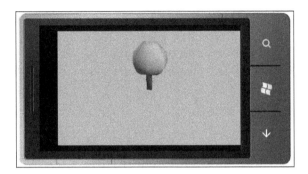

How it works...

In step 1, the model variable will be used to load and show the 3D model.

In step 2, we define the View matrix with position, target, and up vector. After that, we give the definition of the Project matrix.

In step 4, the first two lines define the matrix array depending on the bone count. Then we use the `CopyAbsoluteBoneTransformsTo()` method to assign the actual values to the transform array. In the `foreach` loop, we iterate all of the meshes in the model. In the loop body, we use `BasicEffect` to render the mesh. In Windows Phone 7 XNA programming, so far, it supports five built-in effects; here we just use the simplest one. For effect, `Effect.World` indicates the mesh's position; `Effect.View` represents the View matrix, `Effect.Projection` represents the Projection matrix. When all of the subloop effects are done, `mesh.Draw()`—in the loop for meshes—will render the mesh to the touchscreen.

Drawing the axes for a 3D game

The presentation of 3D lines is completely different from 2D; to draw the 3D axes in 3D will help you have a straightforward sense on the 3D world. The key to drawing the axes is the vertex format and vertex buffer, which holds the vertex data for rendering the lines. `VertexBuffer` is a sequence of allocated memory for storing vertices, which have the vertex position, color, texture coordinates, and the normal vector for rendering shapes or models. In other words, you can also use vertex buffer as an array of vertices. When the XNA application begins to render, it will read the vertex buffer and draw the vertex with the corresponding information that was saved into the game world. Based on the vertex buffer, the rendering performance will be much faster than passing the vertex one by one when requesting. In this recipe, you will learn how to use the vertex buffer to draw the axes in 3D. For a better view, the example will run in landscape view.

How to do it...

1. Create a Windows Phone Game in Visual Studio 2010. Change the name from `Game1.cs` to `Draw3DAxesGame.cs` and then add the following class-level variables:

```
// Basic Effect object
BasicEffect basicEffect;

// Vertex Data with Positon and Color
VertexPositionColor[] pointList;

// Vertex Buffer to hold the vertex data for drawing
VertexBuffer vertexBuffer;

// Camera View and Projection matrix
Matrix viewMatrix;
Matrix projectionMatrix;

// The Left and right hit region on the screen for rotating the
// axes
Rectangle recLeft;
Rectangle recRight;

// The rotation value
float rotation = 45;
```

2. Initialize the 3D world for the axes and axes vertex data. Insert the following code to the `Initialize()` method:

```
// Define the camera View matrix
viewMatrix = Matrix.CreateLookAt(
    new Vector3(0.0f, 0.0f, 150f),
```

```
        Vector3.Zero,
        Vector3.Up
);

// Define the camera Projection matrix
projectionMatrix = Matrix.CreatePerspectiveFieldOfView(
    MathHelper.PiOver4,
    GraphicsDevice.Viewport.AspectRatio,
    0.5f,
    1000.0f);

// Initialize the basic effect
basicEffect = new BasicEffect(GraphicsDevice);

// Initialize the axes world matrix of the position in 3D world
basicEffect.World = Matrix.Identity;

// Initialize the vertex data
pointList = new VertexPositionColor[6];

// Define the vertex data of axis X
pointList[0] = new VertexPositionColor(new Vector3(0, 0, 0),
    Color.Red);
pointList[1] = new VertexPositionColor(new Vector3(50, 0, 0),
    Color.Red);

// Define the vertex data of axis Y
pointList[2] = new VertexPositionColor(new Vector3(0, 0, 0),
    Color.White);
pointList[3] = new VertexPositionColor(new Vector3(0, 50, 0),
    Color.White);

// Define the vertex data of axis Z
pointList[4] = new VertexPositionColor(new Vector3(0, 0, 0),
    Color.Blue);
pointList[5] = new VertexPositionColor(new Vector3(0, 0, 50),
    Color.Blue);

// Initialize the vertex buffer and allocate the space in
//vertex buffer for the vertex data
vertexBuffer = new VertexBuffer(GraphicsDevice,
    VertexPositionColor.VertexDeclaration, 6,
    BufferUsage.None);
```

```
// Set the vertex buffer data to the array of vertices.
vertexBuffer.SetData<VertexPositionColor>(pointList);

// Define the Left and Right hit region on the screen
recLeft = new Rectangle(0, 0,
    GraphicsDevice.Viewport.Width / 2,
    GraphicsDevice.Viewport.Height);

recRight = new Rectangle(GraphicsDevice.Viewport.Width / 2, 0,
    GraphicsDevice.Viewport.Width / 2,
    GraphicsDevice.Viewport.Height);
```

3. Now, we need to check if the user has tapped the screen, so that we can rotate the axis. Add the following lines to the `Update()` method:

```
// Check whether the tapped position is in the Left or the
Right // hit region
TouchCollection touches = TouchPanel.GetState();
if (touches.Count > 0 && touches[0].State ==
    TouchLocationState.Pressed)
{
    Point point = new Point((int)touches[0].Position.X,
        (int)touches[0].Position.Y);

    // Rotate the axis in the landscape mode
    if (recLeft.Contains(point))
    {
        rotation += 10f;
    }
    if (recRight.Contains(point))
    {
        rotation -= 10f;
    }
}
```

4. Draw the axes on screen. Insert the following code to the `Draw()` method:

```
// Rotate the axes
basicEffect.World =
    Matrix.CreateRotationY(MathHelper.ToRadians(rotation)) *
    Matrix.CreateRotationX(MathHelper.ToRadians(50));

// Give the view and projection to the basic effect
basicEffect.View = viewMatrix;
basicEffect.Projection = projectionMatrix;
```

```
// Enable the vertex color in Basic Effect
basicEffect.VertexColorEnabled = true;

// Draw the axes on screen, iterate the pass in Basic Effect
foreach (EffectPass pass in
    basicEffect.CurrentTechnique.Passes)
{
    // Begin Drawing
    pass.Apply();

    // Set the vertex buffer to graphic device
    GraphicsDevice.SetVertexBuffer(vertexBuffer, 0);

    // Draw the axes with LineList Type
    GraphicsDevice.DrawUserPrimitives<VertexPositionColor>(
        PrimitiveType.LineList, pointList, 0, 3);
}
```

5. Let's build and run the example. It will run similar to the following screenshot:

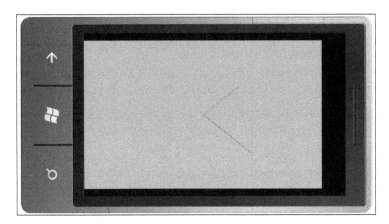

How it works...

In step 1, we declare the `BasicEffect` for axes drawing, the `VertexPositionColor` array to store the vertex information of the axes, and then use the declared `VertexBuffer` object to hold the `VertexPositionColor` data. The following two matrices indicate the camera view and projection. The other two rectangular objects will be used to define the left and right hit regions on the screen. The last `rotation` variable is the controlling factor for axes rotation in 3D.

In step 2, we first define the camera View and Project matrices and then initialize the vertex data for the 3D axes. We use the `Vector3` and `Color` objects to initialize the `VertexPositionColor` structure and then we define the `VertexBuffer` object. The `VertexBuffer` object has two overload constructors. The first one is:

```
public VertexBuffer (
    GraphicsDevice graphicsDevice,
    VertexDeclaration vertexDeclaration,
    int vertexCount,
    BufferUsage usage
)
```

The first parameter is graphic device value; the second is vertex declaration, which describes per-vertex data, the size, and usage of each vertex element; the `vertexCount` parameter indicates how many vertices the vertex buffer will store; and the last parameter `BufferUsage` defines the access right for the vertex buffer, read and write or write only.

The second parameter of the second overload method is a little different. This parameter gets the type of the vertex, especially for the custom vertex type:

```
public VertexBuffer (
    GraphicsDevice graphicsDevice,
    Type vertexType,
    int vertexCount,
    BufferUsage usage
)
```

Here, we use the first overload method and pass 6 as the vertex total number. When the vertex buffer is allocated, you will need to set the vertex data to the vertex buffer for drawing. The last two lines are the definition of left and right regions on the touchscreen.

In step 3, the code checks whether the tapped position is located within the left or right rectangle region and changes the rotation value according to the different rectangles.

In step 4, the first line is to rotate the axes around *Y* based on the value of rotation. Then you give the View and Projection matrices for the camera. Next, you can enable the `BasicEffect.VertexColorEnabled` to color the axes. The last `foreach` loop will draw the vertex data about the 3D axes on the screen. The `DrawUserPrimitives()` method has four parameters:

```
public void DrawUserPrimitives<T> (
    PrimitiveType primitiveType,
    T[] vertexData,
    int vertexOffset,
    int primitiveCount
)
```

The `PrimitiveType` describes the type of primitive to render. Here, we use `PrimitiveType.LineList`, which will draw the line segments as the order of vertex data. The vertex data describes the vertex array information. Vertex offset tells the rendering functions the start index of the vertex data. The `primitiveCount` indicates the number of primitives to render, in this example, the number is three for the three axes.

Implementing a first-person shooter (FPS) camera in your game

Have you ever played a first-person shooter (FPS) game, such as *Counter-Strike, Quake*, or *Doom*? In these kind of games your eyes will be the main view. When you are playing, the game updates the eye view and makes you feel like it is real. On the computer, it is easy to change the view using the mouse or the keyboard; the challenge for Windows Phone 7 FPS camera is how to realize these typical behaviors without the keyboard or the mouse. In this recipe, you will master the technique to overcome it.

Getting ready

It is amazing and exciting to play a FPS game on the PC. In Windows Phone 7, you would want to have similar experiences. Actually, the experiences may be different; you just use the screen for everything. A Windows Phone FPS game also needs to define the camera first. The difference between this and the third-person shooter (TPS) camera is that, in the FPS camera, you should update the position of the camera itself and for the TPS camera you need to make the camera follow the updating position of the main player object at a reasonable distance. In a FPS game, you can use the arrow keys to move the player's position and the mouse to change the direction of your view. In Windows Phone 7, we could use different regions of the touchscreen to move and use FreeDrag to update the view.

How to do it...

Now, let's begin the exciting work:

1. Create a Windows Phone Game in Visual Studio 2010, and change the name from `Game1.cs` to `FPSCameraGame.cs`. Then, add the 3D models `box.fbx` and `tree.fbx`, XNA font object, and `gameFont.font` to content project. After the preparation work, you need to insert the variables in the class field:

   ```
   // Game Font
   SpriteFont spriteFont;

   // Camera View matrix
   Matrix view;
   ```

```
// Camera Projection matrix
Matrix projection;

// Position of Camera
Vector3 position;

// Models
Model modelTree;
Model modelBox;

// Hit regions on the touchscreen
Rectangle recUp;
Rectangle recDown;
Rectangle recRight;
Rectangle recLeft;

// Angle for rotation
Vector3 angle;

// Gesture delta value
Vector2 gestureDelta;
```

2. You need to initialize the camera View matrix and projection and the hit regions on the touchscreen. Now, add the following lines to the `Initialize()` method:

```
angle = new Vector3();

// Enable the FreeDrag gesture
TouchPanel.EnabledGestures = GestureType.FreeDrag;

// Define the camera position and the target position
position = new Vector3(0, 40, 50);
Vector3 target = new Vector3(0, 0, 0);

// Create the camera View matrix and Projection matrix
view = Matrix.CreateLookAt(position, target, Vector3.Up);

projection = Matrix.CreatePerspectiveFieldOfView(
    MathHelper.PiOver4,
    GraphicsDevice.Viewport.AspectRatio, 1, 1000.0f);

// Define the four hit regions on touchscreen
recUp = new Rectangle(GraphicsDevice.Viewport.Width / 4, 0,
    GraphicsDevice.Viewport.Width / 2,
    GraphicsDevice.Viewport.Height / 2);
```

```
recDown = new Rectangle(GraphicsDevice.Viewport.Width / 4,
    GraphicsDevice.Viewport.Height / 2,
    GraphicsDevice.Viewport.Width / 2,
    GraphicsDevice.Viewport.Height / 2);

recRight = new Rectangle( GraphicsDevice.Viewport.Width -
    GraphicsDevice.Viewport.Width / 4, 0,
    GraphicsDevice.Viewport.Width /
    4,GraphicsDevice.Viewport.Height);

recLeft = new Rectangle(0, 0,
    GraphicsDevice.Viewport.Width -
    GraphicsDevice.Viewport.Width / 4,
    GraphicsDevice.Viewport.Height);
```

3. In this step, you have to load the model into your game and add the following code to the `LoadContent()` method:

```
modelBox = Content.Load<Model>("box");
modelTree = Content.Load<Model>("Tree");
spriteFont = Content.Load<SpriteFont>("gameFont");
```

4. Add the core logic code for the FPS camera updating in the `Update()` method. This code reacts to the tap and flick gestures to change the camera view:

```
// Get the touch data
TouchCollection touches = TouchPanel.GetState();

// Check the tapped point whether in the hit regions
if (touches.Count > 0 && touches[0].State ==
    TouchLocationState.Pressed)
{
    // Get the tapped position
    Point point = new Point((int)touches[0].Position.X,
        (int)touches[0].Position.Y);

    // Check whether the point is inside the UP region
    if(recUp.Contains(point))
    {
        // Move the camera forward
        view.Translation += new Vector3(0, 0, 5);
    }
    // Check whether the point is inside the DOWN region
    else if (recDown.Contains(point))
    {
```

```
            // Move the camera backward
            view.Translation += new Vector3(0, 0, -5);
        }
        // Check whether the point is inside the LEFT region
        else if (recLeft.Contains(point))
        {
            // Rotate the camera around Y in clockwise
            view  *= Matrix.CreateRotationY(
                MathHelper.ToRadians(-10));
        }
        // Check whether the point is inside the RIGHT region
        else if (recRight.Contains(point))
        {
            // Rotate the camera around Y in counter-
            // clockwise
            view *= Matrix.CreateRotationY(
                MathHelper.ToRadians(10));
        }
    }


    // Check the available gestures
    while (TouchPanel.IsGestureAvailable)
    {
        // Read the on-going gesture
        GestureSample gestures = TouchPanel.ReadGesture();

        switch (gestures.GestureType)
        {
            // If the GestureType is FreeDrag
            case GestureType.FreeDrag:

            // Read the Delta.Y to angle.X, Delta.X to angle.Y
            // Because the rotation value around axis Y
            // depends on the Delta changing on axis X
            angle.X = gestures.Delta.Y * 0.001f;
            angle.Y = gestures.Delta.X * 0.001f;

            gestureDelta = gestures.Delta;

            // Identify the view and rotate it
            view *= Matrix.Identity;
            view *= Matrix.CreateRotationX(angle.X);
            view *= Matrix.CreateRotationY(angle.Y);
```

```
        // Reset the angle to next coming gesture.
        angle.X = 0;
        angle.Y = 0;
        break;
    }
}
```

5. Render the models on screen. We define a `DrawModel()` method, which will be called in the main `Draw()` method for showing the models:

```
public void DrawModel(Model model)
{
    Matrix[] transforms = new Matrix[model.Bones.Count];
    model.CopyAbsoluteBoneTransformsTo(transforms);

    // Draw the model. A model can have multiple meshes.
    foreach (ModelMesh mesh in model.Meshes)
    {
        foreach (BasicEffect effect in mesh.Effects)
        {
            effect.EnableDefaultLighting();

            effect.World = transforms[mesh.ParentBone.Index];
            effect.View = view;
            effect.Projection = projection;
        }

        mesh.Draw();
    }
}
```

6. Then insert the following code to the `Draw()` method:

```
GraphicsDevice.DepthStencilState = DepthStencilState.Default;
GraphicsDevice.BlendState = BlendState.Opaque;

DrawModel(modelTree);
DrawModel(modelBox);

spriteBatch.Begin();
spriteBatch.DrawString(spriteFont, gestureDelta.ToString(),
    new Vector2(0, 0), Color.White);
spriteBatch.End();
```

7. Now, build and run the application. It will look similar to the following screenshots. Flick on the screen and you will see a different view:

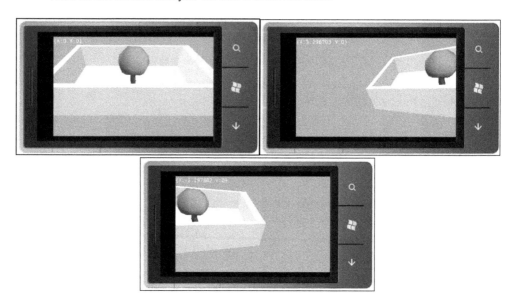

How it works...

In step 1, in this code we declare two matrices, one for camera View matrix and one for Projection matrix. A Vector3 variable, `position,` indicates the camera position. The other two Model variables `modelTree` and `modelBox` will be used to load the 3D model. The following four Rectangle variables individually represent the Up, Down, Right, and Left hit regions on the Windows Phone 7 touchscreen. The `angle` variable will let the game know how to rotate the View matrix and the last variable, `gestureDelta`, will show the actual delta value the gestures take.

In step 2, in the initialize process, you will need to enable the `GestureType.FreeDrag` for the view rotation changing in the Update process. Then define the camera View matrix and Projection matrix. The block of code after that is about the hit region on screen definition. You can understand the basic logic from the following figure:

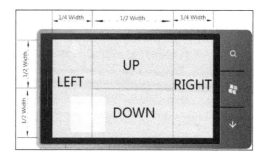

We use four rectangles to divide the screen into four parts, **UP**, **LEFT**, **RIGHT**, and **DOWN**. The width of **UP** and **DOWN** rectangles is half of the screen width in landscape mode and their height is half of the screen height. Similarly, the width of the **LEFT** and **RIGHT** rectangle is a quarter of the screen width in landscape mode and their height is the height of the screen. According to the width and height of each rectangle, it will be easy for you to know their start positions.

In step 3, all the models or fonts must be loaded from the `ContentManager`, which you have used for 2D image manipulation.

In step 4, the first part of code before the `while` loop is to get the tapped position and check whether it is in the four hit regions and do the corresponding operations. If the tapped position is within the **UP** or **DOWN** rectangle, we translate the camera; if it is located at the range of the **LEFT** or **RIGHT** rectangle, the camera view will be rotated. The next part is to react to the `FreeDrag` gesture, which will change the direction of the camera freely. In the code block of step 4, you need to read the gesture after gesture availability checking, and then determine which gesture type is taking place. Here, we deal with the `GestureType.FreeDrag`. If you flick horizontally, the *X* axis will change, you could rotate the camera around the *Y* axis by delta *X*; if you flick vertically, the *Y* axis will change, you could rotate the camera around the *X* axis by delta *Y*. Following the law, we assign `Delta.X` to `angle.Y` for rotation around the *Y* axis and assign `Delta.Y` to `angle.X` for pitch rotation around the *X* axis. When all the necessary gesture delta values are ready, you can do the camera rotation. Identify the View matrix, then use `Matrix.CreateRotationX()` and `Matrix.CreateRotationY()` to rotate the camera around the *Y* and *X* axes. Finally, you need to reset the angle for the next gesture delta value.

In step 5, we also copy and transform model matrices and apply the effect in every mesh in the model.

In step 6, you may be curious on the `DepthStencilState`. The depth stencil state controls how the depth buffer and the stencil buffer are used, from XNA SDK.

During rendering, the z position (or depth) of each pixel is stored in the depth buffer. When rendering pixels more than once—such as when objects overlap—depth data is compared between the current pixel and the previous pixel to determine which pixel is closer to the camera. When a pixel passes the depth test, the pixel color is written to a render target and the pixel depth is written to the depth buffer.

A depth buffer may also contain stencil data, which is why a depth buffer is often called a depth-stencil buffer. Use a stencil function to compare a reference stencil value—a global value you set—to the per-pixel value in the stencil buffer to mask which pixels get saved and which are discarded.

The depth buffer stores floating-point depth or z data for each pixel while the stencil buffer stores integer data for each pixel. The depth-stencil state class, `DepthStencilState`, contains the state that controls how depth and stencil data impact rendering.

Implementing a round rotating camera in a 3D game

When a 3D game reaches the end, sometimes the camera will go up and rotate around the player. On the other hand, when a 3D game just begins, a camera will fly from a very far point to the player's position very fast, like a Hollywood movie. It's impressive and fantastic. In this recipe, you will learn how to create this effect.

How to do it...

1. First of all, we create a Windows Phone Game project, change the name from `Game1.cs` to `RoundRotateCameraGame.cs`. Then, add two 3D models, `tree.fbx` and `box.fbx`, to the content project.

2. Declare the variables used in the game in the `RoundRotateCamerGame` class:

```
// View matrix for camera
Matrix view;

// Projection matrix for camera
Matrix projection;

// Camera position
Vector3 position;

// Tree and box models
Model modelTree;
Model modelBox;
```

3. Define the View and Project matrix and add the following code to the `Initialize()` method:

```
// Camera position
position = new Vector3(0, 40, 50);

// Camera lookat target
Vector3 target = new Vector3(0, 0, 0);

// Define the View matrix
view = Matrix.CreateLookAt(position, target, Vector3.Up);

// Define the Project matrix
projection = Matrix.CreatePerspectiveFieldOfView(
    MathHelper.PiOver4,
    GraphicsDevice.Viewport.AspectRatio, 1, 1000.0f);
```

4. We load and initialize the 3D models and insert the following lines into
`LoadContent()`:

```
modelBox = Content.Load<Model>("box");
modelTree = Content.Load<Model>("Tree");
```

5. This step is most important for rotating the camera. Paste the following code into the
`Update()` method:

```
// Get the game time
float time = (float)gameTime.TotalGameTime.TotalSeconds;

// Get the rotate value from -0.1 to +0.1 around the Sin(time)
Matrix rotate = Matrix.CreateRotationY(
    (float)Math.Sin(time) * 0.1f);

// Update the view camera's position according to the rotate
//value;
position = (Matrix.CreateTranslation(position) *
    rotate).Translation;
view = Matrix.CreateLookAt(position, Vector3.Zero,
    Vector3.Up);
```

6. The last step is to draw the models on the touchscreen. We defined a model
drawing method:

```
public void DrawModel(Model model)
{
    Matrix[] transforms = new Matrix[model.Bones.Count];
    model.CopyAbsoluteBoneTransformsTo(transforms);

    // Draw the model. A model can have multiple meshes, so
    // loop.
    foreach (ModelMesh mesh in model.Meshes)
    {
        foreach (BasicEffect effect in mesh.Effects)
        {
            effect.EnableDefaultLighting();

            effect.World =
            transforms[mesh.ParentBone.Index];
            effect.View = view;
            effect.Projection = projection;
        }

    mesh.Draw();
    }
}
```

7. Then we add the other code to the `Draw()` method:

```
GraphicsDevice.DepthStencilState = DepthStencilState.Default;
GraphicsDevice.BlendState = BlendState.Opaque;

DrawModel(modelTree);
DrawModel(modelBox);
```

8. All done! Build and run the application. You will see a rotating camera around the 3D objects, as shown in the following screenshots:

How it works...

In step 2, we declare the `view` and `projection` matrices for the camera and the `position` vector for the camera's location. The last two model variables will be used to load the 3D model objects.

In step 3, the camera will locate at (X:0, Y:40, Z:50) forwards to (X:0, Y:0, Z:0) and have an Up vector(0, 1, 0), the Projection will have a 45 degree view scope from 1 to 1000.

In step 4, you should always load the content from `ContentManager` with different types as you need. Here, the type is `Model`—a 3D object.

In step 5, we read the game time to rotate the camera automatically as time passes by. Then we use `Math.Sin()` to change the rotation value within the range of `-1` to `+1`. This is required because without this method, the time will keep on increasing and the camera will rotate faster and faster. `Matrix.CreateRotationY()` receives a radian value to rotate around the Y axis, here the value will be -0.1 to +0.1. The last part is about updating the `view` matrix; we translate and rotate the camera's position for creating a new `view` matrix.

In step 6, this code is the basic for drawing a static model, we have discussed in former recipes, here we just need to pay attention on the View matrix and Projection matrix and these two matrices actually impact the rendered effect.

In step 7, notice the `GraphicsDevice.DepthStencilState`, which is important for the rendering order.

Implementing a chase camera

A chase camera will move smoothly around a 3D object and regardless of how the camera view is changed, the camera will restore to its original position. This kind of camera is useful for a racing game or an acceleration effect. In this recipe, you will learn how to make your own chase camera in Windows Phone 7.

How to do it...

1. Create a Windows Phone Game in Visual Studio 2010, change the name from `Game1.cs` to `ChaseCameraGame.cs`. Then add the `box.fbx` 3D model to the content project. After the initial work, you should insert the following code to the `ChaseGameCamera` class as fields:

   ```
   // Loading for box model
   Model boxModel;

   // Camera View and Projection matrix
   Matrix view;
   Matrix projection;

   // Camera's position
   Vector3 position;

   // Camera look at target
   Vector3 target;

   // Offset distance from the target.
   Vector3 offsetDistance;

   // Yaw, Pitch values
   float yaw;
   float pitch;

   // Angle delta for GestureType.FreeDrag
   Vector3 angle;
   ```

2. Instantiate the variables. Add the following lines into the `Initialize()` method:

   ```
   // Enable the FreeDrag gesture type
   TouchPanel.EnabledGestures = GestureType.FreeDrag;

   // Define the camera position and desired position
   position = new Vector3(0, 1000, 1000);
   ```

```
// Define the target position and desired target position
target = new Vector3(0, 0, 0);

// the offset from target
offsetDistance = new Vector3(0, 50, 100);

yaw = 0.0f;
pitch = 0.0f;

// Identify the camera View matrix
view = Matrix.Identity;

// Define the camera Projection matrix
projection = Matrix.CreatePerspectiveFieldOfView(
    MathHelper.PiOver4, GraphicsDevice.Viewport.AspectRatio,
    1f, 1000f);

// Initialize the angle
angle = new Vector3();
```

3. Load the box model in the `LoadContent()` method:

```
boxModel = Content.Load<Model>("box");
```

4. Update the chase camera. First, we define the `UpdateView()` method, as follows:

```
private void UpdateView(Matrix World)
{
    // Normalize the right and up vector of camera world
    // matrix
    World.Right.Normalize();
    World.Up.Normalize();

    // Assign the actual world matrix translation to target
    target = World.Translation;

    // Rotate the right vector of camera world matrix
    target += World.Right * yaw;

    // Rotate the up vector of camera world matrix
    target += World.Up * pitch;

    // Interpolate the increment in every frame until the
    // position is
    // equal to the offset distance from target
    position = Vector3.SmoothStep(position, offsetDistance,
```

```
      0.15f);

      // Interpolate the increment or decrement
      // from current yaw value to 0 to yaw in every frame
      yaw = MathHelper.SmoothStep(yaw, 0f, 0.1f);

      // Interpolate the increment or decrement from current
      // pitch value to 0 to pitch in every frame
      pitch = MathHelper.SmoothStep(pitch, 0f, 0.1f);

      // Update the View matrix.
      view = Matrix.CreateLookAt(position, target, World.Up);
}
```

5. In the `Update()` method, we insert the following code:

```
// Check the available gestures
while (TouchPanel.IsGestureAvailable)
{
    // Read the on-going gesture
    GestureSample gestures = TouchPanel.ReadGesture();

    // Make sure which gesture type is taking place
    switch (gestures.GestureType)
    {
        // If the gesture is GestureType.FreeDrag
        case GestureType.FreeDrag:

        // Read the Delta.Y to angle.X, Delta.X to angle.Y
        // Because the rotation value around axis Y
        // depends on the Delta changing on axis X
        angle.Y += gestures.Delta.X ;
        angle.X += gestures.Delta.Y ;

        // assign the angle value to yaw and pitch
        yaw = angle.Y;
        pitch = angle.X;

        // Reset the angle value for next FreeDrag gesture
        angle.Y = 0;
        angle.X = 0;

        break;
    }
}
```

```
    // Update the viewMatrix
    UpdateView(Matrix.Identity);
```

6. The final step is to draw the model. The drawing code will be as follows:

```
protected override void Draw(GameTime gameTime)
{
    GraphicsDevice.Clear(Color.CornflowerBlue);

    // The following three lines are to ensure that the
    // models
    // are drawn correctly
    GraphicsDevice.DepthStencilState =
        DepthStencilState.Default;
    GraphicsDevice.BlendState = BlendState.AlphaBlend;

    DrawModel(boxModel);

    base.Draw(gameTime);
}

// Draw the model
private void DrawModel(Model model)
{
    Matrix[] modelTransforms = new Matrix[model.Bones.Count];
    model.CopyAbsoluteBoneTransformsTo(modelTransforms);

    foreach (ModelMesh mesh in model.Meshes)
    {
        foreach (BasicEffect effect in mesh.Effects)
        {
            effect.EnableDefaultLighting();
            effect.World =
                modelTransforms[mesh.ParentBone.Index];
            effect.View = view;
            effect.Projection = projection;
        }
        mesh.Draw();
    }
}
```

7. Now, build and run the application. You will see the application runs similar to the following screenshots:

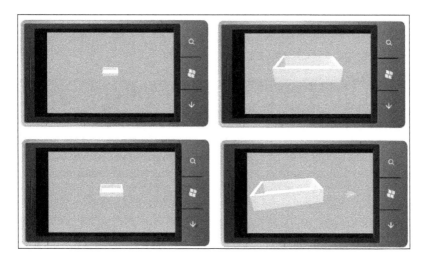

How it works...

In step 1, we declare a `boxModel` object for loading the box model and the `view` and `projection` matrices for camera. The `position` vector specifies the camera position. The `offsetDistance` indicates the distance from the `target`. The `yaw` and `pitch` variables represent the rotation value of the camera and the `angle` stores the actual value that the gesture generates.

In step 2, the initialization phase, you should enable the `FreeDrag` gesture, give the camera the startup position and its target and define the offset distance from the target, assign the initial value to `yaw` and `pitch` and then identify the camera View matrix, which will be used to update the rotation of the camera. Moreover, you still need to specify the camera Projection matrix and instantiate the `angle` variable.

In step 4, the `UpdateView()` method does the actual rotation and chase operations depending on the gesture value. First, we normalize the right and up vectors of the world matrix to make the directions easy and accurate to compute. Then, assign the world translation to the `target` variable, which will be used as the camera look-at position. For camera rotation, we use `World.Right * yaw` to rotate the camera around the *Y* axis and `World.Up * pitch` to rotate the camera around the *X* axis. Next, we interpolate the increment about 0.15 to the camera's position until it is equal to the predefined offset distance in every frame. The `MathHelper.SmoothStep()` method generates smooth values between the source and end settings. Then, we interpolate the increment or decrement about 0.1 from the current `yaw` value to 0 in every frame. The camera will be rotated to the original position around the *Y* axis. Similarly, we interpolate the smooth values to the pitch variable. The final step will update the `view` matrix based on the `position` and `target` values.

In step 5, the first part is to handle the `FreeDrag` gesture. When the gesture is caught, the code will store the gesture delta value to `angle`. `angle.X` saves the delta value around the *Y* axis and `angle.Y` maintains the value around the *X* axis. Then we pass `angle.Y` to the `yaw` variable for the rotation around the *Y* axis and assign `angle.X` to the `pitch` variable for rotating around the *X* axis. After that, we reset the `angle` value for the next gesture. Eventually, we call the `UpdateView()` to update the camera view.

Using culling to remove the unseen parts and texture mapping

In a real 3D game, a large number of objects exist in the game world. Every object has hundreds or thousands of faces. To render all of the faces is a big performance cost. Therefore, we use Frustum to filter the outside objects, and then use the culling algorithm to remove the unseen part of the objects. These approaches cut the unnecessary parts in the 3D game, improving the performance significantly. In this recipe, you will learn how to use the culling method in Windows Phone 7 Game development.

Getting ready

In Windows Phone 7 XNA, the culling method uses the back-face culling algorithm to remove the unseen parts. This culling method is based on the observation that, if all objects in the world are closed, then the polygons, which do not face the viewer, cannot be seen. This directly translates to the vector angle between the direction where the viewer is facing and the normal of the face; if the angle is more than 90 degrees, the polygon can be discarded. Back-face culling is automatically performed by XNA. It can be expected to cull roughly half of the polygons in the view Frustum.

How to do it...

Now, let's see how Windows Phone 7 XNA performs the culling method:

1. Create a Windows Phone Game project in Visual Studio 2010, change the name from `Game1.cs` to `CullingGame.cs`, and add the `Square.png` file to the content project.

2. Declare the variables for the project. Add the following lines to the `CullingGame` class:

```
// Texture
Texture2D texSquare;

// Camera's Position
Vector3 position;
```

```
// Camera look at target
Vector3 target;

//Camera World matrix
Matrix world;

//Camera View matrix
Matrix view;

//Camera Projection matrix
Matrix projection;

BasicEffect basicEffect;

// Vertex Structure
VertexPositionTexture[] vertexPositionTextures;

// Vertex Buffer
VertexBuffer vertexBuffer;

// Rotation for the texture
float rotation;

// Translation for the texture
Matrix translation;

// Bool value for whether keeps rotating the texture
bool KeepRotation = false;
```

3. Initialize the basic effect, camera, `vertexPositionTextures` array, and set the culling mode in Windows Phone 7 XNA. Insert the following code to the `Initialize()` method:

```
// Initialize the basic effect
basicEffect = new BasicEffect(GraphicsDevice);

// Define the world matrix of texture
translation = Matrix.CreateTranslation(new Vector3(25, 0, 0));

// Initialize the camera position and look-at target
position = new Vector3(0, 0, 200);
target = Vector3.Zero;

// Initialize the camera transformation matrices
world = Matrix.Identity;
```

```
view = Matrix.CreateLookAt(position, target, Vector3.Up);

projection = Matrix.CreatePerspectiveFieldOfView(
    MathHelper.PiOver4, GraphicsDevice.Viewport.AspectRatio,
    1, 1000);

// Allocate the VertexPositionTexture array
vertexPositionTextures = new VertexPositionTexture[6];

// Define the vertex information
vertexPositionTextures[0] = new VertexPositionTexture(
    new Vector3(-25, -25, 0), new Vector2(0, 1));

vertexPositionTextures[1] = new VertexPositionTexture(
    new Vector3(-25, 25, 0), new Vector2(0, 0));

vertexPositionTextures[2] = new VertexPositionTexture(
    new Vector3(25, -25, 0), new Vector2(1, 1));

vertexPositionTextures[3] = new VertexPositionTexture(
    new Vector3(-25, 25, 0), new Vector2(0, 0));

vertexPositionTextures[4] = new VertexPositionTexture(
    new Vector3(25, 25, 0), new Vector2(1, 0));

vertexPositionTextures[5] = new VertexPositionTexture(
    new Vector3(25, -25, 0), new Vector2(1, 1));

// Define the vertex buffer
vertexBuffer = new VertexBuffer(
    GraphicsDevice,
    VertexPositionTexture.VertexDeclaration, 6,
    BufferUsage.None);

// Set the VertexPositionTexture array to vertex buffer
vertexBuffer.SetData<VertexPositionTexture>(
    vertexPositionTextures);

// Set the cull mode
RasterizerState rasterizerState = new RasterizerState();
rasterizerState.CullMode = CullMode.CullCounterClockwiseFace;
GraphicsDevice.RasterizerState = rasterizerState;
```

```
    // Set graphic sample state to PointClamp
    graphics.GraphicsDevice.SamplerStates[0] =
        SamplerState.PointClamp;
```

4. Load the square texture in the `LoadContent()` method:

```
    texSquare = Content.Load<Texture2D>("Square");
```

5. React to the Tap to rotate the square texture. Add the following code to the `Update()` method:

```
    TouchCollection touches = TouchPanel.GetState();
    if (touches.Count > 0 && touches[0].State ==
        TouchLocationState.Pressed)
    {
        Point point = new Point((int)touches[0].Position.X,
            (int)touches[0].Position.Y);

        if (GraphicsDevice.Viewport.Bounds.Contains(point))
        {
            KeepRotation = true;
        }
    }

    if (KeepRotation)
    {
        rotation += 0.1f;
    }
```

6. Draw the texture on the screen and add the following lines to the `Draw()` method:

```
    // Set the matrix information to basic effect
    basicEffect.World = world * translation *
    Matrix.CreateRotationY(rotation);

    basicEffect.View = view;
    basicEffect.Projection = projection;

    // Set the texture
    basicEffect.TextureEnabled = true;
    basicEffect.Texture = texSquare;

    // Iterate the passes in the basic effect
    foreach (var pass in basicEffect.CurrentTechnique.Passes)
    {
        pass.Apply();
        GraphicsDevice.SetVertexBuffer(vertexBuffer, 0);
```

```
GraphicsDevice.DrawUserPrimitives<VertexPositionTexture>
(PrimitiveType.TriangleList, vertexPositionTextures,
0, 2);
}
```

7. Now, build and run the application. The application will run similar to the following screenshot:

8. When you tap on the screen, the texture will run similar to the following screenshots. The last one is blank because the rotation is 90 degrees.

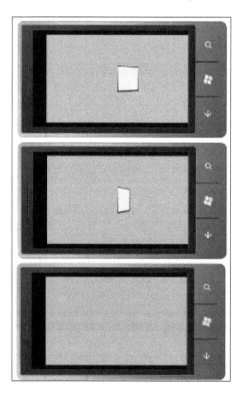

How it works...

In step 2, the `basicEffect` represents the effect for rendering the texture. The `VertexPositionTexture` array will be used to locate and scale the texture on screen. The `VertexBuffer` holds the `VertexPositionTexture` data for the graphic device to draw the texture. The `rotation` variable will determine how much rotation will take place around the *Y* axis. The `translation` matrix indicates the world position of the texture. The `bool` value `KeepRotation` is a flag that signals to the object whether it has to keep rotating or not. This value could be changed by touching the Windows Phone 7 screen.

In step 3, in the code, you need to notice the `VertexPositionTexture` array initialization. The texture is a square composed of two triangles having six vertices. We define the position and texture UV coordinates of every vertex. You can find a detailed explanation of texture coordinates from a computer graphic introduction book such as *Computer Graphics with OpenGL* written by *Donald D. Hearn, M. Pauline Baker, and Warren Carithers*. After the vertex initialization, we define the vertex buffer with the `VertexPositionTexture` type and pass 6 to vertex count and let the vertex buffer be read and written by setting the `BufferUsage` to `None`. Next, we need to fill the vertex buffer with `VertexPositionTexture` data defined previously. After that, the configuration of `CullMode` in `RasterizerState` will impact the culling method for the texture. Here, we set the `CullMode` to `CullMode.CullCounterClockwiseFace`. From the back-face algorithm, the normal will face the camera, and none of the backward polygons will be seen, as they will be removed. The last setting on `GraphicDevice.SamplerState` is important. The `SamplerState` class determines how to sample texture data. When covering a 3D triangle mesh with a 2D texture, you supply 2D texture coordinates that range from (0, 0), the upper-left corner, to (1, 1), the lower-right corner. But you can also supply texture coordinates outside that range, and based on the texture address mode setting the image will be clamped (that is, the outside rim of pixels will just be repeated) or a tiled pattern or wrapped in a flip-flop mirror effect. The `SamplerState` supports `Wrap`, `Mirror`, and `Clamp` effects.

For Windows Phone 7, the GPU on is not compatible with `Wrap`, which is the default setting in XNA, so when you run your application without any setting on `SamplerState`, the application will crash and you cannot get any error message. Consequently, we set the `SamplerState` to `PointClamp` to let the application run smoothly.

In step 5, the code first checks whether the tapped position is within the touchscreen. If so, set the `KeepRotation` value to `true`. Then the updating will increase the rotation value by 0.1 in every frame if the `KeepRotation` is true.

In step 6, the `BasicEffect.World` is used to translate and rotate the texture in 3D, where `BasicEffect.View` and Projection define the camera view. Then, we set the texture to basic effect. When all the necessary settings have been done, the `foreach` loop will use the `Pass` in basic effect technique to draw the primitives. We set the `vertexBuffer` defined before to the current graphic device. Finally, we draw the primitives with texture from the vertex buffer.

4
Heads Up Display (HUD)—Your Phone Game User Interface

In this chapter, we will cover:

- ▶ Scaling an image
- ▶ Creating a simple sprite sheet animation in a 2D game
- ▶ Creating a complex sprite sheet animation in a 2D game
- ▶ Creating a text animation in adventure genre (AVG) game
- ▶ Creating a text-based menu—the easiest menu to create
- ▶ Creating an image-based menu
- ▶ Creating a 3D model-based menu
- ▶ Creating a progress bar for game contents loading and value status
- ▶ Creating buttons in your game
- ▶ Creating a listbox to speed up your information management in a game
- ▶ Creating a text input control to communicate with others in a game

Introduction

Head Up Display (HUD) or Graphic User Interface (GUI) is the core part of games. Players can navigate the different game screens using the menu, click the button to trigger game events, or use the textbox to type messages to other players. In StarCraft 2, you can click a building symbol to create a unit. In Diablo 2, you can change your equipment by selecting the staffs in the bag list panel. A powerful and rich GUI system will make your game more affable and fascinating.

Actually, Windows Phone 7 XNA framework does not support a built-in GUI system such as Silverlight. This means you should implement your own. Fortunately, if you do not hope to do the radical work while focusing on the game logic and the rendering technique, some third-party GUI packages using XNA, such as Neoforce Controls (`http://neoforce.codeplex.com/`) or Nuclex.UserInterface (`http://nuclexframework.codeplex.com/`) will do you a favor. Both the third-party XNA GUI libraries are free, and it is convenient for you to download them including the source code from `http://neoforce.codeplex.com/` or `http://nuclexframework.codeplex.com/`.

As a learner, studying from the source code with basic and essential knowledge should be the fastest way to master a new technique. As guidance, you can write and learn on your own from an existing third-party GUI library. In this chapter, you will master how to create the typical HUD elements: buttons, text animation presentation, menu, listbox, and text control in Windows Phone 7 based on XNA framework.

Scaling an image

Controlling the size of images is a basic technique in Windows Phone 7 XNA programming. Mastering this technique will help you implement many special visual effects in 2D. In this recipe, you will learn how to zoom an image in and out for a special visual effect. As an example, the image will jump up to you and go back. In the jumping phase, the image will fade out gradually. When the image becomes transparent, it will fall back with fading in.

How to do it...

The following mandatory steps will lead you to complete the recipe:

1. Create a Windows Phone Game in Visual Studio 2010 named `ImageZoomInOut`, change `Game1.cs` to `ImageZoomGame.cs`. Then add the `Next.png` file from the code bundle to the content project. After the preparation work, insert the following code to the field of the `ImageZoomGame` class:

```
// Image texture object
Texture2D texImage;

// Image position
Vector2 Position;

// The scale factor
float scale = 1;

// The rotate factor
float rotate = 0;

// Alpha value for controlling the image transparency
```

```
float alpha = 255;

// The color of image
Color color;

// Timer object
float timer;

// Bool value for zooming out or in.
bool ZoomOut = true;
```

2. In the `Initialize()` method, we define the image centered in the middle of the screen and the color:

```
Position = new Vector2(GraphicsDevice.Viewport.Width / 2,
    GraphicsDevice.Viewport.Height / 2);
color = Color.White;
```

3. Load the `Next.png` file in the `LoadContent()` method with the following code:

```
texImage = Content.Load<Texture2D>("Next");
```

4. Add the code to the `Update()` method to control the size transparency and rotation of the image:

```
// Accumulates the game elapsed time
timer += (float)gameTime.ElapsedGameTime.TotalMilliseconds;

// Zoom out
if (ZoomOut && alpha >= 0 && timer > 50)
{
    // If alpha equals 0, zoom the image in
    if (alpha == 0.0f)
    {
        ZoomOut = false;
    }

    // Amplify the image
    scale += 0.1f;

    // Rotate the image in clockwise
    rotate += 0.1f;

    // Fade the image out

    if (alpha > 0)
    {
```

```
            alpha -= 5;
        }

        color.A = (byte)alpha;

        // Reset the timer to 0 for the next interval
        timer = 0;
    }

    // Zoom in
    else if (!ZoomOut && timer > 50)
    {
        // If alpha equals 255, zoom the image out
        if (alpha == 255)
        {
            ZoomOut = true;
        }

        // Scale down the image
        scale -= 0.1f;

        // Rotate the image counter-clockwise
        rotate -= 0.2f;

        // Fade the image in
        if (alpha < 255)
        {
            alpha += 5;
        }

        color.A = (byte)alpha;

        // Reset the timer to 0 for the next interval
        timer = 0;
    }
```

5. To draw the image and effects on the Windows Phone 7 screen, add the code to the `Draw()` method:

```
spriteBatch.Begin(SpriteSortMode.Immediate,
    BlendState.NonPremultiplied);

spriteBatch.Draw(texImage, Position, null, color, rotate, new
    Vector2(texImage.Width / 2, texImage.Height / 2), scale,
    SpriteEffects.None, 0f);

spriteBatch.End();
```

6. Now, build and run the application. The application runs as shown in the following screenshots:

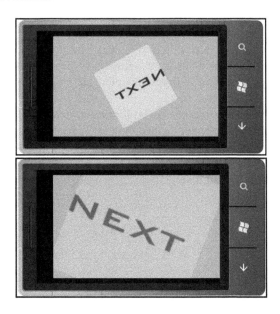

How it works...

In step 1, `texImage` holds the image for controlling; the `Position` variable represents the image position; `scale` will be used to control the image size; as the rotation factor, the `rotate` variable will store the value for rotation; `alpha` in `color` controls the image transparency degree; `timer` accumulates the game elapse milliseconds; the last variable `ZoomOut` determines whether to zoom the image out.

In step 2, we define the `Position` of the image in the center of the screen and set the `color` to `white`.

In step 4, the accumulated timer is used to control the period of time between the two frames. The next part is to check the direction of scale. If `ZoomOut` is true, we will increase the image size, decrease the alpha value and rotate the image in a clockwise direction, then reset the `timer`. Otherwise, the behavior is opposite.

In step 5, we set the `BlendState` in `SpritBatch.Begin()` to `NonPremultiplied` because we change the `alpha` value of `color` linearly, then draw the images with scale and rotation factors around the image center.

Creating a Simple Sprite Sheet animation in a 2D game

In Windows Phone 7 game programming, it is an obvious performance cost if you wanted to render a number of images. You need to allocate the same quantity of texture objects for the images in your game. If this happens in the game initialization phase, the time could be very long. Considering these reasons, the talented game programmers in the early days of the game industry found the solution through the Sprite Sheet technique, using a big image to contain a set of smaller images. It is very convenient for 2D game programming, especially for the sprite animation. The big advantage of using the Sprite Sheet is the ability to create character animation, complex effects, explosions, and so on. Applying the technique will be performance sweet for game content loading.

The Sprite Sheet has two types:

- ▸ Simple Sprite Sheet, where all the smaller images have the same dimensions
- ▸ Complex Sprite Sheet, where all the images in the sheet have different dimensions

In this recipe, you will learn how to create the Simple Sprite Sheet and use it in your Windows Phone 7 game.

In Simple Sprite Sheet, every subimage has the same size, the dimension could be defined when the Sprite Sheet was initiated. To locate the designated sub-image, you should know the X and Y coordinates, along with the width and height, and the offset for the row and column. For Simple Sprite Sheet, the following equation will help you complete the work:

```
Position = (X * Offset, Y * Offset)
```

For convenience, you can define the size of the subimage in digital image processing software, such as Adobe Photoshop, Microsoft Expression Design, Paint.Net, GIMP, and so on.

In this recipe, you will learn how to use the Sprite Sheet in your own Windows Phone 7 Game.

Getting ready

In the image processing tool, we create a Sprite Sheet as the next screenshot. In the image, every subimage is surrounded by a rectangle 50 pixels wide and 58 pixels high, as shown in the left-hand image in the following screenshot.

In a real Windows Phone Game, I am sure you do not want to see the border of the rectangle. As part of the exportation process, we will make the rectangles transparent, you just need to change the alpha value from 100 to 0 in code, and the latest Sprite Sheet should look similar to the right-hand image in the following screenshot:

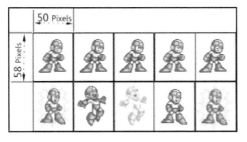 

We name the Sprite Sheet used in our example `SimpleSpriteSheet.png`.

Now the Sprite Sheet is ready, the next part is to animate the Sprite Sheet in our Windows Phone 7 game.

How to do it...

The following steps will give you a complete guidance to animate a Simple Sprite Sheet:

1. Create a Windows Phone Game project in Visual Studio 2010 named `SimpleSpriteSheetAnimation`, change `Game1.cs` to `SimpleSpirteSheetGame.cs`, adding the lines to the field of the `SimpleSpriteSheetGame` class:

```
// Sprite Texture
Texture2D sprite;

// A Timer variable
float timer = 0f;

// The interval
float interval = 200;

// Frame Count
int FrameCount = 4;

// Animation Count
int AnimationCount = 2;

// Current frame holder
int currentFrame = 0;

// Width of a single sprite image, not the whole Sprite
int spriteWidth = 50;
```

```
// Height of a single sprite image, not the whole Sprite
int spriteHeight = 58;

// A rectangle to store which 'frame' is currently being
Rectangle sourceRect;

// The center of the current 'frame'
Vector2 origin;

// Index of Row
int row = 0;

// Position Center
Vector2 screenCenter;
```

2. Load the Sprite Sheet image. Put the code into the LoadContent() method:

```
sprite = Content.Load<Texture2D>("SpriteSheet");

screenCenter = new Vector2(GraphicsDevice.Viewport.Width / 2,
    GraphicsDevice.Viewport.Height / 2);
```

3. This step is to animate the Simple Sprite Sheet. Insert the code in to the Update() method:

```
// Increase the timer by the number of milliseconds since
// update was last called
timer += (float)gameTime.ElapsedGameTime.TotalMilliseconds;

// Check the timer is more than the chosen interval
if (timer > interval)
{
    //Show the next frame
    currentFrame++;

    //Reset the timer
    timer = 0f;
}

// If reached the last frame, reset the current frame back to
// the one before the first frame
if (currentFrame == FrameCount)
{
    currentFrame = 0;
}
```

```
// React to the tap gesture
TouchCollection touches = TouchPanel.GetState();
if (touches.Count > 0 && touches[0].State ==
    TouchLocationState.Pressed)
{
    // Change the sprite sheet animation
    row = (row + 1) % AnimationCount;
}


// Compute which subimage will be rendered
sourceRect = new Rectangle(currentFrame * spriteWidth,
    row * spriteHeight, spriteWidth, spriteHeight);


// Compute the origin position for image rotation and scale.
origin = new Vector2(sourceRect.Width / 2,
    sourceRect.Height / 2);
```

4. Draw the Sprite Sheet on the screen. Add the code in the `Draw()` method:

```
spriteBatch.Begin();

//Draw the sprite in the center of an 800x600 screen
spriteBatch.Draw(sprite, screenCenter, sourceRect,
    Color.White, 0f, origin, 3.0f, SpriteEffects.None, 0);

spriteBatch.End();
```

5. Now, build and run the application. When you tap on the screen, the animation will change, as shown in the following screenshots:

How it works...

In step 1, the `sprite` object will hold the Sprite Sheet image; the `timer` variable will accumulate the game elapsed time; the `interval` variable defines the period of time between two frames in milliseconds; `AnimationCount` shows the number of animations that will be played; `currentFrame` indicates the playing frame, and also presents the column in Sprite Sheet image; `spriteWidth` and `spriteHeight` define the width and height of the currently rendering subimage. In this example the width and height of the Sprite subimage is `50` and `58` pixels respectively; the `sourceRectangle` lets the `SpriteBatch.Draw()` know which part of the Sprite Sheet image will be drawn; the `row` variable shows which animation will be rendered, `0` means the animation starts from the first.

In step 3, we accumulate the game elapsed time. If the accumulated time on the timer is greater than the interval, the current frame goes to the next frame, and then sets the timer to `0` for the next interval. We then check whether the current frame is equal to the `FrameCount`. If yes, it means that the animation ended, then we set the `currentFrame` to `0` to replay the animation. Actually, the `currentFrame` represents the current column of the Sprite Sheet image. Next, we should make sure which animation we want to render, here, the react to the tap gesture to set the row value within the `AnimationCount` to change the animation. When the `currentFrame` for the column and the row are ready, you can use them to locate the sub-image with the rectangle object `sourceRect`; the last line in this code will compute the `origin` position for the image rotation and scale, here we set it to the center of the Sprite Sheet subimage.

In step 4, the `Draw()` method receives the texture parameter; position of texture drawn on screen; the rectangle for defining the part of texture that will be drawn; the color `White` means render the texture in its original color; rotation angle set to `0` stands for no rotation; the `scale` factor will let the rendering device know how big the texture will be, `3` here means the final texture size will be three times larger than the original; `SpriteEffects` means the effects will be applied to render the texture, `SpriteEffects.None` tells the application not to use any effect for the texture; the final parameter `layerDepth` illustrates the texture drawing order.

Creating a Complex Sprite Sheet animation in a 2D game

The Complex Sprite Sheet contains subimages with different sizes. Moreover, for every Complex Sprite Sheet, it has an additional description file. The description file defines the location and size of every subimage. It is the key difference between a Simple Sprite Sheet and a Complex Sprite Sheet. For a Simple Sprite Sheet, you can compute the location and size of the sub-image with the same width and height; however, for a Complex Sprite Sheet, it is harder, because the subimages in this kind of Sprite Sheet are often placed for the efficient use of space. To help identify the coordinates of the sprites in the Complex Sprite Sheet, the description file offers you the subimage location and size information. For the Sprite Sheet animation use, the description file also provides the animation name and attributes. The following screenshot shows an example of a Complex Sprite Sheet:

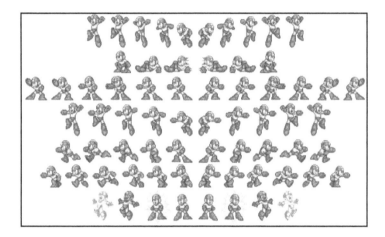

Getting ready

In the Sprite Sheet, you can see that the subimages have different sizes and locations. They are not placed in a regular grid, and that's why we need the description file to control these images. You may ask how we can get the description file for a designated Complex Sprite Sheet. Here, we use the tool SpriteVortex, which you can download from Codeplex at http://spritevortex.codeplex.com/.

The following steps show you how to process a Complex Sprite Sheet using SpriteVortex:

1. When you run **SpriteVortex**, click **Import Spritesheet Image**, at the top-left, as shown in the following screenshot:

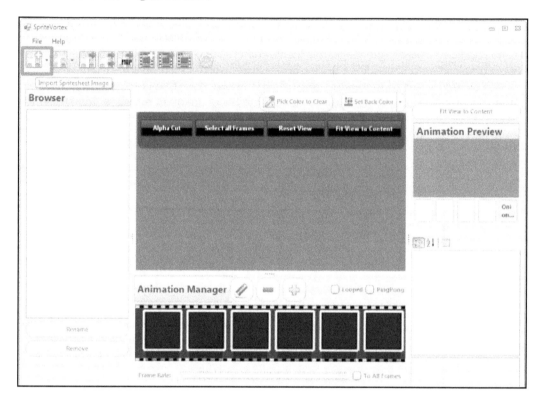

2. After choosing `MegaManSheet.png` from the image folder of this chapter, click on **Alpha Cut**, at the top bar of the main working area. You will see the subimages in the Complex Sprite Sheet individually surrounded by yellow rectangles, as shown in the following screenshot:

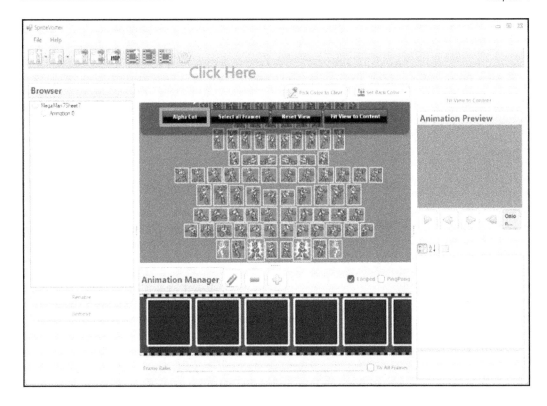

3. Next, you could choose the subimages to create your own animation. In the left **Browser** panel, we change the animation name from **Animation 0** to **Fire**.

4. Then, we choose the sub-images from the Complex Sprite Sheet. After that, we click the button—**Add Selected to Animation**. The selected images will show up in the **Animation Manager** from the first image to the last one frame-by-frame.

5. Similar to these steps, we add other two animations in the project named **Changing** and **Jump**.

6. The final step is to export the animation definition as XML, the important XML will be used in our project to animate the subimages, and the entire process can be seen in the following screenshot:

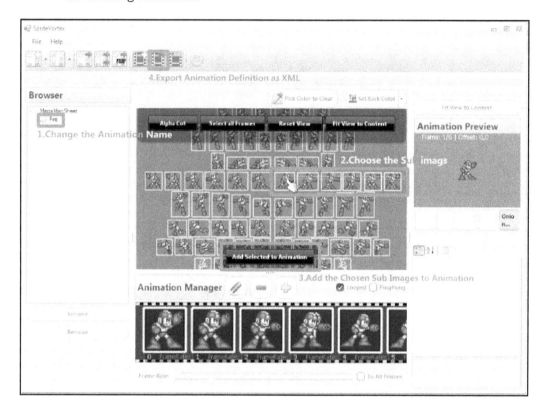

The exported animation XML file named `SpriteDescription.xml` can be found in the project content directory for this recipe.

In the XML file, you will find the XML element—`Texture`, which saves the Sprite Sheet path. The XML—`Animation`—includes the animation name and its frames, the frames contain the subimages' location and size. Next, you will learn how to use the Complex Sprite Sheet and the XML description to animate the sprite.

How to do it...

The following steps will show you how to animate a Complex Sprite Sheet:

1. Create a Windows Phone Game project named `ComplexSpriteSheetAnimation`, change `Game1.cs` to `ComplexSpriteSheetAnimationGame.cs`. Then add the exported Sprite Sheet description file `SpriteDescription.xml` to the content project, changing the **Build Action** property of the XML file from **Compile** to **None** because we customized the content processing code for XML format, and the **Copy to Output Directory** property to **Copy Always**. This will always copy the description file to the game content output directory of the application.

2. The description file is an XML document; we need to parse the animation information when loading it to our game. Subsequently, we add some description parsing classes: `Frame`, `Animation`, `SpriteTexture`, `AnimationSet`, and `SpriteAnimationManager` in the `SpriteAnimationManager.cs` of the main project. Before coding the classes, one more reference `System.Xml.Serialization` must be added to the project reference list as we will use the XML Serialization technique to parse the animation. Now, lets define the basic classes:

```
// Animation frame class
public class Frame
{
    // Frame Number
    [XmlAttribute("Num")]
    public int Num;

    // Sub Image X positon in the Sprite Sheet
    [XmlAttribute("X")]
    public int X;

    // Sub Image Y positon in the Sprite Sheet
    [XmlAttribute("Y")]
    public int Y;

    // Sub Image Width
    [XmlAttribute("Width")]
    public int Width;

    // Sub Image Height
    [XmlAttribute("Height")]
    public int Height;

    // The X offset of sub image
    [XmlAttribute("OffSetX")]
    public int OffsetX;
```

```
        // The Y offset for subimage
        [XmlAttribute("OffsetY")]
        public int OffsetY;

        // The duration between two frames
        [XmlAttribute("Duration")]
        public float Duration;
    }

    // Animation class to hold the name and frames
    public class Animation
    {
        // Animation Name
        [XmlAttribute("Name")]
        public string Name;

        // Animation Frame Rate
        [XmlAttribute("FrameRate")]
        public int FrameRate;

        public bool Loop;

        public bool Pingpong;

        // The Frames array in an animation
        [XmlArray("Frames"), XmlArrayItem("Frame", typeof(Frame))]
        public Frame[] Frames;
    }

    // The Sprite Texture stores the Sprite Sheet path
    public class SpriteTexture
    {
        // The Sprite Sheet texture file path
        [XmlAttribute("Path")]
        public string Path;
    }

    // Animation Set contains the Sprite Texture and animation.
    [XmlRoot("Animations")]
    public class AnimationSet
    {
        // The sprite texture object
        [XmlElement("Texture", typeof(SpriteTexture))]
```

```
    public SpriteTexture SpriteTexture;
    // The animation array in the Animation Set
    [XmlElement("Animation", typeof(Animation))]
    public Animation[] Animations;
```

3. Next, we will extract the Animation information from the XML description file using the XML deserialization technique:

```
// Sprite Animation Manager class
public static class SpriteAnimationManager
{
    public static int AnimationCount;

    // Read the Sprite Sheet Description information from the
    // description xml file
    public static AnimationSet Read(string Filename)
    {
        AnimationSet animationSet = new AnimationSet() ;

        // Create an XML reader for the sprite sheet animation
        // description file
        using (System.Xml.XmlReader reader =
            System.Xml.XmlReader.Create(Filename))
        {
            // Create an XMLSerializer for the AnimationSet
            XmlSerializer serializer = new
                XmlSerializer(typeof(AnimationSet));

            // Deserialize the Animation Set from the
            // XmlReader to the animation set object
          animationSet =
                (AnimationSet)serializer.Deserialize(reader);
        }

        // Count the animations to Animation Count
        AnimationCount = animationSet.Animations.Length;

        return animationSet;
    }
}
```

4. Now, from this step, we will begin to use the parsed `AnimationSet` to animate the Complex Sprite Sheet and switch the animations. So, add the code to the field of `ComplexSpriteSheetAnimationGame` class:

```
// A Timer variable
float timer;

// The interval
float interval = 200;

// Animation Set stores the animations in the sprite sheet
// description file
AnimationSet animationSet;

// Texture object loads and stores the Sprite Sheet image
Texture2D texture;

// The location of subimage
int X = 0;
int Y = 0;

// The size of subimage
int height = 0;
int width = 0;

// A rectangle to store which 'frame' is currently being shown
Rectangle sourceRectangle;

// The center of the current 'frame'
Vector2 origin;

// Current frame holder
int currentFrame = 0;

// Current animation
int currentAnimation = 0;
```

5. Read the Complex Sprite Sheet to the `AnimationSet` object. Add the line to the `Initialize()` method:

```
animationSet =
SpriteAnimationManager.Read(@"Content\SpriteDescription.xml");
```

6. In this step, we animate the Complex Sprite Sheet using the parsed animation set. Add the following lines to the `Update()` method:

```
// Change the animation when tap the Touch screen
TouchCollection touches = TouchPanel.GetState();
if (touches.Count > 0 && touches[0].State ==
    TouchLocationState.Pressed)
{
    // make the animation index vary within the total
    // animation count
    currentAnimation = (currentAnimation + 1) %
        SpriteAnimationManager.AnimationCount;
}

// Accumulate the game elapsed time
timer += (float)gameTime.ElapsedGameTime.TotalMilliseconds;

// If the current frame is equal to the length of the current
// animation frames, reset the current frame to the beginning
if (currentFrame ==
  animationSet.Animations[currentAnimation].Frames.Length - 1)
{
    currentFrame = 0;
}

// Check the timer is more than the chosen interval
if (timer > interval && currentFrame <=
  animationSet.Animations[currentAnimation].Frames.Length - 1)
{
    // Get the location of current subimage
    height = animationSet.Animations[currentAnimation].
        Frames[currentFrame].Height;
    width = animationSet.Animations[currentAnimation].
        Frames[currentFrame].Width;

    // Get the size of the current subimage
    X = animationSet.Animations[currentAnimation].
        Frames[currentFrame].X;
    Y = animationSet.Animations[currentAnimation].
        Frames[currentFrame].Y;

    // Create the rectangle for drawing the part of the
    //sprite sheet on the screen
    sourceRectangle = new Rectangle(X, Y, width, height);
```

```
// Show the next frame
currentFrame++;

// Reset the timer
timer = 0f;
}

// Compute the origin position for image rotation and scale.
origin = new Vector2(sourceRectangle.Width / 2,
    sourceRectangle.Height / 2);
```

7. Draw the animation on the Windows Phone 7 Touch screen, add the code to the `Draw()` method:

```
spriteBatch.Begin();
spriteBatch.Draw(texture, new Vector2(400, 240),
sourceRectangle,
    Color.White, 0f, origin, 2.0f, SpriteEffects.None, 0);
spriteBatch.End();
```

8. Now, build and run the application. When you tap on the Touch screen, the animation will change as shown in the following screenshots:

How it works...

In step 2, the `Frame` class corresponds to the XML element: `Frame` and its attributes in the XML file. The same applies for the `Animation` class, `SpriteTexture` class, and the `AnimationSet` class. The `XmlSerializer` can recognize the `XmlElement` and `XmlAttribute` for every member variable unless the `XmlAttribute` or `XmlElement` attribute is defined above it. If the class type is customized, we also need to use the `typeof()` method to let the serializer know the object size. For identifying the array member variables—Frames and Animations—we should use the `XmlArray` attribute with array root name in the XML file and the `XmlArrayItem` with its element name. Additionally, the `XmlRoot` will help the `XmlSerializer` to locate the root of the whole XML file, here, it is `Animations`.

In step 3, since the loading of this data occurs independently of the instance of the manager class (in this case it deserializes an instance of a class from XML), we can declare it `static` to simplify our code, as an instance of the manager is not necessary as it contains no instance data. The `Read()` method creates an `XmlReader` object to read the Sprite Sheet XML description file. The `XmlReader` class supports reading XML data from a stream or file. It allows you to read the contents of a node. When the `XmlReader` for the description file is created, we instance the `XmlSerializer` object to read the `AnimationSet` type data. We use the `XmlSerializer.Deserialize()` method to decode the description XML file to meet the XML attributes we defined for the `AnimationSet` class, then the `XmlSerializer` will recursively read the subclasses with the XML attributes. After the XML deserialization, the code will set the count of the parsed animations to the `AnimationCount` variable. We will use the `AnimationCount` to control the index of animations for animation playing in the game.

In step 4, the `timer` variable will accumulate the game elapsed time; the `interval` variable defines the period of time between two frames; the `animationSet` variable will store the animations from the Sprite Sheet description file; the `texture` object holds the Complex Sprite Sheet image, with X,Y for the location and `height, width` for the size. The `sourceRectangle` variable will read the location and size information of the to create the region for drawing the subimage on screen; `currentFrame` defines the current animation playing frame; `currentAnimation` indicates the currently playing animation.

In step 6, the first part of the code is to react to the tap gesture for changing the current playing animation. The second part is to increase the currently playing frame, if the current frame reaches the maximum frame count of current animation, we will replay the current animation. The last part will get the location and size of the current subimage according to the current frame and use the location and size information to build the region of the current subimage for playing. Then, increase the frame to next before resetting the timer to 0 for a new frame. This information is controlled by the XML file that was generated from the Codeplex tool we exported in step 1.

Creating a text animation in Adventure Genre (AVG) game

Adventure Genre (**AVG**) game uses the text or dialog to describe game plots. With different branches, you will experience different directions in game underplaying. In most AVG games, text presentation is the key part, if you have ever played one or more of the games, you might have found the text was rendered character-by-character or word-by-word. In this recipe, you will learn how to work with sprite font and how to manipulate the font-related methods to compute the font and properly adjust the character and word positions in real time.

How to do it...

The following steps will lead you to complete text animation effect in Windows Phone 7:

1. Create a Windows Phone Game in Visual Studio 2010 named `AVGText`, change `Game1.cs` to `AVGTextGame.cs`, and add the following code to the `AVGTextGame` class as field:

```
// SpriteFont object
SpriteFont font;

// Game text
string text = "";

// The text showed on the screen
string showedText = "";

// The bound for the showedText
const int TextBound = 20;

// Game timer
float timer = 0;

// Interval time
float interval = 100;

// Index for interate the whole original text
int index = 0;
```

2. Initialize the original text and process it for wrapped showing. Add the initialization and processing code to the `Initialize()` method:

```
// The original text
text = "This is an AVG game text, you will find the text is
    + "showed character by character, I hope "
    + "this recipe is useful for you.";

// Split the original string to a string array
string[] strArray = text.Split(' ');

// Declare the temp string for each row, aheadstring for
// looking ahead one word in this row
string tempStr = strArray[0];
string aheadString = "";
```

```
// Declare the StringBuilder object for holding the sliced
// line
StringBuilder stringBuild = new StringBuilder();

// Iterate the word array, i for current word, j for next word
for (int i = 0 ,j = i ; j < strArray.Length; j++)
{
    // i is before j
    i = j - 1;

    // Check the temp string length whether less than the
    // TextBound
    if (aheadString.Length <= TextBound)
    {
        // If yes, check the string looks ahead one more word
        // whether less than the TextBound
        if ((aheadString = tempStr + " " + strArray[j]).Length
            <= TextBound)
        {
            // If yes, set the look-ahead string to the temp
            // string
            tempStr = aheadString;
        }
    }
    else
    {
        // If not, add the temp string as a row
        // to the StringBuilder object
        stringBuild.Append(tempStr.Trim() + "\n");

        // Set the current word to the temp string
        tempStr = strArray[i];

        aheadString = tempStr;
        j = i;
    }
}
```

3. Load the `SpriteFont` content in the `LoadContent()` method:

```
font = Content.Load<SpriteFont>("gameFont");
```

4. Update for drawing the `showedText` character-by-character. Add the lines to the `Update()` method:

```
// Accumulate the game elapsed
timer += (float)gameTime.ElapsedGameTime.TotalMilliseconds;

// Show the text character by character
if (timer > interval && index < text.Length)
{
    // Every interval add the current index character to the
    // showedText.
    showedText += text.Substring(index, 1);

    // Increse the index
    index++;

    // Set the timer to 0 for the next interval
    timer = 0;
}
```

5. Draw the AVG text effect on the Windows Phone 7 Touch screen. Add the code to the `Draw()` method:

```
// Draw the string on screen
spriteBatch.Begin();
spriteBatch.DrawString(font, showedText, new Vector2(0, 0),
    Color.White);
spriteBatch.End();
```

6. Build and run the application. It should look similar to the following screenshots:

How it works...

In step 1, the `font` object will be used to render the AVG game text; the `text` variable holds the original text for processing; the `showedText` stores the latest showing text; `TextBound` limits the bound for the showing text; the `timer` is used to count the game elapsed time; the `interval` variable represents the period of time between two frames; the `index` variable indicates the current position when showing the original text.

In step 2, we use the `text.Split()` method to split the original text to a word array, then declare three objects `tempStr`, `aheadString`, and `stringBuild`. `tempStr` stores the current row, composed of the words from the original text; `aheadString` saves one more word ahead of the `tempStr` for preventing the actual length of `tempStr` from becoming greater than the `TextBound`. In the `for` loop, we declare two iterating indices i and j: i is the index from the beginning of the original text, j goes after i. In the loop step, if the length of `aheadString` is less than the `TextBound`, one more word following the `tempStr` will be added to it. If the new look-ahead string length is still less than the `Textbound`, we will assign the `aheadString` to `tempStr`. On the other hand, if the length of `aheadString` is greater than `Textbound`, we will do line breaking. At this moment, the `tempStr` is appended to the `stringBuild` object as a row with a line breaking symbol—\n. Then we set the current word to the `tempStr` and `aheadString`, and also set the current i to j for the next row.

In step 4, the first line accumulates the game elapsed milliseconds. If the elapsed time is greater than the `interval`, and the `index` is less than the processed text length, we will append the current character to `showedText`, after that, move the `index` pointer to the next character and set the `timer` to zero for the next interval.

Creating a text-based menu—the easiest menu to create

Menu plays the key role of a complete game; the player could use the menu to navigate to different parts of the game. As guidance to the game, the menu has a lot of appearances depending on the game type, animated or static, and so on. In this chapter, you will learn how to work with three kinds of menu, text-based, image-based, and model-based. As a beginning, this recipe shows you the text-based menu.

Getting ready

The text-based menu is made up of texts. Every menu item is an independent string. In this example, when you tap the item, the reaction will be triggered with the text color changing and text visual effects popping up. OK, let's begin!

How to do it...

The following steps will show you how to create a simple text-based menu:

1. Create a Windows Phone Game project named `TextMenu`, change `Game1.cs` to `TextMenuGame.cs`, and add `gameFont.spriteFont` to content project. Then add `TextMenuItem.cs` to the main project.

2. Open `TextMenuItem.cs` file, in the field of the `TextMenuItem` class, add the following lines:

    ```
    // SpriteBatch
    SpriteBatch spriteBatch;

    // Menu item text font
    SpriteFont font;

    // Menu item text
    public string Text;

    // Menu Item position
    public Vector2 Position;
    public Vector2 textOrigin;

    // Menu Item size
    public Vector2 Size;

    // Bool tap value shows whether tap on the screen
    public bool Tap;

    // Tap event handler
    public event EventHandler OnTap;

    // Timer object
    float timer = 0;

    // Alpha value of text color
    float alpha = 1;
    Color color;

    // The scale of text
    float scale = 1;
    ```

3. Next, we define the `Bound` property of the text menu item:

```
// The Bound of menu item
public Rectangle Bound
{
    get
    {
        return new Rectangle((int)Position.X,
            (int)Position.Y, (int)Size.X, (int)Size.Y);
    }
}
```

4. Define the constructor of the `TextMenuItem` class:

```
// Text menu item constructor
public TextMenuItem(Vector2 position, string text, SpriteFont
    font, SpriteBatch spriteBatch)
{
    Position = position;
    Text = text;
    this.font = font;
    this.spriteBatch = spriteBatch;

    // Compute the text size
    Size = font.MeasureString(Text);
    textOrigin = new Vector2(Size.X / 2, Size.Y / 2);
    color = Color.White;
}
```

5. Then, we implement the `Update()` method:

```
// Text menu item update method, get the tapped position on
screen
public void Update(Vector2 tapPosition)
{
    // if the tapped position within the text menu item bound,
    // set Tap to true and trigger
    // the OnTap event
    if (Bound.Contains((int)tapPosition.X,(int)tapPosition.Y))
    {
        Tap = true;
        OnTap(this, null);
    }
    else
    {
        Tap = false;
    }
}
```

6. The last method in the `TextMenuItem` class is the `Draw()` method, let's add the code:

```
public void Draw(GameTime gameTime)
{
    timer += (float)gameTime.ElapsedGameTime.TotalMilliseconds;

    // Draw the text menu item
    if (Tap)
    {
        // Draw text visual effect
        if (alpha >= 0 && timer > 100)
        {
            // Decrease alpha value of effect text
            alpha -= 0.1f;
            color *= alpha;

            // Increase the effect text scale
            scale++;

            // Draw the first layer of effect text
            spriteBatch.DrawString(font, Text, Position,
                color, 0, new Vector2(Size.X / 2, Size.Y / 2),
                    scale, SpriteEffects.None, 0);

            // Draw the second layer of effect text
            spriteBatch.DrawString(font, Text, Position,
                color, 0, new Vector2(Size.X / 2, Size.Y / 2),
                scale / 2, SpriteEffects.None, 0);

            // Reset the timer for the next interval
            timer = 0;
        }

        // Draw the original text
        spriteBatch.DrawString(font, Text, Position,
            Color.Red);

    }
    else
    {
        // Reset the scale, alpha and color value of original
        // text
        scale = 1;
        alpha = 1;
```

```
color = Color.White;

// Draw the original text
spriteBatch.DrawString(font, Text, Position,
    Color.White);



    }
}
```

7. When the `TextMenuItem` class is done, the following work is about using the class in our game class. Add the code to the `TextMenuGame` field:

```
// SpriteFont object for text menu item
SpriteFont font;

// Menu collection of text menu item
List<TextMenuItem> Menu;

// Random color for background
Random random;
Color backgroundColor;
```

8. This step is to initialize the variables—Menu, `random`, and `backgroundColor`; add the code to the `Initialize()` method:

```
Menu = new List<TextMenuItem>();
random = new Random();
backgroundColor = Color.CornflowerBlue;
```

9. Load the game sprite font and text menu items in Menu, and add the following code to the `LoadContent()` method:

```
font = Content.Load<SpriteFont>("gameFont");

// Initialize the text menu items in Menu
int X = 100;
int Y = 100;

for (int i = 0; i < 5; i++)
{
    TextMenuItem item = new TextMenuItem(
        new Vector2(X, Y + 60 * i), "TextMenuItem", font,
        spriteBatch);
    item.OnTap += new EventHandler(item_OnTap);
    Menu.Add(item);
}
```

10. Define the text menu item event reaction method `item_OnTap()`:

```
void item_OnTap(object sender, EventArgs e)
{
    // Set random color for back in every valid tap
    backgroundColor.R = (byte)random.Next(0, 256);
    backgroundColor.G = (byte)random.Next(0, 256);
    backgroundColor.B = (byte)random.Next(0, 256);
}
```

11. Get the tapped position and pass it to the text menu items for valid tap checking. Insert the code to the `Update()` method:

```
// Get the tapped position
Vector2 tapPosition = new Vector2();
TouchCollection touches = TouchPanel.GetState();
if (touches.Count > 0 && touches[0].State ==
    TouchLocationState.Pressed)
{
    tapPosition = touches[0].Position;

    // Check the tapped positon whether inside one of the text
    // menu items
    foreach (TextMenuItem item in Menu)
    {
        item.Update(tapPosition);
    }
}
```

12. Draw the `Menu`, paste the code into the `Draw()` method:

```
// Replace the existing Clear code with this to
// simulate the effect of the menu item selection
GraphicsDevice.Clear(backgroundColor);

// Draw the Menu
spriteBatch.Begin(SpriteSortMode.Immediate, BlendState.
AlphaBlend);

foreach (TextMenuItem item in Menu)
{
    item.Draw(gameTime);
}
spriteBatch.End();
```

13. Now, build and run the application, and tap the first text menu item. It should look similar to the following screenshot:

How it works...

In step 2, the `spriteBatch` is the main object to draw the text; `font` object holds the `SpriteFont` text definition file; `Text` is the actual string shown in the text menu; `Position` indicates the location of the text menu item on screen; `textOrigin` defines the center of the text menu item for scale or rotation; the `Size`, `Vector2` variable returns the width and height of `Text` through X and Y in `Vector2`; `Tap` represents whether the tap gesture takes place; the event handler `OnTap` listens to the occurrence of the tap gesture; `timer` object accumulates the game elapsed time for text visual effects; `alpha` value will be used to change the transparency of the text `color`; the last variable `scale` stores the scale factor of text menu item size.

In step 3, `Bound` returns a rectangle around the text menu item, and the property will be used to check whether the tapped position is inside the region of the text menu item.

In step 4, notice, we use the `font.MeasureString()` method to compute the size of the `Text`. Then set the origin position to the center of the `Text`.

In step 5, the `Update()` method receives the tapped position and checks whether it is inside the region of the text menu item, if yes, set the Boolean value `Tap` to `true` and trigger the `OnTap` event, otherwise, set `Tap` to `false`.

In step 6, the first line is to accumulate the game elapsed time. When the `Tap` is `false`—which means no tap on the text menu item—we set `scale` and `alpha` to 1, and the `color` to `Color.White`. Else, we will draw the text visual effects with two texts having the same text content of the text menu item; the size of the first layer is two times the second. As time goes by, the two layers will grow up and gradually disappear. After that, we draw the original text of the text menu item to `Color.Red`.

In step 7, the `font` object holds the game sprite font for rendering the `Text` of the text menu item; `Menu` is the collection of text menu items; the `random` variable will be used to generates random number for creating random `backgroundColor`.

In step 10, because the range for *red*, *green*, and *blue* factors of `Color` is from 0 to 255, the random numbers generated for them also meet the rule. With the `random` number, every valid text menu item tap will change the background color randomly.

Creating an image-based menu

The image-based menu is another menu-presentation approach. Unlike the text-based menu, the image-based menu uses 2D picture as the content of every menu item and makes the game navigation user interface more attractive and innovative. It gives graphic designers a much bigger space for conceiving ideas for a game. An image-based menu easily stimulates the designers' and programmers' creativities. The image menu item can swipe in and swipe out, jump in and jump out, or fade in and fade out. In this recipe, you will learn how to create an image-based menu system and use it in your own Windows Phone 7 game.

Getting ready

As an example, the image menu items are placed horizontally on the screen. When you tap one of them, it will grow up and the current item index shows at the top-left of the screen; once the tapped position is outside of its bound, the menu will restore to the initial state. Now, let's build the application.

How to do it...

Follow these steps to create your own image-based menu:

1. Create a Windows Phone Game project in Visual Studio 2010 named `ImageMenu`, change `Game1.cs` to `ImageMenuGame.cs`, and add the `ImageMenuItem.cs` in the main project. Then add `Imageitem.png` and `gameFont.spriteFont` to the content project.

2. Create the `ImageMenuItem` class in the `ImageMenuItem.cs` file. First, add the code to the `ImageMenuItem` class field:

   ```
   // SpriteBatch object
   SpriteBatch spriteBatch;

   // Menu item text font
   Texture2D texture;

   // Menu Item position
   public Vector2 Position;
   ```

```
// Menu Item origin position for translation and rotation
public Vector2 Origin;

// Bool tap value shows whether tap on the screen
public bool Tap;

// Timer object
float timer = 0;

// The scale range from MinScale to MaxScale
const float MinScale = 0.8f;
const float MaxScale = 1;

// The scale of text
float scale = 0.8f;

// Image menu item index
public int Index = 0;
```

3. Next, add the `Bound` property:

```
// The Bound of menu item
public Rectangle Bound
{
    get
    {
        return new Rectangle(
            (int)(Position.X - Origin.X * scale),
            (int)(Position.Y - Origin.Y * scale),
            (int)(texture.Width * scale),
            (int)(texture.Height * scale));
    }
}
```

4. Then, define the constructor of the `ImageMenuItem` class:

```
// Text menu item constructor
public ImageMenuItem(Vector2 Location,Texture2D Texture,
    SpriteBatch SpriteBatch)
{
    Position = Location;
    texture = Texture;
    spriteBatch = SpriteBatch;

    Origin = new Vector2(texture.Width / 2,
        texture.Height / 2);
}
```

5. The following method is the `Update()` method of the `ImageMenuItem` class, so let's add its implementation code:

```
// Text menu item update method, get the tapped position on
// screen
public void Update(GameTime gameTime, Vector2 tapPosition)
{
    // if the tapped position within the text menu item bound,
    // set Tap to true and trigger the OnTap event
    Tap = Bound.Contains((int)tapPosition.X,
      (int)tapPosition.Y);
    // Accumulate the game elapsed time
    timer += (float)gameTime.ElapsedGameTime.TotalMilliseconds;


}
```

6. The last method of the `ImageMenuItem` class is the `Draw()` method, so let's add its implementation code:

```
public void Draw(GameTime gameTime)
{
    // Draw the text menu item
    if (Tap)
    {

        // if tap gesture is valid, gradually scale to
          // MaxScale in
        if (scale <= MaxScale && timer > 200)
        {
            scale += 0.1f;
        }
        spriteBatch.Draw(texture, Position, null, Color.Red,
            0f, Origin, scale, SpriteEffects.None, 0f);

    }
    else
    {

        // If no valid tap, gradually restore scale to
          // MinScale in every frame
        if (scale > MinScale && timer > 200)
        {
            scale -= 0.1f;
        }
        spriteBatch.Draw(texture, Position, null, Color.White,
          0f, Origin, scale, SpriteEffects.None, 0f);
    }
}
```

7. So far, we have seen the `ImageMenuItem` class. Our next job is to use the class in the main class. Add the code to the `ImageMenuGame` class:

```
// SpriteFont object for the current index value
SpriteFont font;

// The image menu item texture
Texture2D texImageMenuItem;

// The collection of image menu items
List<ImageMenuItem> Menu;

// The count of image menu items
int TotalMenuItems = 4;

// The index for every image menu item
int index = 0;

// Current index of tapped image menu item
int currentIndex;
```

8. Initialize the `Menu` object in the `Initialize()` method:

```
// Initialize Menu
Menu = new List<ImageMenuItem>();
```

9. Load the `SpriteFont` and `ImageMenuItem` texture, and initialize the `ImageMenuItem` in `Menu`. Next, insert the code to the `LoadContent()` method:

```
texImageMenuItem = Content.Load<Texture2D>("ImageItem");
font = Content.Load<SpriteFont>("gameFont");

// Initialize the image menu items
int X = 150;
int Y = 240;

// Instance the image menu items horizontally
for (int i = 0; i < TotalMenuItems; i++)
{
    ImageMenuItem item = new ImageMenuItem(
        new Vector2(
            X + i * (texImageMenuItem.Width + 20), Y),
        texImageMenuItem, spriteBatch);
    item.Index = index++;
    Menu.Add(item);
}
```

10. In this step, we will check the valid tapped position and get the index of the tapped image menu item, paste the code to the `Update()` method:

```
// Get the tapped position
Vector2 tapPosition = new Vector2();
TouchCollection touches = TouchPanel.GetState();
if (touches.Count > 0 && touches[0].State ==
    TouchLocationState.Pressed)
{
    tapPosition = touches[0].Position;

    // Check the tapped positon whether inside one of the
    // image menu items
    foreach (ImageMenuItem item in Menu)
    {
        item.Update(gameTime, tapPosition);

        // Get the current index of tapped image menu item
        if (item.Tap)
        {
            currentIndex = item.Index;
        }
    }
}
```

11. Draw the menu and the current index value on the screen, and insert the lines to the `Draw()` method:

```
spriteBatch.Begin();

// Draw the Menu
foreach (ImageMenuItem item in Menu)
{
    item.Draw(gameTime);
}

// Draw the current index on the top-left of screen
spriteBatch.DrawString(font, "Current Index: " +
    currentIndex.ToString(), new Vector2(0, 0), Color.White);

spriteBatch.End();
```

12. Now, build and run the application. Tap the second image menu item, and it should look similar to the following screenshot:

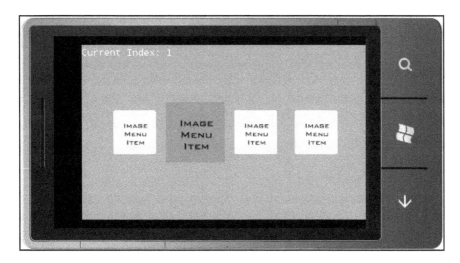

How it works...

In step 2, `spriteBatch` renders the image of the menu item on screen; `texture` loads the graphic content of the image menu item; `Position` represents the position of every image menu item; `Origin` defines the center for menu item rotation and translation; `Tap` is the mark for valid menu item tapping; the `timer` variable accumulates the game elapsed time for changing the scale of the image menu item. The following two objects `MinScale` and `MaxScale` limit the range of scale changing; the `scale` variable indicates the current scale value of the menu item; `index` holds the sequential position of a menu.

In step 3, the `Bound` property returns a rectangle around the image of the menu item according to the menu item position and the image size.

In step 6, we will draw the visual effect for the menu item with image zoom in and zoom out. The first line accumulates the game elapsed time for changing the menu item scale. If the tapped position is inside the image menu item, the item will grow up gradually along with the increasing `scale` value until `MaxScale`; otherwise, it will restore to the initial state.

In step 7, the `font` object will render the current index of the image menu item on the top-left of the screen; `texImageMenuItem` holds the image of the menu item; `Menu` is the collection of `ImageMenuItem`; `TotalMenuItems` declares the total number of image menu items in `Menu`; `index` is used to mark the index of every menu item in Menu; the `currentValue` variable saves the index of the tapped image menu item.

In step 9, we instance the image menu items horizontally and define the gap between each of the items at about 20 pixels wide.

In step 10, after calling the `ImageMenuItem.Update()` method, you can get the current index of the menu item when its `Tap` value is `true`.

Creating a 3D model-based menu

Text- or image-based menus are very common in games. As you know, they are both in 2D, but sometimes you want some exceptional effects for menus in 3D, such as rotating. 3D menus render the model as a menu item for any 3D transformation. They offer a way to implement your own innovative menu presentation in 3D. This recipe will specify the interesting technique in Windows Phone 7.

Getting ready

Programming the 3D model-based menu is an amazing adventure. You can use the 3D model rendering and transformation techniques to control the menu items and control the camera at different positions, getting closer or looking like a bird. As a demo, the model menu item of menu will pop up when selected. I hope this recipe will impress you. Let's look into the code.

How to do it...

The following steps will lead you to build an impressive 3D model-based menu:

1. Create the Windows Phone Game project named `ModelMenu3D`, change `Game1.cs` to `ModelMenuGame.cs`. Add a `ModelMenuItem.cs` to the project; `gameFont.spriteFont` and `ModelMenuItem3D.FBX` to the content project.

2. Create the `ModelMenuItem` class in `ModelMenuItem.cs`. Add the code to its field:

```
// Model of menu item
Model modelItem;

// Translation of model menu item
public Vector3 Translation;

// The view and projection of camera for model view item
public Matrix View;
public Matrix Projection;

// The index of model menu item
public int Index;

// The mark for selection
public bool Selected;

// The offset from menu item original position when selected
public int Offset;
```

3. Next, define the constructor of the `ModelMenuItem` class and set the default offset of the selected model menu item.

```
// Constructor
public ModelMenuItem(Model model, Matrix view, Matrix
projection)
{
    modelItem = model;
    View = view;
    Projection = projection;
    Offset = 5;
}
```

4. This step is to give the definition of the `Draw()` method of the `ModelMenuItem` class:

```
// Draw the model menu item
public void Draw()
{
    Matrix[] modelTransforms = new
        Matrix[modelItem.Bones.Count];
    modelItem.CopyAbsoluteBoneTransformsTo(modelTransforms);

    foreach (ModelMesh mesh in modelItem.Meshes)
    {
        foreach (BasicEffect effect in mesh.Effects)
        {
            // Enable lighting
            effect.EnableDefaultLighting();

            // Set the ambient light color to white
            effect.AmbientLightColor = Color.White.ToVector3();

            if (Selected)
            {
                // If the item is not selected, it restores
                // to the original state
                effect.World =
                    modelTransforms[mesh.ParentBone.Index]
                    * Matrix.CreateTranslation(Translation +
                    new Vector3(0,0, Offset));
            }
            else
            {
                // If the item is selected, it stands out
                effect.World =
                    modelTransforms[mesh.ParentBone.Index]
```

```
                              * Matrix.CreateTranslation(Translation);
                    }
                  effect.View = View;
                  effect.Projection = Projection;
              }
          mesh.Draw();
      }
  }
```

5. Use the `ModelMenuItem` class in our game. Add the code to the field of the `ModelMenuGame` class:

    ```
    // Sprite font object
    SpriteFont font;

    // Model of menu Item
    Model menuItemModel;

    // Camera position
    Vector3 cameraPositon;

    // Camera view and projection matrices
    Matrix view;
    Matrix projection;

    // The collection of Model Menu items
    List<ModelMenuItem> Menu;

    // The count of model menu items in Menu
    int TotalMenuItems = 4;

    // The left and right hit regions for menu item selection
    Rectangle LeftRegion;
    Rectangle RightRegion;

    // Current index of model menu item in Menu
    int currentIndex = 0;

    // Event handler of hit regions
    public event EventHandler OnTap;
    ```

6. Initialize the camera, menu, and hit regions. Insert the code to the `Initialize()` method:

    ```
    // Define the camera position
    cameraPositon = new Vector3(-40, 10, 40);
    ```

```
// Define the camera view and projection matrices
view = Matrix.CreateLookAt(cameraPositon, Vector3.Zero,
    Vector3.Up);
projection =
    Matrix.CreatePerspectiveFieldOfView(MathHelper.PiOver4,
    GraphicsDevice.Viewport.AspectRatio, 1.0f, 1000.0f);

// Initialize the Menu object
Menu = new List<ModelMenuItem>();

// Left hit region occupies the left half of screen
LeftRegion = new Rectangle(
    0, 0,
    GraphicsDevice.Viewport.Width / 2,
    GraphicsDevice.Viewport.Height);

// Right hit region occupies the right half of screen
RightRegion = new Rectangle(GraphicsDevice.Viewport.Width / 2,
    0, GraphicsDevice.Viewport.Width / 2,
    GraphicsDevice.Viewport.Height);

// Define the event handler OnTap with the delegate method
OnTap = new EventHandler(item_OnTap);
```

7. Next, define the reaction method `item_OnTap` of the `OnTap` event:

```
// Make the current index value change within the range of
// total menu items
currentIndex = currentIndex % TotalMenuItems;

// If the current index is less than 0, set it to the last item
if (currentIndex < 0)
{
    // From the last item
    currentIndex = TotalMenuItems - 1;
}

// if the current index is greater than the last index, set it
to the
// first item
else if (currentIndex > TotalMenuItems - 1)
{
    // From the beginning item;
    currentIndex = 0;
}
```

```
// Select the menu item, of which the index equals the
// current index
foreach (ModelMenuItem item in Menu)
{
    if (item.Index == currentIndex)
    {
        item.Selected = true;
    }
    else
    {
        item.Selected = false;
    }
}
```

8. Load the game content and initialize the menu items of `Menu`. Insert the code in the `Initialize()` method:

```
// Load and initialize the model and font objects
menuItemModel = Content.Load<Model>("ModelMenuItem3D");
font = Content.Load<SpriteFont>("gameFont");

// Initialize the model menu items in Menu horizontally
for (int i = 0; i < TotalMenuItems; i++)
{
    int X = -20;

ModelMenuItem item = new ModelMenuItem(
    menuItemModel, view,
    projection);
    item.Translation = new Vector3(X + (i * 20), 0, 0);

    // Set the index of menu item
    item.Index = i;
    Menu.Add(item);
}

// Setting the first menu item to be selected by default
Menu[0].Selected = true;
```

9. In this step, we make the current index value react to the tap on the hit regions. Paste the code to the `Update()` method:

```
// Get the tapped position
Vector2 tapPosition = new Vector2();
TouchCollection touches = TouchPanel.GetState();
if (touches.Count > 0 && touches[0].State ==
```

```
        TouchLocationState.Pressed)
    {
        tapPosition = touches[0].Position;
        Point point = new Point((int)tapPosition.X,
        (int)tapPosition.Y);

        // Check the tapped position whether in the left region
        if (LeftRegion.Contains(point))
        {
            // If yes, decrease the current index
            --currentIndex;
            OnTap(this, null);
        }
        // Check the tapped position whether in the right region
        else if (RightRegion.Contains(point))
        {
            // If yes, increase the current index
            ++currentIndex;
            OnTap(this, null);


        }
    }
```

10. The last step is to draw the menu on screen. Insert the code to the `Draw()` method:

```
    // The following three lines are to ensure that the models are
    // drawn correctly
    GraphicsDevice.DepthStencilState = DepthStencilState.Default;
    GraphicsDevice.BlendState = BlendState.AlphaBlend;

    // Draw the Menu
    foreach (ModelMenuItem item in Menu)
    {
        item.Draw();
    }

    // Draw the current index on the top-left of screen
    spriteBatch.Begin();
    spriteBatch.DrawString(font, "Current Index: " +
        currentIndex.ToString(), new Vector2(0, 0), Color.White);
    spriteBatch.End();
```

11. Now, build and run the application. When you tap the right region, the second model menu will pop up, as shown in the following screenshot:

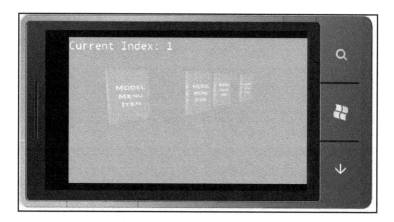

How it works...

In step 2, the `modelitem` holds the model object of the menu item; `Translation` stores the world position of the model menu item; `View` and `Projection` stand for the view and projection matrices of the camera respectively; `index` saves the index of the menu item in the menu; `Selected` indicates the selection state of the model menu item; `Offset` is the offset value from the model menu item's original position.

In step 4 and in the iteration of `Mesh.Effects`, we enable the light through calling the `Effect.EnableDefaultLighting()` method and set the `Effect.AmbientLightColor` to `Color.White.ToVector3()`. Notice, for popping up the model menu item, we create the translation matrix with positive 5 units offset at the Z-axis from the original position. If a menu is selected, it will pop up, otherwise, it will go back or remain in the initial state.

In step 5, `font` object will be used to draw the current index value on the top-left on screen; `menuModel` stores the model object for model menu item; `cameraPosition` defines the position of the camera; `view` and `projection` are the matrices for camera view and projection respectively; `Menu` is the collection of model menu items; `TotalMenuItems` indicates the total number of menu items; `LeftRegion` and `RightRegion` are the areas for item choosing.

In step 6, the first part of the code before is to define the camera; the second part is about initializing the left and right hit regions. `LeftRegion` takes up the left half of the screen; `RightRegion` occupies the other half.

In step 7, the first line is responsible for making the `currentIndex` value not less than `-1` and greater than `TotalMenuItems`. Next, if the current index is less than `0`, the last menu item will be selected; otherwise, if the current index is greater than `TotalMenuItems` minus `1`, the first item will pop up. The following `foreach` loop checks which item is currently selected when its index is equal to the current index.

In step 8, the first two lines are to load the menu item model and the font for presenting the current index. The following `for` loop initializes the menu items of `Menu` horizontally and assigns `i` value to the item index. The last line sets the first selected item.

In step 9, this block of code first gets the tapped position on screen. If the tapped position is in the left region, the current index decreases by `1`, else, current index increases by `1`. Any valid tap on the regions will trigger the `OnTap` event.

Creating a progress bar for game content loading and value status

When playing a game, especially for some big games, at the initialization phase, a progress bar will show you the game object loading status and percents. As a time-based game, the progress bar represents the remaining time. Moreover, a **Role Playing Game** (**RPG**) often uses the progress bar to present the current life value. A progress bar is a very common control in game development and is easy to use. In this recipe, you will find the inner code for creating a progress bar.

Getting ready

In Windows Phone 7 XNA programming, two methods will let you create the progress bar. One is using the *rectangle* for drawing the background and forefront. This is simple but not flexible and stylish. If you want to make some innovative and unusual visual effects, the primitives will not meet your needs. The second method will give you much more space to realize your idea for the progress bar. You can use graphic design tool to draw the background and forefront images as you like, then render these images and change the size of the forefront image to comply with the on going percents; even the round or other shapes can be used for presenting the progress status. In this example, we will use the rectangle images (second method) for implementing the progress bar in Windows Phone 7.

How to do it...

The following steps give you a complete guidance to develop a progress bar in your Windows Phone 7 game:

1. Create a Windows Phone Game project in Visual Studio 2010 named `ProgressBar`, change `Game1.cs` to `ProgressBarGame.cs` and insert a `ProgressBar.cs` in the project. Then add `ProgressBarBackground.png` and `ProgressBarForefront.png` to the content project.

2. Add a `ProgressBar` class in `ProgressBar.cs` to the main project. Add the code to the `ProgressBar` class fields:

    ```
    // SpriteBatch for drawing 2D image
    SpriteBatch spriteBatch;

    // ProgressBar forefront and background images
    Texture2D texForefront;
    Texture2D texBackground;

    // The background and forefront positon
    Vector2 backgroundPosition;
    Vector2 forefrontPosition;

    // The offset of forefront image from the background.
    float forefrontStartOffSetX;
    float forefrontStartOffSetY;

    // Current value of progressbar
    public int Value;

    // The Min and Max values of progressbar
    public int Min;
    public int Max;

    // Percent of current value around 100
    float percent;

    // the actual rendering width of forefront image
    float actualWidth;

    // The direction of progress.
    bool increase = false;
    ```

3. Next, we define the `Increase` property:

```
// The increasing direction
public bool Increase
{
    get
    {
        return increase;
    }
    set
    {
        // When increasing, the Value begins from Min
        if (value)
        {
            increase = value;
            Value = Min;
        }
        // When decreasing, the Value begins from Max
        else
        {
            increase = value;
            Value = Max;
        }

    }
}
```

4. The next step is to define the constructor of the `ProgressBar` class:

```
public ProgressBar(Vector2 position, Texture2D forefront,
    Texture2D background, SpriteBatch spriteBatch)
{
    this.spriteBatch = spriteBatch;
    texForefront = forefront;
    texBackground = background;
    backgroundPosition = position;

    // Calculate the offset for forefront image
    forefrontStartOffSetX = (texBackground.Width -
        texForefront.Width) / 2;
    forefrontStartOffSetY = (texBackground.Height -
        texForefront.Height) / 2;

    // Create the forefront image position
    forefrontPosition = new Vector2(backgroundPosition.X +
        forefrontStartOffSetX,
```

```
                    backgroundPosition.Y + forefrontStartOffSetY);

    // Intitialize the Min and Max
    Min = 0;
    Max = 100;

    // Set the increasing direction from high to low.
    Increase = false;
}
```

5. After the constructor, the following method definition is the `Update()`, so add the method to the `ProgressBar` class:

```
public void Update(GameTime gameTime)
{
    // If decreasing and Value greater than Min, minus the
    // Value by one
    if (Increase && Value < Max)
    {
        Value++;
    }
    else if (Value > Min)
    {
        Value--;
    }

    // Compute the actual forefront image for drawing
    percent = (float)Value / 100;
    actualWidth = percent * texForefront.Width;

}
```

6. The final step of creating the `ProgressBar` class is to define the `Draw()` method:

```
public void Draw()
{
    spriteBatch.Draw(texBackground, backgroundPosition,
        Color.White);
    spriteBatch.Draw(texForefront, forefrontPosition, new
        Rectangle(0, 0, (int)actualWidth,
        texForefront.Height), Color.White);
}
```

7. Use the `ProgressBar` class in our game. First, add the code to the class field:

```
// Texture objects for background and forefront images
Texture2D texForefront;
Texture2D texBackground;

// The background image position
Vector2 position;

// Progress bar object
ProgressBar progressBar;
```

8. Then insert the initialization code to the `LoadContent()` method:

```
// Load the background and forefront images
texForefront =
    Content.Load<Texture2D>("ProgressBarForefront");
texBackground =
    Content.Load<Texture2D>("ProgressBarBackground");

// Initialize the progress bar
position = new Vector2(200, 240);
progressBar = new ProgressBar(position, texForefront,
    texBackground, spriteBatch);
```

9. Next, insert the code to the `Update()` method:

```
// Update the progress bar
progressBar.Update(gameTime);
```

10. Finally, put the code in the `Draw()` method:

```
// draw the progress bar
spriteBatch.Begin();
progressBar.Draw();
spriteBatch.End();
```

11. Now, build and run the application, and it will run as shown in the following screenshots:

How it works...

In step 2, the `texForefront` and `texBackground` are the Texture2D objects that hold the `progressBar` forefront and background images. The next two variables `forefrontStartOffSetX` and `forefrontStartOffSetY` indicate the offset position of forefront from the background; `Value` stores the `progressBar` current value; the `Min` and `Max` defines the range of the `progressBar`; `percent` and `actualWidth` will be used to calculate and store the current width of the forefront image respectively; the last variable `increase` represents the direction of the `progressBar` value increasing.

In step 3, if the `Increase` value is `false`, which means it is decreasing, the `Value` begins from the right with `Max`. Otherwise, the `Value` will begin from the left.

In step 4, notice the computation for forefront image offset, we use the background image width minus the width of the forefront image, get the gap between the left sides of the two images, then use the gap value and divide it by 2, get the offset on the X-axis from the background for the forefront image. The offset on the Y-axis is similar. After getting the offset of the forefront image, we set `Min` to 0 and `Max` to 100—the value range of `progressBar`. The last line is to define the increasing direction. `False`, here, stands for the progress value that will decrease from 100 to 0, right to left.

In step 5, the first part of the `Update()` method is to change `Value` by one, according to the increasing direction. The second part is about computing the actual width of the forefront image for rendering.

In step 6, this code draws the background image and forefront image on screen. Notice the third parameter in the `Drawing()` method for the forefront image. This is a `Rectangle` parameter, which represents the part of the forefront image for rendering in every frame; it helps you to adjust the size of the forefront image for presenting the value variation of the progress bar.

In step 7, the `texForefront` stands for the forefront image of the progress bar; the `texBackground` represents the background image of the progress bar; `position` defines the progress bar position on the Windows Phone 7 screen; the last variable `progressBar` is the progress bar object which will perform the different progress behaviors.

Creating buttons in your game

In any type of game, button control is always the most basic and important part. In a GUI system, button control often plays a role in linking different parts of other controls. When you input some text in a text control, you click the button to send the message or confirm it as a command. When you are using a listbox, the up and down buttons help you look up special information that you need in the game, such as choosing weapons. In the development phase, programmers can define specific behaviors of the button events to implement the game logic or effects. To implement a button in the Windows Phone 7 XNA framework is not a hard mission. In this recipe, you will learn how to build your own button in Windows Phone 7.

How to do it...

The following steps will show you the working code for creating the buttons for your Windows Phone 7 game:

1. Create a Windows Phone Game project named `Button`, change `Game1.cs` to `ButtonGame.cs`. Then add the `Button.cs` to the main project and `button_image.png` and `gameFont.spriteFont` to the content project.

2. Create the `Button` class in the `Button.cs` file. Add the line to the class as a field:

```
// Button texture
Texture2D texButton;

// SpriteBatch for drawing the button image
SpriteBatch spriteBatch;

// Button position on the screen
public Vector2 Position;

// Color alpha value
public int Alpha = 255;

// Button color
Color color;

// Timer for game elapsed time accumulation
float timer;

// The Tapped bool value indicates whether tap in the button
region
public bool Tapped;

// Event handler OnTapped to react with tap gesture
public event EventHandler OnTapped;
```

3. Then, define the `HitRegion` property of the `Button` class:

```
// Get the hit region
public Rectangle HitRegion
{
    get
    {
        return new Rectangle((int)Position.X, (int)Position.Y,
            texButton.Width, texButton.Height);
    }
}
```

4. Next, give the class constructor `Button()` of the `Button` class:

```
// Initialize the button without text
public Button(Texture2D texture, Vector2 position, SpriteBatch
    spriteBatch)
{
    this.texButton = texture;
    this.Position = position;
    this.spriteBatch = spriteBatch;
    color = Color.White;
}
```

5. After the class constructor, the important `Update()` method that reacts to the tap gesture looks similar to the following code:

```
// Update the button
public void Update(GameTime gameTime, Vector2 touchPosition)
{
    // React to the tap gesture
    Point point = new Point((int)touchPosition.X,
        (int)touchPosition.Y);

    // If tapped button, set the Hovered to true and trigger
    // the OnClick event
    if (HitRegion.Contains(point))
    {
        Tapped = true;
        OnTapped(this, null);

    }
    else
    {
        Tapped = false;
    }
}
```

6. The final step to build the `Button` class is to define the `Draw()` method:

```
// Draw the button
public virtual void Draw(GameTime gameTime)
{

    timer += (float)gameTime.ElapsedGameTime.TotalMilliseconds;


    // Draw the button texture
    if (Tapped)
```

```
        {
            // Flash the button through the alpha value changing
            if (timer > 100)
            {
                // If the Alpha is 255, set it to 0
                if (Alpha == 255)
                {
                    Alpha = 0;
                }
                // If the Alpha value is 0, set it to 255
                else if (Alpha == 0)
                {
                    Alpha= 255;
                }

                // Set the color alpha value
                color.A = (byte)Alpha;

                // Set the timer to 0 for next frame
                timer = 0;
            }

            // Draw the button image
            spriteBatch.Draw(texButton, HitRegion, null, color, 0,
                Vector2.Zero, SpriteEffects.None, 0);
        }
        else
        {
            spriteBatch.Draw(texButton, HitRegion,
                null,Color.White, 0,
                Vector2.Zero, SpriteEffects.None, 0);

        }
    }
}
```

7. Use the `Button` class in our main game class. Insert code to the `ButtonGame` class field:

```
// Sprite Font for showing the text
SpriteFont font;

// Text object
string textTapState = "Random Color Text";

// Text color;
```

```
Color textColor = Color.White;

// Random object for showing the random color
Random random;

// Button object
Button button;

// Button texture;
Texture2D buttonTexture;
```

8. Initialize the `random` variable in the `Initialize()` method, and add the following code to the method:

    ```
    random = new Random();
    ```

9. Load the button image and initialize the button object. Add the code to the `LoadContent()` method:

    ```
    font = Content.Load<SpriteFont>("gameFont");

    buttonTexture = Content.Load<Texture2D>("button_image");
    Vector2 position = new Vector2(
        GraphicsDevice.Viewport.Width / 2 - buttonTexture.Width / 2,
        GraphicsDevice.Viewport.Height/2 - buttonTexture.Height / 2);
    button = new Button(buttonTexture, position, spriteBatch);
    button.OnTapped += new EventHandler(button_OnTapped);
    ```

10. Next is the reaction method for the button `OnTapped` event:

    ```
    void button_OnTapped(object sender, EventArgs e)
    {
        textColor.R = (byte)random.Next(0, 256);
        textColor.G = (byte)random.Next(0, 256);
        textColor.B = (byte)random.Next(0, 256);
    }
    ```

11. Get the tapped position and pass it to the `Button.Update()` method, paste the code in to the `Update()` method:

    ```
    TouchCollection touches = TouchPanel.GetState();
    if(touches.Count > 0 && touches[0].State ==
        TouchLocationState.Pressed)
    {
        Vector2 tappostion = touches[0].Position;
        button.Update(gameTime, tappostion);
    }
    ```

12. Draw the button on screen, and put the following lines of code to the `Draw()` method:

```
spriteBatch.Begin(SpriteSortMode.Immediate,
    BlendState.NonPremultiplied);
button.Draw(gameTime);
spriteBatch.DrawString(font, textTapState, new Vector2(0, 0),
    textColor);
spriteBatch.End();
```

13. Ok, we have done the code work. Build and run the project, and the application should run similar to the following screenshot; when we tap the button, it will flicker and generate a random color for the text on the top-left corner.

How it works...

Steps 2–6 are about creating the `Button` class.

In step 2, the `texButton` is the button texture; `spriteBatch` will render the button texture on screen; `Position` specifies the location of the button on screen. `Alpha` represents the alpha value of the button `color`; `timer` will be used to accumulate the game elapsed time; `bool` value tapped will indicate the tapping state of the button; `OnTap` is the event handler to handle the button tap gesture.

In step 3, the `HitRegion` property will return the bound surrounding the button for tap validation.

In step 4, the constructor initializes the button texture, position, and color.

In step 5, within the `Update()` method of the `Button` class, the code checks the tapped position to see whether it's inside the button `HitRegion`. If yes, set `Tapped` to `true` and trigger the `OnTapped` event, else, it will be `false`.

In step 6, the first line is to accumulate the game elapsed time in milliseconds. The following code draws the button image. If the button is tapped and the elapsed time is greater than `100`, it will flicker. The effect is implemented by setting the `Alpha` value of button color. If the `Alpha` value equals `255` (Opaque), we set it to `0` (Transparent). Otherwise, the value will be set from `0` to `255`. After that, the latest alpha value will be assigned to `Color.A`, the alpha factor of `Color`. Then, reset the timer for the next frame. The last line will render the flickering effect on screen.

Steps 7–11 are about using the `Button` class in the main game class.

In step 7, the `font` object will render the text on screen; the `textTapState` stores the text to be displayed; `textColor` specifies the text color; `random` will be used to generate a random `color` for the text; the `button` variable represents the `Button` class instance; the `buttonTexture` loads the button image.

In step 9, the `button_OnTapped()` method will run if the `OnTapped` event happens. In the event reaction method, we set the `R`, `G`, and `B` factors of text color randomly, because the RGB value is from `0` to `255`, so the random value for each of them must be inside the range.

In step 10, we get the tapped position for the button hit region validation.

In step 11, notice we must set the `BlendState.NonPremultiplied` because we change the button image `Alpha` value linearly.

Creating a listbox to speed up your information management in a game

Listbox is a list-style control, which collects the information in the list. For games, list control often plays a role in information management. The items in the listbox are presented one-by-one vertically or horizontally. You can choose the information entry through the control. In this recipe, you will master the technique of building your own listbox.

Getting ready

The example will create a listbox in Windows Phone 7. When you click the scrollbar down or the down button, the listbox will show the list items from the latest index. Once you tap one of the items, the text of the item will be presented at the top-left of the screen. Now, let's begin with building the `Button` class.

How to do it...

The following steps will show you the complete process of creating the GUI listbox control:

1. Create the Windows Phone Game project named `ListBoxControl`, change `Game1.cs` to `ListBoxControlGame.cs`. Add the `Button.cs`, `ScrollBar.cs`, and `ListBox.cs` files to the main project, and add `gameFont.spriteFont`, `ListBoxBackground.png`, `ScrollBarDown.png`, and `ScrollBarUp.png` to the content project.

2. Create the `Button` class in `Button.cs`. First, insert the lines as the field of the `Button` class:

```
// Button texture
Texture2D texButton;

// SpriteBatch for drawing the button image
SpriteBatch spriteBatch;

// Button position on the screen
public Vector2 Position;

// Button color
Color color;

// The Tapped bool value indicates whether tap in the button
region
public bool Tapped;

// Event handler OnTap to react with tap gesture
public event EventHandler OnTapped;
```

3. The next part is the `HitRegion` property:

```
// Get the hit region
public Rectangle HitRegion
{
    get
    {
        return new Rectangle((int)Position.X, (int)Position.Y,
            texButton.Width, texButton.Height);
    }
}
```

4. After the property definition, the constructor will be:

```
// Initialize the button without text
public Button(Texture2D texture, Vector2 position, SpriteBatch
    spriteBatch)
{
    this.texButton = texture;
    this.Position = position;
    this.spriteBatch = spriteBatch;
    color = Color.White;
}
```

5. Then, we define the `Update()` method:

```
// Update the button
public void Update(GameTime gameTime, Vector2 touchPosition)
{
    // React to the tap gesture
    Point point = new Point((int)touchPosition.X,
        (int)touchPosition.Y);

    // If tapped button, set the Hovered to true and trigger
    // the OnClick event
    if (HitRegion.Contains(point))
    {
        Tapped = true;
        OnTapped(this, null);
    }
    else
    {
        Tapped = false;
    }
}
```

6. The final method in the `Button` class is the `Draw()` method:

```
// Draw the button
public virtual void Draw(GameTime gameTime)
{
    // Draw the button texture
    if (Tapped)
    {
        spriteBatch.Draw(texButton, HitRegion, null,
            Color.Red, 0,
            Vector2.Zero, SpriteEffects.None, 0);

    }
```

```
        else
        {

            spriteBatch.Draw(texButton, HitRegion,
                null,Color.White, 0,
                Vector2.Zero, SpriteEffects.None, 0);
        }
    }
```

7. Create the `ScrollBar` class in `ScrollBar.cs`. As the class field, we use the following code:

```
// SpriteBatch for drawing the scrollbar
SpriteBatch spriteBatch;

// ScrollBar up and down buttons
Button scrollUp;
Button scrollDown;

// Textures for scrollbar up and down buttons
Texture2D texScrollUp;
Texture2D texScrollDown;

// The position of scrollbar
public Vector2 Position;

// The positions of scrollbar up and down buttons
public Vector2 scrollUpPosition;
public Vector2 scrollDownPosition;

// Event handler when scrollbar up button tapped
public event EventHandler OnScrollUpTapped;

// Event handler when scrollbar down button tapped
public event EventHandler OnScrollDownTapped;

// The ScrollBar Height and Width
public int ScrollBarHeight;
public int ScrollBarWidth;
```

8. The following code is the `ScrollDownBound` and `ScrollUpBound` property of the `ScrollBar` class:

```
// The Bound of Scrollbar down button
public Rectangle ScrollDownBound
{
```

```
        get
        {
            return new Rectangle((int)scrollDownPosition.X,
                (int)scrollDownPosition.Y,
                (int)texScrollDown.Width,
                (int)texScrollDown.Height);
        }
    }


    // The Bound of Scrollbar up button
    public Rectangle ScrollUpBound
    {
        get
        {
            return new Rectangle((int)scrollUpPosition.X,
                (int)scrollUpPosition.Y,
                (int)texScrollDown.Width,
                (int)texScrollDown.Height);
        }
    }
```

9. After the properties, the constructor of the `ScrollBar` class should be as follows:

```
    // ScrollBar constructor
    public ScrollBar(Vector2 position, int scrollbarHeight,
        ContentManager content, SpriteBatch spriteBatch)
    {
        // Load the textures of scroll bar up and down button
        texScrollDown = content.Load<Texture2D>("ScrollBarDown");
        texScrollUp = content.Load<Texture2D>("ScrollBarUp");

        Position = position;
        this.spriteBatch = spriteBatch;

        // Get the scrollbar width and height
        this.ScrollBarWidth = texScrollDown.Width;
        this.ScrollBarHeight = scrollbarHeight;

        // The position of scrollbar up button
        this.scrollUpPosition = new Vector2(
        Position.X - ScrollBarWidth / 2, Position.Y);

        // The position of scrollbar down button
        this.scrollDownPosition = new Vector2(
        Position.X - ScrollBarWidth / 2,
```

```
        Position.Y + ScrollBarHeight - texScrollDown.Height);

        // Instance the scrollbar up and down buttons
        scrollUp = new Button(texScrollUp, scrollUpPosition,
            spriteBatch);
        scrollDown = new Button(texScrollDown, scrollDownPosition,
            spriteBatch);
    }
```

10. Next, we define the `Update()` method of the `Scrollbar` class:

```
    // Scrollbar Update method
    public void Update(GameTime gameTime, Vector2 tappedPosition)
    {
        // Check whether the tapped position is in the bound of
        // scrollbar up button
        if (ScrollDownBound.Contains((int)tappedPosition.X,
            (int)tappedPosition.Y))
        {
            // If yes, set the Tapped property of scrollbar down
            // button to true
            scrollDown.Tapped = true;

            // Set the Tapped property of scrollbar up button to
            // false
            scrollUp.Tapped = false;

            // Trigger the scrollbar down button event
            OnScrollDownTapped(this, null);
        }
        else if(ScrollUpBound.Contains((int)tappedPosition.X,
            (int)tappedPosition.Y))
        {
            // If yes, set the Tapped property of scrollbar up
            // button to true
            scrollUp.Tapped = true;

            // Set the Tapped property of scrollbar down button to
            // false
            scrollDown.Tapped = false;

            // Trigger the scrollbar up button event
            OnScrollUpTapped(this, null);
        }
    }
```

11. Then, draw the scrollbar on screen by using the `Draw()` method:

```
// Draw the scrollbar
public void Draw(GameTime gameTime)
{
    // Draw the scrollbar down and up buttons
    scrollDown.Draw(gameTime);
    scrollUp.Draw(gameTime);
}
```

12. Create the `ListBox` class in the `ListBox.cs` file. We add the following code as the class field:

```
// Game object holds the listbox
Game game;

// SpriteBatch for drawing listbox
SpriteBatch spriteBatch;

// SpriteFont object for showing the listbox text items
SpriteFont font;

// The listbox background texture
Texture2D texBackground;

// The collection of listbox text items
public List<string> list;

// The position of listbox on screen
public Vector2 Position;

// The count of the listbox text items
public int Count;

// Scrollbar object to control the text items for showing
ScrollBar scrollBar;

// The Index for locating the specified item in listbox
public int Index = 0;

// The bounds of showed items
List<Rectangle> listItemBounds;

// The index of selected items
public int SelectedIndex = 0;
```

```
// The selected item
public string SelectedItem = "";

// The selected area for highlighting the selected item
Texture2D SelectedArea;

// The offset from the position of listbox as the beginning of
// drawing the text items
Vector2 Offset;

// The width and height of listbox
int ListBoxWidth;
int ListBoxHeight;

// The total number of items presenting in listbox
int ShowedItemCount = 0;
```

13. As properties, the `CharacterHeight` and `Bound` look similar to the following:

```
// Get the character height o text item
public float CharacterHeight
{
    get
    {
        if (font != null && list.Count > 0)
        {
            // The Y value represents the character height in
            // the returned Vector2 value
            // of SpriteFont.MeasureString()
            return font.MeasureString(list[0]).Y;
        }
        else
        {
            throw new Exception();
        }
    }
}

// Get the bound of listbox
public Rectangle Bound
{
    get
    {
        return new Rectangle((int)Position.X, (int)Position.Y,
            texBackground.Width, texBackground.Height);
    }
}
```

14. The next block of code is the constructor of the `ListBox` class:

```
// Listbox constructor
public ListBox(Vector2 position, ContentManager content,
SpriteBatch
    spriteBatch, Game game)
{
    this.game = game;
    this.spriteBatch = spriteBatch;

    listItemBounds = new List<Rectangle>();

    list = new List<string>();
    Position = position;

    font = content.Load<SpriteFont>("gameFont");
    texBackground =
        content.Load<Texture2D>("ListBoxBackground");

    ListBoxWidth = texBackground.Width;
    ListBoxHeight = texBackground.Height;

    // Define the scrollbar position relative to the position
    // of listbox
    Vector2 scrollBarPosition = new Vector2(
        Position.X + ListBoxWidth + 40, Position.Y);

    // Instance the scrollbar
    scrollBar = new ScrollBar(scrollBarPosition, ListBoxHeight,
        content, spriteBatch);

    scrollBar.OnScrollUpTapped += new
        EventHandler(scrollBar_OnScrollUpTapped);
    scrollBar.OnScrollDownTapped += new
        EventHandler(scrollBar_OnScrollDownTapped);

    // Define the offset for drawing the text items
    Offset = new Vector2(20, 4);
}
```

15. Now, we define the reaction method of the tap event of the scrollbar's up and down buttons:

```
// The reaction method of scrollbar down button tapping event
void scrollBar_OnScrollDownTapped(object sender, EventArgs e)
{
    // If the current item index plus the ShowedItemCount
    // is less
```

```
    // than count of list items, increase the Index
    if (Index + ShowedItemCount < Count)
    {
        Index++;
    }
}


// The reaction method of scrollbar up button tapping event
void scrollBar_OnScrollUpTapped(object sender, EventArgs e)
{
    // If the current item index is greater than 0, decrease
the
    // Index
    if (Index > 0)
    {
        Index--;
    }
}
```

16. The following important method in the `ListBox` class is the `Update()` method:

```
    // Check the tapping state of scrollbar and the selection of
    // listbox items
    public void Update(GameTime gameTime, Vector2 tapposition)
    {
        scrollBar.Update(gameTime, tapposition);
        CheckSelected(tapposition);
    }
```

17. The definition of `CheckSelected()` is as follows:

```
    // Get the selected index and item in listbox
    private void CheckSelected(Vector2 tappedPosition)
    {
        for (int i = 0; i < ShowedItemCount; i++)
        {
            // Check whether the tapped position is in the region
of
            // listbox and in which one of the item bounds.
            if (Bound.Contains(
                (int)tappedPosition.X, (int)tappedPosition.Y)
                && tappedPosition.Y <
                    listItemBounds[i].Y + CharacterHeight)
            {
                SelectedIndex = i;
                SelectedItem = list[Index + i];
                break;
            }
        }
    }
```

18. Before giving the definitions of the `AddItem()` and `RemoveItem()` methods, let's give the definition of the `GetListItemBound()` method:

```
private void GetListItemBound(List<String> list)
{
    // If the count of the items is greater than 0
    if (list.Count > 0)
    {
        Rectangle itemBound;

        // If the current count of item is less than the
        // ShowedItemCount, set the LoopBound to Count, else,
        // set it to ShowedItemCount.
        int LoopBound = Count < ShowedItemCount ? Count :
            ShowedItemCount;

        // Get the item bounds
        for (int i = 0; i < LoopBound; i++)
        {
            itemBound = new Rectangle(
                (int)Position.X,
                (int)(Position.Y + Offset.Y) +
                    font.LineSpacing * i,
                (int)ListBoxWidth, (int)CharacterHeight);
            listItemBounds.Add(itemBound);
        }
    }
}
```

19. Next it's time for implementing the `AddItem()` and the `RemoveItem()` methods:

```
// Add text item to listbox
public void AddItem(string str)
{
    // Add the text item to the list object
    this.list.Add(str);

    // Update total number of list items
    Count = list.Count;
    // Set the limited count for showing the list items
    if (list.Count == 1)
    {
        ShowedItemCount = (int)(texBackground.Height /
            CharacterHeight);
    }
```

```
        // Get the text item bounds
        listItemBounds.Clear();
        GetListItemBound(list);
    }
```

20. Now, define the `RemoveItem()` method:

```
    public void RemoveItem(string str)
    {
        // Delete the text item from the list items
        this.list.Remove(str);

        // Update the total number of list items
        Count = list.Count;
        GetListItemBound(list);
    }
```

21. After the text item management functions, is the Selection Area creating method:

```
    // Create the texture of the selected area
    private void CreateSelectedArea(Rectangle rectangle)
    {
        // Initialize the selected area texture
        SelectedArea = new Texture2D(game.GraphicsDevice,
            rectangle.Width, rectangle.Height, false,
            SurfaceFormat.Color);

        // Initialize the pixels  for the texture
        Color[] pixels = new Color[SelectedArea.Width *
            SelectedArea.Height];
        for (int y = 0; y < SelectedArea.Height; y++)
        {
            for (int x = 0; x < SelectedArea.Width; x++)
            {
                pixels[x + y * SelectedArea.Width] =
                    new Color(new Vector4(125f, 125f,125f, 0.5f));
            }
        }

        // Set the pixels to the selected area texture
        SelectedArea.SetData<Color>(pixels);
    }
```

22. The final step in building the `ListBox` class is to draw the listbox on screen through the `Draw()` method:

```
public void Draw(GameTime gameTime)
{
    // Draw the listbox background
    spriteBatch.Draw(texBackground, Position, Color.White);

    // The text items exist
    if (Count > 0)
    {
        // If current count of items is less than the
        // ShowedItemCount, show the items one by one
        // from the beginning
        if (Count <= ShowedItemCount)
        {
            for (int i = 0; i < Count; i++)
            {
                spriteBatch.DrawString(font, list[i],
                    Position + new Vector2(
                    Offset.X, Offset.Y + font.LineSpacing * i),
                    Color.White);
            }
        }
        // If current count of items is greater than the
        // ShowedItemCount, show the items from the current
        // index.
        else
        {
            for (int i = 0; i < ShowedItemCount; i++)
            {
                spriteBatch.DrawString(font, list[i + Index],
                    Position + new Vector2(
                    Offset.X, Offset.Y + font.LineSpacing * i),
                    Color.White);
            }
        }

        // If the SelectionArea is not created, creat a new
        // one
        if (SelectedArea == null)
        {
            CreateSelectedArea(listItemBounds[0]);
        }
```

```
            // Draw the SelectedArea texture
            spriteBatch.Draw(SelectedArea,
                listItemBounds[SelectedIndex], Color.White);
        }

        scrollBar.Draw(gameTime);
    }
```

23. Woo! The `ListBox` class and its dependent classes are done. Now, we will use the `ListBox` class in our main project, and this is simple and easy to code. Insert the following lines to the `ListBoxControlGame` class field:

```
SpriteFont spriteFont;
ListBox listBox;
```

24. Initialize the `spriteFont` object and `listBox`. Add the lines in the `LoadContent()` method:

```
// Create a new SpriteBatch, which can be used to draw
textures.
spriteBatch = new SpriteBatch(GraphicsDevice);
spriteFont = Content.Load<SpriteFont>("gameFont");

listBox = new ListBox(new Vector2(200, 100), this.Content,
spriteBatch, this);

listBox.AddItem("Item1");
listBox.AddItem("Item2");
listBox.AddItem("Item3");
listBox.AddItem("Item4");
listBox.AddItem("Item5");
listBox.AddItem("Item6");
listBox.AddItem("Item7");
listBox.AddItem("Item8");
```

25. Get the tapped position on `listBox`. Paste the following code to the `Update()` method:

```
TouchCollection touches = TouchPanel.GetState();
if (touches.Count > 0 && touches[0].State ==
    TouchLocationState.Pressed)
{
    Vector2 tapposition = touches[0].Position;
    listBox.Update(gameTime, tapposition);
}
```

26. Draw the listbox and selected text item on screen, and insert the block of code in to the `Draw()` method:

```
spriteBatch.Begin(SpriteSortMode.Immediate,
    BlendState.NonPremultiplied);

listBox.Draw(gameTime);

spriteBatch.DrawString(spriteFont,
    " SelectedItem: " + listBox.SelectedItem,
    new Vector2(0, 0), Color.White);
spriteBatch.End();
```

27. The whole project is complete. Build and run the application. It should look similar to the following screenshots:

How it works...

Steps 1–6 are about creating the `Button` class.

In step 2, the `texButton` stores the button texture; `spriteBatch` will render the button texture on screen; `Position` defines the button position on screen; the `color` object represents the button color; `Tapped` shows the tapping state of the button; `OnTap` is the event handler of tap gesture.

In step 3, the `HitRegion` property returns the button hit region around the button background texture.

In step 5, the `Update()` method gets the tapped position and checks whether it's inside the button hit region. If yes, set `Tapped` to `true` and trigger the `OnTapped` event. Else, set `Tapped` to `false`.

In step 6, the code draws a button on the Windows Phone 7 screen. If the button is tapped, draw the button in red, or else, in white.

Steps 7-11 are about implementing the `Scrollbar` class.

In step 7, the `spriteBatch` will render the scrollbar background texture on screen; the `scrollUp` and `scrollDown` buttons will be used to increase or decrease the index of listbox items; `Position` stores the position of the scrollbar; `scrollUpPosition` and `scrollDownPosition` maintain the positions of the `scrollUp` and `scrollDown` buttons; the following two event handlers specify the tap events of the two scroll buttons when they are tapped. The two variables `ScrollBarHeight` and `ScrollBarWidth` define the height and width of the scrollbar buttons.

In step 8, the `ScrollDownBound` property returns the bound around the `scrollDown` button, similar to the `ScrollUpBound` property.

In step 9, the constructor initializes the two scrollbar buttons and gets the scrollbar width and height.

In step 10, the `Update()` method checks the tapped position to see whether it's in the `ScrollDownBound`, if yes, set the `Tapped` of `scrollDown` to `true` and the property of `scrollUp` to `false`, then trigger the `OnScrollDownTapped` event; otherwise, do similar things for `ScrollUpBound`.

Steps 12-22 are to build the `ListBox` class using `Button` and `Scrollbar` classes.

In step 12, the `game` is the object of `Game` that supplies the `GraphicDevice` for drawing the selection area texture; `spriteBatch` will draw the listbox on screen; `font` will be used to draw the text of the listbox items; `texBackground` holds the listbox background texture; `list` is the collection of listbox text items; `Position` specifies the position of the listbox; `Count` shows the current total number of listbox items; `scrollbar` is the object of `ScrollBar` used to explore the listbox items; `Index` shows the current beginning index in listbox items; `listItemBounds` is the collection the bounds of list items. The following two variables indicate the index of the selected item in the listbox; if the item is selected, the `SelectedArea` will present a rectangle texture around the item; `Offset` is the position for drawing the text item relative to the position of the listbox; `ShowedItemCount` saves the maximum limitation of the number for rendering listbox items.

In step 13, the `CharacterHeight` returns the character height of the listbox text item. The `Bound` property gets the rectangle surrounding the `listbox`.

In step 15, when the `scrollUp` button is tapped, the `Index` will increase by 1 if the sum of `Index` plus `ShowedItemCount` is less than the amount of listbox items. While the `scrollDown` button is tapped and the `Index` is greater than 0, we will decrease the `Index` by one.

In step 16, first the `Update()` method checks the tapped position, to see whether it's inside the buttons of the scrollbar. Then, use the `CheckSelected()` method to check the listbox item selection.

In step 17, because the `ShowedItemCount` limits the number for showing items, we just need to do the same steps for the loop. In the body of the `for` loop, first we check the tapped position to see whether it's in the bound of the listbox, then we examine the lower-side of the current item bound to see whether it is greater than the `Y` factor of the tapped position. If so, it means the tapped position is in the region of the current item bound that is selected. Now, we set the current `i` to the `SelectedIndex` and the content of the current item to `SelectedItem`. The `break` here is important, as we only need the first selected one.

In step 18, we implement the `GetListItemBound()` method. When the `list.Count` is greater than `0` and if the current count of `listbox` item is less than `ShowedItemCount`, the loop will be equal to the `Count`; otherwise, the `ShowedCount` should be the `LoopBound`. In the loop, the code generates the item bound with the `CharacterHeight` and `ListBoxWidth`.

In step 19, once every new listbox item is added to the `list`, we will update the `Count`. This stands for the total number of listbox items. We get the `ShowedItemCount` when there is an item in the listbox. After that, we obtain the bounds of items through the `GetListItemBound()` method defined in step 18.

In step 21, the `CreateSelectedArea()` method first creates a new texture—`SelectedArea` which has the same size as the method parameter—`rectangle`. The second line defines the dimension of pixels equal to the `SelectedArea`. In the `for` loop, we set the actual color to each pixel of the new texture. Finally, the `SetData()` method copies the pixels to the `SelectedArea` for texture drawing.

In step 22, the first line of the `Draw()` method draws the listbox background texture. When the `Count` is greater than `0` and is equal to, or less than, the `ShowedItemCount`, the list item will be drawn one by one from the beginning of the list. Otherwise, we draw the items from the current index. After that, if one of the list items is selected, the `SelectionArea` will also be rendered around the selected item.

Steps 23–26 are for drawing the listbox on screen in the main game class `ListBoxControlGame`.

Creating a text input control to communicate with others in a game

Textbox is a very common and useful control in applications, reading the input and displaying the symbols in the main area. For multiplayer games, players love to use the control to communicate with each other for exchanging their thoughts. A textbox control can also act like a command line for controlling the game settings. With textbox control and corresponding functions, you can do a lot of things. In this recipe, you will learn how to make your own textbox control in Windows Phone 7.

How to do it...

The following steps will help you to implement a text input control for communicating in your own Windows Phone 7 game:

1. Create a Windows Phone Game project in Visual Studio 2010 named `TextBox`, and change `Game1.cs` to `TextBoxGame.cs`. Then, add `cursor.png`, `button.png`, `backspace.png`, `TextboxBackground.png`, and `gameFont.spriteFont` to the content project.

2. Now, let's develop a button class for input. First of all, in the `Button.cs` file we declare the class field and property:

```
// Button texture
Texture2D texButton;

// SpriteBatch for drawing the button image
SpriteBatch spriteBatch;

// SpriteFont for drawing the button text
SpriteFont font;

// Button text
public String Text = "";

// Button text position on the screen
public Vector2 TextPosition;

// Button text size
public Vector2 TextSize;

// Button position on the screen
public Vector2 Position;

// The Clicked bool value indicates whether tap in the button
public bool Clicked;

// Event handler when tap on the button
public event EventHandler OnClicked;

// Get the hit region
public Rectangle HitRegion
{
    get
    {
        return new Rectangle((int)Position.X, (int)Position.Y,
            texButton.Width, texButton.Height);
    }
}
```

3. Next, we define two overload constructors of the `Button` class:

```
// Initialize the button without text
public Button(Texture2D texture, Vector2 position, SpriteFont
    font, SpriteBatch spriteBatch)
{
    this.texButton = texture;
    this.Position = position;
    this.spriteBatch = spriteBatch;
    this.font = font;
}

// Initialize the button with text
public Button(Texture2D texture, Vector2 position, String
    text, SpriteFont font, SpriteBatch spriteBatch)
{
    this.texButton = texture;
    this.Position = position;
    this.spriteBatch = spriteBatch;
    this.Text = text;

    // Compute the text size and place the text in the center
    // of the button
    TextSize = font.MeasureString(Text);
    this.TextPosition = new Vector2(position.X +
        texture.Width / 2 - TextSize.X / 2, position.Y);
    this.font = font;
}
```

4. In the following step, we will make the button react to the tap gesture. Add the `Update()` code as follows:

```
// Update the button
public void Update(GameTime gameTime, Vector2 touchPosition)
{
    // React to the tap gesture
    Point point = new Point((int)touchPosition.X,
        (int)touchPosition.Y);

    // If tapped button, set the Hovered to true and trigger
    // the OnClick event
    if (HitRegion.Contains(point))
    {
        Clicked = true;
        OnClicked(this, null);
    }
```

```
        else
        {
            Clicked = false;
        }
    }
```

5. The final step for the `Button` class is to draw it on the screen. To do this, we use this block of code:

```
// Draw the button
public virtual void Draw()
{
    // Draw the button texture
    if (!Clicked)
    {
        spriteBatch.Draw(texButton, HitRegion, Color.White);
    }
    else
    {
        spriteBatch.Draw(texButton, HitRegion, Color.Red);
    }

    // Draw the button text
    spriteBatch.DrawString(font, Text, TextPosition,
    Color.White);
}
```

6. In this step, we begin to write the `TextBoxControl` class. In `TextBoxControl.cs`, add the lines to the `TextBoxControl` class as fields:

```
// SpriteBatch for drawing the textbox texture
SpriteBatch spriteBatch;

// SpriteFont for drawing the textbox font
SpriteFont spriteFont;

// Textbox background texture
Texture2D texBackGround;

// Textbox cursor texture
Texture2D texCursor;

// Textbox Bound for showing the text
public Rectangle Bound;

// Textbox position
```

```
public Vector2 Position;

// Textbox cursor position
public Vector2 CursorPosition;

// Timer used to control the cursor alpha value
float timer;

// Text position in the textbox
public Vector2 TextPosition;

// The text size of the showing text
public Vector2 textSize;

// The character size of the textbox text
private float characterSize;

// Alpha value for the cursor
int alpha = 255;

// The cursor color
Color cursorColor;

// TypedText stores the typed letters
public string TypedText = "";

// ShowedText saves the text shown in the textbox
public string ShowedText = "";
```

7. Next, we add the properties to the `TextBoxControl` class:

```
// Get the character size
public float CharacterSize
{
    get
    {
        textSize = spriteFont.MeasureString(TypedText);
        characterSize = textSize.X / TypedText.Length;
        return characterSize;
    }
}

// Get the text size
public Vector2 TextSize
{
```

```
        get
        {
            return textSize = spriteFont.MeasureString(TypedText);
        }
    }

    // Get the bound for showing the text
    public int ShowedCharacterBound
    {
        get
        {
            return (int)(Bound.Width / CharacterSize);
        }
    }
```

8. The following part is about the `TextBoxControl` class initialization, and the constructer looks as follows:

```
    // Initialize the textbox
    public TextBoxControl(Vector2 position, Texture2D texCursor,
        Texture2D texBackground, SpriteFont font, SpriteBatch
        spriteBatch)
    {
        this.Position = position;
        this.spriteBatch = spriteBatch;
        this.texCursor = texCursor;
        this.spriteFont = font;
        this.texBackGround = texBackground;

        // Set the bound of textbox control
        Bound = new Rectangle((int)position.X, (int)position.Y,
        texBackGround.Width, texBackGround.Height);

        // Set the cursor position
        this.CursorPosition = new Vector2(position.X + 10,
            position.Y + 10);

        // Set the text position
        this.TextPosition = new Vector2(position.X + 10,
        position.Y);

        // Set the cursor color with alpha value
        cursorColor = new Color(255, 255, 255, alpha);
    }
```

9. After the initialization, the following code is the definition of the `Update()` method:

```
public void Update(GameTime time)
{
    // Accumulate the game elapsed milliseconds
    timer += (float)time.ElapsedGameTime.TotalMilliseconds;

    // Every 500 milliseconds the alpha value of the cursor will
    // change from 255 to 0 or 0 to 255.
    if (timer > 500)
    {
        if (alpha == 255)
        {
            alpha = 0;
        }
        else if (alpha == 0)
        {
            alpha = 255;
        }
        cursorColor.A = (byte)alpha;
        timer = 0;
    }
}
```

10. Then we define the `Draw()` method :

```
public void Draw()
{
    // Draw the textbox control background
    spriteBatch.Draw(texBackGround, Position, Color.White);

    // Draw the textbox control cursor
    spriteBatch.Draw(texCursor, CursorPosition, cursorColor);

    // Draw the textbox showing text
    spriteBatch.DrawString(spriteFont, ShowedText,
        TextPosition, Color.White);
}
```

11. From this step, we will use the `Button` class and the `TextBoxControl` class in the main game class. Now, add the lines to the `TextBoxGame` class fields:

```
// SpriteFont object
SpriteFont font;

// TextboxControl object
TextBoxControl textBox;
```

```
// Button objects
Button buttonA;
Button buttonB;
Button buttonBackspace;
```

12. Initialize the textbox control and buttons. Insert the code to the `LoadContent()` method:

```
// Load the textbox textures
Texture2D texCursor = Content.Load<Texture2D>("cursor");
Texture2D texTextboxBackground =
    Content.Load<Texture2D>("TextboxBackground");

// Load the button textures
Texture2D texButton = Content.Load<Texture2D>("button");
Texture2D texBackSpace = Content.Load<Texture2D>("Backspace");
font = Content.Load<SpriteFont>("gameFont");

// Define the textbox position
Vector2 position = new Vector2(400, 240);

// Initialize the textbox
textBox = new TextBoxControl(position, texCursor,
    texTextboxBackground, font, spriteBatch);

// Initialize the buttonA
buttonA = new Button(texButton, new Vector2(400, 350), "A",
    font, spriteBatch);
buttonA.OnClicked += new EventHandler(button_OnClicked);

// Initialize the buttonB
buttonB = new Button(texButton, new Vector2(460, 350), "B",
    font, spriteBatch);
buttonB.OnClicked += new EventHandler(button_OnClicked);

// Initialize the backspace button
buttonBackspace = new Button(texBackSpace,
    new Vector2(520, 350), font, spriteBatch);
buttonBackspace.OnClicked += new
    EventHandler(buttonBackspace_OnClicked);
```

13. Define the event handling code for `buttonA` and `button`, which is same for both:

```
void button_OnClicked(object sender, EventArgs e)
{
    // Add the button text to the textbox TypedText

    // Update the position of textbox cursor
    textBox.CursorPosition.X = textBox.TextPosition.X +
    textBox.TypedText += ((Button)sender).Text;

        textBox.TextSize.X;

    // Get the textbox showed character bound
    int showedCharacterBound = textBox.ShowedCharacterBound;

    // check whether the textbox cursor goes outside of the
    // textbox bound
    if (textBox.CursorPosition.X > textBox.Bound.X +
        textBox.Bound.Width)
    {
        // If yes, set cursor positon at the right side of
        // the textbox
        textBox.CursorPosition.X = textBox.TextPosition.X +
            textBox.CharacterSize * showedCharacterBound;

        // Show the TypedText from end to the left in
        // the range for  showing characters of textbox
        textBox.ShowedText =
        textBox.TypedText.Substring(textBox.TypedText.Length -
            showedCharacterBound - 1, showedCharacterBound);
    }
    else
    {
        // If not, just set the current TypedText to the
        // showedText
        textBox.ShowedText = textBox.TypedText;
    }
}
```

14. The next block of code is the handling code for the backspace button:

```
void buttonBackspace_OnClicked(object sender, EventArgs e)
{
    // Get the length of TypedText
    int textLength = textBox.TypedText.Length;

    // Check whether the TypedText is greater than 0
    if (textLength > 0)
```

```
        {
            // If yes, delete the last character
            textBox.TypedText = textBox.TypedText.Substring(0,
                textLength - 1) ;

            // Get the current showed character count.
            int showedCharacterCount = (int)(textBox.TextSize.X /
                textBox.CharacterSize);

            // Check whether the current showed character count is
less than
            // the textbox showed character bound
            if (showedCharacterCount <=
                textBox.ShowedCharacterBound)
            {
                // If yes, just update the cursor position with
                // current text size and the showedText with
                // current text
                textBox.CursorPosition.X = textBox.TextPosition.X
                    + textBox.TextSize.X;
                textBox.ShowedText = textBox.TypedText;
            }
            else
            {
                // If not, show the TypedText from end to the
                // left in the range for showing characters
                // of textbox
                textBox.ShowedText = textBox.TypedText.Substring(
                    textBox.TypedText.Length -
                    textBox.ShowedCharacterBound,
                    textBox.ShowedCharacterBound);
            }
        }
    }
}
```

15. Trigger the button event. Add the code to the `Update()` method:

```
TouchCollection touches = TouchPanel.GetState();
if(touches.Count > 0 && touches[0].State ==
    TouchLocationState.Pressed)
{
    buttonA.Update(gameTime, touches[0].Position);
    buttonB.Update(gameTime, touches[0].Position);
    buttonBackspace.Update(gameTime, touches[0].Position);
}

textBox.Update(gameTime);
```

16. Draw the textbox and buttons on screen. Paste the code into the `Draw()` method:

```
spriteBatch.Begin();
textBox.Draw();
buttonA.Draw();
buttonB.Draw();
buttonBackspace.Draw();
spriteBatch.End();
```

17. Now, build and run the application. When you tap button A and button B, the textbox will show the input as shown in the following screenshot to the left. When you tap the backspace button, it will look similar to the following screenshot on the right:

How it works...

Steps 2–5 are responsible for creating the `Button` class:

In step 2, the `texButton` stores the button texture; `font` will be used to render the button text, we use the button `Text` for the input text; the `position` variable tells you where the button is on the screen; the `bool` value `Clicked` indicates whether the tap gesture takes place in the button hit region; when the button is clicked, the `OnClicked` event will be triggered. The `HitRegion` property returns the bound of the button for clicking.

In step 3, the first constructor initializes the button without text. The second constructor initializes the button with text and places the text in the center of the button. The `SpriteFont.MeasureString()` method computes and returns the text size as a `Vector2`, the X value holds the text width, and the Y value holds the text height.

In step 4, the reacting code first gets the tapped position, then use the `Rectangel.Contains()` method to check whether the position is inside the hit region, if yes, we set the `Clicked` to `true` and trigger the `OnClicked()` event.

Steps 6–10 are about creating the `TextBoxControl` class:

In step 6, the first four variables deal with the textbox texture and font; the following `Bound` variable stores the textbox bound for showing text; `Position` indicates the location of the textbox control on the screen; the `CursorPosition` represents the cursor place within the textbox control bound; the `timer` variable will be used to control the alpha value of the cursor for the flashing effect; the `TextPosition` shows the text position inside the textbox control; `textSize` represents the size of the `TypedText`; the `characterSize` defines the size of a single character of the `TypedText`; the `ShowedText` stores the text that will be presented in the textbox.

In step 7, the `CharacterSize` returns the size of a single character in the `TypedText`, we use `SpriteFont.MeasureString()` to compute the size of the `TypedText`, then use the X value of the `textSize` and divide the `TypedText` length to get the unit character length; the `TextSize` returns the size of `TypedText`; `ShowedCharacterBound` returns the region for showing the `TypedText`.

In step 9, the `Update()` method checks whether the accumulated milliseconds are greater than 500 or not. If yes and the `alpha` value is equal to 255 (opaque), it will be set to 0 (transparent), and vice versa. After setting the latest `alpha` value to alpha factor of cursor color—`cursorColor.A`, we reset the `timer` for the next interval.

Steps 11–16 are about using the `Button` and `TextBoxControl` class in the main class. We will draw the button and textbox control on the Windows Phone 7 screen and perform the reactions for text input and delete.

In step 11, the `textBox` stands for the `TextBoxControl`; `buttonA` represents the button for input character A; `buttonB` is used to input character B; the `buttonBackspace` will delete the character of the `TypedText` from the end to the beginning.

In step 12, the code loads the textures for the textbox and buttons first. Then, it initializes their event handling code.

In step 13, the code reacts to the event triggered from `buttonA` or `buttonB`. The first line casts the `sender` to `Button`. Then add the `Text` value to the `TextBoxControl.TypedText`. After getting the text, the cursor position is updated following the new `TypedText`. The rest of the code deals with the situation when the length of the `TypedText` is greater than the textbox bound. If this happens, the cursor will still stay at the right-side of the textbox, the `showedText` will be the substring of the `TypedText` from the end to the left in the range for showing characters of the textbox. On the other hand, the entire `TypedText` will be drawn.

In step 14, as the reaction code for the backspace button, at the beginning, we get the length of the `TypedText`. Then check whether it is greater than 0. If yes, we delete the last character. The rest of the code works with the state when the deleted `TypedText` length is greater or less than the textbox bound. If greater, the `showedText` will range from the end of the deleted `TypedText` to the left about the showed character count of the textbox. Otherwise, the cursor will follow the current `TypedText`, which will be completely rendered on the screen.

5

Content Processing

In this chapter, we will cover:

- ▶ The architecture and flow of content processing
- ▶ Creating a custom importer and processor for your text
- ▶ Processing XML files
- ▶ Manipulating the extracted information from an image in the content pipeline
- ▶ Extracting BoundingSphere and BoundingBox information from models

Introduction

The management and processing of game assets in Windows Phone 7 XNA are fundamental; you can load and deal with images, music, and model contents as you need. The advantage of XNA content loading is that all the contents will be transformed to binary files as XNB which contain the complete content information that you need to load the contents at the beginning of every game. This approach will obviously speed up the content loading time. In Windows Phone XNA, Microsoft has already written the most common content importer and processor for you. However, sometimes you will still have to process customized data or format. At the moment, the **Extension Content Pipeline Library** is the best way to handle the content material. The Extentsion Content Pipeline is a project template that generates the standard XNA content importer and processor. You can override the importer and processor default methods to read and process a typical file format that XNA does support to meet your own requirements in the game. In this chapter, you will learn how to apply these useful techniques to your games.

The architecture and flow of content processing

Content processing is a special module in Windows Phone 7 Game Programming. It provides the flexibility for different types of game content including images, effects, and models. Besides this, the most powerful aspect of content processing is the extension to customize your game with different types of contents. In a commercial game, the customized game contents are especially relevant. Mastering the technique of dealing with any kind of game content is the key ability to master in your Windows Phone 7 Game Programming life. In this section, you will learn the basics of XNA Content Processing and, for example, we will process the text as game contents.

As a key part of the XNA game framework, the content processing pipeline transforms the original art or information file to a format that can be read and used in the Windows Phone 7 XNA framework. Actually, you don't need to rewrite the importer for some common game content file formats, such as `.FBX`, `.PNG`, `.fx`, and so on. The XNA team has done all the hard work for you, saving you time on learning and researching these formats. Usually, all the built-in content processing components are enough for you to write games. However, if you want to use a new file format that XNA does not support, the best method is to develop your own importer and processor to get the file data. Before doing the job, it is better to have a thorough understanding of how the Window Phone 7 XNA Content Pipeline works, which will help you to fix some weird and unexpected content processing bugs. Believe me, it is true!

The content processing pipeline generally has the following two phases:

- The reading phase: In this phase, the asset file is read from the local disk, the file is then processed, and the process data is stored in a binary form as **exported file** (`.xnb`).

- The loading phase: In this phase, the exported data is loaded from the `.xnb` binary file into the XNA game application memory. This loading operation is completed manually by the user.

By putting the importing and processing operations in the compile phase, the game contents loading time is reduced. When the actual game reads the exported file at runtime, it only needs to get the processed data from the binary file. Another convenience is that the exported file could be used on different platforms, such as Windows, Xbox, and Windows Phone 7.

The following diagram shows the main content processing flow in XNA:

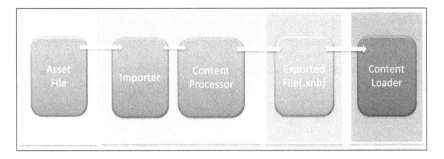

The reading phase

The importer converts the game assets into objects that the standard content processor can recognize, or other specific customized processor could deal with. An importer typically converts the content into managed objects and includes strong typing for such assets as meshes, vertices, and materials. In addition, a custom importer may produce custom objects for a particular custom content processor to consume.

The job of the content processor is to transform the imported game assets and compile them into a managed code object that can be loaded and used by XNA games on Windows, Xbox, or Windows Phone. The managed code object is the .xnb file. Different processors deal with different game asset types.

If the imported file format is recognized by the Windows Phone 7 XNA built-in importers, the corresponding processor will be assigned to it automatically. Otherwise, if the content is not recognized properly, you should manually set the specific importer and processor in the file property panel (don't worry about how to do this just now, as you will learn this later in the chapter). After that, when you build your game, the assigned importer and processor for each asset will build the recognized assets to binary XNB files which can be loaded at runtime.

The loading phase

In the reading phase, the game contents are serialized in a binary file, they are ready for use in your game, and then in the loading phase, you can load the processed file in your game by the **content loader**. When the game needs the game assets, it must call the `ContentManager.Load()` method to invoke the content loader, specifying the expected object type. The content loader then locates and loads the asset data from the .xnb file into the game memory.

Content Document Object Model

When importing the game asset to your Windows Phone 7 XNA game project, the XNA framework will transform the data to a built-in type system named **Content Document Object Model** (**DOM**) which represents the set of classes for standard content processing. Additionally, if the importer and processor are customized, the importer will return ContentItem with the information you specified, or a predefined data type. The following diagram is the main route of the model content processing pipeline specified by Microsoft:

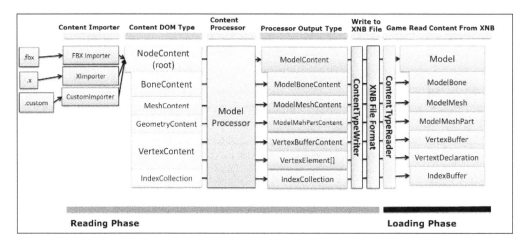

This is how it works:

1. The first step is to import the original model game asset into the game project, where each corresponding content importer converts the input model data into an XNA Document Object Model (DOM) format.

2. The output of the model importers is a root NodeContent object, which describes a graphics type that has its own coordinate system and can have children. The classes: BoneContent, MeshContent, GeometryContent, VertexContent, and IndexCollection are all inherited from the NodeContent class. As a result, the root NodeContent object output from a model importer might have some NodeContent, MeshContent, and BoneContent children. Moreover, the NodeContent.Children property represents the hierarchy of the model.

3. After the models have been imported, they can be processed by their corresponding model processors, or also by your processor. This separation allows you to define two importers for importing X and FBX files, but use the same model processor to process their output. ModelProcessor receives the root NodeContent object as a parameter, generated by the model importer, and returns a ModelContent object.

4. The exported ModelContent model data has a Tag property which is an object, containing vertex and bone data, but no animation data.

5. At the end of the reading phase, this processed data needs to be stored in an XNB binary file. To be able to store the `ModelContent` object in an XNB file, `ModelContent` and each object inside it must have its own `ContentTypeWriter`. `ContentTypeWriter` defines how the data of each object is written into the binary XNB file.

6. During the reading phase, at runtime, `ContentManager` reads the binary XNB file and uses the correct `ContentTypeReader` for each object it finds in the XNB file.

   As the XNA Content Pipeline does not have full support for models with skeletal animation, you need to extend the content pipeline, adding support for skeletal animation.

Creating a custom importer and processor for your text

Most of the time, the standard content importers and processors are enough for Windows Phone Game Development. However, sometimes you need to process a different type of file that the XNA framework does not support. At present, you will need, a custom importer and processor. In this recipe, you will learn how to write your own importer and processor for text in Windows Phone 7 XNA.

Getting ready

In order to read the specific game asset, first you should develop a corresponding importer and processor. Then, write the processed data to an XNB file with the override `Write()` method of `ContentTypeWriter` class in the content pipeline project. After that, override the `Read()` method of `ContentTypeWriter` class in a separate class in the main game project. In this example, you will write a text importer and read the data from the compiled text in an XNB file into your game.

How to do it...

Carry out the following steps to create a custom importer and processor:

1. Create a Windows Phone Game project named `TextContentReader` and a **Content Pipeline Extension Library** project named `TextImporterProcessor` with a clicking sequence: **File | New | Project | XNA Game Studio 4.0 | Content Pipeline Extension Library**. When the content pipeline project is created, we add five new files into it: `Text.cs`, `TextImporter.cs`, `TextOutput.cs`, `TextProcessor.cs`, and `TextWriter.cs`.

2. In this step, we define the `TextInput` class and the `TextOutput` class. The `TextInput` class in the `TextInput.cs` file looks as follows:

```csharp
// TextInput class for importer and processor
public class TextInput
{
  // Text string
  string text;

  // Constructor
  public TextInput(string text)
  {
      this.text = text;
  }

    // Text property
    public string Text
    {
       get
       {
           return text;
       }
    }
}
```

3. The other class `TextOutput` in the `TextOutput.cs` file is:

```csharp
// TextOutput class for processor and ContentTypeWriter and
// ContentTypeReader
public class TextOutput
{
    // Text byte array
    byte[] textOutput;

    public TextOutput(byte[] textOutput)
    {
        this.textOutput = textOutput;
    }

    // Compiled text property
    public byte[] CompiledText
    {
        get
        {
            return textOutput;
        }
    }
}
```

4. Create the `TextImporter` class in the `TextImporter.cs` file as follows:

```
// Text importer
[ContentImporter(".txt", DefaultProcessor = "TextImporter",
    DisplayName = "TextImporter")]
public class TextImporter : ContentImporter<TextInput>
{
    // Override the Import() method
    public override TextInput Import
        (string filename, ContentImporterContext context)
    {
        // Read the text data from .txt file
        string text = System.IO.File.ReadAllText(filename);

        // Return a new TextInput object
        return new TextInput(text);
    }
}
```

5. Create a `TextProcessor` class that uses `TextInput` from `TextImporter` as an input and outputs a `TextOutput` object. Define the class in the `TextProcessor.cs` file as follows:

```
// Text content processor
[ContentProcessor(DisplayName = "TextProcessor")]
public class TextProcessor :
    ContentProcessor<TextInput, TextOutput>
{
    // Override the Process() method
    public override TextOutput Process
        (TextInput input,       ContentProcessorContext context)
    {
        // Return the TextOutput object
        return new
            TextOutput(Encoding.UTF8.GetBytes(input.Text));
    }
}
```

6. The last step in the loading phase is to save the `TextOutput` data into an XNB file. In this step, we will create the `TextWriter` class in `TextWriter.cs` to define the behavior of how to write the `TextOutput` data into an XNB fie. The implementation of `TextWriter` is as follows:

```
// TextWriter for writing the text information into XNB
// file
[ContentTypeWriter]
public class TextWriter : ContentTypeWriter<TextOutput>
{
```

```
    // Override the Write() method
    protected override void Write
        (ContentWriter output, TextOutput value)
    {
        // Write the text length information to XNB file
        output.Write(value.CompiledText.Length);

        // Write the text string into XNB file
        output.Write(value.CompiledText);
    }

    public override string GetRuntimeType
        (TargetPlatform targetPlatform)
    {
        // Get the run time type of TextOutput
        return typeof(TextOutput).AssemblyQualifiedName;
    }

    public override string GetRuntimeReader
        (TargetPlatform targetPlatform)
    {
        // Get the TextOutput assembly information
        return "TextContentReader.TextReader,
            TextContentReader," +
            " Version=1.0.0.0, Culture=neutral";
    }
}
```

7. In the loading phase, the first step is to define the output type of
   `ContentTypeReader`. For `TextReader`, the output type is the `TextOutput`
   class that came with it in the `TextImporterProcessor` project. Now we
   add `TextOutput.cs` and `TextReader.cs` into the main game project
   `TextContentReader`. For `TextOutput.cs`, we should change the namespace
   from `TextImporterProcessor` to `TextContentReader`, and the rest remains
   the same. Then, we define the `TextReader` class in `TextReader.cs` as follows:

```
    public class TextReader : ContentTypeReader<TextOutput>
    {
        // Read the TextOutput data from xnb file
        protected override TextOutput Read
            (ContentReader input, TextOutput existingInstance)
        {
            // Read the text length
            int size = input.ReadInt32();

            // Read the text content
```

```
        byte[] bytes = input.ReadBytes(size);

        // Generate a TextOutput object with the already
        // read text.
        return new TextOutput(bytes);
    }
}
```

8. Load the text of the XNB file into the main game and render the content on the screen. We add `gameSprite.spritefont` into the content project and insert the TextImporterProcessor DLL into the content project reference. In the content project, right-click on the **TextContent.txt** file and choose the **Properties** from the pop-up menu. We then choose the text corresponding to the importer and processor in the property panel, as shown in the following screenshot:

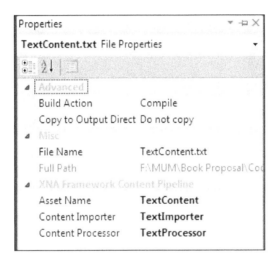

9. Now, insert the following lines into the `TextContentReader` class field, as follows:

```
SpriteFont font;
string str;
```

10. Then, add the following code into the `LoadContent()` method as follows:

```
font = Content.Load<SpriteFont>("gameFont");

TextOutput text = Content.Load<TextOutput>("TextContent");
str = System.Text.Encoding.UTF8.GetString(
text.CompiledText, 0, text.CompiledText.Length);
```

11. The last part is to render the text content on the screen, so add the following code in the `Draw()` method as follows:

```
spriteBatch.Begin();
spriteBatch.DrawString(font, str, new Vector2(0, 0), Color.
White);
spriteBatch.End();
```

12. Now build and run the Windows Phone 7 XNA game, making sure that the **Copy to Output Directory** in the **Property** panel of the `TextContent.txt` text file in the content project has been set to **Copy always**. The application will run as shown in the following screenshot:

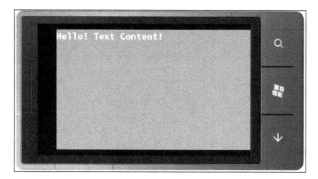

How it works...

In step 2, the `TextInput` class will be used to load the text data from `TextImporter` and send the data to `TextProcessor` as the input.

In step 3, the `TextOutput` class stores the text information compiled by `TextProcessor` as the output text data. All the string data is stored in `TextOutput` as byte array.

In step 4, before the `TextImporter` class, we add a `ContentImporter` attribute to provide some properties for the importer. The first parameter defines the file extension that the importer could recognize when the game asset is imported; the `DefaultProcessor` argument instructs the XNA system which processor will be the default processor corresponding to the importer. The last argument `DisplayName` specifies the display name when you have chosen the importer for your asset. The following is the `ContentImporter` attribute that `TextImporter` must inherit from the `ContentImporter` class and override the `Import()` method. The importer reads a text file containing characters and generates the original file to `TextInput` object. From XNA SDK:

When the game is built, the Content Importer.Import *function is called once for each XNA content item in the current project.*

When invoked against an input file in the appropriate format, a custom importer is expected to parse the file and produce as output one or more content objects of appropriate types. Since an importer's output is passed directly to a Content Pipeline processor, each type that an importer generates must have at least one processor available that can accept it as input.

In step 5, for the TextProcessor class, we declare another class attribute named ContentProcessor. DisplayName shows the display name when it is chosen for a specific game asset. As the Process() method is the default method in ContentProcessor, as a subclass, TextProcessor should override the Process() method to handle the TextInput data from TextImporter. Here, we use the Encoding. UTF8.GetBytes() to transform the text string into a byte array and generate the TextOutput object. The generated TextOutput object is the intermediate data for ContentTypeWriter to write to an XNB file.

In step 6, the TypeWriter class is derived from the ContentTypeWriter class and overrides the Write(), GetRuntimeType(), and GetRuntimeReader() methods. The Write() method performs the key operation of writing the text information into an XNB file. Notice that the text information writing order must comply with the data when read by TextReader at runtime. The GetRuntimeType() method identifies the type of an object your game should load from the XNB file written by the writer object. In this instance, the XNB file contains the binary array from your custom TextOutput type. The GetRuntimeReader() method specifies what reader should be invoked to load the XNB file in your game. It returns the namespace and name of the reader class, followed by the name of the assembly in which that class is physically located. In general, the assembly string of ContentTypeReader should be:

```
GameNamespace.ContentReaderClassName, ContentReaderClassName,
Version=x.x.x.x, Culture=neutral
```

In step 7, TextReader is the subclass of ContentTypeReader and overrides the Read() method to read the XNB file generated in the reading phase. The reading order is the same as the data writing order. Essentially, what we are going to do here is load all the serialized bits of the XNB file. Finally, the method returns a new TextOutput object to the ContentManager.Load() method.

Processing XML files

In game development, the XML file often plays the role of describing the whole game world, configuring the basic game settings or defining the object properties in the game scenario. For processing an XML file, the .NET framework supports several methods. In Windows Phone 7 XNA programming, if XML is a part of the game content, you can process the file in a way to suit your requirements. At present, the technique of writing the XML file importer and processor will help you. In the following recipe, you will learn this useful technique, and it is easy to extend for your own game.

How to do it...

The following steps will lead you to create the content importer and process for XML files:

1. Create a Windows Phone Game project named XMLReader. Change Game1.cs to XMLReaderGame.cs. Then, add a Content Pipeline Extension Library project in the solution named XMLImporterProcessor. Add Person.cs, PersonWriter.cs, PersonXMLInput.cs, XMLImporter.cs, and XMLProcessor.cs files into the project. In the content project, add the PersonInfo.xml file. The XML file looks as follows:

   ```
   <?xml version="1.0" encoding="utf-8" ?>
   <Person>
           <Name>Steven</Name>
           <Age>24</Age>
           <Gender>Male</Gender>
   </Person>
   ```

2. Create the PersonXMLInput class in PersonXMLInput.cs as follows:

   ```
   [XmlRoot("Person")]
   public class PersonXMLInput
   {
           [XmlElement("Name")]
           public string Name;

           [XmlElement("Age")]
           public int Age;

           [XmlElement("Gender")]
           public string Gender;

   }
   ```

3. Then, build the `Person` class in `Person.cs` as follows:

```
public class Person
{
        public string Name;
        public int Age;
        public string Gender;

        public Person(string name, int age, string gender)
        {
            this.Name = name;
            this.Age = age;
            this.Gender = gender;
        }
}
```

4. Create the `XMLImporter` class in `XMLImporter.cs` as follows:

```
[ContentImporter(".xml", DisplayName="XMLImporter",
                 DefaultProcessor="XMLProcessor")]
public class XMLImporter : ContentImporter<PersonXMLInput>
{
    public override PersonXMLInput Import
        (string filename, ContentImporterContext context)
    {
        PersonXMLInput personXMLInput =  new PersonXMLInput();

        // Create an XML reader for XML file
        using (System.Xml.XmlReader reader =
                System.Xml.XmlReader.Create(filename))
        {
            // Create an XMLSerializer for the AnimationSet
            XmlSerializer serializer = new
                XmlSerializer(typeof(PersonXMLInput));

            // Deserialize the PersonXMLInput from the
            // XmlReader to the PersonXMLInput object
            personXMLInput =
                (PersonXMLInput)serializer.Deserialize(reader);
        }

        return personXMLInput;
    }
}
```

5. Implement `XMLProcessor` in `XMLProcessor.cs` as follows:

```
[ContentProcessor(DisplayName="XMLProcessor")]
public class XMLProcessor :
ContentProcessor<PersonXMLInput, Person>
{
    public override Person Process(PersonXMLInput input,
        ContentProcessorContext context)
    {
        return new Person(input.Name, input.Age, input.Gender);
    }
}
```

6. Define the `PersonWriter` class for writing the importer XML person information into an XNB file:

```
[ContentTypeWriter]
class PersonWriter : ContentTypeWriter<Person>
{
    // Override the Write() method
    protected override void Write(ContentWriter output,
                                    Person value)
    {
        output.Write(value.Name);
        output.Write(value.Age);
        output.Write(value.Gender);
    }

    public override string GetRuntimeType
        (TargetPlatform targetPlatform)
    {
        // Get the run time type of TextOutput
        return typeof(Person).AssemblyQualifiedName;
    }

    public override string GetRuntimeReader
        (TargetPlatform targetPlatform)
    {
        // Get the PersonReader assembly information
        return "XMLReader.PersonReader, XMLReader," +
            " Version=1.0.0.0, Culture=neutral";
    }
}
```

7. Load the person information from the XNB file. We should add `PersonReader.cs` and `Person.cs` in the main game project. The only difference between `Person.cs` here and in the `XMLImporterProcessor` project is that the namespace here is `XMLReader`. The `Person` class will be the storage for the person information from the XNB file when loaded by the `content manager`. The `PersonReader` should be:

```
public class PersonReader : ContentTypeReader<Person>
{

    protected override Person Read
        (ContentReader input, Person existingInstance)
    {
        return new Person(input.ReadString(),
                    input.ReadInt32(), input.ReadString());
    }
}
```

8. Read the XML file in the game. First, we add the following lines into the class field:

```
SpriteFont font;
Person person;
string textPersonInfo;
```

9. Then, load the `PersonInfo.xml` in `LoadContent()` as follows::

```
person = Content.Load<Person>("PersonInfo");
font = Content.Load<SpriteFont>("gameFont");

textPersonInfo = "Name: " + person.Name + "\n" + "Age: " +
        person.Age + "\n" + person.Gender;
```

10. Draw the person information on the screen.

```
spriteBatch.Begin();
spriteBatch.DrawString(font, textPersonInfo,
                    new Vector2(0, 0), Color.White);
spriteBatch.End();
```

11. Now build and run the application, and the person information should appear as shown in the following screenshot:

How it works...

In step 2, the `PersonXMLInput` class defines how the person information maps to the `PersonXMLInput` from XML description file. `XmlRoot("Person")` stands for the root name `<Person>` in the XML file, the other three `XmlElement` attributes represent the XML element: `<Name>`, `<Age>`, and `<Gender>`.

In step 3, the `Person` class is the output type of `XMLProcessor` and the input type of `XMLReader`.

In step 4, we create an `XMLReader` object to read the content of the XML file. The following `XMLSerializer` object is used to read the `PersonXMLInput` information from the XML file. The new `personXMLInput` object will be passed to `XMLProcessor` as the input.

In step 5, the processor code is simple; it extracts information from the `PersonXMLInput` object input to generate a new `Person` class object as the output.

In step 6, the `Person` object is the input of `PersonWriter`. The `ContentWriter` writes the `Name`, `Age`, and `Gender` into the XNB file, one by one. The `GetRuntimeType()` method identifies the type of `Person` your game should load from the XNB file written by the `PersonWriter` object. The `GetRuntimeReader()` method specifies the `XMLReader` which will be invoked to load the XNB file in your game.

In step 7, the `PersonReader` reads the person information from the XNB file written by `PersonWriter` and builds a new `Person` object.

Manipulating the extracted information from an image in the content pipeline

Images are irreplaceable in games. They could be the sprites, the game world in 2D or the game user interface. In the 3D world, usually, images represent the appearance of 3D models. In the Windows Phone 7 XNA framework, the default texture or model importers and processors have already dealt with the images for you. Sometimes, you may want to handle the image information as per your needs when loading them from an XNB file. In this recipe, you will learn how to get and operate the image data in the XNA content pipeline.

How to do it...

Carry out the following steps:

1. Create a Windows Phone Game project named ImageProcessorGame and change Game1.cs to ImageProcessorGame.cs. Add the BackgroundMaze.png (shown in the following screenshot) into the content project. Then, add a Content Pipeline Extension Library into the game solution named ImageProcessor, and then add ImageProcessor.cs into the project:

2. Create the ImageProcessor class in the ImageProcessor content library project as follows:

```
[ContentProcessor(DisplayName = "Image Processor")]
public class ImageProcessor : TextureProcessor
{
    public override TextureContent Process
        (TextureContent input, ContentProcessorContext context)
    {
        // Random object to generate random color
        Random random = new Random();

        Color color = Color.White;

        // PixelBitmapContent maintain pixel value in a 2D
        //array
```

```
PixelBitmapContent<Color> image = null;

// TextureContent object get the image content
TextureContent texContent = base.Process(input,
    context);

// Convert the texture content into PixelBitmapContent
texContent.ConvertBitmapType(typeof
    (PixelBitmapContent<Color>));

// Get the pixel color from the image content
for (int face = 0; face < texContent.Faces.Count;
    face++)
{
    MipmapChain mipChain = texContent.Faces[face];
    for (int mipLevel = 0;
    mipLevel < mipChain.Count; mipLevel++)
    {
        image = (PixelBitmapContent<Color>)
            input.Faces[face][mipLevel];
    }
}

int RowSpan = 0;

// Generate the random color strip line by line
for (int i = 0; i < image.Height; i++)
{
    if (RowSpan++ < 20)
    {
        for (int j = 0; j < image.Width; j++)
        {
            // If the pixel color is black,
            // replace it with a random color
            if (image.GetPixel(j, i) == Color.Black)
            {
                image.SetPixel(j, i, color);
            }
        }
    }
    else
    {
        // Begin a new line and generate another random
        //color
        RowSpan = 0;
```

```
                    color.R = (Byte)random.Next(0, 255);
                    color.G = (Byte)random.Next(0, 255);
                    color.B = (Byte)random.Next(0, 255);
                }
            }
            return texContent;
        }
    }
```

3. Now, build the `ImageProcessor` project and you will get the `ImageProcessor.dll` library file. Add the `ImageProcessor.dll` into the reference list of the content project. Right-click on the **BackgroundMaze.png** to change the corresponding processor, as shown in the following screenshot:

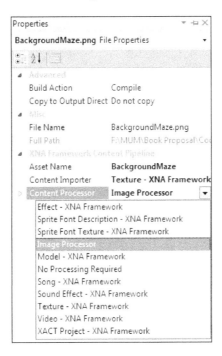

4. In this step, we will draw the processed image on the screen. We add the following code as the field of the `ImageProcessorGame` class:

```
// The Texture2D object
Texture2D image;
```

5. Then, load the image in `LoadContent()` by using the following line:

```
image = Content.Load<Texture2D>("BackgroundMaze");
```

6. Draw the processed image on screen, paste the code in the `Draw()` method:

```
spriteBatch.Begin();
spriteBatch.Draw(image, new Vector2(0,0), Color.White);
spriteBatch.End();
```

7. Now build and run the application. It runs as shown in the following screenshot:

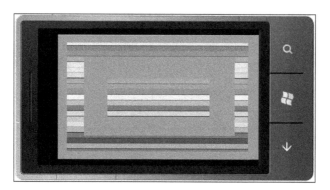

How it works...

In step 2, the `ImageProcessor` inherits from `TextureProcessor` for dealing with the image information imported by the built-in importer which supports `.bmp`, `.dds`, `.dib`, `.hdr`, `.jpg`, `.pfm`, `.png`, `.ppm`, and `.tga` image formats. If the importer does not support the image format, such as `.gif`, then you should implement the corresponding one.

As the input of `ImageProcessor`, `TextureContent` contains basic methods to manipulate the image content. The `random` and `color` objects will be used to generate random colors. `Image` is an object of `PixelBitmapContent<Color>` and the `PixelBitmapContent` is a subclass of `BitmapContent`. The `BitmapContent` class represents a single two-dimensional image with a fixed size and fixed format. Various pixel encodings are supported by subclasses of the bitmap type. Higher-level constructs, such as textures, that may contain multiple mipmap images or cube map faces are stored as collections of multiple bitmaps. The `image` object declares the type to which the `texContent` will be converted. The following methods `base.Process()` and `TexContent.ConvertBitmapType` change the `texContent` to a designated format. Here we change the contents to colors. By default, the `texContent` will be converted to `TextureContent2D`, but could also be `TextureContent3D`. This means that the image can have multiple faces and mipmaps. For a simple image, it has only one face and one mipmap. Our job here is to iterate the mipmaps in every face in an image. After the first `for` loop, you will get the image color set. The second `for` loop is easy; we go through all of the colors pixel by pixel in the image. If the pixel color is black, we use the `image.SetPixel()` method to set the color to a randomly generated color.

Extracting BoundingSphere and BoundingBox information from models

Extracting the `BoundingSphere` and `BoundingBox` information often helps you in detecting collisions in a 3D game. The BoundingSphere and BoundingBox come from the model vertices. For BoundingSphere, you should know the center and radius, whereas for BoundingBox, you need the min and max points. In this recipe, you will learn how to build and get the BoundingSphere and BoundingBox from 3D models produced by 3D modeling tool such as 3DS MAX or Maya. The default format in XNA is FBX, a compatible format shared between most 3D modeling tools in the content processing phase for Windows Phone 7 XNA game.

Getting ready

BoundingBox is actually specified by eight points, whereas BoundingSphere consists of a center point and the radius. BoundingBox is axis aligned, where each face is perpendicular to the axis.

The reason to use BoundingBox is for performance and ease. BoundingBox has the advantage that it fits the non-rotated rectangular objects very well. Mostly, game objects are static, so there is no need to perform accurate collision detection. Even if you want to make a more precise collision detection, BoundingBox can still help you to eliminate the non-collided object to gain better performance. The disadvantage of BoundingBox is that when it is applied to an object that is not axis aligned and rotating, you have to recreate the BoundingBox. This means performing the rotation matrix multiplication of every BoundingBox point, and this will slow down the game running speed.

As compared to BoundingBox, BoundingSphere needs less information: only the center point vector and the radius are required. If the object encompassed by BoundingBox is rotated, you need to recreate the BoundingBox. When the game objects are bounded by BoundingSphere, any collision detection between them will be fast. You only need to compute the distance of the center points of the two objects. As a suggestion, the BoundingSphere could be the first choice when you want to perform the basic collision detection. The disadvantage of BoundingSphere is that if the object is a long box, there will be a log space which will be wasted.

The following steps show you the best practice approach to extracting the BoundingBox and BoundingSphere from 3D models, which will help you to perform the collision detection in the real game:

1. Create a Windows Phone Game project named `ObjectBoundings`. Change `Game1.cs` to `ObjectBoundingsGame.cs`. Add a Content Pipeline Extension Library named `ModelBoundsProcessor` and insert a new processor definition file named `ModelBoundingBoxProcessor.cs`. Then, in the content project, we add a `box.fbx` model file.

2. Define `ModelBoundingBoxProcessor`. We add the following lines into the class field:

   ```
   // The collection for MeshBoundingSpheres
   Dictionary<string, BoundingBox> MeshBoundingBoxes = new
       Dictionary<string, BoundingBox>();

   // The collection for MeshBoundingBoxes
   Dictionary<string, BoundingSphere> MeshBoundingSpheres = new
       Dictionary<string, BoundingSphere>();

   // The dictionary stores the BoundingSphere and BoundingBox
   // information of a model
   Dictionary<string, object> bounds = new Dictionary<string,
       object>();
   ```

3. Next, we implement the `Process()` method for `ModelBoundingBoxProcessor` as follows:

   ```
   public override ModelContent Process(NodeContent input,
       ContentProcessorContext context)
   {
       // Get the children NodeContents
       NodeContentCollection nodeContentCollection =
           input.Children;

       // If the input NodeContent does not have children mesh,
       // the input is the NodeContent for processing
       if (input.Children.Count == 0)
       {
           // Cast the input to MeshContent
           MeshContent meshContent = (MeshContent)input;

           // Get the points of the mesh
           PositionCollection vertices = new PositionCollection();
   ```

```
        // Get the world transformation of current meshcontent
        Matrix absoluteTransform =
            meshContent.AbsoluteTransform;

        // Translate the points' positions from object
        //coordinates to world coordinates
        foreach (Vector3 vec in meshContent.Positions)
        {
            Vector3 vector =
                Vector3.Transform(vec, absoluteTransform);

            // Add the transformed vector to the vertice list
            vertices.Add(vector);
        }

        // Generate the BoundingBox of the mesh from the
        // transformed vertice list
        BoundingBox boundingbox =
            BoundingBox.CreateFromPoints(vertices);
        MeshBoundingBoxes.Add(input.Name, boundingbox);

        // Generate the BoundingSpere of the mesh from the
        // transformed vertice list
        BoundingSphere boundingSphere =
            BoundingSphere.CreateFromPoints(vertices);
        MeshBoundingSpheres.Add(input.Name, boundingSphere);

    }
    else
    {
        // If the root NodeContent has children, process them
        ParseChildren(nodeContentCollection);
    }

    // Deal with model in default
    ModelContent modelContent = base.Process(input, context);

    // Add the output BoundingBoxes and BoundingSpere to the
    //bounds
    bounds.Add("BoundingBoxes", MeshBoundingBoxes);
    bounds.Add("BoundingSpheres", MeshBoundingSpheres);

    // Assign the bounds to Tap for using in the game.
    modelContent.Tag = bounds;

    return modelContent;
}
```

4. Read `BoundingSphere` and `BoundingSphere` information of model in the main game project `ObjectBoundings`. Insert the following code as the class fields:

```
Model modelBox;
Dictionary<string, object> bounds;
Dictionary<string, BoundingSphere> boundingSpheres;
Dictionary<string, BoundingBox> boundingBoxes;
```

5. Then, add the following code into the `LoadContent()` method:

```
modelBox = Content.Load<Model>("box");

// Read the the bounds dictionary object from Tag property
bounds = (Dictionary<string, object>)modelBox.Tag;

// Get the BoundingSphere dictionary
boundingSpheres = (Dictionary<string,
    BoundingSphere>)bounds["BoundingSpheres"];

// Get the BoundingBox dictionary
boundingBoxes = (Dictionary<string,
    BoundingBox>)bounds["BoundingBoxes"];
```

How it works...

In step 2, `MeshBoundingBoxes` is the dictionary that holds the BoundingBox of every mesh of a model by name. `MeshBoundingSpheres` stores the BoundingSphere of every mesh of model by name. `bounds` is the final dictionary where both BoundingSphere and BoundingBox collections are saved.

In step 3, the `input` is a `NodeContent` object that represents the root of the model tree. The first thing is to get the children `NodeContents` of input to hold the submeshes. The following condition judgment checks the count of children `NodeObjects` of `input`. If the input does have children, we will deal with the input itself. Understand this condition as we transform the `input` to `MeshContent`, which represents the model mesh. The following vertex is a `PositionCollection` object that stores the collection of `Vector3`. Then, we use `MeshContent.AbsoluteTransform` to get the world transformation matrix of model. After that, we iterate every point in the mesh and transform them from object coordinate to world coordinate. Finally, we use the `BoundingBox.CreateFromPoints()` and `BoundingSphere.CreateFromPoints()` methods to generate the `BoundingBox` and `BoundingSphere` of the model. Otherwise, if the model has more than one submesh, we use `ParseChildren()` to work on. The only difference is that we should traverse all the submeshes, and the `ParseChildren ()` method should be:

```
private void ParseChildren(NodeContentCollection
nodeContentCollection)
{
```

```
    //Iterate every NodeContent in the children NodeContent collection
    foreach (NodeContent nodeContent in nodeContentCollection)
    {
        // Cast the input to MeshContent
        MeshContent meshContent = (MeshContent)nodeContent;

        // Get the points of the mesh
        PositionCollection vertices = new PositionCollection();

        // Get the world transformation of current meshcontent
        Matrix absoluteTransform = meshContent.AbsoluteTransform;

        // Translate the points' positions from object
        // coordinates to world coordinates
        foreach (Vector3 vec in meshContent.Positions)
        {
            Vector3 vector = Vector3.Transform(vec,
                absoluteTransform);
            // Add the transformed vector to the vertice list
            vertices.Add(vector);
        }

        // Generate the BoundingBox of the mesh from the
        // transformed vertice list
        BoundingBox boundingbox = BoundingBox.
CreateFromPoints(vertices);
        MeshBoundingBoxes.Add(nodeContent.Name, boundingbox);

        // Generate the BoundingSpere of the mesh from the
        // transformed vertice list
        BoundingSphere boundingSphere =
            BoundingSphere.CreateFromPoints(vertices);
        MeshBoundingSpheres.Add(nodeContent.Name, boundingSphere);
    }
}
```

Now you have learned how to get the BoundingSphere and BoundingBox information from a model, you can use this information in your game for efficient collision detection.

6
Entering the Exciting World of 3D Models

In this chapter, we will cover:

- ▶ Controlling a model with the help of trackball rotation
- ▶ Translating the model in world coordinates
- ▶ Scaling a model
- ▶ Viewing the model hierarchy information
- ▶ Highlighting individual meshes of a model
- ▶ Implementing a rigid model animation
- ▶ Creating a terrain with texture mapping
- ▶ Customizing vertex formats
- ▶ Calculating the normal vectors from a model vertex
- ▶ Simulating an ocean on your CPU

Introduction

3D games are almost the main stream in modern times; StarCraft 2 has been transformed from 2D to 3D, the same with Diablo 3. 3D games are different from their 2D counterparts in that they provide more realistic experiences for players. You can easily explore the entire game world just with your eyes, and also drive a Porsche Boxster Spyder around San Francisco at high speed, which is not allowed in real life. To make a 3D game on your own is amazing and fun. In every 3D game, the models from the modeling software are the vital components. The game player, game level, outdoor terrain, and so on, compose the game world. Besides the static 3D models, the animation is another major component. When you are playing action games such as Assassin's Creed 2, the main character has a lot of moves such as jumping, running, climbing, and crawling. In 2D games, these actions are easy to achieve using the sprite sheet. In 3D games, the predefined animations from the animation modeling tool will do the job. In this chapter, you will go through the fundamental model operation techniques, understand the hierarchy of models, and learn how to control the animation.

Controlling a model with the help of trackball rotation

To rotate a model from any direction in Windows Phone 7 could let the game player have extra choices to view the model. For programming, the trackball viewer will help the programmer to check whether the output model from the model software works well. In this recipe, you will learn how to control a model in trackball rotation.

How to do it...

Follow these steps to control a model in trackball rotation:

1. Create a Windows Phone Game named `ModelTrackBall`, change `Game1.cs` to `ModelTrackBallGame.cs`. Then add the `tree.fbx` model file to the content project.

2. Declare the variables for rotating and rendering the model in `ModelTrackBall` class field:

```
// Tree model
Model modelTree;

// Tree model world position
Matrix worldTree = Matrix.Identity;

// Camera Position
Vector3 cameraPosition;
```

```
// Camera look at target
Vector3 cameraTarget;

// Camera view matrix
Matrix view;

// Camera projection matrix
Matrix projection;

// Angle for trackball rotation
Vector2 angle;
```

3. Initialize the camera and enable the `GestureType.FreeDrag`. Add the code into the `Initialize()` method:

```
// Initialize the camera
cameraPosition = new Vector3(0, 40, 40);
cameraTarget = Vector3.Zero + new Vector3(0, 10, 0);
view = Matrix.CreateLookAt(cameraPosition, cameraTarget,
    Vector3.Up);
projection = Matrix.CreatePerspectiveFieldOfView(
    MathHelper.PiOver4, GraphicsDevice.Viewport.AspectRatio,
    0.1f, 1000.0f);

// Instance the angle
angle = new Vector2();

// Enable the FreeDrag gesture
TouchPanel.EnabledGestures = GestureType.FreeDrag;
```

4. Rotate the tree model. Please insert the code into the `Update()` method:

```
// Check if the gesture is enabled or not
if (TouchPanel.IsGestureAvailable)
{
    // Read the on-going gesture
    GestureSample gesture = TouchPanel.ReadGesture();

    if (gesture.GestureType == GestureType.FreeDrag)
    {
        // If the gesture is FreeDrag, read the delta value
        // for model rotation
        angle.Y = gesture.Delta.X * 0.001f;
        angle.X = gesture.Delta.Y * 0.001f;
    }
}
```

```
// Rotate the tree model around axis Y
worldTree *= Matrix.CreateRotationY(angle.Y);

// Read the tree model around axis X
worldTree *= Matrix.CreateRotationX(angle.X);
```

5. Render the rotating tree model to the screen. First, we define the `DrawModel()` method:

```
// Draw the model on screen
public void DrawModel(Model model, Matrix world, Matrix view,
    Matrix projection)
{
    Matrix[] transforms = new Matrix[model.Bones.Count];
    model.CopyAbsoluteBoneTransformsTo(transforms);

    foreach (ModelMesh mesh in model.Meshes)
    {
        foreach (BasicEffect effect in mesh.Effects)
        {
            effect.EnableDefaultLighting();
            effect.World = transforms[mesh.ParentBone.Index] *
                world;
            effect.View = view;
            effect.Projection = projection;
        }
        mesh.Draw();
    }
}
```

6. Then add the reference to the `Draw()` method:

```
DrawModel(modelTree, worldTree, view, projection);
```

7. Build and run the application. It should run as shown in the following screenshots:

How it works...

In step 2, `modelTree` will load and store the tree model for rendering; `worldTree` represents the world position of the model tree. The following four variables, `cameraPosition`, `cameraTarget`, `view`, and `projection` are responsible for initializing and manipulating the camera; the last variable `angle` specifies the angle value when `GestureType.FreeDrag` takes place.

In step 3, we define the camera world position and look at the target in the first two lines. Then we create the view and projection matrices for camera view. After that, we have the code for initiating the `angle` object and enabling the `FreeDrag` gesture using `TouchPanel.EnabledGesture`.

In step 4, the first part of the code before rotation is to read the delta value for the `FreeDrag` gesture. We use `TouchPanel.IsGestureAvailable` to check whether the gestures are enabled. Then we call `TouchPanel.ReadGesture()` to get the on-going gesture. After that, we determine whether the gesture is `FreeDrag` or not. If so, then read `Delta.X` to `angle.Y` for rotating the model around the Y-axis and assign `Delta.Y` to `angle.X` for rotating around the X-axis. Once the latest `angle` value is known, it is time for rotating the tree model. We use `Matrix.CreateRotationY` and `Matrix.CreateRotationX` to rotate the tree model around the X- and Y-axes.

Translating the model in world coordinates

Translating the model in 3D world is a basic operation of Windows Phone 7 games; you can move the game object from one place to another. Jumping, running, or crawling is based on the translation. In this recipe, you will learn how to gain the knowledge necessary to do this.

How to do it...

The following steps will show you how to do the basic and useful operations on 3D models—Translation:

1. Create a Windows Phone Game project named `TranslateModel`, change `Game1.cs` to `TranslateModelGame.cs`. Next, add the model file `ball.fbx` and font file `gameFont.spritefont` to the content project.

2. Declare the variables for ball translation. Add the following lines to the `TranslateModelGame` class:

   ```
   // Sprite font for showing the notice message
   SpriteFont font;

   // The beginning offset at axis X
   float begin;
   ```

```
// The ending offset at axis X
float end;

// the translation value at axis X
float translation;

// Ball model
Model modelBall;

// Ball model position
Matrix worldBall = Matrix.Identity;

// Camera position
Vector3 cameraPosition;

// Camera view and projection matrix
Matrix view;
Matrix projection;

// Indicate the screen tapping state
bool Tapped;
```

3. Initialize the camera, and define the start and end position for the ball. Insert the
    following code to the `Initialize()` method:

```
// Initialize the camera position
cameraPosition = new Vector3(0, 5, 10);

// Initialize the camera view and projection matrices
view = Matrix.CreateLookAt(cameraPosition, Vector3.Zero,
    Vector3.Up);
projection = Matrix.CreatePerspectiveFieldOfView(
    MathHelper.PiOver4, GraphicsDevice.Viewport.AspectRatio,
    0.1f, 1000.0f);

// Define the offset of beginning position from Vector.Zero at
// axis X.
begin = -5;

// Define the offset of ending position from Vector.Zero at
// axis X.
end = 5;

// Translate the ball to the beginning position
worldBall *= Matrix.CreateTranslation(begin, 0, 0);
```

4. In this step, you will translate the model smoothly when you touch the phone screen. Add the following code into the `Update()` method:

```
// Check the screen is tapped
TouchCollection touches = TouchPanel.GetState();
if (touches.Count > 0 && touches[0].State ==
    TouchLocationState.Pressed)
{
    if (GraphicsDevice.Viewport.Bounds.Contains
        ((int)touches[0].Position.X, (int)touches[0].
Position.Y))
    {
        Tapped = true;
    }
}


// If the screen is tapped, move the ball in straight along
// the axis X
if (Tapped)
{
    begin = MathHelper.SmoothStep(begin, end, 0.1f);
    translation = begin;
    worldBall += Matrix.CreateTranslation(translation, 0, 0);
}
```

5. Draw the ball model and display the instructions on screen. Paste the following code to the `Draw()` method:

```
// Draw the ball model
DrawModel(modelBall, worldBall, view, projection);

// Draw the text
spriteBatch.Begin();
spriteBatch.DrawString(font, "Please Tap the Screen",
    new Vector2(0, 0), Color.White);
spriteBatch.End();
```

6. We still need to add the `DrawModel()` method to the `TranslateModelGame` class:

```
public void DrawModel(Model model, Matrix world, Matrix view,
    Matrix projection)
{
    Matrix[] transforms = new Matrix[model.Bones.Count];
    model.CopyAbsoluteBoneTransformsTo(transforms);

    foreach (ModelMesh mesh in model.Meshes)
    {
        foreach (BasicEffect effect in mesh.Effects)
```

```
        {
            effect.EnableDefaultLighting();
            effect.World = transforms[mesh.ParentBone.Index] *
                world;
            effect.View = view;
            effect.Projection = projection;
        }
        mesh.Draw();
    }
}
```

7. Now build and run the application. It will look similar to the following screenshots:

How it works...

In step 2, the SpriteFont is used to render the text on screen; begin and end specifies the offset at the X-axis; translation is the actual value for ball translation along the X-axis; modelBall loads and stores the ball model; worldBall represents the ball world position in 3D; the following three variables cameraPosition, view, and projection are used to initialize the camera. The bool value Tapped indicates whether Windows Phone 7 was tapped.

In step 4, the first part before if (Tapped) is to check whether the tapped position locates inside the screen bound. If yes, set Tapped to true. Once the screen is tapped, MathHelper. SmoothStep() will increase the begin value to end value defined previously frame-by-frame using the cubic interpolation algorithm and add the latest step value to the translation variable. It will then use the Matrix.CreateTranslation() method to generate a translation matrix for moving the ball model in 3D world.

Scaling a model

In order to change the scale of a model you can adjust the model meets the scene size or construct special effects, such as when a little sprite takes magical water, it suddenly becomes much stronger and bigger. In this recipe, you will learn how to change the model size at runtime.

How to do it...

Follow these steps to scale a 3D model:

1. Create a Windows Phone Game project named `ScaleModel`, change `Game1.cs` to `ScaleModelGame.cs`. Then add the model file `ball.fbx` and font file `gameFont.fle` to the content project.

2. Declare the necessary variables. Add the following lines to the `ScaleModel` class field:

```
// SpriteFont for showing the scale value on screen
SpriteFont font;

// Ball model
Model modelBall;

// Tree model world position
Matrix worldBall = Matrix.Identity;

// Camera Position
Vector3 cameraPosition;

// Camera view matrix
Matrix view;

// Camera projection matrix
Matrix projection;

// Scale factor
float scale = 1;

// The size the model will scale to
float NewSize = 5;
```

3. Initialize the camera. Insert the following code into the `Initialize()` method:

```
// Initialize the camera
cameraPosition = new Vector3(0, 5, 10);

view = Matrix.CreateLookAt(cameraPosition, Vector3.Zero,
    Vector3.Up);
projection = Matrix.CreatePerspectiveFieldOfView(
    MathHelper.PiOver4, GraphicsDevice.Viewport.AspectRatio,
    0.1f, 1000.0f);
```

4. Load the ball model and game font. Paste the following code into the `LoadContent()` method:

```
// Load the tree model
modelBall = Content.Load<Model>("ball");
font = Content.Load<SpriteFont>("gameFont");
```

5. This step will change the scale value of the ball model to the designated size. Add the following lines to the `Update()` method:

```
scale = MathHelper.SmoothStep(scale, NewSize, 0.1f);

worldBall = Matrix.Identity;
worldBall *= Matrix.CreateScale(scale);
```

6. Draw the ball and font on the Windows Phone 7 screen. Add the following code to the `Draw()` method:

```
// Draw the ball
DrawModel(modelBall, worldBall, view, projection);

// Draw the scale value
spriteBatch.Begin();
spriteBatch.DrawString(font, "scale: " + scale.ToString(), new
    Vector2(0, 0), Color.White);
spriteBatch.End();
```

7. The `DrawModel()` method should be as follows:

```
// Draw the model on screen
public void DrawModel(Model model, Matrix world, Matrix view,
    Matrix projection)
{
    Matrix[] transforms = new Matrix[model.Bones.Count];
    model.CopyAbsoluteBoneTransformsTo(transforms);

    foreach (ModelMesh mesh in model.Meshes)
    {
        foreach (BasicEffect effect in mesh.Effects)
        {
            effect.EnableDefaultLighting();
            effect.World = transforms[mesh.ParentBone.Index] *
                world;
            effect.View = view;
            effect.Projection = projection;
        }
        mesh.Draw();
    }
}
```

8. The application. It will run similar to the following screenshots:

How it works...

In step 3, the `font` variable is responsible for the draw-the-scale value on screen; `modelBall` loads the ball model; `worldBall` is the key matrix that specifies the world position and scale of the ball model; `scale` stands for the size of the ball model. When the initiative value is `1`, it means the ball is in its original size; `NewSize` indicates the new size the ball model will scale to.

In step 4, the `MathHelper.SmoothStep()` method uses the cubic interpolation algorithm to change the current scale to a new value smoothly. Before calling the `Matrix.CreateScale()` method to create the scale matrix and multiply the `worldBall` matrix, we must restore the `worldBall` to `Matrix.Identity`, otherwise the new scale will change from the previous value.

Viewing the model hierarchy information

In Windows Phone 7 3D game programming, the models come from the modeling software, such as 3DS MAX or Maya, which are used frequently. Sometimes, it you do not want to control a complete animation, just part of it. At that moment, you should know the subdivisions where they are. Actually, the models are organized as a tree, and you can find a specified mesh or bone using a tree-based binary search algorithm; however, there is no need to write an algorithm, as the XNA framework has done them for you. As a handy reference, you should know the hierarchy of the model and the name of every part. In the recipe, you will learn how to get the model hierarchy information.

How to do it...

1. Create a Windows Phone Game project named `ModelHierarchy`, and change `Game1.cs` to `ModelHierarchyGame.cs`. Then, add the `tank.fbx` model file from the XNA APP sample to the content project. After that, create a content pipeline extension library named `ModelHierarchyProcessor` and replace `ContentProcessor1.cs` to `ModelHierarchyProcessor.cs`.

2. Create the `ModelHierarchyProcessor` class in the `ModelHierarchyProcessor.cs` file.

```
[ContentProcessor(DisplayName = "ModelHierarchyProcessor")]
public class ModelHierarchyProcessor : ModelProcessor
{
    public override ModelContent Process(NodeContent input,
        ContentProcessorContext context)
    {
        context.Logger.LogImportantMessage(
            "---- Model Bone Hierarchy ----");

        // Show the model hierarchy
        DemonstrateNodeTree(input, context, "");
        return base.Process(input, context);
    }

    private void DemonstrateNodeTree(NodeContent input,
        ContentProcessorContext context, string start)
    {
        // Output the name and type of current model part
        context.Logger.LogImportantMessage(
            start + "- Name: [{0}] - {1}", input.Name,
            input.GetType().Name);

        // Iterate all of the sub content of current
                //NodeContent
        foreach (NodeContent node in input.Children)
            DemonstrateNodeTree(node, context, start + "- ");
    }
}
```

3. Add `ModelHierarchyProcessor.dll` to the content project reference list and the content processor of the tank model to `ModelHierarchyProcessor`, as shown in the following screenshot:

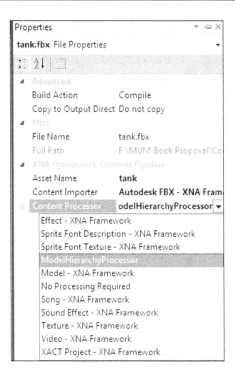

4. Build the `ModelHierarchy`. In the Output window, the model hierarchy information will show up as follows:

```
---- Model Bone Hierarchy ----
 - Name: [tank_geo] - MeshContent
 - - Name: [r_engine_geo] - MeshContent
 - - - Name: [r_back_wheel_geo] - MeshContent
 - - - Name: [r_steer_geo] - MeshContent
 - - - - Name: [r_front_wheel_geo] - MeshContent
 - - Name: [l_engine_geo] - MeshContent
 - - - Name: [l_back_wheel_geo] - MeshContent
 - - - Name: [l_steer_geo] - MeshContent
 - - - - Name: [l_front_wheel_geo] - MeshContent
 - - Name: [turret_geo] - MeshContent
 - - - Name: [canon_geo] - MeshContent
 - - - Name: [hatch_geo] - MeshContent
```

Compare it to the model information in 3DS MAX, as shown in the following screenshot. They should completely match. For looking up the information in 3DS MAX, you could click **Tools | Open Container Explorer**.

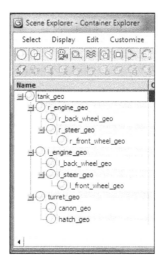

How it works...

In step 2, `ModelHierarchyProcessor` directly inherits from the `ModelProcessor` because we just need to print out the model hierarchy. In the `DemonstrateNodeTree()` method—which is the key method showing the model mesh and bone tree—the `Context.Logger.LogImportantMessage()` shows the name and type of the current `NodeContent`. Mostly, the `NodeContent` is `MeshContent` or `BoneContent` in the model processing phase when building the main project. The following recursion is to check whether the current `NodeContent` has sub node contents. If so, we will process the children one by one at a lower level. Then, the `Process()` method calls the method before returning the processed `ModelContent`.

Highlighting individual meshes of a model

The 3D game model object is made up of different meshes. In a real 3D game development, sometimes you want to locate the moving mesh and see the bounding wireframe. This will help you to control the designated mesh more accurately. In this recipe, you will learn how to draw and highlight the mesh of the model individually.

How to do it...

The following steps will help you understand how to highlight different parts of a model for better comprehension of model vertex structure:

1. Create a Windows Phone Game project named `HighlightModelMesh` and change `Game1.cs` to `HighlightModelMeshGame.cs`. Then, add a new `MeshInfo.cs` file to the project. Next, add the model file `tank.fbx` and font file `gameFont.spritefont` to the content project. After that, create a Content Pipeline Extension Library named `MeshVerticesProcessor` and replace `ContentProcessor1.cs` with `MeshVerticesProcessor.cs`.

2. Define the `MeshVerticesProcessor` in `MeshVerticesProcessor.cs` of `MeshVerticesProcessor` Content Pipeline Extension Library project. The processor is the extension of `ModelProcessor`:

   ```
   // This custom processor attaches vertex position data of every
   mesh to a model's tag property.
   [ContentProcessor]
   public class MeshVerticesProcessor : ModelProcessor
   ```

3. In the `MeshVerticesProcessor` class, we add a `tagData` dictionary in the class field:

   ```
   Dictionary<string, List<Vector3>> tagData =
       new Dictionary<string, List<Vector3>>();
   ```

4. Next, we define the `Process()` method:

   ```
   // The main method in charge of processing the content.
   public override ModelContent Process(NodeContent input,
       ContentProcessorContext context)
   {
       FindVertices(input);

       ModelContent model = base.Process(input, context);

       model.Tag = tagData;

       return model;
   }
   ```

5. Build the `MeshVerticesProcessor` project. Add a reference to `MeshVerticesProcessor.dll` in the content project and change the **Content Processor** of `tank.fbx`, as shown in the following screenshot:

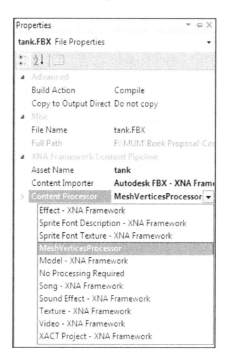

6. Define the `MeshInfo` class in `MeshInfo.cs`.

```
public class MeshInfo
{
    public string MeshName;
    public List<Vector3> Positions;

    public MeshInfo(string name, List<Vector3> positions)
    {
        this.MeshName = name;
        this.Positions = positions;
    }
}
```

7. From this step, we will start to render the individual wireframe mesh and the whole tank object on the Windows Phone 7 screen. First, declare the necessary variable in the `HighlightModelMeshGame` class fields:

```
// SpriteFont for showing the model mesh name
SpriteFont font;
```

```
// Tank model
Model modelTank;

// Tank model world position
Matrix worldTank = Matrix.Identity;

// Camera position
Vector3 cameraPosition;

// Camera view and projection matrix
Matrix view;
Matrix projection;

// Indicate the screen tapping state
bool Tapped;

// The model mesh index in MeshInfo list
int Index = 0;

// Dictionary for mesh name and vertices
Dictionary<string, List<Vector3>> meshVerticesDictionary;

// Store the current mesh vertices
List<Vector3> meshVertices;

// Mesh Info list
List<MeshInfo> MeshInfoList;

// Vertex array for drawing the mesh vertices on screen
VertexPositionColor[] vertices;

// Vertex buffer store the vertex buffer
VertexBuffer vertexBuffer;

// The WireFrame render state
static RasterizerState WireFrame = new RasterizerState
{
    FillMode = FillMode.WireFrame,
    CullMode = CullMode.None
};

// The noraml render state
static RasterizerState Normal = new RasterizerState
{
```

```
        FillMode = FillMode.Solid,
        CullMode = CullMode.None
    };
```

8. Initialize the camera. Insert the code into the `Initialize()` method:

```
cameraPosition = new Vector3(35, 15, 35);

// Initialize the camera view and projection matrices
view = Matrix.CreateLookAt(cameraPosition, Vector3.Zero,
    Vector3.Up);
projection = Matrix.CreatePerspectiveFieldOfView(
    MathHelper.PiOver4, GraphicsDevice.Viewport.AspectRatio,
    0.1f, 1000.0f);

meshVertices = new List<Vector3>();
```

9. Load the tank model and font in the game. Then, map the model Tag dictionary data with mesh info to `MeshInfo` list. Insert the following code to the `LoadContent()` method:

```
// Create a new SpriteBatch, which can be used to draw
// textures.
spriteBatch = new SpriteBatch(GraphicsDevice);

// Load the font
font = Content.Load<SpriteFont>("gameFont");

// Load the ball model
modelTank = Content.Load<Model>("tank");

// Get the dictionary data with mesh name and its vertices
meshVerticesDictionary = (Dictionary<string, List<Vector3>>)
    modelTank.Tag;

// Get the mapped MeshInfo list
MeshInfoList = MapMeshDictionaryToList(meshVerticesDictionary);

// Set the mesh for rendering
SetMeshVerticesToVertexBuffer(Index);
```

10. Change the mesh for rendering. Add the following code to the `Update()` method:

```
// Check the screen is tapped and change the rendering mesh
TouchCollection touches = TouchPanel.GetState();
if (touches.Count > 0 && touches[0].State ==
TouchLocationState.Pressed)
    {
```

```
        if (GraphicsDevice.Viewport.Bounds.Contains(
            (int)touches[0].Position.X, (int)touches[0].
            Position.Y))
        {
            // Clamp the Index value within the amount of model
            meshes
            Index = ++Index % MeshInfoList.Count;

            // Set the mesh index for rendering
            SetMeshVerticesToVertexBuffer(Index);
        }
    }
}
```

11. Draw the tank mode, current mesh, and its name on the Windows Phone 7 screen.
    Paste the following code into the `Draw()` method:

```
GraphicsDevice device = graphics.GraphicsDevice;

device.Clear(Color.CornflowerBlue);

// Set the render state for drawing the tank model
device.BlendState = BlendState.Opaque;
device.RasterizerState = Normal;
device.DepthStencilState = DepthStencilState.Default;

DrawModel(modelTank, worldTank, view, projection);

// Set the render state for drawing the current mesh
device.RasterizerState = WireFrame;
device.DepthStencilState = DepthStencilState.Default;

// Declare a BasicEffect object to draw the mesh wireframe
BasicEffect effect = new BasicEffect(device);
effect.View = view;
effect.Projection = projection;

// Enable the vertex color
effect.VertexColorEnabled = true;

// Begin to draw
effect.CurrentTechnique.Passes[0].Apply();

// Set the VertexBuffer to GraphicDevice
device.SetVertexBuffer(vertexBuffer);
```

```
    // Draw the mesh in TriangleList mode
    device.DrawPrimitives(PrimitiveType.TriangleList, 0,
        meshVertices.Count / 3);

    // Draw the mesh name on screen
    spriteBatch.Begin();
    spriteBatch.DrawString(font, "Curent Mesh Name: " +
        MeshInfoList[Index].MeshName, new Vector2(0, 0),
        Color.White);
    spriteBatch.End();
```

12. Now, build and run the application. It should run as shown in the following screenshots. When you tap the screen the current mesh will change to another.

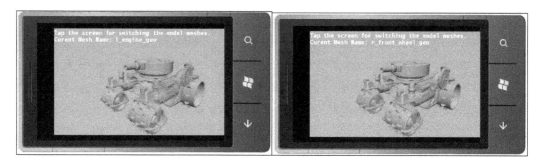

How it works...

In step 3, the `tagData` receives the mesh name as the key and the corresponding mesh vertices as the value.

In step 4, the `input`, a `NodeContent` object, represents the root `NodeContent` of the input model. The key called **method** is the `FindVertices()` method. It iterates the meshes in the input model and stores the mesh vertices in `tagData` with the mesh name. The method should be as follows:

```
// Extracting a list of all the vertex positions in
// a model.
void FindVertices(NodeContent node)
{
    // Transform the current NodeContent to MeshContent
    MeshContent mesh = node as MeshContent;

    if (mesh != null)
    {
        string meshName = mesh.Name;
        List<Vector3> meshVertices = new List<Vector3>();
```

```
            // Look up the absolute transform of the mesh.
            Matrix absoluteTransform = mesh.AbsoluteTransform;

            // Loop over all the pieces of geometry in the mesh.
            foreach (GeometryContent geometry in mesh.Geometry)
            {
                // Loop over all the indices in this piece of
                // geometry. Every group of three indices
                // represents one triangle.
                foreach (int index in geometry.Indices)
                {
                    // Look up the position of this vertex.
                    Vector3 vertex =
                        geometry.Vertices.Positions[index];

                    // Transform from local into world space.
                    vertex = Vector3.Transform(vertex,
                        absoluteTransform);

                    // Store this vertex.
                    meshVertices.Add(vertex);
                }
            }

            tagData.Add(meshName, meshVertices);
        }

        // Recursively scan over the children of this node.
        foreach (NodeContent child in node.Children)
        {
            FindVertices(child);
        }
    }
```

The first line is to transform the current `NodeContent` to `MeshContent` so that we can get the mesh vertices. If the current `NodeContent` is a `MeshContent`, declare the `meshName` variable for holding the current mesh name, `meshVertices` for saving the mesh vertices, and store the world absolute transformation matrix to the `absoluteTransform` matrix using `MeshContent.AbsoluteTransform`. The following `foreach` loop iterates every vertex of the model geometries and transforms it from the object coordinate to the world coordinate, then stores the current vertex to the `meshVertices`. When all the vertices of the current mesh are processed, we add `meshVertices` to the `tagData` dictionary with `meshName` as key. The last part is to recursively process the vertices of the child `NodeContent`s of the temporary `MeshContent`.

In step 6, the `MeshInfo` class assembles the mesh name and its vertices.

In step 7, the `font` will be used to render the current mesh name on screen; `modelTank` loads the tank model; `worldTank` indicates the tank world position; `Index` determines which mesh will be rendered; `meshVerticesDictionary` stores the model Tag information, which stores the mesh name and mesh vertices; `meshVertices` saves the vertices of the current mesh for rendering; `MeshInfoList` will hold the mesh information mapped from `meshVerticesDictionary`; `vertices` represents the `VertexPositionColor` array for rendering the current mesh vertices on screen; `vertexBuffer` will allocate the space for the current mesh vertex array. `WireFrame` and `Normal` specify the render state for the individual mesh and the tank model.

In step 9, we call two other methods: `MapMeshDictionaryToList()` and `SetMeshVerticesToVertexBuffer()`.

The `MapMeshDictionaryToList()` method is to map the mesh info from the dictionary to the `MeshInfo` list, as follows:

```
// Map mesh info dictionary to MeshInfo list
public List<MeshInfo> MapMeshDictionaryToList(
    Dictionary<string, List<Vector3>>  meshVerticesDictionary)
{
    MeshInfo meshInfo;
    List<MeshInfo> list = new List<MeshInfo>();

    // Iterate the item in dictionary
    foreach (KeyValuePair<string, List<Vector3>> item in
        meshVerticesDictionary)
    {
        // Initialize the MeshInfo object with mesh name and
        // vertices
        meshInfo = new MeshInfo(item.Key, item.Value);

        // Add the MeshInfo object to MeshInfoList
        list.Add(meshInfo);
    }
    return list;
}
```

We iterate and read the item of `meshVerticesDictionary` to `meshInfo` with the mesh name and vertices. Then, add the mesh info to the `MeshInfoList`.

The `SetMeshVerticesToVertexBuffer()` method is to set the current mesh vertices to vertex buffer. The code is as follows:

```
// Set the mesh index for rendering
private void SetMeshVerticesToVertexBuffer(int MeshIndex)
{
```

```
    if (MeshInfoList.Count > 0)
    {
        // Get the mesh vertices
        meshVertices = MeshInfoList[MeshIndex].Positions;

        // Declare the VertexPositionColor array
        vertices = new VertexPositionColor[meshVertices.Count];

        // Initialize the VertexPositionColor array with the
        // mesh vertices data
        for (int i = 0; i < meshVertices.Count; i++)
        {
            vertices[i].Position = meshVertices[i];
            vertices[i].Color = Color.Red;
        }

        // Initialize the VertexBuffer for VertexPositionColor
        // array
        vertexBuffer = new VertexBuffer(GraphicsDevice,
            VertexPositionColor.VertexDeclaration,
            meshVertices.Count, BufferUsage.WriteOnly);

        // Set VertexPositionColor array to VertexBuffer
        vertexBuffer.SetData(vertices);
    }
}
```

We use `MeshIndex` to get the current vertices from `MeshInfoList`. Then allocate the space for `vertices`—a `VertexPositionColor` array—and initialize the array data using `meshVertices`. After that, we initialize the `vertexBuffer` to store the `VertexPositionColor` array for drawing the current mesh on screen.

In step 10, this code will react to the valid tap gesture and change the mesh index for choosing different meshes to show.

In step 11, the first part of the code is to draw the tank model in `Normal` render state defined in the class field. The second part is responsible for rendering the current mesh in `WireFrame` render state. For rendering the current mesh, we declare a new `BasicEffect` object and enable the `VertexColorEnabled` attribute to highlight the selected mesh. The following is the code snippet for the `DrawModel()` method:

```
//Draw the model
public void DrawModel(Model model, Matrix world, Matrix view, Matrix
    projection)
{
    Matrix[] transforms = new Matrix[model.Bones.Count];
```

```
model.CopyAbsoluteBoneTransformsTo(transforms);

foreach (ModelMesh mesh in model.Meshes)
{
    foreach (BasicEffect effect in mesh.Effects)
    {
        effect.EnableDefaultLighting();
        effect.World = transforms[mesh.ParentBone.Index] * world;
        effect.View = view;
        effect.Projection = projection;
    }
    mesh.Draw();
}
```

Implementing a rigid model animation

Since 1997, 3D animation has made modern games more fun, and has given them more possibilities. You can take different actions in role-playing games. 3D model animation will make the game more fun and realistic. In this recipe, you will learn how to process and play the rigid model animation in Windows Phone 7.

How to do it...

The following steps will help you look into detail on implementing a rigid model animation:

1. Create a Windows Phone Game project named `RigidModelAnimationGame`, change `Game1.cs` to `RigidAnimationGame.cs` and add the 3D animated model file `Fan.FBX` to the content project. Then create a Windows Phone Class Library project called `RigidModelAnimationLibrary` to define the animation data and add the class files `ModelAnimationClip.cs`, `AnimationClip.cs`, `AnimationPlayerBase.cs`, `ModelData.cs`, `Keyframe.cs`, `RigidAnimationPlayer.cs`, and `RootAnimationPlayer.cs` to this project.

2. Next, build a new Content Pipeline Extension Library project named `RigidAnimationModelProcessor` to process the animated model and return the model animation data to the `Model` object when initializing the game.

3. Define the `Keyframe` class in `Keyframe.cs` of `RigidModelAnimationLibrary` project. `Keyframe` class is responsible for storing an animation frame for a bone in the mode. An animation frame is required to refer to a corresponding bone. If you have not created a bone, or there is no bone in the mesh, XNA frame will automatically create a bone for this kind of mesh, so that the system can locate the mesh. The class should be as follows:

```
// Indicate the position of a bone of a model mesh

public class Keyframe
{
    public Keyframe() { }

    // Gets the index of the target bone that is animated by
    // this keyframe.
    [ContentSerializer]
    public int Bone;

    // Gets the time offset from the start of the animation to
    // this keyframe.
    [ContentSerializer]
    public TimeSpan Time;

    // Gets the bone transform for this keyframe.
    [ContentSerializer]
    public Matrix Transform;

    // Constructs a new Keyframe object.
    public Keyframe(int bone, TimeSpan time, Matrix transform)
    {
        Bone = bone;
        Time = time;
        Transform = transform;
    }
}
```

4. Implement the `AnimationClip` class in `AnimationClip.cs` of `RigidModelAnimationLibrary` project. `AnimationClip` class is the runtime equivalent of the `Microsoft.Xna.Framework.Content.Pipeline.Graphics.AnimationContent` type, which holds all the key frames needed to describe a single model animation. The class is as follows:

```
public class AnimationClip
{
    private AnimationClip() { }

    // The total length of the model animation
    [ContentSerializer]
    public TimeSpan Duration;

    // The collection of key frames, sorted by time, for all
    // bones
```

```
        [ContentSerializer]
        public List<Keyframe> Keyframes;

        // Animation clip constructor
        public AnimationClip(TimeSpan duration, List<Keyframe>
            keyframes)
        {
            Duration = duration;
            Keyframes = keyframes;
        }
    }
```

5. Implement the `AnimationPlayerBase` class in `AnimationPlayerBase.cs` of `RigidModelAnimationLibrary` project. This class is the base class for rigid animation players. It deals with a clip, playing it back at speed, notifying clients of completion, and so on. We add the following lines to the class field:

```
    // Clip currently being played
    AnimationClip currentClip;

    // Current timeindex and keyframe in the clip
    TimeSpan currentTime;
    int currentKeyframe;

    // Speed of playback
    float playbackRate = 1.0f;

    // The amount of time for which the animation will play.
    // TimeSpan.MaxValue will loop forever. TimeSpan.Zero will
    // play once.
    TimeSpan duration = TimeSpan.MaxValue;

    // Amount of time elapsed while playing
    TimeSpan elapsedPlaybackTime = TimeSpan.Zero;

    // Whether or not playback is paused
    bool paused;

    // Invoked when playback has completed.
    public event EventHandler Completed;
```

6. We define the attributes of the `AnimationPlayerBase` class:

```
    // Gets the current clip
    public AnimationClip CurrentClip
    {
```

```csharp
        get { return currentClip; }
}


// Current key frame index
public int CurrentKeyFrame
{
    get { return currentKeyframe; }
    set
    {
        IList<Keyframe> keyframes = currentClip.Keyframes;
        TimeSpan time = keyframes[value].Time;
        CurrentTime = time;
    }
}


// Get and set the current playing position.
public TimeSpan CurrentTime
{
    get { return currentTime; }
    set
    {
        TimeSpan time = value;

        // If the position moved backwards, reset the keyframe
        // index.
        if (time < currentTime)
        {
            currentKeyframe = 0;
            InitClip();
        }

        currentTime = time;

        // Read keyframe matrices.
        IList<Keyframe> keyframes = currentClip.Keyframes;

        while (currentKeyframe < keyframes.Count)
        {
            Keyframe keyframe = keyframes[currentKeyframe];

            // Stop when we've read up to the current time
            // position.
            if (keyframe.Time > currentTime)
                break;
```

```
            // Use this keyframe
            SetKeyframe(keyframe);

            currentKeyframe++;
        }
    }
}
```

7. Give the definition of the `StartClip()` method to the `AnimationPlayerBase` class:

```
// Starts the specified animation clip.
public void StartClip(AnimationClip clip)
{
    StartClip(clip, 1.0f, TimeSpan.MaxValue);
}

// Starts playing a clip, duration (max is loop, 0 is once)
public void StartClip(AnimationClip clip, float playbackRate,
    TimeSpan duration)
{
    if (clip == null)
        throw new ArgumentNullException("Clip required");

    // Store the clip and reset playing data
    currentClip = clip;
    currentKeyframe = 0;
    CurrentTime = TimeSpan.Zero;
    elapsedPlaybackTime = TimeSpan.Zero;

    // Store the data about how we want to playback
    this.playbackRate = playbackRate;
    this.duration = duration;

    // Call the virtual to allow initialization of the clip
    InitClip();
}
```

8. Add the implementation of `Update()` to the `AnimationPlayerBase` class:

```
// Called during the update loop to move the animation forward
public virtual void Update(GameTime gameTime)
{
    if (currentClip == null)
        return;
```

```
        TimeSpan time = gameTime.ElapsedGameTime;

        // Adjust for the rate
        if (playbackRate != 1.0f)
            time = TimeSpan.FromMilliseconds(
                time.TotalMilliseconds * playbackRate);

        elapsedPlaybackTime += time;

        // Check the animation is end
    if (elapsedPlaybackTime > duration && duration !=
        TimeSpan.Zero ||
        elapsedPlaybackTime > currentClip.Duration &&
        duration == TimeSpan.Zero)
        {
            if (Completed != null)
                Completed(this, EventArgs.Empty);

            currentClip = null;

            return;
        }

        // Update the animation position.
        time += currentTime;

        CurrentTime = time;
    }
```

9. Implement two virtual methods for subclass to custom its special behaviors:

```
        // Subclass initialization when the clip is
        // initialized.
        protected virtual void InitClip()
        {
        }

        // For subclasses to set the associated data of a particular
        // keyframe.
        protected virtual void SetKeyframe(Keyframe keyframe)
        {
        }
```

10. Define the `RigidAnimationPlayer` class in `RigidAnimationPlayer.cs` of the `RigidModelAnimationLibrary` project. This animation player knows how to play an animation on a rigid model, applying transformations to each of the objects in the model over time. The class is as follows:

```
public class RigidAnimationPlayer : AnimationPlayerBase
{
    // This is an array of the transforms to each object in the
    // model
    Matrix[] boneTransforms;

    // Create a new rigid animation player, receive count of
    // bones
    public RigidAnimationPlayer(int count)
    {
        if (count <= 0)
            throw new Exception("Bad arguments to model
            animation player");

        this.boneTransforms = new Matrix[count];
    }

    // Initializes all the bone transforms to the identity
    protected override void InitClip()
    {
        int boneCount = boneTransforms.Length;
        for (int i = 0; i < boneCount; i++)
            this.boneTransforms[i] = Matrix.Identity;
    }

    // Sets the key frame for a bone to a transform
    protected override void SetKeyframe(Keyframe keyframe)
    {
        this.boneTransforms[keyframe.Bone] =
            keyframe.Transform;
    }

    // Gets the current bone transform matrices for the
    // animation
    public Matrix[] GetBoneTransforms()
    {
        return boneTransforms;
    }
}
```

11. Define the `RootAnimationPlayer` class in `RootAnimationPlayer.cs` of the `RigidModelAnimationLibrary` project. The root animation player contains a single transformation matrix to control the entire model. The class should be as follows:

```
public class RootAnimationPlayer : AnimationPlayerBase
{
    Matrix currentTransform;

    // Initializes the transformation to the identity
    protected override void InitClip()
    {
        this.currentTransform = Matrix.Identity;
    }

    // Sets the key frame by storing the current transform
    protected override void SetKeyframe(Keyframe keyframe)
    {
        this.currentTransform = keyframe.Transform;
    }

    // Gets the current transformation being applied
    public Matrix GetCurrentTransform()
    {
        return this.currentTransform;
    }
}
```

12. Define the `ModelData` class in `ModelData.cs` of `RigidModelAnimationLibrary` project. The `ModelData` class combines all the data needed to render an animated rigid model, the `ModelData` object will be used to store the animated data in `Tag` property. The class looks similar to the following:

```
public class ModelData
{
    [ContentSerializer]
    public Dictionary<string, AnimationClip>
        RootAnimationClips;

    [ContentSerializer]
    public Dictionary<string, AnimationClip>
        ModelAnimationClips;

    public ModelData(
        Dictionary<string, AnimationClip> modelAnimationClips,
```

```
                    Dictionary<string, AnimationClip> rootAnimationClips
                    )
            {
                ModelAnimationClips = modelAnimationClips;
                RootAnimationClips = rootAnimationClips;
            }

            private ModelData()
            {
            }
        }
```

13. Now, build the `RigidModelAnimationLibrary` project and you will get `RigidModelAnimationLibrary.dll`.

14. From this step, we will begin to create the `RigidModelAnimationProcessor`. The `RigidModelAnimationProcessor` extends from the `ModelProcessor` because we only want to get the model animation data.

```
[ContentProcessor(DisplayName = "Rigid Model Animation
    Processor")]
public class RigidModelAnimationProcessor : ModelProcessor
```

15. Define the maximum number of bones. Add the following line to the class field:

```
const int MaxBones = 59;
```

16. Define the `Process()` method:

```
// The main Process method converts an intermediate format
// content pipeline NodeContent tree to a ModelContent object
// with embedded animation data.
public override ModelContent Process(NodeContent input,
    ContentProcessorContext context)
{
    ValidateMesh(input, context, null);

    List<int> boneHierarchy = new List<int>();

    // Chain to the base ModelProcessor class so it can
    // convert the model data.
    ModelContent model = base.Process(input, context);

    // Animation clips inside the object (mesh)
    Dictionary<string, AnimationClip> animationClips =
        new Dictionary<string, AnimationClip>();

    // Animation clips at the root of the object
```

```
Dictionary<string, AnimationClip> rootClips =
    new Dictionary<string, AnimationClip>();

// Process the animations
ProcessAnimations(input, model, animationClips, rootClips);

// Store the data for the model
model.Tag = new ModelData(animationClips, rootClips);

return model;
}
```

17. Define the `ProcessAnimations()` method:

```
// Converts an intermediate format content pipeline
// AnimationContentDictionary object to our runtime
// AnimationClip format.
static void ProcessAnimations(
    NodeContent input,
    ModelContent model,
    Dictionary<string, AnimationClip> animationClips,
    Dictionary<string, AnimationClip> rootClips)
{
    // Build up a table mapping bone names to indices.
    Dictionary<string, int> boneMap =
        new Dictionary<string, int>();
    for (int i = 0; i < model.Bones.Count; i++)
    {
        string boneName = model.Bones[i].Name;

        if (!string.IsNullOrEmpty(boneName))
            boneMap.Add(boneName, i);
    }

    // Convert each animation in the root of the object
    foreach (KeyValuePair<string, AnimationContent> animation
        in input.Animations)
    {
        AnimationClip processed = ProcessRootAnimation(
            animation.Value, model.Bones[0].Name);

        rootClips.Add(animation.Key, processed);
    }

    // Get the unique names of the animations on the mesh
```

```
        // children
        List<string> animationNames = new List<string>();
        AddAnimationNodes(animationNames, input);

        // Now create those animations
        foreach (string key in animationNames)
        {
            AnimationClip processed = ProcessAnimation(key,
                boneMap, input, model);

            animationClips.Add(key, processed);
        }
    }
```

18. Define the `ProcessRootAnimation()` method, in the
    `RigidModelAnimationProcessor` class, to convert an intermediate
    format content pipeline `AnimationContent` object to the runtime
    `AnimationClip` format. The code is as follows:

```
    public static AnimationClip ProcessRootAnimation(
        AnimationContent animation, string name)
    {
      List<Keyframe> keyframes = new List<Keyframe>();

        // The root animation is controlling the root of the bones
        AnimationChannel channel = animation.Channels[name];

        // Add the transformations on the root of the model
        foreach (AnimationKeyframe keyframe in channel)
        {
            keyframes.Add(new Keyframe(0, keyframe.Time,
                keyframe.Transform));
        }

        // Sort the merged keyframes by time.
        keyframes.Sort(CompareKeyframeTimes);

        if (keyframes.Count == 0)
            throw new InvalidContentException("Animation has no"
            + "keyframes.");

        if (animation.Duration <= TimeSpan.Zero)
            throw new InvalidContentException("Animation has a"
            + "zero duration.");

        return new AnimationClip(animation.Duration, keyframes);
    }
```

19. Define the `AddAnimationNames()` static method, in the `RigidModelAnimationProcessor` class, which assembles the animation names to locate different animations. It is as follows:

```
static void AddAnimationNames(List<string> animationNames,
    NodeContent node)
{
    foreach (NodeContent childNode in node.Children)
    {
        // If this node doesn't have keyframes for this
        // animation we should just skip it
        foreach (string key in childNode.Animations.Keys)
        {
            if (!animationNames.Contains(key))
                animationNames.Add(key);
        }

        AddAnimationNames(animationNames, childNode);
    }
}
```

20. Define the `ProcessAnimation()` method, in the `RigidModelAnimationProcessor` class, to process the animations of individual model meshes. The method definition should be as follows:

```
// Converts an intermediate format content pipeline
// AnimationContent object to the AnimationClip format.
static AnimationClip ProcessAnimation(
    string animationName,
    Dictionary<string, int> boneMap,
    NodeContent input)
{
    List<Keyframe> keyframes = new List<Keyframe>();
    TimeSpan duration = TimeSpan.Zero;

    // Get all of the key frames and duration of the input
    // animated model
    GetAnimationKeyframes(animationName, boneMap, input,
        ref keyframes, ref duration);

    // Sort the merged keyframes by time.
    keyframes.Sort(CompareKeyframeTimes);

    if (keyframes.Count == 0)
        throw new InvalidContentException("Animation has no
        + "keyframes.");
```

```
        if (duration <= TimeSpan.Zero)
            throw new InvalidContentException("Animation has a
            + "zero duration.");

        return new AnimationClip(duration, keyframes);
    }
```

21. Define the `GetAnimationKeyframe()` method referenced by
    `ProcessAnimation()` in the `RigidModelAnimationProcessor` class.
    This is mainly responsible for processing the input animated model and gets
    all of its key frames and duration. The complete implementation of the method
    is as follows:

```
// Get all of the key frames and duration of the input
// animated model
static void GetAnimationKeyframes(
    string animationName,
    Dictionary<string, int> boneMap,
    NodeContent input,
    ref List<Keyframe> keyframes,
    ref TimeSpan duration)
{
    // Add the transformation on each of the meshes from the
    // animation key frames
    foreach (NodeContent childNode in input.Children)
    {
        // If this node doesn't have keyframes for this
        // animation we should just skip it
        if (childNode.Animations.ContainsKey(animationName))
        {
            AnimationChannel childChannel =
                childNode.Animations[animationName].Channels[
                childNode.Name];
            if(childNode.Animations[animationName].Duration !=
                duration)
            {
                if (duration < childNode.Animations[
                    animationName].Duration)
                    duration = childNode.Animations[
                        animationName].Duration;
```

```
                    }

                    int boneIndex;
                    if(!boneMap.TryGetValue(childNode.Name,
                        out boneIndex))
                    {
                        throw new InvalidContentException(
                            string.Format("Found animation for"
                            + "bone '{0}', which is not part of the"
                            + "model.", childNode.Name));
                    }

                    foreach (AnimationKeyframe keyframe in
                        childChannel)
                    {
                        keyframes.Add(new Keyframe(boneIndex,
                            keyframe.Time, keyframe.Transform));
                    }
                }

                // Get the child animation key frame by animation
                // name of current NodeContent
                GetAnimationKeyframes(animationName, boneMap,
                    childNode, ref keyframes, ref duration);
            }
        }
```

22. Define the `CompareKeyframeTimes()` method for sorting the animation key frames along the animation running sequence.

```
    // Comparison function for sorting keyframes into ascending
    // time order.
    static int CompareKeyframeTimes(Keyframe a, Keyframe b)
    {
        return a.Time.CompareTo(b.Time);
    }
```

23. Now the `RigidModelAnimationProcessor` class is complete, you need to build the `RigidModelAnimationProcessor` project. You will get a `RigidModelAnimationProcessor.dll` library file. Add the `RigidModelAnimationProcessor.dll` to the content project reference list and change the model processor of `Fan.fbx` to `RigidModelAnimationProcessor`, as shown in the following screenshot:

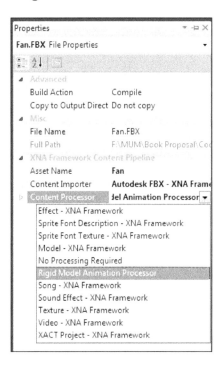

24. From this step, you will begin to draw the animated model on the Windows Phone 7 screen. Add the code to the `RigidAnimationGame` class:

```
// Rigid model, animation players, clips
Model rigidModel;
Matrix rigidWorld;
bool playingRigid;
RootAnimationPlayer rigidRootPlayer;
AnimationClip rigidRootClip;
RigidAnimationPlayer rigidPlayer;
AnimationClip rigidClip;

// View and Projection matrices used for rendering
Matrix view;
Matrix projection;
```

```
RasterizerState Solid = new RasterizerState()
{
    FillMode = FillMode.Solid,
    CullMode = CullMode.None
};
```

25. Now, build and run the application. It runs as shown in the following screenshots:

How it works...

In step 3, we use the key frames to change the bone from original transformation to a new one. The transformation, the `Transform` variable, saved as a `Matrix`. `TimeSpan` will store the animation time when the key frame is played. The `ContentSerializer` is an attribute that marks a field or property showing how it is serialized or included in serialization.

In step 5, the `currentClip` represents the current animation that will be played; `currentTime` indicates the index of time; `currentKeyframe` is the current playing key frame; `playbackRate` stands for how fast the animation will be played; `duration` represents the total length of time of the current animation being played; `elapsedPlaybackTime` shows the amount of time that the current animation has played.

In step 6, `CurrentKeyFrame` attribute returns the index of current key frame. When the attribute is set by an integer value, the attribute will read the `Time` value of the current frame and assign it to the `CurrentTime` attribute for getting the transformation of the current bone.

In step 7, the `StartClip()` method is to initialize the necessary data for playing the current clip.

In step 8, the `Update()` method counts the elapsed time of animation being played. Then, it checks the `elapsedPlaybackTime` to see whether it is greater than the valid `duration` value or `currentClip.Duration` when duration is `TimeSpan.Zero`. If yes, it means the current animation is ended. `Completed` will be triggered when it has been initialized. After that, we should update the animation position, `time`, plus the `currentTime`, to compute the total time from the beginning. Finally, update the `CurrentTime` attribute.

In step 10, the `boneTransforms` will store all of the transformation matrices of model bones. The `SetKeyframe()` method is responsible for assigning the transformation matrix of the designated key frame of the corresponding element in `boneTransforms` based on the bone index of the current key frame. The `GetBoneTransforms()` method returns the processed `boneTransforms` for actual transformation computation on the model.

In step 11, based on the class, we could transform the entire model, not the individual mesh, which has its own animation. Now, please notice the difference between the `RootAnimationPlayer` class and the `RigidAnimationPlayer` class. The `RigidAnimationPlayer` class constructor receives a `count` parameter, but the other one does not. The reason is that the `RootAnimationPlayer` controls the transformation of the entire model; it just needs to get the root bone information, which will be passed to it at runtime. On the other hand, `RigidAnimationPlayer` is responsible for playing the animation of every individual mesh; it should know how many bones there are for the meshes, which will help it to allocate enough space to store the transformation matrices.

In step 16, the `Process()` method is the root method to read the animations from an animated model including the root animation for the entire model transformation and the animations of every single model mesh. Finally, you then assign the generated `ModelData` with root animations and mesh animations to the `Model.Tag` property for animating the model at runtime.

In step 17, first the code creates a `boneMap` dictionary that stores the bone name and its index in the model. Then, the `ProcessAnimations()` will process the animated model into two animation clips, one for the `rootClips` using the `ProcessRootAnimation()` method with the input root bone, and one for `animationClips` using the `ProcessAnimation()` method.

In step 18, the first line we declare is a `Keyframe` collection, which stores all of the key frames of animation. Then, the code gets `AnimationChannel` from `AnimationContent.Channel` by the root bone name, where the animation channel data has the necessary transformation data to transform the child bones of the root. Since XNA will generate a corresponding bone for every model for its position, the mesh will be transformed when the root bone is transformed. After getting the animation channel data, the following `foreach` loop will read all the content pipeline type `AnimationKeyFrame` objects from the current `AnimationChannel` data and store the key frame information to the animation runtime type `Keyframe` defined in the `RigidModelAnimationLibrary`. Notice the digit 0 in the `Keyframe` constructor parameter list stands for the root bone index. Next, the `keyframes.Sort()` is to sort the `keyframes` collection along the actual animation running sequence, `CompareKeyFrameTimes` is a key frame time comparing method, which will be discussed later on. Next, we use two lines to validate the `keyframes` and `animation`. Finally, return a new `AnimationClip` object with `Duration` and `keyframes` to the caller.

In step 19, the first `foreach` loop iterates the child `NodeContent` of the input, the second `foreach` loop looks into every key of animation of the current `NodeContent`. The key is the animation name. For example, `Take001` will be the animation name when you export an FBX format 3D model from AutoDesk 3DS MAX. Then, the `animationNames.Contains()` method will check whether the animation name is already in the collection or not. If not, the new animation name will be added to the `animationNames` collection.

In step 20, the two variables `keyframes` and `duration` represent the total key frames and running time of the current model mesh animation. Then, we call the `GetAnimationKeyframes()` method to get all the key frames and duration of the current animation by animation name. After that, the `keyframes.Sort()` method sorts the key frames along the animation running order. The following two lines are to check whether the current animation is valid. At last, this method returns a new `AnimationClip` object corresponding to the input animation name.

In step 21, the `foreach` loop iterates the every child `NodeContent` of input. In the loop body, the first job is to check whether the current `NodeContent` has the animation with the input animation using the `NodeContent.Animations.ContainsKey()` method. If yes, then the `childNode.Animations[animationName].Channels[childNode.Name]` is responsible for finding the animation channel, which stores the total key frames of a mesh or bone, such as `Plane001`, from the specified animation by the name of the current `NodeContent`. The next line is on returning the duration time of the unique animation. So far, we have collected the necessary `AnimationChannel` data and duration time for creating the runtime `KeyFrame` collection. Before generating the runtime `Keyframe` set, we should get the bone index the set will attach to. Depending on the `bone.TryGetValue()` method, the `boneIndex` value is returned according to the current `NodeContent` name. After that, the following `foreach` loop goes through all of `AnimationKeyFrame` in the `childChannel`, and `AnimationChannel` that we got earlier. Then add a new `KeyFrame` object to the `keyframes` with bone index, key frame time, and the related transformation matrix. The last line recursively gets the animation key frames and duration of the child content of the current node.

In step 22, the `CompareTo()` method of `KeyFrame.TimeSpan` compares the `KeyFrame` object a to the `TimeSpan` of another `Keyframe` object b and returns an integer that indicates whether the `TimeSpan` of a is earlier than, equal to, or later than the `TimeSpan` of b. This method lets the `keyframes.Sort()` method in `ProcessAnimation()` and `ProcessRootAnimation()` know how to sort the `keyframes`.

Creating a terrain with texture mapping

In most of the modern outdoor games, such as Delta Force and Crysis, you will see the trees, rivers, mountains, and so on, all of which are dedicated to simulating the real world, as the game developer hopes to bring a realistic environment when you are playing. In order to achieve this aim, a key technique called **Terrain Rendering** is used. In the following recipe, you will learn how to use this technique in your game.

Getting ready

In this recipe, we will build the terrain model based on **height map**. In computer graphics, a `heightmap` or `heightfield` is a raster image used to store values, such as surface elevation data. A `heightmap` contains one channel interpreted as a distance of displacement or *height* from the *floor* of a surface and is sometimes visualized as luma of a grayscale image, with black representing minimum height and white representing maximum height. Before rendering, the terrain presentation application will process the grey image to get the grey value of each pixel, which will represent the vertex in the terrain model, then calculate the height depending on the value, with higher values having greater height, and vice versa. When the process is done, the application will have a set of terrain vertices with specified height (the Y-axis or the Z-axis value). Finally, the application should read and process the vertex set to render the terrain.

How to do it...

Follow the steps below to master the technique for creating a texture-mapped terrain:

1. Create a Windows Phone Game project named `TerrainGeneration`, change `Game1.cs` to `TerrainGenerationGame.cs`. In the content project, add two images—`Grass.dds` and `HeightMap.png`. Then, we add a Content Pipeline Extension Project named `TerrainProcessor` to the solution, replacing `ContentProcessor1.cs` with `TerrainProcessor.cs` in the content pipeline library.

2. Implement the `TerrainProcessor` class for the terrain processor in `TerrainProcessor.cs`. At the beginning, put the following code into the class field:

   ```
   // Scale of the terrain
   const float terrainScale = 4;

   // The terrain height scale
   const float terrainHeightScale = 64;

   // The texture coordinate scale
   const float texCoordScale = 0.1f;

   // The texture file name
   const string terrainTexture = "grass.dds";
   ```

3. Next, the `Process()` method is the main method of the `TerrainProcessor` class:

   ```
   // Generate the terrain mesh from the heightmap image
   public override ModelContent Process(Texture2DContent input,
       ContentProcessorContext context)
   {
       // Initialize a MeshBuilder
   ```

```
MeshBuilder builder = MeshBuilder.StartMesh("terrain");

// Define the data type of every pixel
input.ConvertBitmapType(typeof(PixelBitmapContent<float>));

// Get the bitmap object from the imported image.
PixelBitmapContent<float> heightmap =
    (PixelBitmapContent<float>)input.Mipmaps[0];

// Create the terrain vertices.
for (int y = 0; y < heightmap.Height; y++)
{
    for (int x = 0; x < heightmap.Width; x++)
    {
        Vector3 position;

        // Put the terrain in the center of game
        //world and scale it to the designated size
        position.X = (x - heightmap.Width / 2) *
            terrainScale;
        position.Z = (y - heightmap.Height / 2) *
            terrainScale;

        // Set the Y factor for the vertex
        position.Y = (heightmap.GetPixel(x, y) - 1) *
            terrainHeightScale;

        // Create  the vertex in MeshBuilder
        builder.CreatePosition(position);
    }
}

// Create a vertex channel for holding texture coordinates.
int texCoordId = builder.CreateVertexChannel<Vector2>(
    VertexChannelNames.TextureCoordinate(0));



// Create a material and map it on the terrain
// texture.
BasicMaterialContent material = new BasicMaterialContent();

// Get the full path of texture file
string directory =
    Path.GetDirectoryName(input.Identity.SourceFilename);
```

```
string texture = Path.Combine(directory, terrainTexture);

// Set the texture to the meshbuilder
material.Texture = new
    ExternalReference<TextureContent>(texture);

// Set the material of mesh
builder.SetMaterial(material);


// Create the individual triangles that make up our terrain.
for (int y = 0; y < heightmap.Height - 1; y++)
{
    for (int x = 0; x < heightmap.Width - 1; x++)
    {
        // Draw a rectancle with two triangles, one at top
        // right, one at bottom-left
        AddVertex(builder, texCoordId, heightmap.Width,
            x, y);
        AddVertex(builder, texCoordId, heightmap.Width,
            x + 1, y);
        AddVertex(builder, texCoordId, heightmap.Width,
            x + 1, y + 1);

        AddVertex(builder, texCoordId, heightmap.Width,
            x, y);
        AddVertex(builder, texCoordId, heightmap.Width,
            x + 1, y + 1);
        AddVertex(builder, texCoordId, heightmap.Width,
            x, y + 1);
    }
}

// Finish creating the terrain mesh.
MeshContent terrainMesh = builder.FinishMesh();

// Convert the terrain from MeshContent to ModelContent
return context.Convert<MeshContent,
ModelContent>(terrainMesh, "ModelProcessor");
}
```

4. From this step, we will render the terrain model to the screen in the game. In this step, we declare the terrain model in the `TerrainGenerationGame` class field:

```
// Terrain Model
```

```
Model terrain;

// Camera view and projection matrices
Matrix view;
Matrix projection;
```

5. Create the projection matrix in the `Initialize()` method with the following code:

```
projection =
    Matrix.CreatePerspectiveFieldOfView(MathHelper.PiOver4,
    GraphicsDevice.Viewport.AspectRatio,1, 10000);
```

6. Then, load the height map image. Insert the following code in to `LoadContent()`:

```
terrain = Content.Load<Model>("HeightMap");
```

7. Rotate the camera around a circle:

```
float time = (float)gameTime.TotalGameTime.TotalSeconds * 0.2f;

// Rotate the camera around a circle
float cameraX = (float)Math.Cos(time) * 64;
float cameraY = (float)Math.Sin(time) * 64;

Vector3 cameraPosition = new Vector3(cameraX, 0, cameraY);

view =
    Matrix.CreateLookAt(cameraPosition,Vector3.Zero,Vector3.Up);
```

8. Draw the terrain on-screen. First, we should define the `DrawTerrain()` method for drawing the terrain model.

```
void DrawTerrain(Matrix view, Matrix projection)
{
    foreach (ModelMesh mesh in terrain.Meshes)
    {
        foreach (BasicEffect effect in mesh.Effects)
        {
            effect.View = view;
            effect.Projection = projection;
            effect.AmbientLightColor = Color.White.ToVector3();

            effect.EnableDefaultLighting();

            // Set the specular lighting
            effect.SpecularColor = new Vector3(
                0.6f, 0.4f, 0.2f);
            effect.SpecularPower = 8;
```

```
                        effect.FogEnabled = true;
                        effect.FogColor = Color.White.ToVector3();
                        effect.FogStart = 100;
                        effect.FogEnd = 500;
                    }

                    mesh.Draw();
                }
            }
```

9. Then, add the reference of the `DrawTerrain()` method in the `Draw()` method:

   ```
   DrawTerrain(view, projection);
   ```

10. The whole project is complete. Build and run the example. The application should run as shown in the following screenshots:

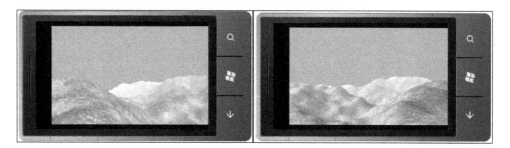

How it works...

In step 2, the `TerrainScale` defines the size of the terrain in a 3D world; `terrainHeightScale` amplifies height change when generating the terrain; `texCoordScale` stands for displaying the portion of texture image when sampling; `terrainTexture` is the name of the texture file.

In step 3, since the `Terrain Processor` is to generate terrain mesh from an image, the input of the content processor is `Texture2DContent`, the output is `ModelContent`. The first line in the method body is to initialize the `MeshBuilder`. `MeshBuilder` is a helper class to ease the way to create a mesh object with internal `MeshContent` and `GeometryContent` classes. A general procedure to build a mesh consists of six steps:

1. Call the `StartMesh()` method to instance a `MeshBuilder` object.
2. Call the `CreatePosition()` method to fill the position's buffer with data.

3. Call the `CreateVertexChannel()` method to get the types of vertex channels and create a vertex data channel for use by the mesh. Typically, the data channel holds texture coordinates, normals, and other per-vertex data. A vertex channel is a list of arbitrary data with one value for each vertex. The types of vertex channels include:

   ❑ Binormal

   ❑ Color

   ❑ Normal

   ❑ Tangent

   ❑ TextureCoordinate

   ❑ Weights

4. After building the position and vertex data channel buffers, start creating the triangles. For setting the data of each triangle use the `SetMaterial()` method. The `SetVertexChannelData()` method will set the individual vertex data of each triangle.

5. Call `AddVertex()` to add a vertex into the index collection for forming a triangle. `MeshBuilder` supports triangle lists only. Therefore, calls to the `AddTriangleVertex()` method must occur in groups of three. That means the code snippet should look similar to the following:

   ```
   // Create a Triangle
   AddTriangleVertex(…);
   AddTriangleVertex(…);
   AddTriangleVertex(…);
   ```

6. In addition, `MeshBuilder` automatically determines which `GeometryContent` object receives the current triangle based on the state data. This data is set by the last calls to `SetMaterial()` and `SetOpaqueData()`.

7. Call the `FinishMesh()` method to finish the mesh building. All of the vertices in the mesh will be optimized with calls to the `MergeDuplicateVertices()` method for merging any duplicate vertices and to the `CalculateNormals()` method for computing the normals from the specified mesh.

So far, you have seen the procedure to create a mesh using `MeshBuilder`. Now, let's go on looking into the `Process()` method. After creating the `MeshBuilder` object, we use the `input.ConvertBitmapType()` method to convert the image color information to float, because we want to use the different color values to determine the height of every vertex of the terrain mesh. The following `for` loop is used to set the position of every vertex, `x - heightmap.Width / 2` and `y - heightmap.Width / 2`, define the X and Y positions to make the terrain model locate at the center in 3D world. The code (`heightmap.GetPixel(x, y)` is the key method to get the height data from image pixels. With this value, we could set the Y value of the vertex position. After defining the vertex position, we call the `MeshBuilder.CreatePosition()` to create the vertex position data in the `MeshBuilder`:

```
MeshBuilder.CreateVertexChannel<Vector2>(
    VertexChannelNames.TextureCoordinate(0));
```

This code creates a vertex texture coordinate channel for terrain mesh use. Then we get the texture file's absolute filepath, set it to the terrain mesh material and assign the material to `MeshBuilder`. When the material is assigned, we begin building the triangles with texture based on the vertices defined earlier. In the following `for` loop, every step creates two triangles, a top right and bottom left. We will discuss the `AddVertex()` method later. When mesh triangles are created, we will call `Mesh.FinishMesh()`. Finally, call `ContentProcessorContext.Convert()`, which converts the `MeshContent` to `ModelContent`.

Now it's time to explain the `AddVertex()` method:

```
// Adding a new triangle vertex to a MeshBuilder,
// along with an associated texture coordinate value.
static void AddVertex(MeshBuilder builder, int texCoordId, int w,
    int x, int y)
{
    // Set the vertex channel data to tell the MeshBuilder how to
    // map the texture
    builder.SetVertexChannelData(texCoordId,
        new Vector2(x, y) * 0.1f);

    // Add the triangle vertices to the indices array.
    builder.AddTriangleVertex(x + y * w);
}
```

The first `MeshBuilder.SetVertexChannelData()` method sets the location and portion of the texture coordinate for the specified vertex. `MeshBuilder.AddTriangleVertex()` adds the triangle vertex to the `MeshBuilder` indices buffer.

In step 7, the camera rotation meets the law as shown in the following diagram:

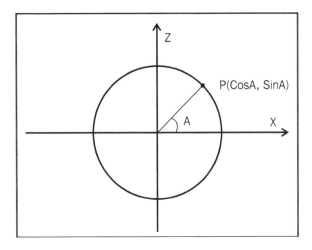

```
P.X = CosA * Radius, P.Y = SinA * Radius
```

The previous formula is easy to understand, `CosA` is cosine value of angle `A`, it multiplies with the `Radius` to produce the horizontal value of X; Similarly, the `SinA * Radius` will produce the vertical value of Y. Since the formula is computing with angle `A`, the radius is constant when rotating around the center; the formula will generate a point set for representing a circle.

Customizing vertex formats

In XNA 4.0, a vertex format has a description about how the data stored in the vertex allows the system to easily locate the specified data. The XNA framework provides some built-in vertex formats, such as `VertexPositionColor` and `VertexPositionNormalTexture` format. Sometimes, these built-in vertex formats are limited for special effects such as particles with life limitation. At that moment, you will need to define a custom vertex format. In this recipe, you will learn how to define the custom vertex format.

How to do it...

Now let's begin to program our sample application:

1. Create a Windows Phone Game project named `CustomVertexFormat`, change `Game1.cs` to `CustomVertexFormatGame.cs`. Add a new class file `CustomVertexPositionColor.cs` to the project.

2. Define the `CustomVertexPositionColor` class in the `CustomVertexPositionColor.cs` file:

```
// Define the CustomVertexPositionColor class
public struct CustomVertexPositionColor : IVertexType
{
    public Vector3 Position;
    public Color Color;

    public CustomVertexPositionColor(Vector3 Position,
        Color Color)
    {
        this.Position = Position;
        this.Color = Color;
    }

    // Define the vertex declaration
    public static readonly VertexDeclaration
        VertexDeclaration = new
            Microsoft.Xna.Framework.Graphics.VertexDeclaration
        (
            new VertexElement(0, VertexElementFormat.Vector3,
                VertexElementUsage.Position, 0),

            new VertexElement(12, VertexElementFormat.Color,
                VertexElementUsage.Color, 0)
        );

    // Override the VertexDeclaration attribute
    VertexDeclaration IVertexType.VertexDeclaration
    {
        get { return VertexDeclaration; }
    }
}
```

3. From this step, we will begin to use the `CustomVertexPositionColor` array to create a cubic and render it on the Windows Phone 7 screen. First, declare the variables in the field of the `CustomVertexFormatGame` class:

```
// CustomVertexPositionColor array
CustomVertexPositionColor[] vertices;

// VertexBuffer stores the custom vectex data
VertexBuffer vertexBuffer;

// BasicEffect for rendering the vertex array
```

```
BasicEffect effect;

// Camera position
Vector3 cameraPosition;

// Camera view matrix
Matrix view;

// Camera projection matrix
Matrix projection;

// The WireFrame render state
static RasterizerState WireFrame = new RasterizerState
{
    FillMode = FillMode.Solid,
    CullMode = CullMode.None
};
```

4. Define the faces of cubic and initialize the camera. Add the following code to the `Initialize()` method:

```
// Allocate the CustomVertexPositonColor array on memory
vertices = new CustomVertexPositionColor[24];

// Initialize the vertices of cubic front, right, left and
// bottom faces.
int i = 0;

// Front Face
vertices[i++] = new CustomVertexPositionColor(
    new Vector3(-10, -10, 0), Color.Blue);
vertices[i++] = new CustomVertexPositionColor(
    new Vector3(-10, 10, 0), Color.Blue);
vertices[i++] = new CustomVertexPositionColor(
    new Vector3(10, 10, 0), Color.Blue);

vertices[i++] = new CustomVertexPositionColor(
    new Vector3(10, 10, 0), Color.Blue);
vertices[i++] = new CustomVertexPositionColor(
    new Vector3(-10, -10, 0), Color.Blue);
vertices[i++] = new CustomVertexPositionColor(
    new Vector3(10, -10, 0), Color.Blue);

// Right Face
vertices[i++] = new CustomVertexPositionColor(
```

```
                new Vector3(10, 10, 0), Color.Red);
    vertices[i++] = new CustomVertexPositionColor(
        new Vector3(10, -10, 0), Color.Red);
    vertices[i++] = new CustomVertexPositionColor(
        new Vector3(10, 10, -20), Color.Red);

    vertices[i++] = new CustomVertexPositionColor(
        new Vector3(10, -10, 0), Color.Red);
    vertices[i++] = new CustomVertexPositionColor(
        new Vector3(10, -10, -20), Color.Red);
    vertices[i++] = new CustomVertexPositionColor(
        new Vector3(10, 10, -20), Color.Red);

    // Left Face
    vertices[i++] = new CustomVertexPositionColor(
        new Vector3(-10, 10, 0), Color.Green);
    vertices[i++] = new CustomVertexPositionColor(
        new Vector3(-10, -10, 0), Color.Green);
    vertices[i++] = new CustomVertexPositionColor(
        new Vector3(-10, 10, -20), Color.Green);

    vertices[i++] = new CustomVertexPositionColor(
        new Vector3(-10, -10, 0), Color.Green);
    vertices[i++] = new CustomVertexPositionColor(
        new Vector3(-10, -10, -20), Color.Green);
    vertices[i++] = new CustomVertexPositionColor(
        new Vector3(-10, 10, -20), Color.Green);

    // Bottom Face
    vertices[i++] = new CustomVertexPositionColor(
        new Vector3(-10, -10, 0), Color.Yellow);
    vertices[i++] = new CustomVertexPositionColor(
        new Vector3(10, -10, 0), Color.Yellow);
    vertices[i++] = new CustomVertexPositionColor(
        new Vector3(-10, -10, -20), Color.Yellow);

    vertices[i++] = new CustomVertexPositionColor(
        new Vector3(-10, -10, -20), Color.Yellow);
    vertices[i++] = new CustomVertexPositionColor(
        new Vector3(10, -10, 0), Color.Yellow);
    vertices[i++] = new CustomVertexPositionColor(
        new Vector3(10, -10, -20), Color.Yellow);

    // Initialze the vertex buffer for loading the vertex array
```

```
vertexBuffer = new VertexBuffer(GraphicsDevice,
    CustomVertexPositionColor.VertexDeclaration,
    vertices.Length, BufferUsage.WriteOnly);

// Set the vertex array data to vertex buffer
vertexBuffer.SetData <CustomVertexPositionColor>(vertices);

// Initialize the camera
cameraPosition = new Vector3(0, 0, 100);
view = Matrix.CreateLookAt(cameraPosition, Vector3.Zero,
    Vector3.Up);
projection = Matrix.CreatePerspectiveFieldOfView(
    MathHelper.PiOver4, GraphicsDevice.Viewport.AspectRatio,
    0.1f, 1000.0f);

// Initialize the basic effect for drawing
effect = new BasicEffect(GraphicsDevice);
```

5. Draw the cubic on the Windows Phone 7 screen. Insert the following code into `Draw()` method:

```
GraphicsDevice device = GraphicsDevice;

// Set the render state
device.BlendState = BlendState.Opaque;
device.RasterizerState = WireFrame;

// Rotate the cubic
effect.World *=
    Matrix.CreateRotationY(MathHelper.ToRadians(1));

// Set the basic effect parameters for drawing the cubic
effect.View = view;
effect.Projection = projection;
effect.VertexColorEnabled = true;

// Set the vertex buffer to device
device.SetVertexBuffer(vertexBuffer);

// Drawing the traingles of the cubic from vertex buffer on
// screen
foreach (EffectPass pass in effect.CurrentTechnique.Passes)
{
    pass.Apply();
```

```
        // The count of triangles = vertices.Length / 3 = 24 / 3
        // = 8
        device.DrawPrimitives(PrimitiveType.TriangleList, 0, 8);
    }
```

6. Now, build and run the application. It runs as shown in the following screenshots:

How it works...

In step 2, the `CustomVertexPositionColor` derives from the `IVertexType` interface, which declares a `VertexDeclaration` that the class must override and implement the `VertexDeclaration` attribute to describe the layout custom vertex format data and their usages. The custom vertex format `CustomVertexPositionColor` is a customized version of the built-in vertex format `VertexPositionColor`; it also has the `Position` and `Color` data members. The class constructor `CustomVertexPositionColor()` is the key data member `VertexDeclaration`. Here, the `VertexElement` class defines the properties of `Position` and `Color` includes the offset in memory, `VertexElementFormat` and the vertex usage. The `Position` is a `Vector3` object, that has three float parameters occupying `12` bytes. Because the `Color` variable is following the `Position`, the offset of `Color` should begin from the end of `Position` at the 12th byte in memory. Finally, the `IVertexType. VertexDeclaration` attribute will return the `VertexDeclaration` data when initializing the `VertexBuffer` or you can manually read it.

In step 3, the `vertices` is a `CustomVertexPositionColor` array that will store the vertices of the cubic faces; `vertexBuffer` stores the `CustomVertexPositionColor` array data for rendering; `effect` defines the rendering method. The following three variables: `cameraPosition`, `view`, and `projection` will be used to initialize the camera: `WireFrame` specifies the device render state, because the triangles of every face of cubic are composed of two triangles, we should disable the culling method that triangles could be seen from the back.

In step 4, as we want to draw four faces of cubic and every face is made up of two triangles, the amount of `CustomVertexPositionColor` is 4 * 2 * 3 = 24. After initializing the vertices of the triangles with position and color information, it is time to create the vertex buffer to store the defined vertex array and assign the vertex array to the vertex buffer for rendering. The next part of code is about establishing the camera and instancing the `BasicEffect` object.

In step 5, the code assigns the `WireFrame` defined in a class field to disable the culling that you could see the graphics in any perspective. The settings of `effect` are rotating the cubic and coloring the vertices. After that, the iteration of `EffectPass` collection is to draw the triangles of cubic on screen using `GraphicDevice.DrawPrimitives()`. Since the `PrimitiveType` is `TriangleList`, the third parameter of the `DrawPrimitives()` method is 8 and stands for the total count of triangles, which comes from the equation total vertex count / 3 = 24 / 3 = 8.

Calculating the normal vectors from a model vertex

In mathematics, normal is the vector perpendicular to a plane or a surface. In computer graphics, normal is often used to calculate the lighting, angle of tilting, and collision detection. In this recipe, you will learn how to calculate the normal from vertices.

Getting ready

The 3D model mesh is made up of triangles and every triangle in a plane has a normal vector and is stored in the vertex. (You can find out more information about normal vectors in any computer graphic or linear algebra books.) Some typical and realistic lighting techniques will use the average normal vector of a vertex shared by several triangles. To calculate the normal of a triangle is not hard. Suppose the triangle has three points: A, B, and C. Choose point A as the root, Vector AB equals B - A; Vector AC equals C - A, and normal Vector N is the cross product of the two vectors AB and AC. Our example will illustrate the actual working code.

How to do it...

The following steps will show you a handy way to get the normal vectors of a model:

1. Create a Windows Phone Game project named `NormalGeneration`, change `Game1.cs` to `NormalGenerationGame.cs`.

2. Add the `GenerateNormalsForTriangleStrip()` method for normal calculation to the `NormalGenerationGame` class:

```
private VertexPositionNormalTexture[]
    GenerateNormalsForTriangleStrip(VertexPositionNormalTextu
re[]
    vertices, short[] indices)
{
    // Set the Normal factor of every vertex
    for (int i = 0; i < vertices.Length; i++)
        vertices[i].Normal = new Vector3(0, 0, 0);
```

```
// Compute the length of indices array
int indiceLength = indices.Length;

// The winding sign
bool IsNormalUp = false;

// Calculate the normal vector of every triangle
for (int i = 2; i < indiceLenngth; i++)
{
    Vector3 firstVec = vertices[indices[i - 1]].Position -
        vertices[indices[i]].Position;
    Vector3 secondVec = vertices[indices[i - 2]].Position -
        vertices[indices[i]].Position;
    Vector3 normal = Vector3.Cross(firstVec, secondVec);
    normal.Normalize();

    // Let the normal of every triangle face up
    if (IsNormalUp)
        normal *= -1;

    // Validate the normal vector
    if (!float.IsNaN(normal.X))
    {
        // Assign the generated normal vector to the
        // current triangle vertices
        vertices[indices[i]].Normal += normal;
        vertices[indices[i - 1]].Normal += normal;
        vertices[indices[i - 2]].Normal += normal;
    }

    // Swap the winding sign for the next triangle when
    // create mesh as TriangleStrip
    IsNormalUp = !IsNormalUp;
}

return vertices;
}
```

How it works...

In step 2, this method receives the array of mesh vertices and indices. The indices tell the drawing system how to index and draw the triangles from vertices. The `for` loop starts from the third vertex. With the former two indices i − 1 and i − 2, they form a triangle and use the indices to create two vectors in the same plain representing two sides of the current triangle.

Then call the `Vector3.Cross()` method to compute the normal perpendicular to the triangle plain. After that, we should normalize the normal for accurate computing such as lighting. Since the indices are organized in `TriangleStrip`, every new added index will generate a new triangle, but the normal of the new triangle is opposite to the previous one. We should reverse the direction of the new normal by multiplying by `-1` when `IsNormalUp` is true.

Next, we should validate the normal using `float.IsNaN()`, which returns a value indicating whether the specified number evaluates to a number. When two vectors used to compute the normal vector and the current triangle have completely the same direction, another vector, the cross product will return a `Vector3` object with three `NaN` values, meanwhile the invalid data must be eliminated. Finally, the method returns the processed vertices with correct normal vectors.

Simulating an ocean on your CPU

The ocean simulation is an interesting and challenging topic in computer graphic rendering that has been covered in many papers and books. In Windows, it is easier to render a decent ocean or water body depending on the GPU HLSL or Cg languages. In Windows Phone 7 XNA, so far, the customized HLSL shader is not supported. The only way to solve the problem is to do the simulation on CPU of Windows Phone 7. In this recipe, you will learn to realize the ocean effect on Windows Phone 7 CPU.

How to do it...

The following steps demonstrate one approach to emulating an ocean on the Windows Phone CPU:

1. Create a Windows Phone Game project named `OceanGenerationCPU`, change `Game1.cs` to `OceanGenerationCPUGame.cs`. Then add a new file `Ocean.cs` to the project and image file to the content project.

2. Define the `Ocean` class in the `Ocean.cs` file. Add the following lines to the class field as a data member:

```
// The graphics device object
GraphicsDevice device;

// Ocean width and height
int PlainWidth = 64;
int PlainHeight = 64;

// Random object for randomly generating wave height
Random random = new Random();

// BasicEffect for drawing the ocean
```

```
BasicEffect basicEffect;

// Texture2D object loads the water texture
Texture2D texWater;

// Ocean vertex buffer
VertexBuffer oceanVertexBuffer;

// Ocean vertices
VertexPositionNormalTexture[] oceanVertices;

// The index array of the ocean vertices
short[] oceanIndices;

// Ocean index buffer
IndexBuffer oceanIndexBuffer;

// The max height of wave
int MaxHeight = 2;

// The wind speed
float Speed = 0.02f;

// Wave directions
protected int[] directions;
```

3. Next, implement the `Ocean` constructor as follows:

```
public Ocean(Texture2D texWater, GraphicsDevice device)
{
    this.device = device;
    this.texWater = texWater;
    basicEffect = new BasicEffect(device);

    // Create the ocean vertices
    oceanVertices = CreateOceanVertices();

    // Create the ocean indices
    oceanIndices = CreateOceanIndices();

    // Generate the normals of ocean vertices for lighting
    oceanVertices =
        GenerateNormalsForTriangleStrip(oceanVertices,
        oceanIndices);
```

```
        // Create the vertex buffer and index buffer to load the
        // ocean vertices and indices
        CreateBuffers(oceanVertices, oceanIndices);
    }
```

4. Define the `Update()` method of the `Ocean` class.

```
    // Update the ocean height for the waving effect
    public void Update(GameTime gameTime)
    {
        for (int i = 0; i < oceanVertices.Length; i++)
        {
            oceanVertices[i].Position.Y += directions[i] * Speed;

            // Change direction if Y component has ecxeeded the
            // limit
            if (Math.Abs(oceanVertices[i].Position.Y) > MaxHeight)
            {
                oceanVertices[i].Position.Y =
                    Math.Sign(oceanVertices[i].Position.Y) *
                    MaxHeight;
                directions[i] *= -1;
            }
        }
        oceanVertices =
            GenerateNormalsForTriangleStrip(oceanVertices,
            oceanIndices);
    }
```

5. Implement the `Draw()` method of the `Ocean` class:

```
    public void Draw(Matrix view, Matrix projection)
    {
        // Draw Ocean
        basicEffect.World = Matrix.Identity;
        basicEffect.View = view;
        basicEffect.Projection = projection;
        basicEffect.Texture = texWater;
        basicEffect.TextureEnabled = true;

        basicEffect.EnableDefaultLighting();
        basicEffect.AmbientLightColor = Color.Blue.ToVector3();
        basicEffect.SpecularColor = Color.White.ToVector3();

        foreach (EffectPass pass in
            basicEffect.CurrentTechnique.Passes)
```

```
    {
        pass.Apply();

        oceanVertexBuffer.SetData<VertexPositionNormalTexture>
            (oceanVertices);
        device.SetVertexBuffer(oceanVertexBuffer, 0);

        device.Indices = oceanIndexBuffer;
        device.DrawIndexedPrimitives(
            PrimitiveType.TriangleStrip, 0, 0, PlainWidth *
            PlainHeight, 0,
            PlainWidth * 2 * (PlainHeight - 1) - 2);

        // This is important, because you need to update the
        // vertices
        device.SetVertexBuffer(null);
    }
}
```

6. From this step, we will use the `Ocean` class to actually draw the ocean on the Windows Phone 7 CPU. Please add the following code to the `OceanGenerationCPUGame` class field:

```
// Ocean water texture
Texture2D texWater;

// Ocean object
Ocean ocean;

// Camera view and projection matrices
Matrix view;
Matrix projection;
```

7. Initialize the camera in the `Initialize()` method:

```
Vector3 camPosition = new Vector3(80, 20, -100);
view = Matrix.CreateLookAt(camPosition, Vector3.Zero,
    Vector3.Up);
projection = Matrix.CreatePerspectiveFieldOfView(
    MathHelper.PiOver4, GraphicsDevice.Viewport.AspectRatio,
    0.1f, 1000);
```

8. Load the ocean water texture and initiate the `ocean` object. Insert the code into the `LoadContent()` method:

```
texWater = Content.Load<Texture2D>("Water");

ocean = new Ocean(texWater, GraphicsDevice);
```

9. Update the `ocean` state. Add the following line to the `Update()` method:

```
ocean.Update(gameTime);
```

10. Draw the `ocean` on the Windows Phone 7 screen.

```
ocean.Draw(view, projection);
```

11. Now, build and run the application. You will see the ocean as shown in the following screenshot:

How it works...

In step 2, `PlainWidth` and `PlainHeight` define the dimensions of the ocean; the `random` object will be used to generate the random height of every ocean vertex; `texWater` loads the ocean texture; `oceanVertexBuffer` will store the ocean vertices; `oceanVertices` is the `VertexPositionNormalTexture` array representing the entire ocean vertices; `oceanIndices` represents the indices of ocean vertices. It is a short array because XNA only supports the 16 bytes index format; `oceanIndexBuffer` is the `IndexBuffer` to store the ocean indices; `directions` indicates the waving direction of every vertex.

In step 3, for the constructor, we will discuss the `CreateOceanVertices()`, `CreateOceanIndices()`, `GenerateNormalsForTriangleStrip()`, and the `CreateBuffers()` method.

1. Define the `CreateOceanVertices()` method:

```
// Create the ocean vertices
private VertexPositionNormalTexture[] CreateOceanVertices()
{
    // Creat the local ocean vertices
    VertexPositionNormalTexture[] oceanVertices =
        new VertexPositionNormalTexture[PlainWidth *
```

```
                    PlainHeight];

        directions = new int[PlainHeight * PlainWidth];

        // Initialize the ocean vertices and wave direction array
        int i = 0;
        for (int z = 0; z < PlainHeight; z++)
        {
            for (int x = 0; x < PlainWidth; x++)
            {
                // Generate the vertex position with random
                // height
                Vector3 position = new
                    Vector3(x, random.Next(0, 4), -z);
                Vector3 normal = new Vector3(0, 0, 0);
                Vector2 texCoord =
                    new Vector2((float)x / PlainWidth,
                        (float)z / PlainWidth);

                // Randomly set the direction of the vertex up or
                // down
                directions[i] = position.Y > 2 ? -1 : 1;

                // Set the position, normal and texCoord to every
                // element of ocean vertex array
                oceanVertices[i++] = new
                    VertexPositionNormalTexture(position, normal,
                    texCoord);
            }
        }

        return oceanVertices;
    }
```

First you find the width and height of the ocean. Then, create an array that stores all the vertices for the ocean about `PlainWidth * PlainHeight` in total. After that, we use two `for` loops to initiate the necessary information for the ocean vertices. The height of the vertex is randomly generated, the normal is zero which will get changed in the `Update()` method; `texCoord` specifies how to map the texture on the ocean vertices so that every `PlainWidth` vertex will repeat the water texture. Next, the code on `position.Y` is to determine the wave direction of every ocean vertex. When all the needed information is done, the last line in the `for` loop is about initializing the vertices one by one.

2. The `CreateOceanIndices()` method: when the ocean vertices are ready, it is time to define the indices array to build the ocean mesh in triangle strip mode.

```
// Create the ocean indices
private short[] CreateOceanIndices()
{
    // Define the resolution of ocean indices
    short width = (short)PlainWidth;
    short height = (short)PlainHeight;

    short[] oceanIndices =
        new short[(width) * 2 * (height - 1)];

    short i = 0;
    short z = 0;

    // Create the indices row by row
    while (z < height - 1)
    {
        for (int x = 0; x < width; x++)
        {
            oceanIndices[i++] = (short)(x + z * width);
            oceanIndices[i++] = (short)(x + (z + 1) * width);
        }
        z++;

        if (z < height - 1)
        {
            for (short x = (short)(width - 1); x >= 0; x--)
            {
                oceanIndices[i++] = (short)
                    (x + (z + 1) * width);
                oceanIndices[i++] = (short)(x + z * width);
            }
        }
        z++;
    }

    return oceanIndices;
}
```

In this code, we store all the indices of the ocean vertices and in each row we define the `PlainWidth * 2` triangles. Actually, every three rows of indices represent two rows of triangles, so we have `PlainHeight - 1` rows of triangles. The total indices are `PlainWidth * 2 * (PlainHeight - 1)` in `TriangleStrip` drawing mode where each index indicates a new triangle based on the index and its previous two indices.

The z variable indicates the current row from 0, the first row created from left to right. Next, you increment z by one for moving to the next row created from right to left. You repeat the process until the rows are all built when z is equal to PlainHeight - 1.

1. GenerateNormalsForTriangleStrip() method: we use the method to calculate the normal of each vertex of ocean mesh triangles. For a more detailed explanation, please refer to the *Calculating the normal vectors from a model vertex* recipe.

2. CreateBuffers() method: this method is to create the vertex buffer for ocean vertices and index buffer for ocean indices for rendering the ocean on the Windows Phone 7 CPU. The code is as follows:

```
// Create the vertex buffer and index buffer for ocean
// vertices and indices
private void CreateBuffers(VertexPositionNormalTexture[]
    vertices, short[] indices)
{
    oceanVertexBuffer = new VertexBuffer(device,
        VertexPositionNormalTexture.VertexDeclaration,
        vertices.Length, BufferUsage.WriteOnly);
    oceanVertexBuffer.SetData(vertices);

    oceanIndexBuffer = new IndexBuffer(device, typeof(short),
        indices.Length, BufferUsage.WriteOnly);
    oceanIndexBuffer.SetData(indices);
}
```

In step 4, the code iterates all the ocean vertices and changes the height of every vertex. Once the absolute value of height is greater than MaxHeight, the direction of the vertex will be reversed to simulate the wave effect. After the ocean vertices are updated, we need to compute the vertex normal again since the vertex positions are different.

In step 5, when rendering the 3D object manually with mapping texture, the basicEffect. TextureEnabled should be true and set the Texture2D object to the BasicEffect. Texture attribute. Then, we open the light to highlight the ocean. Finally, the foreach loop is used to draw the ocean on the Windows Phone 7 CPU. Here, we should set the updated ocean vertices to the vertex buffer in every frame.

7
Collision Detection

In this chapter, we will cover:

- ▸ Detecting the intersection of line segments
- ▸ Implementing per pixel collision detection in a 2D game
- ▸ Implementing BoundingBox collision detection in a 3D game
- ▸ Implementing BoundingSphere collision detection in a 3D game
- ▸ Implementing ray-triangle collision detection
- ▸ Mapping a tapped location to 3D
- ▸ Implementing sphere-triangle collision detection
- ▸ Making a 3D ball move along a curved surface

Introduction

Collision detection is the fundamental for computer games in 2D and 3D. Collision detection can be used to compute whether a bullet shoots at an object or prevents a game character from going through a wall. Based on collision detection, you can simulate the physics. If two moving balls collide, collision detection will compute the moment for their new directions and velocities. In modern 3D games, collision detection has already played an important role in bringing people realistic experiences. While playing Need for Speed, when the car crashes on an obstacle, you can see that the car moves backward with vibration depending on the speed. In Crysis, if an explosion happens in a building, the bricks will bump out and the whole construction will go down from the top to the bottom gradually. Collision detection provides possibilities to people for making and having more desirable realistic sensations from computer games. Besides computer games, collision detection can also be applied to many other situations, especially in simulation applications, such as airplane driving, car crash testing, war mimic training, and so on. In this chapter, you will learn how to use some of these techniques; for example, bounding box, bounding sphere, ray, and triangles.

Detecting the intersection of line segments

Basically, line segments' intersection is a mathematical concept. To detect the intersection of two line segments, find their intersection points. For 2D games, it is very helpful when an explosion animation appears at a position where the two lines intersect; for example, two laser shoots collide. The line segments' intersection can also help you to make a decision in pool games as a guideline, especially for beginners. In this recipe, you will learn how to detect the line segments' intersection.

Getting ready

To define the two line segments, we need the following two formulae:

$$P_a = P_1 + U_a(P_2 - P_1) \qquad \text{where } 0 \le U_a \le 1$$
$$P_b = P_3 + U_b(P_4 - P_3) \qquad \text{where } 0 \le U_b \le 1$$

If you put in 0 for U, you'll get the start point, if you put in 1, you'll get the end point.

With the two equations, if the intersection happens between the two line segments:

$$P_a = P_b$$

The equation could be rewritten as follows:

$$P_1 + U_a(P_2 - P_1) = P_3 + U_b(P_4 - P_3)$$

In order to get the Ua and Ub values, we need two equations. The previous equation could also be written using x and y factors of the points:

$$x_1 + U_a(x_2 - x_1) = x_3 + U_b(x_4 - x_3)$$
$$y_1 + U_a(y_2 - y_1) = y_3 + U_b(y_4 - y_3)$$

You can use the two equations to solve for Ua and Ub:

$$U_a = \frac{(x_4 - x_3)(y_1 - y_3) - (y_4 - y_3)(x_1 - x_3)}{(y_4 - y_3)(x_2 - x_1) - (x_4 - x_3)(y_2 - y_1)}$$

$$U_b = \frac{(x_2 - x_1)(y_1 - y_3) - (y_2 - y_1)(x_1 - x_3)}{(y_4 - y_3)(x_2 - x_1) - (x_4 - x_3)(y_2 - y_1)}$$

The denominator of both of the equations is the same. Solve it first. If it is zero, the lines are parallel. If both numerators are also zero, then the two line segments are coincident.

Since these equations treat the lines as infinitely long lines instead of line segments, there is a guarantee of having an intersection point if the lines aren't parallel. To determine if it happens with the segments we've specified, we need to see if U is between zero and one. Verify that both of the following are true:

$$0 \leq U_a \leq 1$$

$$0 \leq U_b \leq 1$$

If we've gotten this far, then our line segments intersect, and we just need to find the point at which they do and then we're done:

$$x = x_1 + U_a(x_2 - x_1)$$

$$y = y_1 + U_a(y_2 - y_1)$$

The following pseudo code describes the line segments' intersection algorithm coming from the previous description:

```
ua = (p4.x - p3.x)*(p1.y - p3.y) - (p4.y - p3.y)*(p1.x - p3.x)
ub = (p2.x - p1.x)*(p1.y - p3.y) - (p2.y - p1.y)*(p1.x - p3.x)

denominator = (p4.y p2.y)*(p2.x-p1.x) - (p4.x-p2.x)(p2.y-p1.y)


if( | denominator | < epsilon)
{
    // Now, two line segments are parallel
    If(| ua | <= epsilon && | ub | <= epsilon)
    {
        // Now, two line segments are coincident
    }
}
else
{
    ua /= denominator;
    ub /= denominator

    if( |ua| < 1 && |ub| < 1)
    {
        // Intersected
        intersectionPoint.x = p1.x + ua * (p2.x - p1.x)
        intersectionPoint.y = p1.y + ua * (p2.y - p1.y)
    }
}
```

Translate the pseudo code to an XNA version, as follows:

```
// Line segments' intersection detection
private void DetectLineSegmentsIntersection(
    ref bool intersected,  ref bool coincidence,
    ref Vector2 intersectedPoint,
    ref Vector2 point1, ref Vector2 point2,
    ref Vector2 point3, ref Vector2 point4)
{
    // Compute the ua, ub factor of two line segments
    float ua = (point4.X - point3.X) * (point1.Y - point3.Y) -
        (point4.Y - point3.Y) * (point1.X - point3.X);
    float ub = (point2.X - point1.X) * (point1.Y - point3.Y) -
        (point2.Y - point1.Y) * (point1.X - point3.X);

    // Calculate the denominator
    float denominator = (point4.Y - point3.Y) * (point2.X -
        point1.X) - (point4.X - point3.X)*(point2.Y - point1.Y);

    // If the denominator is very close to zero, it means
    // the two line segments are parallel
    if (Math.Abs(denominator) <= float.Epsilon)
    {
        // If the ua and ub are very close to zero, it means
        // the two line segments are coincident
        if (Math.Abs(ua) <= float.Epsilon && Math.Abs(ub) <=
            float.Epsilon)
        {
            intersected = coincidence = true;
            intersectedPoint = (point1 + point2) / 2;
        }
    }
    else
    {
        // If the denominator is greater than zero, it means
        // the two line segments have different directions.
        ua /= denominator;
        ub /= denominator;

        // Check the ua and ub are both between 0 and 1 to
        // take the line segments' intersection detection
        if (ua >= 0 && ua <= 1 && ub >= 0 && ub <= 1)
        {
            intersected = true;
```

```
            // Compute the position of the intersection point
            intersectedPoint.X = point1.X +
                ua * (point2.X - point1.X);
            intersectedPoint.Y = point1.Y +
                ua * (point2.Y - point1.Y);
        }
        else
        {
            intersected = false;
        }
    }
}
```

The method receives the four points of the two line segments and two flags for indicating the intersected and coincident states. The first two lines are to compute the numerators of `ua` and `ub`, then the following line is on calculating the denominator. After that, we begin to check the value of the `denominator` to see whether the two line segments intersected. If the `denominator` is almost zero, it means the two line segments are parallel. Meanwhile, if the numerators of `Ua` and `Ub` are both almost zero, the two line segments are coincident. Otherwise, if the `denominator` is greater than zero, it means the two lines where the two line segments lie intersect. In order to make sure the two line segments intersect, we need to check that the absolute values of `ua` and `ub` are both less than or equal to 1. If true, the intersection between them happens; now we can use `ua` or `ub` to calculate the `intersectionPoint`.

How to do it...

The following steps will show you how to master the practical method of using the line segments' intersection:

1. Create a Windows Phone Game project named `LineSegmentIntersection`, change `Game1.cs` to `LineSegmentsIntersectionGame.cs`. Then, add `Line.cs` to the project.

2. In the next step, we need to define the `Line` class in `Line.cs`. The class will draw the line between two points on the Windows Phone 7 screen.

   Declare the indispensable variables of the class, and then add the following code to the class field:

   ```
   // Line Texture
   private Texture2D lineTexture;

   // Origin point of line texture for translation, scale and
   // rotation
   ```

```
        private Vector2 origin;

        // Scale factor
        private Vector2 scale;

        // Rotation factor
        private float rotation;

        // Axis X
        Vector2 AxisX = new Vector2(1, 0);

        // Dictance vector
        Vector2 distanceVector;

        // Line direction
        Vector2 Direction = Vector2.Zero;

        // The angle between the line and axis X
        float theta = 0;

        // Line thickness
        private int Thickness = 2;

        // Line color
        private Color color;
```

3. Create the constructor of the `Line` class:

```
        public void Load(GraphicsDevice graphicsDevice)
        {
            // Initialize the line texture and its origin point
            lineTexture = CreateLineUnitTexture(graphicsDevice,
                Thickness, color);
            origin = new Vector2(0, Thickness / 2f);
        }
```

4. Define the `CalculateRotation()` method called in the previous step in the `Line` class. This method calculates the angle between the line and the X-axis:

```
        private void CalculateRotation(Vector2 distanceVector)
        {
            // Normalize the distance vector for line direction
            Vector2.Normalize(ref distanceVector, out Direction);

            // Compute the angle between axis X and line
            Vector2.Dot(ref AxisX, ref Direction, out theta);
```

```
        theta = (float)Math.Acos(theta);



        // If the Y factor of distanceVector is less than 0
        // this means the start point is lower than the end point,
        // the rotation direction should be in the opposite
        // direction.
        if (distanceVector.Y < 0)
        {
            theta = -theta;
        }

        // return the angle value for rotation
        rotation = theta;
    }
```

5. Implement the `CalculateScale()` method in the `Line` class. The method will calculate a scale represented as a `Vector2` object. The X factor stores the number of textures while the Y factor stores the scale degree.

```
    private void CalculateScale(Vector2 distanceVector)
    {
        // The Vector2 object scale determines how many textures
        // will be drawn based on the input rotation and start
        // point, X for the number, Y for the scale factor
        float desiredLength = distanceVector.Length();
        scale.X = desiredLength / lineTexture.Width;
        scale.Y = 1f;
    }
```

6. Define the `CreateLineUnitTexture()` method, in the `Line` class, which creates the line unit texture according to the input line thickness.

```
    // Create a unit texture of line, the texture will be used to
    // generate a line with desired number
    public static Texture2D CreateLineUnitTexture(
        GraphicsDevice graphicsDevice,
        int lineThickness, Color color)
    {
        // Initialize the line unit texture according to the line
        // thickness
        Texture2D texture2D = new Texture2D(graphicsDevice,
            lineThickness, lineThickness, false,
            SurfaceFormat.Color);

        // Set the color of every pixel of the line texture
```

```
        int count = lineThickness * lineThickness;
        Color[] colorArray = new Color[count];

        for (int i = 0; i < count; i++)
        {
            colorArray[i] = color;
        }

        texture2D.SetData<Color>(colorArray);
        return texture2D;
    }
```

7. Define the `Draw()` method in the `Line` class that draws the line segment on Windows Phone 7.

```
// Draw the line
public void Draw(SpriteBatch spriteBatch, Vector2 startPoint,
    Vector2 endPoint)
{
    // Compute the distance vector between the line start
    // point and end point
    Vector2.Subtract(ref endPoint, ref startPoint,
        out distanceVector);

    // Calculate the rotation angle
    CalculateRotation(distanceVector);

    // Calculate the scale factor
    CalculateScale(distanceVector);

    // Draw the line texture on screen
    spriteBatch.Draw(lineTexture, startPoint, null, color,
        rotation, origin, scale, SpriteEffects.None, 0);
}
```

8. From this step, we will begin to interact with the tap gesture and draw the line segments and the intersection point if intersection takes place on the Windows Phone 7 screen. First, add the following lines to the `LineSegmentsIntersectionGame` class field:

```
// Line Object
Line line;

// Circle Texture
Texture2D circleTexture;
```

```
// Points of two lines for intersection testing
Vector2 point1, point2, point3, point4, intersectionPoint;

// The flag for intersection
bool Intersection;

// The flag for coincidence
bool Coincidence;
```

9. Initialize the four points of the two line segments. Insert the following lines to the `Initialize()` method:

```
// Initialize the points of two lines
point1 = Vector2.Zero;
point2 = newVector2(600, 300);
point3 = newVector2(0, 200);
point4 = newVector2(800, 200);
```

10. Initialize the `line` and `circleTexture` objects. Add the following code to the `LoadContent()` method:

```
// Initialize the two line objects with white color
line = new Line(Color.White);
line.Load(GraphicsDevice);

// Initialize the texture of circle
circleTexture = CreateCircleTexture(GraphicsDevice, 5, Color.
White);
```

11. This step is the key to detecting the line segment intersection. Add the following code to the `Update()` method:

```
// Do the line segments' intersection testing
DetectLineSegmentsIntersection(ref Intersection,
    ref Coincidence, ref intersectionPoint,
    ref point1, ref point2, ref point3, ref point4);

// Check the tapped position to see whether it is inside the
//TopHitRegion
// or BottomHitRegion
TouchCollection touches = TouchPanel.GetState();
if (touches.Count > 0 && touches[0].State ==
    TouchLocationState.Pressed)
{
    Point point = new Point((int)touches[0].Position.X,
        (int)touches[0].Position.Y);
    if (GraphicsDevice.Viewport.Bounds.Contains(point))
    {
        point1.X = point.X;
        point1.Y = point.Y;
    }
}
```

12. Insert the `DetectLineSegmentsIntersection()` method into the `LineSegmentsIntersectionGame` class. This method is the same as the definition we gave at the beginning of the method.

13. Define the `CreateCircleTexture()` method. This method creates the circle textures for showing the end points of the line segments:

```
// Create the circle texture
public static Texture2D CreateCircleTexture(GraphicsDevice
    graphicsDevice, int radius, Color color)
{
    int x = 0;
    int y = 0;

    // Compute the diameter of circle
    int diameter = radius * 2;

    // Calculate the center of circle
    Vector2 center = new Vector2(radius, radius);

    // Initialize the circle texture
    Texture2D circle = new Texture2D(graphicsDevice, diameter,
        diameter, false, SurfaceFormat.Color);

    // Initialize the color array of circle texture
    Color[] colors = new Color[diameter * diameter];

    // Set the color of the circle texture
    for (int i = 0; i < colors.Length; i++)
    {
        // For raw
        if (i % diameter == 0)
        {
            y += 1;
        }

        // For column
        x = i % diameter;

        // Calculate the distance from current position to
        // circle center
        Vector2 diff = new Vector2(x, y) - center;
        float distance = diff.Length();

        // Check the position whether inside the circle
```

```
            if (distance > radius)
            {
                // If not, set the pixel color to transparent
                colors[i] = Color.Transparent;
            }
            else
            {
                // If yes, set the pixel color to desired color
                colors[i] = color;
            }
        }

        // Assign the processed circle color array to circle
        // texture
        circle.SetData<Color>(colors);
        return circle;
    }
```

14. Draw the line segments on screen with end points and intersection point on the Windows Phone 7 screen. Add the following code to the `Draw()` method:

```
    spriteBatch.Begin();

    // Draw the two lines segments
    line.Draw(spriteBatch, point1, point2);
    line.Draw(spriteBatch, point3, point4);

    // Draw the circles to indicate the endpoints of the two lines
    // with red color
    Vector2 circleOrigin = new Vector2(
    circleTexture.Width / 2, circleTexture.Height / 2);
    spriteBatch.Draw(circleTexture, point1, null, Color.Red, 0,
        circleOrigin, 1, SpriteEffects.None, 0);
    spriteBatch.Draw(circleTexture, point2, null, Color.Red, 0,
        circleOrigin, 1, SpriteEffects.None, 0);
    spriteBatch.Draw(circleTexture, point3, null, Color.Red, 0,
        circleOrigin, 1, SpriteEffects.None, 0);
    spriteBatch.Draw(circleTexture, point4, null, Color.Red, 0,
        circleOrigin, 1, SpriteEffects.None, 0);

    // If the intersection takes place, draw the intersection
    // point
    if (Intersection)
    {
        // If the two lines are coincident, draw the intersection
```

```
        // point in green else in yellow
        spriteBatch.Draw(circleTexture, intersectionPoint, null,
            Coincidence ? Color.Green : Color.Yellow, 0,
            circleOrigin, 1, SpriteEffects.None, 0);
    }

    spriteBatch.End();
```

15. Now, build and run the application. When you tap on the screen, it should run as shown in the following screenshots:

How it works...

We need to draw the line from a texture since there is no drawing method in XNA 4.0.

In step 2, the `lineTexture` holds the texture for the drawing line; the `origin` is the center point for rotation, translation, and scale. The scale, a `Vector2` object, the X-factor tells `SpriteBatch.Draw()` method how many texture units will be drawn. The Y-factor stands for the scaling degree; `rotation` specifies the rotating degrees; `AxisX` is the vector represents the X-axis; `distanceVector` holds the vector between two designated points; `Direction` indicates the line segment direction; the `theta` variable shows the angle between the X-axis and the line segment; the `Thickness` means how thick the line segment should be; `color` defines the color of the line segment.

In step 4, the first line normalizes the `distanceVector`, which stores the vector between two points to `Direction`, a unit vector variable. Then, we use `Vector2.Dot()` and the `Math.Acos()` method to calculate the angle between `Direction` and `distanceVector`. When we get `theta`, if the `distanceVector.Y` is less than 0, this means the start point is lower than the end point, but the `theta`, which should be a negative angle, is still greater than 0 because in the XNA coordinate system, all the location coordinates are greater than 0, so the dot product is always greater than 0. Thus, we should negate the `theta` value to meet the actual angle value. Finally, return the `theta` value to the `rotation` variable.

In step 5, first `distanceVector.Length()` returns the length between the two end points of the given line segment. Then, we calculate the number of line unit textures based on the texture width and assign the value to `scale.X`. After that, we save the scale degree to `scale.Y`.

In step 6, this method first initializes the line unit texture, of which the size depends on the line thickness. Then, we set the input color to every pixel of the texture. Finally, we return the generated line unit texture.

In step 8, the `line` will be used to draw the line segments; `circle` is responsible for drawing the end points and the intersection points of the lines; the `Intersection` is the flag indicating whether the line segments' intersection happens; the `Coincidence` shows whether the line segments are coincident or not.

In step 10, the line has white color; the radius of circle textures is 5.

In step 11, the first line of the method is to detect the line segments' intersection. The `DetectLineSegmentsIntersection()` method uses the `point1`, `point2`, `point3`, and `point4` to compute the intersection equation. If there is an intersection, the `Intersection` variable will be `true` and the `intersectionPoint` will return the intersected point. We have discussed a more detailed explanation of this method at the beginning of the recipe. The second part is to control the position of the first point to make an interactive manipulation on one of the line segments. If the tapped position is valid, the position of the first point will be changed to the current tapped position on screen.

In step 13, the method first computes `diameter` for the width and height of the circle textures. The `center` specifies the center point of the circle. After that, we initialize the `circle` texture and the texture color array of which the length is `diameter*diameter` and then we will iterate each pixel in the array. If the position is outside the region of the circle, the pixel color will be set to transparent, or the color what you want.

Implementing per pixel collision detection in a 2D game

In a 2D game, a general method for detecting collision is by using bounding box. This is the solution for a lot of situations where precision is not the most important factor. However, if your game cares whether two irregular objects collide with each other or overlap, the bounding box will not be comfortable with the. At this moment, per pixel collision will help you. In this recipe, you will learn how to use this technique in your game.

How to do it...

1. Create a Windows Phone Game project named `PixelCollision2D`, change `Game1.cs` to `PixelCollision2DGame.cs`. Then, add the `PixelBall.png` and `PixelScene.png` file to the content project.

2. Add the indispensable data members to the field of `PixelCollision2DGame`.

   ```
   // SpriteFont object
   SpriteFont font;

   // The images we will draw
   Texture2D texScene;
   Texture2D texBall;

   // The color data for the images; used for per pixel collision
   Color[] textureDataScene;
   Color[] textureDataBall;

   // Ball position and bound rectangle
   Vector2 positionBall;
   Rectangle boundBall;

   // Scene position and bound rectangle
   Vector2 positionScene;
   Rectangle boundScene;

   // Collision flag
   bool Collided;

   // Ball selected flag
   bool Selected;
   ```

3. Initialize the positions of ball and scene and enable the `FreeDrag` gesture. Insert the following code in to the `Initialize()` method:

   ```
   // Initialize the position of ball
   positionBall = new Vector2(600, 10);

   // Initialize the position of scene
   positionScene = new Vector2(400, 240);

   TouchPanel.EnabledGestures = GestureType.FreeDrag;
   ```

4. Load the textures of ball and scene. Then, extract the color data of these textures and create their bounding box based on the initial position.

```
// Load Font
font = Content.Load<SpriteFont>("gameFont");

// Load textures
texScene = Content.Load<Texture2D>("PixelScene");
texBall = Content.Load<Texture2D>("PixelBall");

// Extract scene texture color array
textureDataScene =
    new Color[texScene.Width * texScene.Height];
texScene.GetData(textureDataScene);

// Extract ball texture color array
textureDataBall =
    new Color[texBall.Width * texBall.Height];
texBall.GetData(textureDataBall);

// Create the ball bound
boundBall = new Rectangle((int)positionBall.X,
    (int)positionBall.Y,
texBall.Width, texBall.Height);
boundScene = new Rectangle((int)positionScene.X,
    (int)positionScene.Y, texScene.Width, texScene.Height);
```

5. Define the `IntersectPixels()` method. This method determines if there is overlap of the non-transparent pixels between two textures.

```
static bool IntersectPixels(
    Rectangle rectangleA, Color[] dataA,
    Rectangle rectangleB, Color[] dataB)
{
    // Find the bounds of the rectangle intersection
    int top = Math.Max(rectangleA.Top, rectangleB.Top);
    int bottom = Math.Min(rectangleA.Bottom,
        rectangleB.Bottom);

    int left = Math.Max(rectangleA.Left, rectangleB.Left);
    int right = Math.Min(rectangleA.Right, rectangleB.Right);

    // Check every point within the intersection bounds
    for (int y = top; y < bottom; y++)
    {
        for (int x = left; x < right; x++)
```

```
        {
            // Get the color of both pixels at this point
            Color colorA = dataA[(x - rectangleA.Left) +
                (y - rectangleA.Top) * rectangleA.Width];
            Color colorB = dataB[(x - rectangleB.Left) +
                (y - rectangleB.Top) * rectangleB.Width];

            // If both pixels are not completely transparent,
            if (colorA.A != 0 && colorB.A != 0)
            {
                // then an intersection has been found
                return true;
            }
        }
    }

    // No intersection found
    return false;
}
```

6. Call the `IntersectPixels()` method within the `Update()` method for examining the per pixel collision. Add the following code to the `Update()` method:

```
// Move the ball
TouchCollection touches = TouchPanel.GetState();
if (touches.Count > 0 && touches[0].State ==
    TouchLocationState.Pressed)
{
    Point point = new Point((int)touches[0].Position.X,
        (int)touches[0].Position.Y);
    if (boundBall.Contains(point))
    {
        Selected = true;
    }
    else
    {
        Selected = false;
    }
}

// Check whether the gesture is enabled
while (TouchPanel.IsGestureAvailable)
{
    // Read the taking place gesture
    GestureSample gestures = TouchPanel.ReadGesture();
```

```
        switch (gestures.GestureType)
        {
            // If the on-going gesture is FreeDrag
            case GestureType.FreeDrag:
                if (Selected)
                {
                    // If the ball is selected, update the
                    // position of ball texture and the ball bound
                    positionBall += gestures.Delta;
                    boundBall.X += (int)gestures.Delta.X;
                    boundBall.Y += (int)gestures.Delta.Y;
                }
            break;
        }
    }

    // Check collision with Scene
    if (IntersectPixels(boundBall, textureDataBall,
        boundScene, textureDataScene))
    {
        Collided = true;
    }
    else
    {
        Collided = false;
    }
}
```

7. Draw the ball, scene, and collision state on the Windows Phone 7 screen.

```
    spriteBatch.Begin();

    // Draw the scene
    spriteBatch.Draw(texScene, boundScene, Color.White);

    // Draw the ball
    spriteBatch.Draw(texBall, positionBall, Color.White);
    spriteBatch.DrawString(font, "Collided: " +
        Collided.ToString(), new Vector2(0, 0), Color.White);
    spriteBatch.End();
```

8. Now, build and run the application. It will run as shown in the following screenshots:

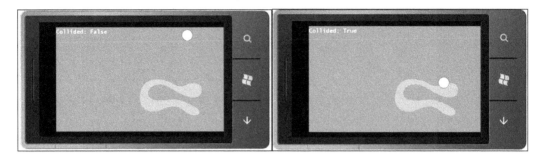

How it works...

In step 2, the `font` is used to draw the collision state; `texScene` loads the scene image; `texBall` holds the ball texture; `textureDataScene` and `textureDataBall` store their texture color array data; `positionBall` and `positionScene` specify the position of ball and scene textures; `boundBall` and `boundScene` define the bound around the ball and scene texture; `Collided` is the flag that shows the collision state; `Selected` indicates whether the ball is tapped.

In step 5, the `IntersectPixels()` method is the key method that detects the per pixel collision. The first four variables `top`, `bottom`, `left`, and `right` individually represent the top, bottom, left, and right side of the intersection rectangle of the two bound boxes around the two textures in the example. Then, in the `for` loop, we check whether the color alpha value of every pixel of both the textures within the intersection rectangle is completely transparent. If yes, the collision occurs; the method will return `true`, otherwise, it will return `false`.

In step 6, the first part is to check whether the ball is selected. If yes, then `Selected` will be `true`. The second part is about reading the on-going gesture; if the gesture type is `FreeDrag`, we will update the position of the ball and its bounding box. The third part calls the `IntersectPixels()` method to detect the pixel-by-pixel collision.

Implementing BoundingBox collision detection in a 3D game

Regardless of whether you are programming 2D or 3D games, collision detection based on bounding box is straightforward, i simple and easy to understand. You can imagine that every object is individually covered by a box. The boxes are moving along with the corresponding boxes; when the boxes collide, the objects collide too. The boxes are called the `BoundingBox`. To compose the `BoundingBox`, you only need to go through all the points or vertices, and then find the min and max ones. After that, the `BoundingBox` collision detection will depend on the min and max information of every BoundingBox to examine whether their min and max values are inside its own range to make the collision decision. Even in a more accurate collision detection system, bounding box collision detection will be taken first, before using the more precise, but costly method. In this recipe, you will learn how to apply the technique to a simple game.

How to do it...

The following steps will help you build your own BoundingBox information content processor and use the BoundingBox in your game:

1. Create a Windows Phone Game project named BoundingBoxCollision and change Game1.cs to BoundingBoxCollisionGame.cs. Then, create a Content Pipeline Extension Library named MeshVerticesProcessor and replace the ContentProcessor1.cs with MeshVerticesProcessor.cs. We create the content pipeline processor for processing and extracting the BoundingBox information from the model objects before running the game. This will accelerate the game loading speed because your application won't need to do this work again and again. After that, add the model file BigBox.FBX to the content project.

2. Next, we need to define the MeshVerticesProcessor class in MeshVerticesProcessor.cs of the MeshVerticesProcessor project.

    Extend the MeshVerticesProcessor class from ModelProcessor, because we need the model vertices information based on the original model.

    ```
    [ContentProcessor]
    publicclass MeshVerticesProcessor : ModelProcessor
    ```

3. Add the Dictionary object in the class field.

    ```
    Dictionary<string, List<Vector3>> tagData =
        new Dictionary<string, List<Vector3>>();
    ```

4. Define the Process() method in the MeshVerticesProcessor class:

    ```
    // The main method in charge of processing the content.
    public override ModelContent Process(NodeContent input,
        ContentProcessorContext context)
    {
        FindVertices(input);

        ModelContent model = base.Process(input, context);

        model.Tag = tagData;

        return model;
    }
    ```

5. Define the `FindVertices()` method in the `MeshVerticesProcessor` class:

```
// Extracting a list of all the vertex positions in
// a model.
void FindVertices(NodeContent node)
{
    // Transform the current NodeContent to MeshContent
    MeshContent mesh = node as MeshContent;

    if (mesh != null)
    {
        string meshName = mesh.Name;
        List<Vector3> meshVertices = new List<Vector3>();

        // Look up the absolute transform of the mesh.
        Matrix absoluteTransform = mesh.AbsoluteTransform;

        // Loop over all the pieces of geometry in the mesh.
        foreach (GeometryContent geometry in mesh.Geometry)
        {
            // Loop over all the indices in this piece of
            // geometry. Every group of three indices
            // represents one triangle.
            foreach (int index in geometry.Indices)
            {
                // Look up the position of this vertex.
                Vector3 vertex =
                    geometry.Vertices.Positions[index];

                // Transform from local into world space.
                vertex = Vector3.Transform(vertex,
                    absoluteTransform);

                // Store this vertex.
                meshVertices.Add(vertex);
            }
        }

        tagData.Add(meshName, meshVertices);
    }

    // Recursively scan over the children of this node.
    foreach (NodeContent child in node.Children)
```

```
        {
            FindVertices(child);
        }
    }
}
```

6. Build the `MeshVerticesProcessor` project. Add a reference to
    `MeshVerticesProcessor.dll` in the content project and change
    the **Content Processor** of `BigBox.FBX` to `MeshVerticesProcessor`,
    as shown in the following screenshot:

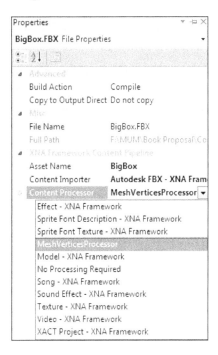

7. From this step, we will begin to draw the two boxes on screen and detect the
    bounding box collision between them in the `BoundingBoxCollisionGame` class
    in `BoundingBoxCollisionGame.cs` of the `BoundingBoxCollision` project.
    First, add the following lines to the class field:

```
// The sprite font for drawing collision state
SpriteFont font;

// Model box A and B
Model modelBoxA;
Model modelBoxB;

// The world transformation of box A and B
Matrix worldBoxA;
```

```
Matrix worldBoxB;

// BoundingBox of model A and B
BoundingBox boundingBoxA;
BoundingBox boundingBoxB;

// The bounding box stores the transformed boundingBox
BoundingBox boundingBox;

// Camera
Vector3 cameraPosition;
Matrix view;
Matrix projection;

// Hit regions
Rectangle LeftHitRegion;
Rectangle RightHitRegion;

// Collided state
bool Collided;
```

8. Initialize the world matrix of box A and B, the camera, and the left and right hit regions. Paste the following code into the `Initialize()` method in the `BoundingBoxCollisionGame` class:

```
// Translate the model box A and B
worldBoxA = Matrix.CreateTranslation(new Vector3(-10, 0, 0));
worldBoxB = Matrix.CreateTranslation(new Vector3(10, 0, 0));

// Initialize the camera
cameraPosition = new Vector3(0, 10, 40);
view = Matrix.CreateLookAt(cameraPosition, Vector3.Zero,
    Vector3.Up);
projection = Matrix.CreatePerspectiveFieldOfView(
    MathHelper.PiOver4, GraphicsDevice.Viewport.AspectRatio,
    0.1f, 1000.0f);

// Initialize the left and right hit regions
Viewport viewport = GraphicsDevice.Viewport;
LeftHitRegion = new Rectangle(0, 0, viewport.Width / 2,
    viewport.Height);
RightHitRegion = new Rectangle(viewport.Width / 2, 0,
    viewport.Width / 2, viewport.Height);
```

9. Load the box model and sprite font. Then extract the box model vertices. With the extracted vertices, create the bounding box for box A and B. Insert the following code into the `LoadContent()` method in the `BoundingBoxCollisionGame` class:

```
// Create a new SpriteBatch, which can be used to draw
// textures.
spriteBatch = new SpriteBatch(GraphicsDevice);

// Load the sprite font
font = Content.Load<SpriteFont>("gameFont");

// Load the box model
modelBoxA = Content.Load<Model>("BigBox");
modelBoxB = Content.Load<Model>("BigBox");

// Get the vertices of box A and B
List<Vector3> boxVerticesA =
    ((Dictionary<string, List<Vector3>>)modelBoxA.Tag)
    ["Box001"];
List<Vector3> boxVerticesB =
    ((Dictionary<string, List<Vector3>>)modelBoxA.Tag)
    ["Box001"];

// Create the bounding box for box A and B
boundingBoxA = BoundingBox.CreateFromPoints(boxVerticesA);
boundingBoxB = BoundingBox.CreateFromPoints(boxVerticesB);

// Translate the bounding box of box B to designated position
boundingBoxB.Min = Vector3.Transform(boundingBoxB.Min,
    worldBoxB);
boundingBoxB.Max = Vector3.Transform(boundingBoxB.Max,
    worldBoxB);
```

10. Move the box A and the corresponding bounding box and detect the bounding box collision between box A and box B. Add the following code to the `Update()` method in the `BoundingBoxCollisionGame` class:

```
// Interact with tapping
TouchCollection touches = TouchPanel.GetState();
if (touches.Count > 0 && touches[0].State ==
    TouchLocationState.Pressed)
{
    Point point = new Point(
        (int)touches[0].Position.X, (int)touches[0].Position.Y);

    // If the tapped position is inside the left hit region,
```

```
        // move the box A left
        if (LeftHitRegion.Contains(point))
        {
            worldBoxA.Translation -= new Vector3(1, 0, 0);
        }

        // If the tapped position is inside the right hit region,
        //move the box A right
        if (RightHitRegion.Contains(point))
        {
            worldBoxA.Translation += new Vector3(1, 0, 0);
        }
    }

    // Create a bounding box for the transformed bounding box A
    boundingBox = new BoundingBox(
    Vector3.Transform(boundingBoxA.Min, worldBoxA),
    Vector3.Transform(boundingBoxA.Max, worldBoxA));

    // Take the collision detection between the transformed
    // bounding box A and bounding box B
    if (boundingBox.Intersects(boundingBoxB))
    {
        Collided = true;
    }
    else
    {
        Collided = false;
    }
```

11. Define the `DrawModel()` method.

```
    // Draw model
    public void DrawModel(Model model, Matrix world, Matrix view,
        Matrix projection)
    {
        Matrix[] transforms = new Matrix[model.Bones.Count];
        model.CopyAbsoluteBoneTransformsTo(transforms);

        foreach (ModelMesh mesh in model.Meshes)
        {
            foreach (BasicEffect effect in mesh.Effects)
            {
                effect.PreferPerPixelLighting = true;
                effect.EnableDefaultLighting();
                effect.DiffuseColor = Color.White.ToVector3();
                effect.World = transforms[mesh.ParentBone.Index] *
```

```
                    world;
                effect.View = view;
                effect.Projection = projection;
            }
            mesh.Draw();
        }
    }
```

12. Draw the boxes on the Windows Phone 7 screen. Add the code to the `Draw()` method.

    ```
    GraphicsDevice.DepthStencilState = DepthStencilState.Default;

    // Draw the box model A and B
    DrawModel(modelBoxA, worldBoxA, view, projection);
    DrawModel(modelBoxB, worldBoxB, view, projection);

    // Draw the collision state
    spriteBatch.Begin();
    spriteBatch.DrawString(font, "Collided: " + Collided.
        ToString(), new Vector2(0, 0), Color.White);
    spriteBatch.End();
    ```

13. Now, build and run the application. The application should run as shown in the following screenshots:

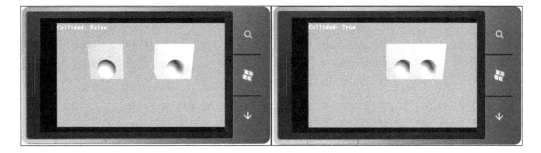

How it works...

In step 2, the `[ContentProcessor]` attribute is required. It makes the `MeshVerticesProcessor` class in to a content processor, which will show up in the content project when you change the model processor.

In step 3, the `tagData` receives the mesh name as the key and the corresponding mesh vertices as the value.

In step 4, the `input`—a `NodeContent` object—represents the root `NodeContent` of the input model. The key called method is the `FindVertices()` method, which iterates the meshes in the input model and stores the mesh vertices in the `tagData` with the mesh name.

In step 5, the first line transforms the current `NodeContent` to `MeshContent` so that we can get the mesh vertices. If the current `NodeContent` is `MeshContent`, declare `meshName` variable for holding the current mesh name, `meshVertices` saves the mesh vertices and stores the world absolute transformation matrix to the `absoluteTransform` matrix using `MeshContent.AbsoluteTransform`. The following `foreach` loop iterates every vertex of the model geometries and transforms it from object coordinate to world coordinate; it then stores the current vertex to the `meshVertices`. When all the vertices of the current mesh are processed, we add the `meshVertices` to the `tagData` dictionary with the `meshName` as the key. The last part is to recursively process the vertices of the child `NodeContent` objects of the temporary `MeshContent`.

In step 7, the `font` is responsible for drawing the collision state on screen; `modelBoxA` and `modelBoxB` hold the two box models; `worldBoxA` and `worldBoxB` represent the world transformation of the two boxes; `boundingBoxA` and `boundingBoxB` store the bound boxes individually around the two boxes; `boundingBox` will save the transformed bounding box A for collision detection; the `cameraPosition`, `view`, and `projection` will be used to initialize the camera; `LeftHitRegion` and `RightHitRegion` define the left and right hit regions on the Windows Phone 7 screen.

In step 9, in this method, we read the vertices of box A and B from the `Model.Tag` property. Then, we use `BoundingBox.CreateFromPoints()` to create the bounding box from the extracted vertices of the box model. Notice, so far, the generated bounding boxes are in the same place; we need to translate them to the place where the corresponding box model locates. Since we will use box A as the moving object, the position will be updated in real time. Now, we just translate the bounding box for box B.

In step 10, in the first part, we check whether the tapped position is in the left or right hit region and move box A. After that, we create a new `boundingbox` for representing the transformed bounding box A. Then, we take the bounding box collision detection between the `boundingBoxA` and `boundingBoxB` using the `BoundingBox.Intersects()` method. If a collision happens, the method will return `true`, otherwise it will return `false`.

Implementing BoundingSphere collision detection in a 3D game

Unlike the bounding box, bounding sphere based collision detection is faster. The technique just needs to compute the length between two points or vertices whether less, equal, or greater than the sum of radii. In modern games, bounding sphere based collision detection is preferred rather than the bounding box. In this recipe, you will learn how to use the technique in an XNA application.

How to do it...

Follow the steps below to master the technique of using `BoundingSphere` in your game:

1. Create a Windows Phone Game project named `BoundingSphereCollision` and change `Game1.cs` to `BoundingSphereCollisionGame.cs`. Then, create a Content Pipeline Extension Library named `MeshVerticesProcessor` and replace the `ContentProcessor1.cs` with `MeshVerticesProcessor.cs`. After that, add the model file `BallLowPoly.FBX` to the content project.

2. Define the `MeshVerticesProcessor` class in `MeshVerticesProcessor.cs` of the `MeshVerticesProcessor` project. The class is the same as the one mentioned in the last recipe *Implementing BoundingBox collision detection in a 3D game*. For a full explanation, please refer back to it.

3. Build the `MeshVerticesProcessor` project. Add a reference to `MeshVerticesProcessor.dll` in the content project and change the **Content Processor** of `BallLowPoly.FBX` to `MeshVerticesProcessor`, as shown in the following screenshot:

4. From this step, we will begin to draw the two balls on screen and detect the bounding sphere collision between them in the `BoundingSphereCollisionGame` class in `BoundingSphereCollisionGame.cs` of the `BoundingSphereCollision` project. First, add the following lines to the class field:

```
// The sprite font for drawing collision state
SpriteFont font;

// Model ball A and B
Model modelBallA;
Model modelBallB;

// The world transformation of ball A and B
Matrix worldBallA;
Matrix worldBallB;

// BoundingSphere of model A and B
BoundingSphere boundingSphereA;
BoundingSphere boundingSphereB;

// Camera
Vector3 cameraPosition;
Matrix view;
Matrix projection;

// Hit regions
Rectangle LeftHitRegion;
Rectangle RightHitRegion;

// Collided state
bool Collided;
```

5. Load the ball model and sprite font. Then, extract the vertices of the ball model. With the extracted vertices, create the bounding spheres for ball A and B. Insert the following code into the `LoadContent()` method:

```
// Translate the model ball A and B
worldBallA = Matrix.CreateTranslation(new Vector3(-10, 0, 0));
worldBallB = Matrix.CreateTranslation(new Vector3(10, 0, 0));

// Initialize the camera
cameraPosition = new Vector3(0, 10, 40);
view = Matrix.CreateLookAt(cameraPosition, Vector3.Zero,
    Vector3.Up);
projection = Matrix.CreatePerspectiveFieldOfView(
    MathHelper.PiOver4, GraphicsDevice.Viewport.AspectRatio,
```

```
    0.1f, 1000.0f);

// Initialize the left and right hit regions
Viewport viewport = GraphicsDevice.Viewport;
LeftHitRegion = new Rectangle(0, 0, viewport.Width / 2,
    viewport.Height);
RightHitRegion = new Rectangle(viewport.Width / 2, 0,
    viewport.Width / 2, viewport.Height);
```

6. Move the ball A and the corresponding bounding sphere. Then, detect the bounding sphere collision between ball A and B. Add the following code to the `Update()` method:

```
// Check the tapped position
TouchCollection touches = TouchPanel.GetState();
if (touches.Count > 0 && touches[0].State ==
    TouchLocationState.Pressed)
{
    Point point = new Point((int)touches[0].Position.X,
        (int)touches[0].Position.Y);

    // If the tapped position is inside the left hit region,
    // move ball A to left
    if (LeftHitRegion.Contains(point))
    {
        worldBallA.Translation -= new Vector3(1, 0, 0);
    }

    // If the tapped position is inside the left right region,
    // move the ball A right
    if (RightHitRegion.Contains(point))
    {
        worldBallA.Translation += new Vector3(1, 0, 0);
    }
}

// Update the position of bounding sphere A
boundingSphereA.Center = worldBallA.Translation;

// Detect collision between bounding sphere A and B
if (boundingSphereA.Intersects(boundingSphereB))
{
    Collided = true;
}
else
```

```
    {
        Collided = false;
    }
```

7. Define the `DrawModel()` method.

```
// Draw model
public void DrawModel(Model model, Matrix world, Matrix view,
    Matrix projection)
{
    Matrix[] transforms = new Matrix[model.Bones.Count];
    model.CopyAbsoluteBoneTransformsTo(transforms);

    foreach (ModelMesh mesh in model.Meshes)
    {
        foreach (BasicEffect effect in mesh.Effects)
        {
            effect.PreferPerPixelLighting = true;
            effect.EnableDefaultLighting();
            effect.DiffuseColor = Color.White.ToVector3();
            effect.World = transforms[mesh.ParentBone.Index] *
                world;
            effect.View = view;
            effect.Projection = projection;
        }
        mesh.Draw();
    }
}
```

8. Draw the spheres on screen. Add the following code to the `Draw()` method.

```
GraphicsDevice.DepthStencilState = DepthStencilState.Default;

// Draw the ball model A and B
DrawModel(modelBallA, worldBallA, view, projection);
DrawModel(modelBallB, worldBallB, view, projection);

// Draw the collision state
spriteBatch.Begin();
spriteBatch.DrawString(font, "Collided:" + Collided.ToString(),
    new Vector2(0, 0), Color.White);
spriteBatch.End();
```

9. Now, build and run the application. The application should run as shown in the following screenshots:

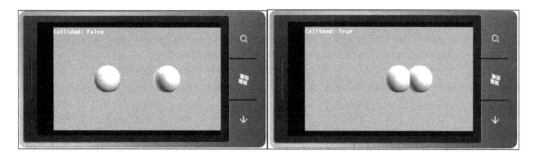

How it works...

In step 4, the `font` is responsible for drawing the collision state on screen; `modelBallA` and `modelBallB` hold the two box models; `worldBallA` and `worldBallB` represent the world transformation of the two boxes; `boundingSphereA` and `boundingSphereB` store the bound boxes individually around the two boxes; the `cameraPosition`, `view`, and `projection` will be used to initialize the camera; `LeftHitRegion` and `RightHitRegion` define the left and right hit regions on the Windows Phone 7 screen.

In step 6, the first part is to check whether the tapped position is in the left or the right hit region and to move ball A. After that, we update the center position of bounding sphere A with the newest position of ball A. Then, we take the bounding sphere collision detection between the `boundingSphereA` and `boundingSphereB` using the `BoundingSphere. Intersects()` method. If the collision happens, the method will return `true`, otherwise it will return `false`.

Implementing ray-triangle collision detection

Ray-triangle collision gives very accurate collision detection in games. Depending on the return value of the distance from the ray start position to the triangle, it is easy for you to decide whether a collision occurs. As you might know, all the models in 3D games are made of triangles, whether static or dynamic. The ray is like a bullet fired from a gun; here, you can consider the gun as another object, with a straight thin rope behind. Once the bullet hits the triangle—an object, the collision happens. A lot of methods on ray-triangle are available; in this recipe, you will learn how to implement the method which has the best time and space complexity to make your game run faster with less memory usage.

Getting ready...

The ray-triangle collision detection method provides more accurate data than other methods using `BoundingBox` or `BoundingSphere`. Before the best ray-triangle collision detection method was invented by Moller and Trumbore, most of the existing methods first compute the intersection point between the ray and the triangle's plane. After that, the intersection point will be projected to the axis-aligned plane to determine whether it is inside the 2D projected triangle. These kinds of methods need the plain equation of triangle based on the computed normal every frame, for a triangle mesh; to do this will cost considerable memory space and CPU resources. However, the method from Moller and Trumbore requires only two cross product computations and also gives us an intersection point.

As a detailed explanation, a point v in a triangle is represented by Barycentric coordinates and not Cartesian coordinates. Since the Barycentric coordinate is the most suitable coordinate system to describe a point position in a triangle, the point could be represented by the following formula:

$$P = (1 - u - v)P_0 + uP_1 + vP_2 \qquad where\ u, v \geq 0\ and\ u + v \leq 1$$

The u and v coordinates—two of the Barycentric coordinates—are also used in texture mapping, normal interpolation like the Phong lighting algorithm, and color interpolation.

For a ray, a point on the ray is given by:

$$P = O + tD \qquad where\ 0 \leq t \leq 1$$

The intersection point between the ray and the triangle means the point is both on the ray and the triangle. To get the point, we have the formula:

$$O + tD = (1 - u - v)P_0 + uP_1 + vP_2$$

We rearrange the previous equation to an expression in matrix notation:

$$[-D \quad P_1 - P_0 \quad P_2 - P_0]\begin{bmatrix} t \\ u \\ v \end{bmatrix} = O - P_0$$

The previous equation means the distance t from the ray origin to the intersection point and the Barycentric coordinate (u,v) can be found in the equation solution. If $[-D \quad P_1 - P_0 \quad P_2 - P_0][-D \quad P_1 - P_0 \quad P_2 - P_0]$ is a matrix M, our job is to find the M-1. The equation will be:

$$\begin{bmatrix} t \\ u \\ v \end{bmatrix} = (O - P_0)M^{-1}$$

Now, let $E_1 = P_1 - P_0$, $E_2 = P_2 - P_0$, $S = O - P_0$. With the Cramer's rule, we find the following solution:

$$\begin{bmatrix} t \\ u \\ v \end{bmatrix} = \frac{1}{\det(-D, E_1, E_2)} \begin{bmatrix} \det(S, E_1, E_2) \\ \det(-D, S, E_2) \\ \det(-D, E_1, S) \end{bmatrix}$$

From linear algebra, the determinant is computed using the Triple Product:

$$\det(A, B, C) = -(A \times C) \cdot B = -(C \times B) \cdot A$$

The solution can be rewritten as follows:

$$\begin{bmatrix} t \\ u \\ v \end{bmatrix} = \frac{1}{(D \times E_2) \cdot E_1} \begin{bmatrix} (S \times E_1) \cdot E_2 \\ (D \times E_2) \cdot S \\ (S \times E_1) \cdot D \end{bmatrix} = \frac{1}{P \cdot E_1} \begin{bmatrix} Q \cdot E_2 \\ P \cdot S \\ Q \cdot D \end{bmatrix}$$

The following pseudo code describing the algorithm comes from the solution of the previous equation:

```
E1 = P1 - P0;
E2 = P2 - P0;
P = D × E2;
determinate = P ' E1;

if(determinate > -epsilon && determinate < epsilon)
return null;

inverse = 1 / determinate;

S = O - P0
u = P · S * inverse;
if( u < 0) return null;

Q = S × E1;

v = Q ' D * inverse
if(v < 0) return null;

t = Q ' E2 * inverse;
if( t < 0) return null;

return (t, u, v)
```

The XNA code to implement the pseudo code should be:

```
public void RayIntersectsTriangle(ref Ray ray,
    ref Vector3 vertex1,
    ref Vector3 vertex2,
    ref Vector3 vertex3, out float? result)
{
    // Compute vectors along two edges of the triangle.
    Vector3 edge1, edge2;

    Vector3.Subtract(ref vertex2, ref vertex1, out edge1);
    Vector3.Subtract(ref vertex3, ref vertex1, out edge2);

    // Compute the determinant.
    Vector3 directionCrossEdge2;
    Vector3.Cross(ref ray.Direction, ref edge2,
        out directionCrossEdge2);

    float determinant;
    Vector3.Dot(ref edge1, ref directionCrossEdge2,
        out determinant);

    // If the ray is parallel to the triangle plane, there is
    // no collision.
    if (determinant > -float.Epsilon &&
        determinant < float.Epsilon)
    {
        result = null;
        return;
    }

    float inverseDeterminant = 1.0f / determinant;

    // Calculate the U parameter of the intersection point.
    Vector3 distanceVector;
    Vector3.Subtract(ref ray.Position, ref vertex1,
        out distanceVector);

    float triangleU;
    Vector3.Dot(ref distanceVector, ref directionCrossEdge2,
        out triangleU);
    triangleU *= inverseDeterminant;

    // Make sure it is inside the triangle.
```

```
    if (triangleU < 0 || triangleU > 1)
    {
        result = null;
        return;
    }

    // Calculate the V parameter of the intersection point.
    Vector3 distanceCrossEdge1;
    Vector3.Cross(ref distanceVector, ref edge1,
        out distanceCrossEdge1);

    float triangleV;
    Vector3.Dot(ref ray.Direction, ref distanceCrossEdge1,
        out triangleV);
    triangleV *= inverseDeterminant;

    // Make sure it is inside the triangle.
    if (triangleV < 0 || triangleU + triangleV > 1)
    {
        result = null;
        return;
    }

    // Compute the distance along the ray to the triangle.
    float rayDistance;
    Vector3.Dot(ref edge2, ref distanceCrossEdge1,
        out rayDistance);
    rayDistance *= inverseDeterminant;

    // Is the triangle behind the ray origin?
    if (rayDistance < 0)
    {
        result = null;
        return;
    }

    result = rayDistance;
}
```

As the parameters of the `RayIntersectsTriangle()` method, the `vertex1`, `vertex2`, and `vertex3` are the three points of a triangle, `ray` is the object of the XNA built-in type ray, which specifies the origin point and the ray direction; the result will return the distance between the ray start point and the intersection point. In the body of the method, the first three lines compute the two triangle edges, then they use the `ray.Direction` and `edge2` to compute the cross product `directionCrossEdge1` that represents P, which equals P=D×E2. Next, we use `directionCrossEdge2` that takes the dot multiplication with `edge1` to compute the `determinate` with the equation `determinate=P·E1`. The following `if` statement is to validate the `determinate`. If the value tends to `0`, the `determinate` will be rejected. Then, we use `inverseDeterminant` to represent the following fraction:

$$\frac{1}{P \cdot E_1}$$

Now you have got the denominator of the fraction of Cramer's rule. With the value, the `u`, `v`, and `t` could be solved as the solution equation. Following the pseudo code, the next step is to calculate the P with equation S=O-P0. Here, `ray.Position` is O, `vertex1` is P0, `distanceVector` is S. Based on the S value, you could get the u value from the equation u=P·S*inverse, the code calls the `Vector3.Dot()` method between `directionCrossEdge2` and `distanceVector` for the intermediate `TriangleU`, then the returned value multiplies with the `inverseDeterminant` for the final `TriangleU`. The v value `triangleV` comes from the equation v=Q×D*inverse in which Q=S×E1. Similarly, you could gain the t value `rayDistance` from the equation t=Q×E2*inverse.

How to do it...

Now, let's look into an example for a direct experience:

1. Create a Windows Phone Game project named `RayTriangleCollisionGame`, change `Game1.cs` to `RayTriangleCollisionGame.cs`. Then, add the `gameFont.spritefont` file to the content project.

2. Declare the necessary variables of the `RayTriangleCollisionGame` class. Add the following lines to the class field:

```
// SpriteFont draw the instructions
SpriteFont font;

// Triangle vertex array
VertexPositionColor[] verticesTriangle;
VertexBuffer vertexBufferTriangle;

// Line vertex array
VertexPositionColor[] verticesLine;
VertexBuffer vertexBufferLine;
```

```
Matrix worldRay = Matrix.CreateTranslation(-10, 0, 0);

// Camera view matrix
Matrix view;

// Camera projection matrix
Matrix projection;

// Ray object
Ray ray;

// Distance
float? distance;

// Left region on screen
Rectangle LeftRectangle;

// Right region on screen
Rectangle RightRectangle;

// Render state
RasterizerState Solid = new RasterizerState()
{
    FillMode = FillMode.Solid,
    CullMode = CullMode.None
};
```

3. Initialize the camera and the hit regions. Insert the code into the
   `Initialize()` method:

```
view = Matrix.CreateLookAt(new Vector3(20, 5, 20),
    Vector3.Zero, Vector3.Up);
projection = Matrix.CreatePerspectiveFieldOfView(
    MathHelper.PiOver4,
    GraphicsDevice.Viewport.AspectRatio, 0.1f, 1000.0f);

LeftRectangle = new Rectangle(0, 0,
    GraphicsDevice.Viewport.Bounds.Width / 2,
    GraphicsDevice.Viewport.Bounds.Height);

RightRectangle = new Rectangle(
    GraphicsDevice.Viewport.Bounds.Width / 2, 0,
    GraphicsDevice.Viewport.Bounds.Width / 2,
    GraphicsDevice.Viewport.Bounds.Height);
```

4. Initialize the vertices and vertex buffer of the triangle and the line. Then, instance the ray object. Add the following code to the `LoadContent()` method:

```
// Load the font
font = Content.Load<SpriteFont>("gameFont");

// Create a triangle
verticesTriangle = new VertexPositionColor[3];
verticesTriangle[0] = new VertexPositionColor(
    new Vector3(0, 0, 0), Color.Green);
verticesTriangle[1] = new VertexPositionColor(
    new Vector3(10, 0, 0), Color.Green);
verticesTriangle[2] = new VertexPositionColor(
    new Vector3(5, 5, 0), Color.Green);

// Allocate the vertex buffer for triangle vertices
vertexBufferTriangle = new VertexBuffer(
    GraphicsDevice, VertexPositionColor.VertexDeclaration, 3,
    BufferUsage.WriteOnly);

// Set the triangle vertices to the vertex buffer of triangle
vertexBufferTriangle.SetData(verticesTriangle);

// Create the line
verticesLine = new VertexPositionColor[2];
verticesLine[0] = new VertexPositionColor(
    new Vector3(5, 2.5f, 10), Color.Red);
verticesLine[1] = new VertexPositionColor(
    new Vector3(5, 2.5f, -10), Color.Red);

// Allocate the vertex buffer for line points
vertexBufferLine = new VertexBuffer(GraphicsDevice,
    VertexPositionColor.VertexDeclaration, 2,
    BufferUsage.WriteOnly);

// Set the line points to the vertex buffer of line
vertexBufferLine.SetData(verticesLine);

// Compute the ray direction
Vector3 rayDirection = verticesLine[1].Position -
    verticesLine[0].Position;
rayDirection.Normalize();

// Initialize the ray with position and direction
ray = new Ray(verticesLine[0].Position, rayDirection);
```

```
    // Transform the ray
    ray.Position = Vector3.Transform(ray.Position, worldRay);
```

5. Perform the ray-triangle collision detection. Paste the following code into the `Update()` method:

```
    TouchCollection touches = TouchPanel.GetState();
    if (touches.Count > 0 && touches[0].State ==
        TouchLocationState.Pressed)
    {
        Point point = new Point((int)touches[0].Position.X,
            (int)touches[0].Position.Y);
        if (LeftRectangle.Contains(point))
        {
            worldRay *= Matrix.CreateTranslation(
                new Vector3(-1, 0, 0));
            ray.Position.X -= 1;
        }

        if (RightRectangle.Contains(point))
        {
            worldRay *= Matrix.CreateTranslation(
                new Vector3(1, 0, 0));
            ray.Position.X += 1;
        }
    }

    RayIntersectsTriangle(
        ref ray,
        ref verticesTriangle[0].Position,
        ref verticesTriangle[1].Position,
        ref verticesTriangle[2].Position,
        out distance);

    if (distance != null)
    {
        verticesTriangle[0].Color = Color.Yellow;
        verticesTriangle[1].Color = Color.Yellow;
        verticesTriangle[2].Color = Color.Yellow;
    }
    else
    {
        verticesTriangle[0].Color = Color.Green;
        verticesTriangle[1].Color = Color.Green;
```

```
            verticesTriangle[2].Color = Color.Green;
        }

        vertexBufferTriangle.SetData(verticesTriangle);
```

6. Define the `DrawColoredPrimitives()` method in the `RayTriangleCollisionGame` class, for drawing the line and triangle on the Windows Phone 7 screen.

```
public void DrawColoredPrimitives(VertexBuffer buffer,
    PrimitiveType primitiveType, int primitiveCount,
    Matrix world)
{
    BasicEffect effect = new BasicEffect(GraphicsDevice);
    effect.VertexColorEnabled = true;
    effect.World = world;
    effect.View = view;
    effect.Projection = projection;

    effect.CurrentTechnique.Passes[0].Apply();
    GraphicsDevice.SetVertexBuffers(buffer);
    GraphicsDevice.DrawPrimitives(primitiveType, 0,
        primitiveCount);
}
```

7. Draw the ray and triangle on the Windows Phone 7 screen. Insert the following code into the `Draw()` method:

```
GraphicsDevice.RasterizerState = Solid;

// Draw the triangle
DrawColoredPrimitives(vertexBufferTriangle,
    PrimitiveType.TriangleList, 1, Matrix.Identity);

// Draw the line which visualizes the ray
DrawColoredPrimitives(vertexBufferLine, PrimitiveType.LineList,
    1, worldRay);

spriteBatch.Begin();
spriteBatch.DrawString(font,
    "Tap the Left or Right Part of \nScreen to Move the ray",
    new Vector2(0, 0), Color.White);
spriteBatch.End();
```

8.   Now, build and run the application. It runs as shown in the following screenshots:

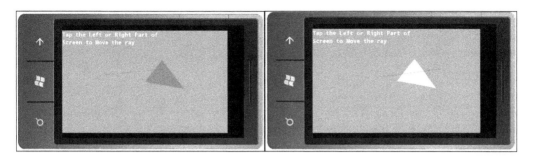

How it works...

In step 2, the font object will draw the instruction about how to play with the example on screen; `verticesTriangle` is the vertex array of the testing triangle; `vertexBufferTriangle` is the vertex buffer that stores the triangle vertices; `verticesLine` holds the two points of a line, which visually represents the testing ray; the matrix `worldRay` stands for the ray world position. The following two matrices `view` and `projection` will be used to define the camera; the ray object will be the real tested ray; the `distance` indicates the actual distance from ray origin position to the ray-triangle intersection point; the `LeftRectangle` and `RightRectangle` are the hit regions for moving the ray to the left or to the right. The `Solid` variable specifies the render state of the graphics device.

In step 3, the `LeftRectangle` occupies the left half of the screen; the `RightRectangle` takes up the right half of the screen.

In step 4, the first part is to initialize three of the triangle vertices with the position and color. The original color is green, and when ray collides with the triangle, the color will be yellow. Then we set the triangle vertices to the triangle vertex buffer. The second part is about initiating the line that visualizes the ray and putting the data into the vertex buffer for line data. The final part defines the ray object with position and direction.

In step 5, before the `RayIntersectsTriangle()` method, the code is to check the tapped position to see whether it is in the `LeftRectangle` or the `RightRectangle`. When a valid tapping takes place, the ray will move along the X-axis by one unit, then we call the `RayIntersectsTriangle()` method to judge whether there is a collision between the ray and the triangle. If the returned `distance` is not `null`, this means that the collision happened, and we change the color of the triangle vertices to `Color.Yellow`. Otherwise, the color will be restored to `Color.Green`. The `RayIntersectsTriangle()` method has been discussed at the beginning of this recipe and inserts the definition of the `RayIntersectsTriangle()` method to the `RayTriangleCollisionGame` class.

In step 6, in the DrawColoredPrimitives() method, the effect receives the view and project matrices for the camera, the world matrix for the world position and transformation. The effect.VertexColorEnabled is set to true to make vertices have color. Then, we use the first pass of the current technique of BasicEffect and GraphicsDevice. The DrawPrimitives() method draws the primitives from the beginning of the vertex array in the vertex buffer.

In step 7, the DrawColoredPrimitives() method is used to draw the triangle that receives a parameter PrimitiveType.TriangleList, where 1 means the count of triangles. When drawing the line the PrimitiveType is LineList.

Mapping a tapped location to 3D

To pick an object in a 3D game is relevant in terms of real-time strategy. For example, in StarCraft2, you can choose a construction from a 2D panel, then a semi-transparent 3D model will show up in the game view that lets you choose the best location for building the construction. Or, you can select your army by just clicking the left button of the mouse and drawing a rectangle covering the units you want to control. All of these happen between 2D and 3D. This is magic! Actually, this technique maps the clicking position in screen coordinate from 2D to 3D world. In this recipe, you will learn how this important mapping method works in the Windows Phone 7 game.

How to do it...

The following steps will lead you to make your own version of picking an object in a 3D game:

1. Create the Windows Phone Game project named Pick3DModel, change Game1.cs to Pick3DModelGame.cs and add a new Marker.cs to the project. Then, we create a Content Pipeline Extension Library called ModelVerticesPipeline, replace ContentProcessor1.cs with ModelVerticesPipeline.cs. After that, add the model file BallLowPoly.FBX and image Marker.png to the content project.

2. Create ModelVerticesProcessor in ModelVerticesProcessor.cs of the ModelVerticesPipeline project. Since the ray-triangle collision detection between ray and model needs the triangle information, in the extension model process, we will extract all of the model vertices and the model global bounding sphere. The returned bounding sphere will serve for the ray-sphere collision detection, before model ray-triangle collision detection, as a performance consideration; the extracted vertices will be used to generate the triangles for the model ray-triangle collision detection when the ray collides with the model bounding sphere. Add the definition of ModelVerticesProcessor class to ModelVerticesProcessor.cs.

3. `ModelVerticesProcessor` inherits from the `ModelProcessor` for extracting extra model vertices. The beginning of the class should be:

```
publicclass ModelVerticesProcessor : ModelProcessor {. . .}
```

4. Add the variable `vertices` to store the model vertices in the `ModelVerticesProcessor` class field.

```
List<Vector3> vertices = new List<Vector3>();
```

5. Override the `Process()` method of the `ModelVerticesProcessor` class. This is the main method in charge of processing the content. In the method, we extract the model vertices and `BoundingSphere`, and store them into the `ModelContent.Tag` property as a `Dictionary` object.

```
// Chain to the base ModelProcessor class.
ModelContent model = base.Process(input, context);

// Look up the input vertex positions.
FindVertices(input);

// Create a dictionary object to store the model vertices and
// BoundingSphere
Dictionary<string, object> tagData =
    new Dictionary<string, object>();

model.Tag = tagData;

// Store vertex information in the tag data, as an array of
// Vector3.
tagData.Add("Vertices", vertices.ToArray());

// Also store a custom bounding sphere.
tagData.Add("BoundingSphere",
    BoundingSphere.CreateFromPoints(vertices));

return model;
```

6. Define the `FindVertices()` method of the `ModelVerticesProcessor` class:

```
// Helper for extracting a list of all the vertex positions in
// a model.
void FindVertices(NodeContent node)
{
    // Convert the current NodeContent to MeshContent if it is
    // a mesh
    MeshContent mesh = node as MeshContent;
```

```
        if (mesh != null)
        {
            // Get the absolute transform of the mesh
            Matrix absoluteTransform = mesh.AbsoluteTransform;

            // Iterate every geometry in the mesh
            foreach (GeometryContent geometry in mesh.Geometry)
            {
                // Loop over all the indices in geometry.
                // Every group of three indices represents one
                // triangle.
                foreach (int index in geometry.Indices)
                {
                    // Get the vertex position
                    Vector3 vertex =
                        geometry.Vertices.Positions[index];

                    // Transform from local into world space.
                    vertex = Vector3.Transform(vertex,
                        absoluteTransform);

                    // Store this vertex.
                    vertices.Add(vertex);
                }
            }
        }

        // Recursively scan over the children of this node.
        foreach (NodeContent child in node.Children)
        {
            FindVertices(child);
        }
    }
```

7. Now, build the `ModelVerticesPipeline` project. You will get the runtime library `ModelVerticesProcessor.dll` in which the `ModelVerticesProcessor` stores.

8. In the next few steps, we will define the `Marker` class in `Marker.cs` of the `Pick3DModel` project.

9. The `Marker` class inherits from `DrawableGameComponent`. Add the variables to the `Marker` class field:

```
    // SpriteBatch for drawing the marker texture
    SpriteBatch spriteBatch;

    // ContentManager for loading the marker texture
```

```
ContentManager content;

// Marker texture
Texture2D texMarker;

// Texture origin position for moving or rotation
Vector2 centerTexture;

// Texture position on screen
publicVector2 position;
```

10. Add the constructor of the `Marker` class.

```
public Marker(Game game, ContentManager content)
    : base(game)
{
    this.content = content;
}
```

11. Implement the `LoadContent()` method, which will load the marker texture and define the texture origin position.

```
protected override void LoadContent()
{
    spriteBatch = new SpriteBatch(GraphicsDevice);

    texMarker = content.Load<Texture2D>("Marker");
    centerTexture = new Vector2(texMarker.Width / 2,
    texMarker.Height / 2);

    base.LoadContent();
}
```

12. Let the marker inside the Windows Phone 7 screen. We define the `Update()` method to achieve this.

```
// Calculate where the marker's position is on the screen. The
// position is clamped to the viewport so that the marker
// can't go off the screen.
publicoverridevoid Update(GameTime gameTime)
{
    TouchCollection touches = TouchPanel.GetState();
    if (touches.Count > 0 && touches[0].State ==
    TouchLocationState.Pressed)

    {
        position.X = touches[0].Position.X;
```

```
                   position.Y = touches[0].Position.Y;
             }

       base.Update(gameTime);
       }
```

13. Define the `CalculateMarkerRay()` method that calculates a world space ray starting at the camera's eye and pointing in the direction of the cursor. The `Viewport.Unproject()` method is used to accomplish this.

```
       publicRay CalculateMarkerRay(Matrix projectionMatrix,
           Matrix viewMatrix)
       {
           // Create 2 positions in screenspace using the tapped
           // position. 0 is as close as possible to the camera, 1 is
           // as far away as possible.
           Vector3 nearSource = newVector3(position, 0f);
           Vector3 farSource = newVector3(position, 1f);

           // Use Viewport.Unproject to tell what those two screen
           // space positions would be in world space.
           Vector3 nearPoint =
           GraphicsDevice.Viewport.Unproject(nearSource,
           projectionMatrix, viewMatrix, Matrix.Identity);

           Vector3 farPoint =
           GraphicsDevice.Viewport.Unproject(farSource,
           projectionMatrix, viewMatrix, Matrix.Identity);

           // Find the direction vector that goes from the nearPoint
           // to the farPoint and normalize it
           Vector3 direction = farPoint - nearPoint;
           direction.Normalize();

           // Return a new ray using nearPoint as the source.
           returnnewRay(nearPoint, direction);
       }
```

14. From this step we begin to compute the ray-model collision and draw the collided triangle and model mesh on Windows Phone 7 in the game main class `Pick3DModelGame`. Now, insert the lines to the class field as data member:

```
       // Marker Ray
       Ray markerRay;

       // Marker
```

```
        Marker marker;

        // Model object and model world position
        Model modelObject;
        Matrix worldModel = Matrix.Identity;

        // Camera view and projection matrices
        Matrix viewMatrix;
        Matrix projectionMatrix;

        // Define the picked triangle vertex array
        VertexPositionColor[] pickedTriangle =
        {
                newVertexPositionColor(Vector3.Zero, Color.Black),
                newVertexPositionColor(Vector3.Zero, Color.Black),
                newVertexPositionColor(Vector3.Zero, Color.Black),
        };

        // Vertex array to represent the selected model
        VertexPositionColor[] verticesModel;
        VertexBuffer vertexBufferModel;

        // The flag indicates whether the ray collides with the model
        float? intersection;

        // The effect of the object is to draw the picked triangle
        BasicEffectwireFrameEffect;

        // The wire frame render state
        staticRasterizerState WireFrame = newRasterizerState
        {
            FillMode = FillMode.WireFrame,
            CullMode = CullMode.None
        };
```

15. Initialize the camera, marker, and `wireFrameEffect`. Add the code to the `Initialize()` method:

```
        // Intialize the camera
        viewMatrix = Matrix.CreateLookAt(new Vector3(0, 5, 15),
            Vector3.Zero, Vector3.Up);
        projectionMatrix = Matrix.CreatePerspectiveFieldOfView(
            MathHelper.ToRadians(45.0f),
            GraphicsDevice.Viewport.AspectRatio, .01f, 1000);
```

```
    // Initialize the marker
    marker = new Marker(this, Content);
    Components.Add(marker);


    wireFrameEffect = new BasicEffect(graphics.GraphicsDevice);
```

16. Load the ball model and read the ball vertices. Then initialize the vertex array of the ball model for drawing the ball mesh on the Windows Phone 7 screen. Insert the following code in to the `LoadContent()` method:

```
    // Load the ball object
    modelObject = Content.Load<Model>("BallLowPoly");


    // Read the vertices
    Dictionary<string, object> tagData =
        (Dictionary<string, object>)modelObject.Tag;
    Vector3[] vertices = (Vector3[])tagData["Vertices"];


    // Initialize the model vertex array for drawing on screen
    verticesModel = new VertexPositionColor[vertices.Length];
    for (int i = 0; i < vertices.Length; i++)
    {
        verticesModel[i] =
            new VertexPositionColor(vertices[i], Color.Red);
    }


    vertexBufferModel = new VertexBuffer(
        GraphicsDevice, VertexPositionColor.VertexDeclaration,
        vertices.Length, BufferUsage.WriteOnly);
    vertexBufferModel.SetData(verticesModel);
```

17. Define the ray-model collision detection method `UpdatePicking()` in the `Pick3DModelGame` class.

```
    void UpdatePicking()
    {
        // Look up a collision ray based on the current marker
        // position.
        markerRay = marker.CalculateMarkerRay(projectionMatrix,
            viewMatrix);


        // Keep track of the closest object we have seen so far,
        // so we can choose the closest one if there are several
        // models under the cursor.
        float closestIntersection = float.MaxValue;
```

```
Vector3 vertex1, vertex2, vertex3;

// Perform the ray to model intersection test.
intersection = RayIntersectsModel(markerRay, modelObject,
    worldModel, out vertex1, out vertex2,out vertex3);

// Check whether the ray-model collistion happens
if (intersection != null)
{
    // If so, is it closer than any other model we might
    // have previously intersected?
    if (intersection < closestIntersection)
    {
        // Store information about this model.
        closestIntersection = intersection.Value;

        // Store vertex positions so we can display the
        // picked triangle.
        pickedTriangle[0].Position = vertex1;
        pickedTriangle[1].Position = vertex2;
        pickedTriangle[2].Position = vertex3;
    }
}
}
```

18. Define the `RayIntersectsModel()` method in the `Pick3DModelGame` class:

```
float? RayIntersectsModel(Ray ray, Model model, Matrix
    modelTransform, out Vector3 vertex1, out Vector3 vertex2,
    out Vector3 vertex3)
{
    bool insideBoundingSphere;
    vertex1 = vertex2 = vertex3 = Vector3.Zero;

    Matrix inverseTransform = Matrix.Invert(modelTransform);

    ray.Position = Vector3.Transform(ray.Position,
        inverseTransform);
    ray.Direction = Vector3.TransformNormal(ray.Direction,
        inverseTransform);

    // Look up our custom collision data from the Tag property
    // of the model.
    Dictionary<string, object> tagData =
    (Dictionary<string, object>)model.Tag;
```

```
BoundingSphere boundingSphere =
    (BoundingSphere)tagData["BoundingSphere"];

if (boundingSphere.Intersects(ray) == null)
{
    // If the ray does not intersect the bounding sphere,
    // there is  no need to do the the ray-triangle
    // collision detection
    insideBoundingSphere = false;

    return null;
}
else
{
    // The bounding sphere test passed, do the ray-
    // triangle test
    insideBoundingSphere = true;

    // Keep track of the closest triangle we found so far,
    // so we can always return the closest one.
    float? closestIntersection = null;

    // Loop over the vertex data, 3 at a time for a
    // triangle
    Vector3[] vertices = (Vector3[])tagData["Vertices"];

    for (int i = 0; i < vertices.Length; i += 3)
    {
        // Perform a ray to triangle intersection test.
        float? intersection;

        RayIntersectsTriangle(ref ray,
            ref vertices[i],
            ref vertices[i + 1],
            ref vertices[i + 2],
            out intersection);

        // Does the ray intersect this triangle?
        if (intersection != null)
        {
            // If so, find the closest one
            if ((closestIntersection == null) ||
                (intersection < closestIntersection))
```

```
                    {
                        // Store the distance to this triangle.
                        closestIntersection = intersection;

                        // Transform the three vertex positions
                        // into world space, and store them into
                        // the output vertex parameters.
                        Vector3.Transform(ref vertices[i],
                            ref modelTransform, out vertex1);

                        Vector3.Transform(ref vertices[i + 1],
                            ref modelTransform, out vertex2);

                        Vector3.Transform(ref vertices[i + 2],
                            ref modelTransform, out vertex3);
                    }
                }
            }

            return closestIntersection;
        }
    }
```

19. Draw the ball on the Windows Phone 7 screen with the model heighted wireframe and the picked triangle. Add the following code to the `Draw()` method:

```
GraphicsDevice.BlendState = BlendState.Opaque;
GraphicsDevice.DepthStencilState = DepthStencilState.Default;

// Draw model
DrawModel(modelObject, worldModel);

// Draw the model wire frame
DrawPickedWireFrameModel();

// Draw the outline of the triangle under the cursor.
DrawPickedTriangle();
```

20. Now we should give the definitions of the called methods: `DrawPickedWireFrameModel()`, `DrawPickedTriangle()`, and `DrawModel()`.

21. Define the `DrawPickedWireFrameModel()` method in the `Pick3DModelGame` class:

```
void DrawPickedWireFrameModel()
{
    if (intersection != null)
    {
        GraphicsDevice device = graphics.GraphicsDevice;

        device.RasterizerState = WireFrame;
        device.DepthStencilState = DepthStencilState.None;

        // Activate the line drawing BasicEffect.
        wireFrameEffect.Projection = projectionMatrix;
        wireFrameEffect.View = viewMatrix;

        wireFrameEffect.CurrentTechnique.Passes[0].Apply();

        // Draw the triangle.
        device.DrawUserPrimitives(PrimitiveType.TriangleList,
            verticesModel, 0, verticesModel.Length / 3);

        // Reset renderstates to their default values.
        device.RasterizerState =
            RasterizerState.CullCounterClockwise;
        device.DepthStencilState = DepthStencilState.Default;
    }
}
```

22. Implement the `DrawPickedTriangle()` method in the `Pick3DModelGame` class:

```
void DrawPickedTriangle()
{
    if (intersection != null)
    {
        GraphicsDevice device = graphics.GraphicsDevice;

        // Set line drawing renderstates. We disable backface
        // culling and turn off the depth buffer because we
        // want to be able to see the picked triangle outline
        // regardless of which way it is facing, and even if
        // there is other geometry in front of it.
        device.RasterizerState = WireFrame;
        device.DepthStencilState = DepthStencilState.None;

        // Activate the line drawing BasicEffect.
```

```
                wireFrameEffect.Projection = projectionMatrix;
                wireFrameEffect.View = viewMatrix;
                wireFrameEffect.VertexColorEnabled = true;
                wireFrameEffect.CurrentTechnique.Passes[0].Apply();

                // Draw the triangle.
                device.DrawUserPrimitives(PrimitiveType.TriangleList,
                    pickedTriangle, 0, 1);

                // Reset renderstates to their default values.
                device.RasterizerState =
                    RasterizerState.CullCounterClockwise;
                device.DepthStencilState = DepthStencilState.Default;
            }
        }
```

23. Give the definition of the `DrawModel()` method in the `Pick3DModelGame` class:

```
        private void DrawModel(Model model, Matrix worldTransform)
        {
            Matrix[] transforms = new Matrix[model.Bones.Count];
            model.CopyAbsoluteBoneTransformsTo(transforms);

            foreach (ModelMesh mesh in model.Meshes)
            {
                foreach (BasicEffect effect in mesh.Effects)
                {
                    effect.EnableDefaultLighting();
                    effect.PreferPerPixelLighting = true;

                    effect.View = viewMatrix;
                    effect.Projection = projectionMatrix;
                    effect.World = transforms[mesh.ParentBone.Index] *
                        worldTransform;
                }
                mesh.Draw();
            }
        }
```

24. Now, build and run the application. It should run as shown in the following screenshots:

How it works...

In step 5, after processing the model basic information as usual in the `base` class, we call the `FindVertices()` method to get all of the model vertices. After that, the dictionary object `tagData` will receive the vertices information and the generated `BoundingSphere` from the model vertices, the `tagData` will be assigned to `ModelContent.Tag` for the game application to read the model vertices and `BoundingSphere` from the model XNB file.

In step 6, the first line is to convert the current `NodeContent` to `MeshContent` if the current `ModelContent` holds a model mesh and not a bone or other types. If `mesh`, an object of `MeshContent`, is not null, we begin to extract its vertices. First of all, the code reads the `mesh.AbsoluteTransform` for transforming the model vertices from object coordinate to world coordinate. Then, we iterate the geometry of the current mesh to get the vertices. In the loop for looping over each of the vertices, we use the `Vector3.Transform()` with `absoluteTransform` matrix to actually transform the vertex from object coordinate to world. After that, the transformed vertex will be saved to the vertices collection. When all of the vertices of the current mesh are processed, the code will deal with the current child content for retrieving the vertices.

In step 8, the `spriteBatch` is the main object in charge of rendering the texture on the Windows Phone 7 screen; the content object of `ContentManager` manages the game contents; `texMarker` represents the marker texture; the `centerTexture` specifies the origin point of texture for rotating and moving; the variable `position` holds the texture position on screen.

In step 10, the constructor receives the `Game` and `ContentManager` objects. The game object provides `GraphicsDevice` and the content offers access to the texture file.

In step 13, this is the key method to generate the ray from the screen coordinates to the world coordinates. The `nearSource` is used for generating the closest point to the camera; `farSource` is for the point that is far away. Then, call the `Viewport.Unproject()` method to generate the `nearPoint` and `farPoint`. After that, convert the `nearSource` and `farSource` from screen space to the `nearPoint` and `farPoint` in world space. Next, use the unprojected points `farPoint` and `nearPoint` to compute the ray direction. Finally, return the new ray object with the `nearPoint` and normalized direction.

In step 14, the `markerRay` specifies the ray from the tapped position to world space; `marker` is the visual sign on screen that indicates the start point of `markerRay`; `modelObject` will load the model; `worldModel` stands for the transformation matrix of `modelObject`; the view and projection will be used to initialize the camera and help generate the `markerRay`; `pickedTriangle` is the triangle vertex array which will be used to draw the triangle on the model where it collides with the `markerRay`; the `verticesModel` reads and stores all of the model vertices and will serve the picked model draw in wireframe; `intersection` indicates the collision state. If not null, the value is the distance between the intersection point and the `markerRay` start point. The final `WireFrame` defines the device render state.

Implementing sphere-triangle collision detection

In FPS game, when the character moves forward to a building or a wall and contacts the object, it will stop and stand there. And you know there is no object around you, because the camera is your eye in the FPS game. If you wonder how the game developers achieve this, you will find the answer in this recipe.

How to do it...

The following steps will show you the best practice of applying the sphere-triangle collision detection for first-person perspective camera:

1. Create a Windows Phone Game project named `CameraModelCollision`, change `Game1.cs` to `CameraModelCollisionGame.cs`. Meanwhile, add `Triangle.cs` and `TriangleSphereCollisionDetection.cs` to the project. Then, create a Content Pipeline Extension Library project named `MeshVerticesProcessor` and replace the `ContentProcessor1.cs` with `MeshVerticesProcessor.cs`. After that, insert the 3D model file `BigBox.fbx` and sprite font file `gameFont.spriteFont` to the content project.

2. Define the `MeshVerticesProcessor` class in `MeshVerticesProcessor.cs` of `MeshVerticesProcessor` project. The class is the same as the processor defined in the *Implementing BoundingSphere collision detection in a 3D game* recipe.

3. Implement the `Triangle` class in `Triangle.cs` in the `CameraModelCollision` project.

    Declare the necessary data members of the `Triangle` class. Add the following lines to the class field:

    ```
    // The triangle corners
    public Vector3 A;
    ```

```
public Vector3 B;
public Vector3 C;
```

4. Define the constructors for the class:

```
// Constructor
public Triangle()
{
    A = Vector3.Zero;
    B = Vector3.Zero;
    C = Vector3.Zero;
}

// Constructor
public Triangle(Vector3 v0, Vector3 v1, Vector3 v2)
{
    A = v0;
    B = v1;
    C = v2;
}
```

5. Implement the `Normal` class of the `Triangle` class. This method returns a unit length normal vector perpendicular to the plane of the triangle.

```
public void Normal(outVector3 normal)
{
    normal = Vector3.Zero;
Vector3 side1 = B - A;
Vector3 side2 = C - A;
    normal = Vector3.Normalize(Vector3.Cross(side1, side2));
}
```

6. Define the `InverseNormal()` method of the `Triangle` class. This method gets a normal that faces away from the point specified (faces in).

```
// Get a normal that faces away from the point specified
// (faces in)
public void InverseNormal(ref Vector3 point,
    out Vector3 inverseNormal)
{
    Normal(out inverseNormal);

    // The direction from any corner of the triangle to the
    //point
    Vector3 inverseDirection = point - A;

    // Roughly facing the same way
```

```
if (Vector3.Dot(inverseNormal, inverseDirection) > 0)
{
    // Same direction therefore invert the normal to face
    // away from the direction to face the point
    Vector3.Multiply(ref inverseNormal, -1.0f,
        out inverseNormal);
}
}
```

7. Create the `TriangleSphereCollisionDetection` class. This class contains the methods to take the triangle sphere collision detection.

   Define the `IsSphereCollideWithTringles()` method. This method is the root method that kicks off the sphere triangle collision detection:

```
public static bool IsSphereCollideWithTringles(
    List<Vector3> vertices,
    BoundingSphere boundingSphere, out Triangle triangle)
{
    bool result = false;
    triangle = null;

    for (int i = 0; i < vertices.Count; i += 3)
    {
        // Create triangle from the tree vertices
        Triangle t = new Triangle(vertices[i], vertices[i + 1],
            vertices[i + 2]);

        // Check if the sphere collides with the triangle
        result = SphereTriangleCollision(ref boundingSphere,
            ref t);

        if (result)
        {
            triangle = t;
            return result;
        }
    }
    return result;
}
```

8. Implement the `SphereTriangleCollision()` method. This method will generate a ray from the center of the sphere and perform the ray-triangle collision check:

```
private static bool SphereTriangleCollision(
    ref BoundingSphere sphere, ref Triangle triangle)
{
```

```
Ray ray = new Ray();
ray.Position = sphere.Center;

// Create a vector facing towards the triangle from the
// ray starting point.
Vector3 inverseNormal;

triangle.InverseNormal(
    ref ray.Position, out inverseNormal);

ray.Direction = inverseNormal;

// Check if the ray hits the triangle
float? distance = RayTriangleIntersects(ref ray,
    ref triangle);
if (distance != null && distance > 0 &&
    distance <= sphere.Radius)
{
    // Hit the surface of the triangle
    return true;
}

return false;
}
```

9. Give the definition of `RayTriangleIntersects()` to the `TriangleSphereCollisionDetection` class. This is the method that performs the ray-triangle collision detection and returns a distance value if the collision takes place:

```
public static float? RayTriangleIntersects(ref Ray ray, ref
    Triangle triangle)
{
    float? result;
    RayIntersectsTriangle(ref ray, ref triangle.A,
    ref triangle.B, ref triangle.C, out result);
    return result;
}
```

10. Add `MeshVerticesProcessor.dll` to the content project reference list, and change the processor of `BigBox.FBX` to `MeshVerticesProcessor`, as shown in the following screenshot:

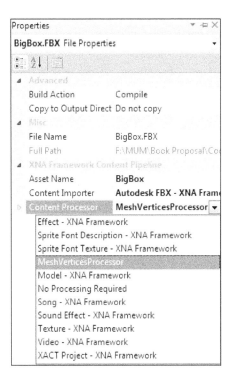

11. From this step, we will begin to take the real-time collision between the camera
    bounding sphere and the model in the main game project `CameraModelCollision`.
    Add the code to the `CameraModelCollision` class field:

```
// SpriteFont for showing instructions
SpriteFont font;

// Box model
Model modelBox;

// Box model world transformation
Matrix worldBox = Matrix.Identity;

// Camera position and look at target
Vector3 cameraPosition;
Vector3 targetOffset;

// Camera view and projection matrices
public Matrix view;
public Matrix projection;

// Camera BoundingSphere
```

```
BoundingSphere boundingSphereCamera;

// Vertices of Box Model
List<Vector3> verticesBox;

// Collided triangle
Triangle triangleCollided;

// Normal of collided triangle
Vector3 normalTriangle;

// The moving forward flag
bool ForwardCollide;
bool BackwardCollide;

// The top and bottom hit regions on screen
Rectangle TopHitRegion;
Rectangle BottomHitRegion;
```

12. Initialize the camera and hit regions. Add the code to the `Initialize()` method in the `CameraModelCollision` class:

```
// Initialize camera
cameraPosition = new Vector3(0, 5, 50);
targetOffset = new Vector3(0, 0, -1000);
view = Matrix.CreateLookAt(cameraPosition, targetOffset,
Vector3.Up);
projection = Matrix.CreatePerspectiveFieldOfView(
    MathHelper.PiOver4, GraphicsDevice.Viewport.AspectRatio,
    0.1f, 1000.0f);

// Initialize the top and bottom hit regions
Viewport viewport = GraphicsDevice.Viewport;
TopHitRegion = new Rectangle(0, 0, viewport.Width,
    viewport.Height / 2);
BottomHitRegion = new Rectangle(0, viewport.Height / 2,
    viewport.Width, viewport.Height / 2);
```

13. Load the box model and initialize the camera bounding sphere. Insert the following code into the `LoadContent()` method in the `CameraModelCollision` class:

```
// Load the game font
font = Content.Load<SpriteFont>("gameFont");

// Load the box model
modelBox = Content.Load<Model>("BigBox");
```

```
    // Get the vertex collection of box model
    verticesBox = ((Dictionary<string,
        List<Vector3>>)modelBox.Tag)["Box001"];

    // Create the BoundingSphere of camera
    boundingSphereCamera = new BoundingSphere(cameraPosition, 5);
```

14. Move the camera and take camera-sphere collision detection. Insert the code into the `Update()` method in the `CameraModelCollision` class.

```
    // Check whether the tapped position is inside the TopHitRegion
    // or BottomHitRegion
    TouchCollection touches = TouchPanel.GetState();
    if (touches.Count > 0 && touches[0].State ==
        TouchLocationState.Pressed)
    {
        Point point = new Point((int)touches[0].Position.X,
            (int)touches[0].Position.Y);
        if (TopHitRegion.Contains(point))
        {
            if (!ForwardCollide)
            {
                // If the tapped position is within the
                // TopHitRegion and the camera has not collided
                // with the model, move the camera forward
                view.Translation += new Vector3(0, 0, 1);
            }
        }

        if (BottomHitRegion.Contains(point))
        {
            // If the tapped position is within the
            // BottomHitRegion and the camera has not
            // collided with the model, move the camera
            // backward
            if (!BackwardCollide)
            {
                view.Translation -= new Vector3(0, 0, 1);
            }
        }
    }

    // Update the center position of camera bounding sphere
```

```
boundingSphereCamera.Center = view.Translation;

// Detect the collision between camera bounding sphere and
// model triangles
TriangleSphereCollisionDetection.IsSphereCollideWithTriangles(
    verticesBox, boundingSphereCamera,
    out triangleCollided);

// If the collision happens, the collided  triangle
// is not null
if (triangleCollided != null)
{
    // Get the normal of the collided triangle
    triangleCollided.Normal(out normalTriangle);

    // Get the direction from the center of camera
    //  BoundingSphere to the collided triangle
    Vector3 Direction = view.Translation - triangleCollided.A;

    // If the camera faces the model, the dot
    // product between the triangle normal
    // and direction is less than 0
    float directionChecker =
        Vector3.Dot(normalTriangle, Direction);

    if (directionChecker < 0)
    {
        ForwardCollide = true;
    }
}
else
{
    ForwardCollide = false;
}
```

15. Define the `DrawModel()` method in the `CameraModelCollision` class to draw the 3D model.

```
// Draw model
public void DrawModel(Model model, Matrix world, Matrix view,
    Matrix projection)
{
    Matrix[] transforms = new Matrix[model.Bones.Count];
    model.CopyAbsoluteBoneTransformsTo(transforms);
```

```
foreach (ModelMesh mesh in model.Meshes)
{
    foreach (BasicEffect effect in mesh.Effects)
    {
        effect.PreferPerPixelLighting = true;
        effect.EnableDefaultLighting();
        effect.DiffuseColor = Color.White.ToVector3();
        effect.World = transforms[mesh.ParentBone.Index] *
            world;
        effect.View = view;
        effect.Projection = projection;
    }
    mesh.Draw();
}
}
```

16. Draw the model and instructions on the Windows Phone 7 screen. Add the code to the `Draw()` method:

```
// Draw the box model
DrawModel(modelBox, worldBox, view, projection);

// Draw the instructions
spriteBatch.Begin();
spriteBatch.DrawString(font, "1.Tap the top half of screen"
    + "for moving the camera forward\n2.Tap the bottom half"
    + "of" screen for moving the camera backward.",
    new Vector2(0, 0), Color.White);
spriteBatch.End();
```

17. Now, build and run the application. It should run as shown in the following screenshots:

How it works...

In step 3, A, B, and C represent the three corners of a triangle; you can use them to calculate the triangle edges.

In step 5, first we calculate the two edges of the triangle. Then we use the `Vector3.Cross()` method to get the normal vector and the `Vector3.Normalize()` method to normalize the normal vector to a unit length vector.

In step 6, first we get the normal of the triangle. Then, calculate the direction from the triangle corner A to the point outside the triangle. After that, we examine the return value of the `Vector3.Dot()` method between the triangle normal vector and the direction from the triangle to the outside point. If the dot product is greater than `0`, this means the two vectors are in the same direction or on the same side.

In step 7, this method goes through all of the vertices of a model and creates a triangle in every three vertices. With the triangle `t` and the given `boundingSphere`, it calls the `SphereTriangleCollision()` method to take the sphere triangle collision detection. If the result is `true`, it means the sphere triangle collision happens and the collided triangle will be returned. If not true, the method return value will be `false` and the triangle `t` will be null.

In step 8, the first line is to initialize a ray object with the original information. Then, we assign the translation of the sphere center to the `ray.Position`. After that, we use the `Triangle.InverseNormal()` method for getting the direction from the point to the current triangle. Now, the ray is ready, the next part is to take the core ray triangle collision detection using the `RayTriangleIntersects()` method. If the returned `distance` is not null, greater than zero and less than the radius of the given bounding sphere, a ray triangle collision happens. The method will return `true` to the caller.

In step 9, insert the definition of the inner `RayIntersectsTriangle()` method to the class, which we had discussed in the *Implementing ray-triangle collision detection* recipe in this chapter. Refer to the recipe for a detailed explanation.

In step 11, the `font` is responsible for showing the instructions; the `modelBox` loads the box model; `worldBox` stands for the transformation of the box model; the following four variables `cameraPosition`, `targetOffset`, `view`, and `projection` are used to initialize the camera; `boundingSphereCamera` is the bounding sphere around the camera; `verticesBox` holds the vertices of the box model; `triangleCollided` specifies the triangle when sphere-triangle collision happens; `normalTriangle` stores the normal vector of the collided triangle; `ForwardCollide` and `BackwardCollide` show that the camera is moving forward or backward; `TopHitRegion` and `BottomHitRegion` are the hit regions if you want to move the camera forward or backward.

In step 12, the camera target is `-1000` at the Z-axis for realistic viewing when you move the camera. `TopHitRegion` occupies the top half of the screen; `BottomHitRegion` takes up the bottom half of the screen.

In step 13, after loading the box model and getting its vertices, we initialize the `boundingSphereCamera` with a radius of about five units at the camera position.

In step 14, the first part is to check whether the tapped position is inside the `TopHitRegion` or `BottomHitRegion` to move the camera forward or backward. After that, we should update the position of the camera bounding sphere, as this is important for us to take the collision detection between camera bounding sphere and model triangles. In the next line, we call the `TriangleSphereCollisionDetection.IsSphereCollideWithTriangles()` method to detect the collision detection. If the returned triangle is not null, we will calculate the dot product between the camera ray direction and the normal of the collided triangle. If it is less than zero, it means the camera is moving forward, otherwise, it is moving backward.

Making a 3D ball move along a curved surface

No doubt, the real modern 3D games are much more complex; they are not a simple ball or a box with a few triangles. Thousands of polygons for games is common, millions is not unheard of. As a technique, the differences in how to do collision detection between different shape objects are not that much. You should already know the core concept or idea behind how to do it. In this recipe, you will learn the idea of dealing with collisions between models of different shapes.

How to do it...

The following steps will show you how to perform collision detection between a ball and a curved surface:

1. Create a Windows Phone Game project named `BallCollideWithCurve`, change `Game1.cs` to `BallCollideWithCurveGame.cs`. Then, add `triangle.cs` and `TriangleSphereCollisionDetection.cs` to the project. Next, add the Content Pipeline Extension Project named `MeshVerticesProcessor`, replace the `ContentProcessor1.cs` with `MeshVerticesProcessor.cs`. After that, insert the model file `ball.FBX` and `CurveSurface.FBX` to the content project.

2. Define the `MeshVerticesProcessor` in `MeshVerticesProcessor.cs` of the `MeshVerticesProcessor` project. The class definition is the same as the class in the *Implementing BoundingBox collision detection in a 3D game* recipe in this chapter. For the full explanation, please refer to that recipe.

3. Define `Triangle` in `Triangle.cs` and `TriangleSphereCollisionDetection` in `TriangleSphereCollisionDetection.cs` of the `CameraModelCollision` project. The two class definitions are the same as the classes implemented in the last *Implementing sphere-triangle collision detection* recipe in this chapter. For a full explanation, please take a look at that recipe.

4. Change the processor of `ball.FBX` and `CurveSurface.FBX` in content project, as shown in the following screenshot:

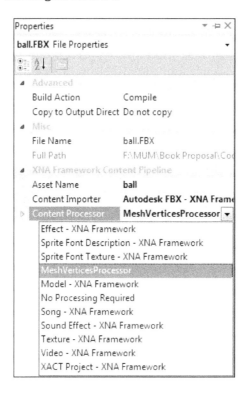

5. Now it is time to draw the ball and curve surface models on screen and take the collision detection in the main game project `BallCollideWithCurve`. First, add the following lines to the class field:

```
// Ball model and the world transformation matrix
Model modelBall;
Matrix worldBall = Matrix.Identity;

// Curve model and the world transformation matrix
Model modelSurface;
Matrix worldSurface = Matrix.Identity;

// Camera
Vector3 cameraPosition;
publicMatrix view;
publicMatrix projection;

// The bounding sphere of ball model
BoundingSphere boundingSphereBall;
```

```
// The vertices of curve model
List<Vector3>verticesCurveSurface;

// Collided triangle
Triangle CollidedTriangle;

// The velocity of ball model
Vector3 Velocity = Vector3.Zero;

// The acceleration factor
Vector3 Acceleration = newVector3(0, 0.0098f, 0);
```

6. Initialize the camera and the collided triangle. Insert the following code into the `Initialize()` method:

```
// Initialize the camera
cameraPosition = new Vector3(0, 0, 20);
view = Matrix.CreateLookAt(cameraPosition, Vector3.Zero,
    Vector3.Up);
projection = Matrix.CreatePerspectiveFieldOfView(
    MathHelper.PiOver4, GraphicsDevice.Viewport.AspectRatio,
    0.1f, 1000.0f);

// Initialize the collided triangle
CollidedTriangle = new Triangle();
```

7. Load the ball and curve surface models and extract their vertices. Then, create the bounding sphere of the ball model from the extracted vertices.

```
modelBall = Content.Load<Model>("Ball");
modelSurface = Content.Load<Model>("CurveSurface");

worldBall = Matrix.CreateTranslation(new Vector3(-2, 5, 0));

Dictionary<string, List<Vector3>> o =
    (Dictionary<string, List<Vector3>>)modelBall.Tag;
boundingSphereBall =
    BoundingSphere.CreateFromPoints(o["Sphere001"]);
boundingSphereBall.Center = worldBall.Translation;

verticesCurveSurface = ((Dictionary<string, List<Vector3>>)
    modelSurface.Tag)["Tube001"];
```

8. Take the sphere-triangle collision and update the position of the ball model and its bounding sphere. Insert the following code into the `Update()` method:

```
// Take the sphere triangle collision detection
TriangleSphereCollisionDetection.IsSphereCollideWithTriangles(
    verticesCurveSurface, boundingSphereBall,
    out CollidedTriangle);

float elapsed;

// If no collision happens, move the ball
if (CollidedTriangle == null)
{
    elapsed = (float)gameTime.ElapsedGameTime.TotalSeconds;
    Velocity += -Acceleration * elapsed;
    worldBall.Translation += Velocity;
}

// Update the translation of ball bounding sphere
boundingSphereBall.Center = worldBall.Translation;
```

9. Define the `DrawModel()` method to draw the model:

```
public void DrawModel(Model model, Matrix world, Matrix view,
    Matrix projection)
{
    Matrix[] transforms = new Matrix[model.Bones.Count];
    model.CopyAbsoluteBoneTransformsTo(transforms);

    foreach (ModelMesh mesh in model.Meshes)
    {
        foreach (BasicEffect effect in mesh.Effects)
        {
            effect.PreferPerPixelLighting = true;
            effect.EnableDefaultLighting();
            effect.DiffuseColor = Color.White.ToVector3();
            effect.World = transforms[mesh.ParentBone.Index] *
                world;
            effect.View = view;
            effect.Projection = projection;
        }
        mesh.Draw();
    }
}
```

10. Draw the ball model and curve surface ball on the Windows Phone 7 screen. Paste the following code into the `Draw()` method:

```
GraphicsDevice.DepthStencilState = DepthStencilState.Default;

// Draw the ball model and surface model
DrawModel(modelBall, worldBall, view, projection);
DrawModel(modelSurface, worldSurface, view, projection);
```

11. Now, build and run the application. The application runs as shown in the following screenshots:

How it works...

In step 5, the `modelBall` loads the ball model object; `worldBall` specifies world transformation of the ball model. Similarly, `modelSurface` for curve surface model, `worldSurface` for its world matrix; the next three variables `cameraPosition`, `view`, and `projection` serve for the camera; `boundingSphereBall` is the bounding sphere around the ball model; `verticesCurveSurface` is a vertex collection of the curve surface model; `CollidedTriangle` stores the collided triangle when the ball bounding sphere collides with the curve surface model triangles; `Velocity` specifies the ball moving velocity; `Acceleration` defines how the velocity will be changed.

In step 7, we use the `BoundingSphere.CreateFromPoints()` method to create the bounding sphere of the ball model using the vertices extracted from the `Tag` property of its model file. For `verticesCurveSurface`, we just read the vertex collection from its model file.

In step 8, the first line is to detect collision between ball bounding sphere and the triangles of the curve surface model. If the collision happens, `CollidedTriangle` is not null. At this moment, we start to move the ball. Anytime, it is required that updating the center position of the ball bounding sphere along with the ball model

8
Embedding Audio in your Game

In this chapter, we will cover:

- ▸ Controlling an audio file
- ▸ Adding sound effects to your game
- ▸ Adding stereo sounds to your game

Introduction

Do you remember the song from the Titanic movie, *My Heart Will Go On*, or the music of *Super Mario?*. A great song or piece of music will be a defining label of media products such as movies or video games. It will help the audience to easily remember and recall the special movie or game. In the modern game industry, sound designers and composers always play the key role in a game studio. They compose the music and sound effects with special style to suit the theme of designated games. In other famous examples, such as *Medal of Honor*, produced by Electronic Arts, the orchestra will be another important part of game producing. The master pieces from symphony could bring players more exceptional and spectacular playing experiences. Besides orchestra, digital music is also a key player in game music production. One of the early games, *Pac-Man*, developed by Namco, used the advanced sound mixing and synthesis technology to build the background music and sound effects. The midi sound is simple and small and could be easily stored and read in the game consoles 20 years ago. A successful and impressive piece of music or sound is a vital standard by which to evaluate a potentially successful game. Whenever you are programming a game, at the design phase, you should spend sufficient time and effort on conceiving the ideas and determining the most suitable styles for associated music and sounds. Fortunately, when developing a game on Windows Phone 7, the XNA framework prepares the essential classes and functions for you to control the audio in advance. In this chapter, we will see how to control music, how to use different sound effects in different scenarios, and how to simulate a 3D sound effect for your game. Moreover, you will experience Doppler Effect in a game, to tell how the sound works based on the distance. Having a better understanding of sound or sound effects will do you a big favor when making your own games. The effect of sounds will make your games more realistic, attractive, and fun to play with. Let's begin the journey.

Controlling an audio file

Music has the ability to impact the emotions of human beings. Different styles of music produce different feelings. Fast tempo music makes people feel nervous or excited; when the tempo becomes slow, people feel relaxed and safe. In modern video games, music often plays an important role in creating the atmosphere. Game designers and composers work together to tailor the music to the plot. When a player goes into a beautiful scene, a euphonious and harmonious song will accompany it; when immersed in a dangerous situation, the music will sound oppressive. In this recipe, you will learn how to use the media technology to control music in your Windows Phone 7 game.

Getting ready

In Windows Phone 7 XNA, a song or music is encapsulated as a `Song` class. This class provides the metadata of a song and includes the song's name, artist, album, and duration. The `Name` and `Duration` are the most direct properties for your song. We will use them in our example. As a class design consideration, the `Song` class does not have a `Play()` method to play a song. You should use the `MediaPlayer` class, which provides methods and properties for playing songs. To control song playback, we can use the following methods:

- `Play()`: The `Play()` method kicks off the song.
- `Stop()`: The `Stop()` method stops the song playing and sets the playing position to the song's beginning.
- `Pause()`: The `Pause()` method also stops the song playing, the difference between the `Pause()` and the `Stop()` method is that the `Pause()` method will not reset the playing position to the start. Instead, it keeps the playing position at the place where the song is paused.
- `Resume()`: The `Resume()` method replays the song from the paused position.

Besides these essential methods, if you have more than one song in your playing queue, the `MoveNext()` and `MovePrevious()` methods will help you to do circular playing. The two methods move to the next or previous song in the queue. They operate as if playing the queue was circular. That is, when the last song is playing the `MoveNext()` method moves to the first song and when the first song is playing the `MovePrevious()` method moves to the last song. If the `IsShuffled` property is set, the `MoveNext()` and `MovePrevious()` methods will randomly choose a song in the playing queue to play. To use these methods, there is no need to instantiate the `MediaPlayer` class, which is actually a static class. You can directly call the method using the following pattern:

```
MediaPlayer.MethodName()
```

In this example, we will play, pause, resume, and stop a song using the `MediaPlayer` and `Song` classes. Besides this, the song's name, playing state, and position will be displayed on the Windows Phone 7 screen.

How to do it...

The following steps show you how to load, play, pause, and resume a song in the Windows Phone7 XNA application:

1. Create a Windows Phone Game named `PlayMusic`, and change `Game1.cs` to `PlayMusicGame.cs`. Add the audio file `music.wma` and the sprite font file `gameFont.spritefont` to the content project.

2. Declare the indispensable variable. Add the following lines to the field of the `PlayMusicGame` class:

    ```
    // SpriteFont object for showing song information
    SpriteFont font;

    // Text presents the song playing position
    string textPlayingPosition = "";

    // Song's name
    string textSongName;

    // Playing state
    MediaState PlayingState;

    // Song object stores a song
    Song song;
    ```

3. Load the game font and the audio file. Then get the song's name and play it. Add the following code to the `LoadContent()` method:

    ```
    // Load the game font
    font = Content.Load<SpriteFont>("gameFont");

    // Load the song
    song = Content.Load<Song>("music");

    // Get the song's name
    ```

```
    textSongName = song.Name;

    // Play the song
    MediaPlayer.Play(song);
```

4. Use the `MediaPlayer` class to play, pause, resume, and stop the song. Meanwhile, update the playing state and position. Insert the following code to the `Update()` method:

```
// Get the tapped position
TouchCollection touches = TouchPanel.GetState();
if (touches.Count > 0 && touches[0].State ==
    TouchLocationState.Pressed)
{
    Point point = new Point((int)touches[0].Position.X,
        (int)touches[0].Position.Y);

    // If the tap gesture is valid
    if (GraphicsDevice.Viewport.Bounds.Contains(point))
    {
        // If the the media player is playing, pause the
        // playing song
        if (MediaPlayer.State == MediaState.Playing)
        {
            MediaPlayer.Pause();
            PlayingState = MediaState.Paused;
        }
        else if (MediaPlayer.State == MediaState.Paused)
        {
            // If the song is paused and not stopped, resume
            //it
            MediaPlayer.Resume();
            PlayingState = MediaState.Playing;
        }
        else if (MediaPlayer.State == MediaState.Stopped)
        {
            // If the song is stopped, replay it
            MediaPlayer.Play(song);
            PlayingState = MediaState.Playing;
        }
    }
}

if (MediaPlayer.State == MediaState.Playing)
{
    // If the song's playing position meets the end, stop
```

```
    // playing
    if (MediaPlayer.PlayPosition == song.Duration)
    {
        MediaPlayer.Stop();
        PlayingState = MediaState.Stopped;
    }

    // Show the song's playing position and the total duration
    textPlayingPosition = MediaPlayer.PlayPosition.ToString()
        + " / " + song.Duration.ToString();
}
```

5. Draw the song's name, playing state, and playing position on the Windows Phone 7 screen. Add the following code to the `Draw()` method:

```
spriteBatch.Begin();

// Draw the instruction text
spriteBatch.DrawString(font, "Tap Screen to Play, Pause and "
    +"Resume the Song", new Vector2(0, 0), Color.White);

// Draw the song's name
spriteBatch.DrawString(font, "Song's Name: " + textSongName,
    new Vector2(0,200 ), Color.White);

// Draw the song's playing state
spriteBatch.DrawString(font, "State: " +
    PlayingState.ToString(),
    new Vector2(0, 240), Color.White);
spriteBatch.DrawString(font, textPlayingPosition,
    new Vector2(0, 280), Color.White);

spriteBatch.End();
```

6. Now, build and run the application; it should run as shown in the following screenshot:

How it works...

In step 2, `font` will be used to show the instructions, song's name, playing state, and position; the `texPlayingPosition` stores the song's current playing position; `textSongName` saves the song's name; `PlayingState` shows the song's playing state: `Playing`, `Paused`, or `Stopped`; the song is the object of the `Song` class and will be used to process and load an audio file.

In step 4, the first part of the `Update()` method is to check whether the player taps on the Windows Phone 7 screen; if he/she does, it has three `MediaState` options for controlling the song. When the song is `Playing`, the tap gesture will pause it; if the song is `Paused`, the gesture will replay it from the paused position using the `MediaPlayer.Resume()` method; once the song's current `MediaState` is `Stopped`, we will replay the song from the beginning when a valid tap gesture takes place. The second part is about updating the song's current playing position with its total duration using the two properties of the `Song` class: `PlayPosition` and `Duration`. Besides these, when the current playing position equals the song's duration, it means the song has ended. In this example, we will replay the song once. You can change it in another way by moving to the next song.

Adding sound effects to your game

"The sound effects are artificially created or enhanced sounds or sound processes used to emphasize artistic or other content of films, television shows, live performance, animation, video game, music, or other media." – Wiki.

When you are playing games such as *Counter Strike* or *Quake*, the sound you hear while firing is the sound effect. Every weapon has its corresponding sound effect. In the early times, the sound effect came from the sound synthesis, a kind of midi rhythm. Today, the game studio can sample the sound from real instances. In making a racing game, the engine sound of every car is different. The game studio can record the sound from a real car, maybe a Lamborghini or a Panamera Turbo, to make the game more realistic. The Windows Phone 7 XNA framework simplifies the work needed to control sound effects. It is up to you to use the sound effects in your game. In this recipe, you will learn how to make your game more interesting by applying sound effects.

Getting ready

In XNA, a `SoundEffect` contains the audio data and metadata (such as wave data and loop information) loaded from a sound file. You can create multiple `SoundEffectInstance` objects, and play them from a single `SoundEffect`. These objects share the resources of that `SoundEffect`. The only limit to the number of loaded `SoundEffect` instances is memory. A loaded `SoundEffect` will continue to hold its memory resources throughout its lifetime. When a `SoundEffect` instance is destroyed, all `SoundEffectInstance` objects previously created by that `SoundEffect` will stop playing and become invalid. Unlike the

Song class, SoundEffect has a Play() method; usually, the sound effect is fast and short, plays once and then stops. If you do not want to loop a sound, the Play() method is enough. Otherwise, you should create an instance of the sound effect using the SoundEffect. CreateInstance() method. As the basic metadata, the SoundEffect class also has Name and Duration properties, and it is easy to get the name of any sound effect and its duration. The DistanceScale and DopplerScale properties will help you to simulate a realistic 3D sound effect, especially when you use the SoundEffectInstance.Apply3D() method.

For DistanceScale, if sounds are attenuating too fast, which means that the sounds get quiet too quickly as they move away from the listener, you need to increase the DistanceScale. If sounds are not attenuating fast enough, decrease the DistanceScale. This property will also affect Doppler sound.

The DopplerScale changes the relative velocities of emitters and listeners. If sounds are shifting (pitch) too much for the given relative velocity of the emitter and listener, decrease the DopplerScale. If sounds are not shifting enough for the given relative velocity of the emitter and listener, increase the DopplerScale.

In this example, we will use the SoundEffect class to play two different weapons' sounds.

How to do it...

The following steps present a complete guide for controlling a sound effect in a Windows Phone 7 XNA game using a .wav file:

1. Create a Windows Phone Game named PlaySoundEffect, and change the Game1. cs to PlaySoundEffectGame.cs. Add the audio file Laser.wav, MachineGun. wav and the sprite font file gameFont.spritefont to the project content.

2. Add the following code as the required variables to the field of PlaySoundEffectGame class:

```
// Sprite font for showing the name of current sound effect
SpriteFont font;

// Current weapon's name
string CurrentWeapon;

//  Sound effect variables
SoundEffect SoundEffectLaser;
SoundEffect soundEffectMachineGun;

//  Current Sound effect
SoundEffect soundEffectPlaying;
```

3. Enable the Hold gesture for Windows Phone 7 `TouchPanel`. Add the following line to the `Initialize()` method:

```
// Enable the hold gesture
TouchPanel.EnabledGestures = GestureType.Hold;
```

4. Load the game font, sound effects of weapons, and set the current sound effect of a weapon for playing. Paste the following code into the `LoadContent()` method:

```
// Load the font
font = Content.Load<SpriteFont>("gameFont");

// Load the sound effect of laser gun
SoundEffectLaser = Content.Load<SoundEffect>("Laser");

// Load the sound effect of machine gun
soundEffectMachineGun = Content.Load<SoundEffect>("MachineG
un");

// Set the sound effect of laser to the current sound effect
// for playing
soundEffectPlaying = SoundEffectLaser;

// Set the name of current sound effect
CurrentWeapon = "Laser";
```

5. Play the sound effect and use the Hold gesture to switch the sound effects between different weapons. Add the following code to the `Update()` method:

```
// Play the current sound effect when tap on the screen
TouchCollection touches = TouchPanel.GetState();
if (touches.Count > 0 && touches[0].State ==
    TouchLocationState.Pressed)
{
    Point point = new Point((int)touches[0].Position.X,
    (int)touches[0].Position.Y);
    if (GraphicsDevice.Viewport.Bounds.Contains(point))
    {
        if (soundEffectPlaying != null)
        {
            soundEffectPlaying.Play();
        }
    }
}

// Using Hold gesture to change the sound effect of weapons
while(TouchPanel.IsGestureAvailable)
```

```
{
    // Read the gesture
    GestureSample gestures = TouchPanel.ReadGesture();

    if (gestures.GestureType == GestureType.Hold)
    {
        // If the Hold gesture is taking place, change the
        // sound effect.
        if (soundEffectPlaying.Equals(soundEffectLaser))
        {
            soundEffectPlaying = soundEffectMachineGun;
            CurrentWeapon = "Machine Gun";
        }
        else if (soundEffectPlaying.Equals
            (soundEffectMachineGun))
        {
            soundEffectPlaying = soundEffectLaser;
            CurrentWeapon = "Laser";
        }
    }
}
```

6. Draw the instructions and the name of the current sound effect. Insert the following code to the `Draw()` method.

```
spriteBatch.Begin();

// Draw the instructions
spriteBatch.DrawString(font, "Tap and hold on for changing
your" + "weapon.\nTap for firing", new Vector2(0,0), Color.
White);

// Draw the current weapon's name
spriteBatch.DrawString(font, "Current Weapon: " +
    CurrentWeapon, new Vector2(0, 70), Color.White);
spriteBatch.End();
```

7. Build and run the application. It should run as shown in the screenshot to the left. When you tap the screen and hold it for a few seconds, the sound effect will be something similar to the screenshot on the right:

How it works...

In step 2, the `font` will be used to draw the name of the current sound effect and the controlling instructions; the `CurrentWeapon` indicates the name of the current weapon; `soundEffectLaser` and `soundEffectMachineGun`, the `SoundEffect` instances, individually represent the laser and machine gun sounds; `soundEffectPlaying` is the currently playing sound effect.

In step 3, we use the `Hold` gesture to switch the playing sound effect. It is required to enable the gesture type in `TouchPanel`.

In step 5, the first part is to check whether the user taps on the Windows Phone 7 screen. If so, then play the current sound effect if it is not null. The second part is to switch the sound effect for playing using the Hold gesture. If the on-going gesture is Hold, we will alternate the sound effects between the laser and the machine gun for playing.

Adding stereo sounds to your game

Sometimes, the music and simple sound effects are not enough for you, if you are pursuing the realistic feeling. You cannot determine the place where the sound comes from in your game world. If you have experience of playing *Counter-Strike*, it is easy to know how many enemies are near you when you stop moving, by listening to the sound. This technique is called Stereo Sound. It uses two or more independent audio channels through a symmetrical configuration of loudspeakers to create the impression of the sound heard from different directions, similar to natural hearing. For the stereo sound, Windows Phone 7 XNA simulates a sound emitter and listener, so that when the position of the emitter is changing, the listener will get a processed sound effect according to the distance between them. In this recipe, you will learn how to use the XNA framework to implement a stereo sound.

Getting ready

In this example, we will use the `SoundEffectInstance` class with its methods to simulate a 3D sound effect. `SoundEffectInstance` provides the single playing, paused, and stopped methods to control an instance of sound effect. You can create a `SoundEffectInstance` by calling the `SoundEffect.CreateInstance()` method. Initially, the `SoundEffectInstance` is created as stopped, but you can play it by calling the `SoundEffectInstance.Play()` method. The volume, panning, and pitch of `SoundEffectInstance` can be modified by setting the `Volume`, `Pitch`, and `Pan` properties. On Windows Phone 7, a game can have a maximum of 16 total playing `SoundEffectInstance` instances at one time, combined across all loaded `SoundEffect` objects. Attempts to play a `SoundEffectInstance` beyond this limit will fail.

The `SoundEffectInstance.Apply3D()` method simulates the 3D sound effect. It receives two parameters, the object of `AudioEmitter` and `AudioListener` classes. This method will calculate the 3D audio values between an `AudioEmitter` and an `AudioListener` object, and will apply the resulting values to the `SoundEffectInstance` instance. If you want to apply the 3D effect to a `SoundEffectInstance`, you must call the method before you call the `SoundEffectInstance.Play()` method. Calling this method automatically sets the Windows Phone 7 speaker mix for any sound played by this `SoundEffectInstance` to a value calculated by the difference in `Position` property values between the listener and the emitter. In preparation for the mix, the sound is converted to mono. Any stereo information in this sound is discarded.

How to do it...

The following steps give you a complete guide to implementing a stereo sound effect:

1. Create a Windows Phone Game named `PlayStereoSound` and change the `Game1.cs` to `PlayStereoSoundGame.cs`. Add the audio file `drums.wma` and the model file `BallLowPoly.fbx` to the project content.

2. Declare the essential variables to the field of the `PlayStereoSoundGame` class. Add the following code to the class:

```
// Sound effect object loads the sound effect file
SoundEffect soundEffect;

// Instance of a SoundEffect sound.
SoundEffectInstance soundEffectInstance;

// AudioEmitter and AudioListener simulate 3D audio effects
AudioEmitter emitter;
AudioListener listener;

// The world position represents the 3D position for
AudioEmitter
```

```
Vector3 objectPos;

// A ball for visually presenting the varying AudioEmitter
// world position.
Model modelBall;
Matrix worldBall = Matrix.Identity;

// Camera
Vector3 cameraPosition;
Matrix view;
Matrix projection;
```

3. Initialize the camera, the audio emitter, and the audio listener. Add the following code to the `Initialize()` method:

```
// Initialize the camera
cameraPosition = new Vector3(0, 30, 50);
view = Matrix.CreateLookAt(cameraPosition, Vector3.Zero,
    Vector3.Up);
projection = Matrix.CreatePerspectiveFieldOfView(
    MathHelper.PiOver4, GraphicsDevice.Viewport.AspectRatio,
    1.0f, 1000.0f);

// Initialize the AudioEmitter and AudioListener
emitter = new AudioEmitter();
listener = new AudioListener();
```

4. Load the ball model and the drum sound effect. Then, create the instance of the drum sound effect and apply the audio emitter to the audio listener of the instance. Finally, play the sound effect. Add the following code to the `LoadContent()` method:

```
// Load the ball model
modelBall = Content.Load<Model>("BallLowPoly");

// Load the sound effect
soundEffect = Content.Load<SoundEffect>("drums");

// Create an instance of the sound effect
soundEffectInstance = soundEffect.CreateInstance();

// Apply 3D position to the sound effect instance
soundEffectInstance.Apply3D(listener, emitter);

soundEffectInstance.IsLooped = true;

// Play the sound
```

```
soundEffectInstance.Play();
```

5. Rotate the audio emitter around the *Y axis*. Add the following lines to the `Update()` method:

```
// Rotate around axis Y
objectPos = new Vector3(
    (float)Math.Cos(gameTime.TotalGameTime.TotalSeconds) / 2,
    0,
    (float)Math.Sin(gameTime.TotalGameTime.TotalSeconds) /
    2);

// Update the position of the audio emitter
emitter.Position = objectPos;

// Apply the new position of the audio emitter to the audio
listener

soundEffectInstance.Apply3D(listener, emitter);
```

6. Define the `DrawModel()` method. Add the following code to the `PlayStereoSoundGame` class:

```
// Draw the 3D model
public void DrawModel(Model model, Matrix world, Matrix view,
Matrix projection)
{
    Matrix[] transforms = new Matrix[model.Bones.Count];
    model.CopyAbsoluteBoneTransformsTo(transforms);

    foreach (ModelMesh mesh in model.Meshes)
    {
        foreach (BasicEffect effect in mesh.Effects)
        {
            effect.EnableDefaultLighting();
            effect.World = transforms[mesh.ParentBone.Index] *
                world;
            effect.View = view;
            effect.Projection = projection;
        }
        mesh.Draw();
    }
}
```

7. Draw the ball model and rotate it around the *Y axis* to coincide with the position of the audio emitter. Add the following code to the `Draw()` method:

```
// Draw the rotating ball
DrawModel(modelBall, worldBall *
    Matrix.CreateTranslation(objectPos * 30), view,
    projection);
```

8. Build and run the application, and it should run similar to the following screenshots:

How it works...

In step 2, the `soundEffect` will be used to load the sound effect file; the `soundEffectInstance` plays and applies the 3D sound effect; `emitter` and `listener` will combine with each other to simulate the 3D audio effects; `objectPos` represents the position changes around the *Y axis*, the latest value will be used to update the position value of the `AudioEmitter` object; `modelBall` loads the ball model; `worldBall` stores the world position of a ball model in 3D; the next three variables `cameraPosition`, `view`, and `project` depict the camera.

In step 4, after loading the ball model sound effect, we create a `SoundEffectInstance` object using the `soundEffect.CreateInstance()` method. Note that it is required to call the `SoundEffectInstance.Apply3D()` method with `AudioListener` and `AudioEmitter` objects before the `Play()` method. If you do not do so, the next time you call the `Apply3D()` method, it will throw an exception.

In step 5, we compute the `objectPos` for rotating around the *Y axis*. The X value comes from the `Math.Cos()` method; the Z value comes from the `Math.Sin()`. These two factors are equal to the value of a round in the XZ plain. After that, we use the newly created `objectPos` to update the position of the `emitter` and then call the `SoundEffectInstance.Apply3D()` method to re-calculate the playing 3D sound effect in the surroundings. In step 7, for the world parameter of the `DrawModel()` method, we use the latest `objectPos` to update the translation of the ball model in the 3D world. This will make the ball rotate around the *Y axis* along with the position of the sound effect emitter.

9
Special Effects

In this chapter, we will cover:

- ▶ Using dual texture effects
- ▶ Using environment map effects
- ▶ Rendering different parts of a character into textures using RenderTarget2D
- ▶ Creating a screen transition effect using RenderTarget2D

Introduction

Special effects in computer graphics is fascinating. A lot of Hollywood movies use special effects, and *Avatar* is the flagship. In this movie, the Pandora planet, the blue-skinned Na'vi, the smoke, fog, and the dreamlike world surrounded by the lighting sprites are produced from modeling software with special effects. It is not only used in movies, as modern video games also benefit from these special effect techniques. *Crysis 2*, from EA, integrates dozens of latest special effects to the game engine. The explosion particle system, the water simulation, the volume cloud, the normal mapping, the environment mapping, and so on, help the game to provide distinguished and leading visual experience to players. Everybody will be surprised by what they see in the game. In Windows Phone 7, due to the hardware, writing your own shader code for special effects is not supported. As a consideration of the needs of special effects in Windows Phone 7 games, the XNA team has developed some typical built-in effects. In this chapter, you will learn how to use two new built-in effects, `DualTextureEffect` and `EnvironmentMapEffect`.

The `DualTextureEffect` uses two textures. The recipe on the effect will tell you how to apply a second lightmap texture generated from modeling software 3DS MAX onto the mapped original texture on a model to simulate lighting effect without any computing on 3D normal vectors. The detailed steps for building the lightmap in 3DS MAX are listed. Next, the recipe on using `EnvironmentMapEffect` will present you with the technique to create the `Cubemap` and how to work with this effect using the `Cubemap`. The last two recipes are both on the topic of `RenderTarget2D`. These two will give you full explanations on showing the different parts of a model in 2D and the core thought of screen transitions.

Using dual texture effects

Dual texture is very useful when you want to map two textures onto a model. The Windows Phone 7 XNA built-in `DualTextureEffect` samples the pixel color from two texture images. That is why it is called dual texture. The textures used in the effect have their own texture coordinate and can be mapped individually, tiled, rotated, and so on. The texture is mixed using the pattern:

```
finalTexture.color = texture1.Color * texture2.Color;
finalTexture.alpha = texture1.Alpha * texture2.Alpha;
```

The `color` and `alpha` of the final texture come from a separate computation. The best practice of `DualTextureEffect` is to apply the lightmap on the model. In computer graphics, computing the lighting and shadows is a big performance job in real time. The lightmap texture is pre-computed and stored individually. A lightmap is a data set comprising the different surfaces of a 3D model. This will save the performance cost on lighting computation. Sometimes, you might want to use the ambient occlusion effect, which is costly. At this point, lightmap can be used as a texture, then mapped to the special model or scene for realistic effect. As the lightmap is pre-computed in 3D modeling software (you will learn how to deal with this in 3DS MAX), it is easy for you to use the most complicated lighting effects (shadows, ray-tracing, radiosity, and so on.) in Windows Phone 7. You can use the dual texture effect if you just want the game scene to have shadows and lighting. In this recipe, you will learn how to create the lightmap and apply it on your game model using the `DualTextureEffect`.

How to do it...

The following steps show you the process for creating the lightmap in 3DS MAX and how to use the lightmap in your Windows Phone 7 game using `DualTextureEffect`:

1. Create the Sphere lightmap in 3DS MAX 2011. Open 3DS MAX 2011, in the **Create** panel, click the **Geometry** button, then create a sphere by choosing the **Sphere** push button, as shown in the following screenshot:

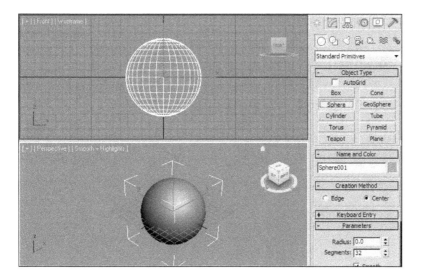

2. Add the texture to the **Material Compact Editor** and apply the material to the sphere. Click the following menu items of 3DS MAX 2011: **Rendering | Material Editor | Compact Material Editor**. Choose the first material ball and apply the texture you want to the material ball. Here, we use the **tile1.png**, a checker image, which you can find in the `Content` directory of the `example` bundle file. The applied material ball looks similar to the following screenshot:

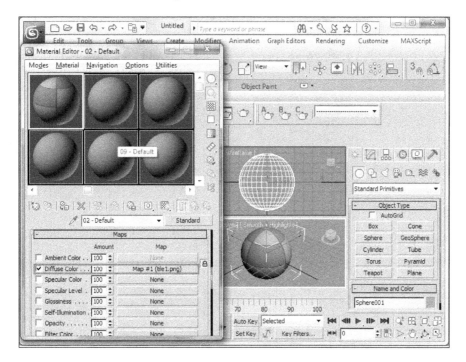

3. Apply the Target Direct Light to the sphere. In the **Create** panel—the same panel for creating sphere—click the **Lights** button and choose the **Target Direct** option. Then drag your mouse over the sphere in the **Perspective** viewport and adjust the **Hotspot/Beam** to let the light encompass the sphere, as shown in the following screenshot:

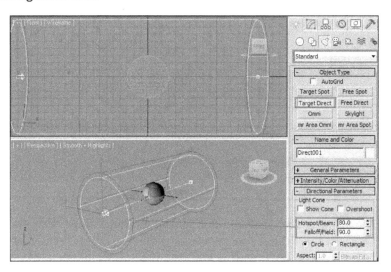

4. Render the Lightmap. When the light is set as you want, the next step is to create the lightmap. After you click the sphere that you plan to build the lightmap for, click the following menu items in 3DS MAX: **Rendering | Render To Texture**. In the **Output** panel of the pop-up window, click the **Add** button. Another pop-up window will show up; choose the **LightingMap** option, and then click **Add Elements**, as shown in the following screenshot:

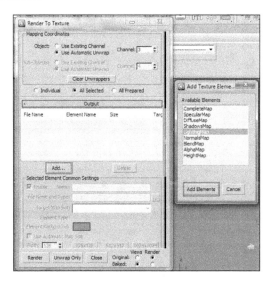

5. After that, change the setting of the lightmap:

  ❑ Change the **Target Map Slot** to **Self-Illumination** in the **Output** panel.

  ❑ Change the **Baked Material Settings** to **Output Into Source** in the **Baked Material** panel.

  ❑ Change the **Channel** to **2** in the **Mapping Coordinates** panel.

  ❑ Finally, click the **Render** button. The generated lightmap will look similar to the following screenshot:

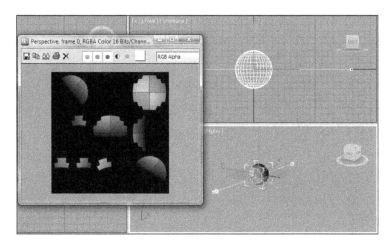

By default, the lightmap texture type is .tga, and the maps are placed in the \images subfolder of the folder where you installed 3DS MAX. The new textures are flat. In other words, they are organized according to groups of object faces. In this example, the lightmap name is Sphere001LightingMap.tga.

6. Open the **Material Compact Editor** again by clicking the menu items **Rendering | Material Editor | Compact Material Editor**. You will find that the first material ball has a mixed texture combined with the original texture and the lightmap. You can also see that **Self-Illumination** is selected and the value is **Sphere001LightingMap. tga**. This means the lightmap for the sphere is applied successfully.

7. Select the sphere and export to an FBX model file named DualTextureBall.FBX, which will be used in our Windows Phone 7 game.

8. From this step, we will render the lightmap of the sphere in our Windows Phone 7 XNA game using the new built-in effect DualTextureEffect. Now, create a Windows Phone Game project named DualTextureEffectBall in Visual Studio 2010 and change Game1.cs to DualTextureEffectBallGame.cs. Then, add the texture file tile1.png, the lightmap file Sphere001LightingMap.tga, and the model DualTextureBall.FBX to the content project.

9. Declare the indispensable variables in the `DualTextureEffectBallGame` class. Add the following code to the `class` field:

```
// Ball Model
Model modelBall;

// Dual Texture Effect
DualTextureEffect dualTextureEffect;

// Camera
Vector3 cameraPosition;
Matrix view;
Matrix projection;
```

10. Initialize the camera. Insert the following code to the `Initialize()` method:

```
// Initialize the camera
cameraPosition = new Vector3(0, 50, 200);
view = Matrix.CreateLookAt(cameraPosition, Vector3.Zero,
    Vector3.Up);
projection = Matrix.CreatePerspectiveFieldOfView(
    MathHelper.PiOver4,
    GraphicsDevice.Viewport.AspectRatio,
    1.0f, 1000.0f);
```

11. Load the ball model and initialize the `DualTextureEffect`. Paste the following code to the `LoadContent()` method:

```
// Load the ball model
modelBall = Content.Load<Model>("DualTextureBall");

// Initialize the DualTextureEffect
dualTextureEffect = new DualTextureEffect(GraphicsDevice);
dualTextureEffect.Projection = projection;
dualTextureEffect.View = view;

// Set the diffuse color
dualTextureEffect.DiffuseColor = Color.Gray.ToVector3();

// Set the first and second texture
dualTextureEffect.Texture =
    Content.Load<Texture2D>("tile1");
dualTextureEffect.Texture2 =
    Content.Load<Texture2D>("Sphere001LightingMap");

Define the DrawModel() method in the class:
// Draw model
private void DrawModel(Model m, Matrix world,
```

```
        DualTextureEffect effect)
    {
        foreach (ModelMesh mesh in m.Meshes)
        {
            // Iterate every part of current mesh
            foreach (ModelMeshPart meshPart in mesh.MeshParts)
            {
                // Change the original effect to the designed
                // effect
                meshPart.Effect = effect;

                // Update the world matrix
                effect.World *= world;
            }
            mesh.Draw();
        }
    }
```

12. Draw the ball model using `DualTextureEffect` on the Windows Phone 7 screen. Add the following lines to the `Draw()` method:

```
// Rotate the ball model around axis Y.
float timer =
    (float)gameTime.ElapsedGameTime.TotalSeconds;

DrawModel(modelBall, Matrix.CreateRotationY(timer),
    dualTextureEffect);
```

13. Build and run the example. It should run as shown in the following screenshot:

14. If you comment the following line in `LoadContent()` to disable the lightmap texture, you will find the difference when lightmap is on or off:

```
dualTextureEffect.Texture2 =
    Content.Load<Texture2D>("Sphere001LightingMap");
```

15. Run the application without lightmap. The model will be in pure black as shown in the following screenshot:

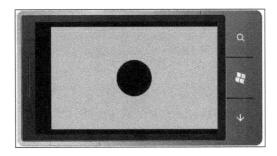

How it works...

Steps 1–6 are to create the sphere and its lightmap in 3DS MAX 2011.

In step 8, the `modelBall` is responsible for loading and holding the ball model. The `dualTextureEffect` is the object of XNA 4.0 built-in effect `DualTextureEffect` for rendering the ball model with its original texture and the lightmap. The following three variables `cameraPosition`, `view`, and `projection` represent the camera.

In step 10, the first line is to load the ball model. The rest of the lines initialize the `DualTextureEffect`. Notice, we use the `tile1.png` for the first and original texture, and the `Sphere001LightingMap.tga` for the lightmap as the second texture.

In step 11, the `DrawModel()` method is different from the definition in previous chapters. Here, we need to replace the original effect of each mesh with the `DualTextureEffect`. When we iterate the mesh parts of every mesh of the current model, we assign the `effect` to the `meshPart.Effect` for applying the `DualTextureEffect` to the mesh part.

Using environment map effects

In computer games, environment mapping is an efficient image-based lighting technique for aligning the reflective surface with the distant environment surrounding the rendered object. In *Need for Speed*, produced by Electronic Arts, if you open the special visual effect option while playing the game, you will find the car body reflects the scene around it, which may be trees, clouds, mountains, or buildings. They are amazing and attractive. This is environment mapping, it makes games more realistic. The methods for storing the surrounding environment include sphere mapping and cube mapping, pyramid mapping, and the octahedron mapping. In XNA 4.0, the framework uses cube mapping, in which the environment is projected onto the six faces of a cube and stored as six square textures unfolded into six square regions of a single texture. In this recipe, you will learn how to make a cubemap using the DirectX texture tool, and apply the cube map on a model using `EnvironmentMappingEffect`.

Getting ready

Cubemap is used in real-time engines to fake refractions. It's way faster than ray-tracing because they are only textures mapped as a cube. So that's six images (one for each face of the cube).

For creating the cube map for the environment map effect, you should use the **DirectX Texture Tool** in the `DirectX SDK Utilities` folder. The latest version of Microsoft DirectX SDK can be downloaded from the URL `http://www.microsoft.com/downloads/en/details.aspx?FamilyID=3021d52b-514e-41d3-ad02-438a3ba730ba`.

How to do it...

The following steps lead you to create an application using the Environment Mapping effect:

1. From this step, we will create the cube map in DirectX Texture Tool. Run this application and create a new Cube Map. Click the following menu items: **File | New Texture**. A window will pop-up; in this window, choose the **Cubemap Texture** for **Texture Type**; change the dimension to 512 * 512 in the **Dimensions** panel; set the **Surface/Volume Format** to **Four CC 4-bit: DXT1**. The final settings should look similar to the following screenshot:

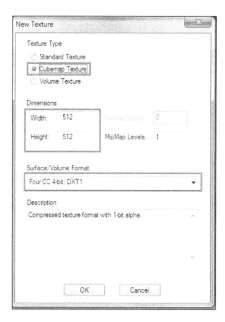

2. Set the texture of every face of the cube. Choose a face for setting the texture by clicking the following menu items: **View | Cube Map Face | Positive X**, as shown in the following screenshot:

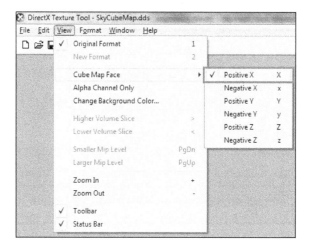

3. Then, apply the image for the Positive X face by clicking: **File | Open Onto This Cubemap Face**, as shown in the following screenshot:

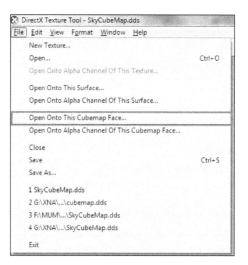

4. When you click the item, a pop-up dialog will ask you to choose a proper image for this face. In this example, the Positive X face will look similar to the following screenshot:

5. It is similar for the other five faces, **Negative X**, **Positive Y**, **Negative Y**, **Positive Z**, and **Negative Z**. When all of the cube faces are appropriately set, we save cubemap as `SkyCubeMap.dds`. The cube map will look similar to the following figure:

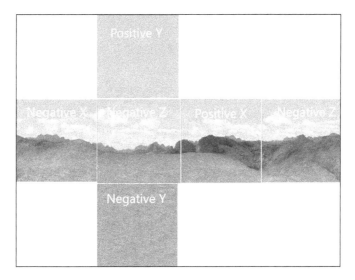

6. From this step, we will start to render the ball model using the XNA 4.0 built-in effect called `EnvironmentMapEffect`. Create a Windows Phone Game project named `EnvironmentMapEffectBall` in Visual Studio 2010 and change `Game1.cs` to `EnvironmentMapEffectBallGame.cs`. Then, add the ball model file `ball.FBX`, ball texture file `silver.jpg`, and the generated cube map from DirectX Texture Tool `SkyCubemap.dds` to the content project.

7. Declare the necessary variables of the `EnvironmentMapEffectBallGame` class. Add the following lines to the class:

```
// Ball model
Model modelBall;

// Environment Map Effect
EnvironmentMapEffect environmentEffect;

// Cube map texture
TextureCube textureCube;

// Ball texture
Texture2D texture;

// Camera
Vector3 cameraPosition;
Matrix view;
Matrix projection;
```

8. Initialize the camera. Insert the following lines to the `Initialize()` method:

```
// Initialize the camera
cameraPosition = new Vector3(2, 3, 32);
view = Matrix.CreateLookAt(cameraPosition, Vector3.Zero,
    Vector3.Up);
projection = Matrix.CreatePerspectiveFieldOfView(
    MathHelper.PiOver4,
    GraphicsDevice.Viewport.AspectRatio,
    1.0f, 100.0f);
```

9. Load the ball model, ball texture, and the sky cube map. Then initialize the environment map effect and set its properties. Paste the following code in the `LoadContent()` method:

```
// Load the ball model
modelBall = Content.Load<Model>("ball");

// Load the sky cube map
textureCube = Content.Load<TextureCube>("SkyCubeMap");
```

```
// Load the ball texture
texture = Content.Load<Texture2D>("Silver");

// Initialize the EnvironmentMapEffect
environmentEffect = new EnvironmentMapEffect(GraphicsDevice);
environmentEffect.Projection = projection;
environmentEffect.View = view;

// Set the initial texture
environmentEffect.Texture = texture;

// Set the environment map
environmentEffect.EnvironmentMap = textureCube;

environmentEffect.EnableDefaultLighting();

// Set the environment effect factors
environmentEffect.EnvironmentMapAmount = 1.0f;
environmentEffect.FresnelFactor = 1.0f;
environmentEffect.EnvironmentMapSpecular = Vector3.Zero;
```

10. Define the `DrawModel()` of the class:

```
// Draw Model
private void DrawModel(Model m, Matrix world,
EnvironmentMapEffect environmentMapEffect)
{
    foreach (ModelMesh mesh in m.Meshes)
    {
        foreach (ModelMeshPart meshPart in mesh.MeshParts)
        {
            meshPart.Effect = environmentMapEffect;
            environmentMapEffect.World = world;
        }
        mesh.Draw();
    }
}
```

11. Draw and rotate the ball with `EnvironmentMapEffect` on the Windows Phone 7 screen. Insert the following code to the `Draw()` method:

```
// Draw and rotate the ball model
float time = (float)gameTime.TotalGameTime.TotalSeconds;
DrawModel(modelBall, Matrix.CreateRotationY(time * 0.3f) *
    Matrix.CreateRotationX(time), environmentEffect);
```

12. Build and run the application. It should run similar to the following screenshot:

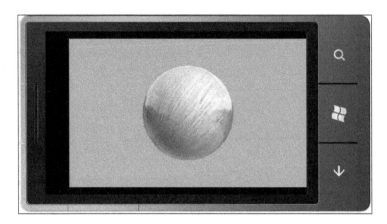

How it works...

Steps 1 and 2 use the DirectX Texture Tool to generate a sky cube map for the XNA 4.0 built-in effect `EnvironmentMapEffect`.

In step 4, the `modelBall` loads the ball model, `environmentEffect` will be used to render the ball model in `EnvironmentMapEffect`, and `textureCube` is a cube map texture. The `EnvironmentMapEffect` will receive the texture as an `EnvironmentMap` property; texture represents the ball texture; the last three variables `cameraPosition`, `view`, and `projection` are responsible for initializing and controlling the camera.

In step 6, the first three lines are used to load the required contents including the ball model, texture, and the sky cube map. Then, we instantiate the object of `EnvironmentMapEffect` and set its properties. `environmentEffect.Projection` and `environmentEffect. View` are for the camera; `environmentEffect.Texture` is for mapping ball texture onto the ball model; `environmentEffect.EnvironmentMap` is the environment map from which the ball model will get the reflected color and mix it with its original texture.

The `EnvironmentMapAmount` is a float that describes how much of the environment map could show up, which also means how much of the cube map texture will blend over the texture on the model. The values range from 0 to 1 and the default value is 1.

The `FresnelFactor` makes the environment map visible independent of the viewing angle. Use a higher value to make the environment map visible around the edges; use a lower value to make the environment map visible everywhere. Fresnel lighting only affects the environment map color (RGB values); alpha is not affected. The value ranges from 0.0 to 1.0. 0.0 is used to disable the Fresnel Lighting. 1.0 is the default value.

The EnvironmentMapSpecular implements cheap specular lighting, by encoding one or more specular highlight patterns into the environment map alpha channel, then setting the EnvironmentMapSpecular to the desired specular light color.

In step 7, we replace the default effect of every mesh part of the model meshes with the EnvironmentMapEffect, and draw the mesh with replaced effect.

Rendering different parts of a character into textures using RenderTarget2D

Sometimes, you want to see a special part of a model or an image, and you also want to see the original view of them at the same time. This is where, the render target will help you. From the definition of render target in DirectX, a render target is a buffer where the video card draws pixels for a scene that is being rendered by an effect class. In Windows Phone 7, the independent video card is not supported. The device has an embedded processing unit for graphic rendering. The major application of render target in Windows Phone 7 is to render the viewing scene, which is in 2D or 3D, into 2D texture. You can manipulate the texture for special effects such as transition, partly showing, or something similar. In this recipe, you will discover how to render different parts of a model into texture and then draw them on the Windows Phone 7 screen.

Getting ready

Render target, by default, is called the back buffer. This is the part of the video memory that contains the next frame to be drawn. You can create other render targets with the RenderTarget2D class, reserving new regions of video memory for drawing. Most games render a lot of content to other render targets besides the back buffer (offscreen), then assemble the different graphical elements in stages, combining them to create the final product in the back buffer.

A render target has a width and height. The width and height of the back buffer are the final resolution of your game. An offscreen render target does not need to have the same width and height as the back buffer. Small parts of the final image can be rendered in small render targets, and copied to another render target later. To use a render target, create a RenderTarget2D object with the width, height, and other options you prefer. Then, call GraphicsDevice.SetRenderTarget to make your render target the current render target. From this point on, any Draw calls you make will draw into your render target because the RenderTarget2D is the subclass of Texture2D. When you are finished with the render target, call GraphicsDevice.SetRenderTarget to a new render target (or null for the back buffer).

How to do it...

In the following steps, you will learn how to use `RenderTarget2D` to render different parts of a designated model into textures and present them on the Windows Phone 7 screen:

1. Create a Windows Phone Game project named `RenderTargetCharacter` in Visual Studio 2010 and change `Game1.cs` to `RenderTargetCharacterGame.cs`. Then, add the character model file `character.FBX` and the character texture file `Blaze.tga` to the content project.

2. Declare the required variables in the `RenderTargetCharacterGame` class field. Add the following lines of code to the `class` field:

    ```
    // Character model
    Model modelCharacter;

    // Character model world position
    Matrix worldCharacter = Matrix.Identity;

    // Camera
    Vector3 cameraPosition;
    Vector3 cameraTarget;
    Matrix view;
    Matrix projection;

    // RenderTarget2D objects for rendering the head, left //fist,
    and right foot of character
    RenderTarget2D renderTarget2DHead;
    RenderTarget2D renderTarget2DLeftFist;
    RenderTarget2D renderTarget2DRightFoot;
    ```

3. Initialize the camera and render targets. Insert the following code to the `Initialize()` method:

    ```
    // Initialize the camera
    cameraPosition = new Vector3(0, 40, 350);
    cameraTarget = new Vector3(0, 0, 1000);
    view = Matrix.CreateLookAt(cameraPosition, Vector3.Zero,
        Vector3.Up);

    projection = Matrix.CreatePerspectiveFieldOfView(
        MathHelper.PiOver4,
        GraphicsDevice.Viewport.AspectRatio,
        0.1f, 1000.0f);

    // Initialize the RenderTarget2D objects with different sizes
    renderTarget2DHead = new RenderTarget2D(GraphicsDevice,
    ```

```
        196, 118, false, SurfaceFormat.Color,
    DepthFormat.Depth24, 0,
    RenderTargetUsage.DiscardContents);

renderTarget2DLeftFist = new RenderTarget2D(GraphicsDevice,
    100, 60, false, SurfaceFormat.Color,
    DepthFormat.Depth24,
    0, RenderTargetUsage.DiscardContents);

renderTarget2DRightFoot = new
    RenderTarget2D(GraphicsDevice, 100, 60, false,
    SurfaceFormat.Color, DepthFormat.Depth24, 0,
    RenderTargetUsage.DiscardContents);
```

4. Load the character model and insert the following line of code to the
    `LoadContent()` method:

    ```
    modelCharacter = Content.Load<Model>("Character");
    ```

5. Define the `DrawModel()` method:

    ```
    // Draw the model on screen
    public void DrawModel(Model model, Matrix world, Matrix view,
    Matrix projection)
    {
        Matrix[] transforms = new Matrix[model.Bones.Count];
        model.CopyAbsoluteBoneTransformsTo(transforms);

        foreach (ModelMesh mesh in model.Meshes)
        {
            foreach (BasicEffect effect in mesh.Effects)
            {
                effect.EnableDefaultLighting();
                effect.DiffuseColor = Color.White.ToVector3();
                effect.World =
                    transforms[mesh.ParentBone.Index] * world;
                effect.View = view;
                effect.Projection = projection;
            }
            mesh.Draw();
        }
    }
    ```

6. Get the `rendertargets` of the right foot, left fist, and head of the character. Then draw the `rendertarget` textures onto the Windows Phone 7 screen. Insert the following code to the `Draw()` method:

```
// Get the rendertarget of character head
GraphicsDevice.SetRenderTarget(renderTarget2DHead);

GraphicsDevice.Clear(Color.Blue);
cameraPosition = new Vector3(0, 110, 60);
cameraTarget = new Vector3(0, 110, -1000);
view = Matrix.CreateLookAt(cameraPosition, cameraTarget,
    Vector3.Up);
DrawModel(modelCharacter, worldCharacter, view,
    projection);

GraphicsDevice.SetRenderTarget(null);

// Get the rendertarget of character left fist
GraphicsDevice.SetRenderTarget(renderTarget2DLeftFist);

GraphicsDevice.Clear(Color.Blue);
cameraPosition = new Vector3(-35, -5, 40);
cameraTarget = new Vector3(0, 5, -1000);
view = Matrix.CreateLookAt(cameraPosition, cameraTarget,
    Vector3.Up);
DrawModel(modelCharacter, worldCharacter, view,
    projection);

GraphicsDevice.SetRenderTarget(null);

// Get the rendertarget of character right foot
GraphicsDevice.SetRenderTarget(renderTarget2DRightFoot);

GraphicsDevice.Clear(Color.Blue);
cameraPosition = new Vector3(20, -120, 40);
cameraTarget = new Vector3(0, -120, -1000);
view = Matrix.CreateLookAt(cameraPosition, cameraTarget,
    Vector3.Up);
DrawModel(modelCharacter, worldCharacter, view,
    projection);

GraphicsDevice.SetRenderTarget(null);

// Draw the character model
cameraPosition = new Vector3(0, 40, 350);
```

```
view = Matrix.CreateLookAt(cameraPosition, Vector3.Zero,
    Vector3.Up);
GraphicsDevice.Clear(Color.CornflowerBlue);
DrawModel(modelCharacter, worldCharacter, view,
    projection);

// Draw the generated rendertargets of different parts of
// character model in 2D
spriteBatch.Begin();
spriteBatch.Draw(renderTarget2DHead, new Vector2(500, 0),
    Color.White);
spriteBatch.Draw(renderTarget2DLeftFist, new Vector2(200,
    220),
    Color.White);
spriteBatch.Draw(renderTarget2DRightFoot, new Vector2(500,
    400),
    Color.White);

spriteBatch.End();
```

7. Build and run the application. The application will run as shown in the following screenshot:

How it works...

In step 2, the `modelCharacter` loads the character 3D model and the `worldCharacter` represents the world transformation matrix of the character. The following four variables `cameraPosition`, `cameraTarget`, `view`, and `projection` are used to initialize the camera. Here, the `cameraTarget` will have the same *Y* value as the `cameraPosition` and large enough *Z* value, which is far away behind the center, because we want the camera's look-at direction to be parallel to the *XZ* plane. The last three `RenderTarget2D` objects, `renderTarget2DHead`, `renderTarget2DLeftFist`, and `renderTarget2DRightFoot`, are responsible for rendering the different parts of the character from 3D real-time view to 2D texture.

In step 3, we initialize the camera and the three render targets. The initialization code for the camera is nothing new. The `RenderTarget2D` has three overloaded constructers, and the most complex one is the third. If you understand the third, the other two are easy. This constructor looks similar to the following code:

```
public RenderTarget2D (
    GraphicsDevice graphicsDevice,
    int width,
    int height,
    bool mipMap,
    SurfaceFormat preferredFormat,
    DepthFormat preferredDepthFormat,
    int preferredMultiSampleCount,
    RenderTargetUsage usage
)
```

Let's have a look at what all these parameters stand for:

- `graphicsDevice`: This is the graphic device associated with the render target resource.

- `width`: This is an integer, in pixels, of the render target. You can use `graphicsDevice.PresentationParameters.BackBufferWidth` to get the current screen width. Because the `RenderTarget2D` is a subclass of `Texture2D`, the value for width and height of `RenderTarget2D` objects are used to define the size of the final `RenderTarget2D` texture. Notice, the maximum size for `Texture2D` in Windows Phone 7 is less than 2048, so the width value of `RenderTarget2D` cannot be beyond this limitation.

- `height`: This is an integer, in pixels, of the render target. You can use `graphicsDevice.PresentationParameters.BackBufferHeight` to get the current screen height. The additional information is similar to the `width` parameter.

- `mipMap`: This is true to enable a full mipMap chain to be generated, otherwise false.

- `preferredFormat`: This is the preferred format for the surface data. This is the format preferred by the application, which may or may not be available from the hardware. In the XNA Framework, all two-dimensional (2D) images are represented by a range of memory called a surface. Within a surface, each element holds a color value representing a small section of the image, called a pixel. An image's detail level is defined by the number of pixels needed to represent the image and the number of bits needed for the image's color spectrum. For example, an image that is 800 pixels wide and 600 pixels high with 32 bits of color for each pixel (written as 800 x 600 x 32) is more detailed than an image that is 640 pixels wide and 480 pixels tall with 16 bits of color for each pixel (written as 640 x 480 x 16). Likewise, the more detailed image requires a larger surface to store the data. For an 800 x 600 x 32 image, the surface's array dimensions are 800 x 600, and each element holds a 32-bit value to represent its color.

All formats are listed from left to right, most-significant bit to least-significant bit. For example, ARGB formats are ordered from the most-significant bit channel A (alpha), to the least-significant bit channel B (blue). When traversing surface data, the data is stored in memory from least-significant bit to most-significant bit, which means that the channel order in memory is from least-significant bit (blue) to most-significant bit (alpha).

The default value for formats that contain undefined channels (Rg32, Alpha8, and so on) is 1. The only exception is the Alpha8 format, which is initialized to 000 for the three color channels. Here, we use the `SurfaceFormat.Color` option. The `SurfaceFormat.Color` is an unsigned format, 32-bit ARGB pixel format with alpha, using 8 bits per channel.

▶ `preferredDepthFormat`: This is a depth buffer containing depth data and possibly stencil data. You can control a depth buffer using a `state` object. The depth format includes `Depth16`, `Depth24`, and `Depth24 Stencil`.

▶ `usage`: This is the object of `RenderTargetUsage`. It determines how render target data is used once a new target is set. This enumeration has three values: `PreserveContents`, `PlatformContents`, and `DiscardContents`. The default value `DiscardContents` means whenever a `rendertarget` is set onto the device, the previous one will be destroyed first. On the other hand, when you choose the `PreserveContents` option, the data associated with the render target will be maintained if a new `rendertarget` is set. This method will impact the performance greatly because it stores data and copies it all back to `rendertarget` when you use it again. The `PlatformContents` will either clear or keep the data, depending on the current platform. On Xbox 360 and Windows Phone 7, the render target will discard contents. On PC, the render target will discard the contents if multi-sampling is enabled, and preserve the contents if not.

In step 6, the first part of the `Draw()` method gets the render target texture for the head of the character, the `GraphicDevice.SetRenderTarget()` sets a new render target for this device. As the application runs on Windows Phone 7 and the `RenderTargetUsage` is set to `DiscardContents`, every time a new render target is assigned onto the device, the previous one will be destroyed. From XNA 4.0 SDK, the method has some restrictions while calling. They are as follows:

▶ The multi-sample type must be the same for the render target and the depth stencil surface

▶ The formats must be compatible for the render target and the depth stencil surface

▶ The size of the depth stencil surface must be greater than, or equal to, the size of the render target

These restrictions are validated only while using the debug runtime when any of the `GraphicsDevice` drawing methods are called. Then, the following lines until the `GraphicsDevice.SetRenderTarget(null)` are used to adjust the camera position and the look-at target for rendering the head of the character. The block of code points out the view for transforming and rendering the model from 3D to 2D texture as render target, which will be displayed at the designated place on the Windows Phone screen. The method calling of `GraphicsDevice.SetRenderTarget(null)` will reset the render target currently on the graphics device for the next render target using it. It is similar to `renderTarget2DRightFoot` and `renderTarget2DLeftFist` in the second and third part of the `Draw()` method. The fourth part is to draw the actual character 3D model. After that, we will present all of the generated render targets on the Windows Phone 7 screen using the 2D drawing methods.

Creating a screen transition effect using RenderTarget2D

Do you remember the scene transition in *Star Wars*? The scene transition is a very common method for smoothly changing the movie scene from current to next. The frequent transition patterns are Swiping, Rotating, Fading, Checkerboard Scattering, and so on. With the proper transition effects, the audience will know that the plots go well when the stage changes. Besides movies, the transition effects also have a relevant application in video games, especially in 2D games. Every game state change will trigger a transition effect.
In this recipe, you will learn how to create a typical transition effect using `RenderTarget2D` for your Windows Phone 7 game.

How to do it...

The following steps will draw a spinning squares transition effect using the `RenderTarget2D` technique:

1. Create a Windows Phone Game named `RenderTargetTransitionEffect` and change `Game1.cs` to `RenderTargetTransitionEffectGame.cs`. Then, add `Image1.png` and `Image2.png` to the content project.

2. Declare the indispensable variables. Insert the following code to the `RenderTargetTransitionEffectGame` code field:

```
// The first forefront and background images
Texture2D textureForeFront;
Texture2D textureBackground;

// the width of each divided image
int xfactor = 800 / 8;

// the height of each divided image
int yfactor = 480 / 8;
```

```
// The render target for the transition effect
RenderTarget2D transitionRenderTarget;

float alpha = 1;

// the time counter
float timer = 0;

const float TransitionSpeed = 1.5f;
```

3. Load the forefront and background images, and initialize the render target for the jumping sprites transition effect. Add the following code to the `LoadContent()` method:

```
// Load the forefront and the background image
textureForeFront = Content.Load<Texture2D>("Image1");
textureBackground = Content.Load<Texture2D>("Image2");

// Initialize the render target
transitionRenderTarget = new RenderTarget2D(GraphicsDevice,
    800, 480, false, SurfaceFormat.Color,
    DepthFormat.Depth24, 0,
    RenderTargetUsage.DiscardContents);
```

4. Define the core method `DrawJumpingSpritesTransition()` for the jumping sprites transition effect. Paste the following lines into the `RenderTargetTransitionEffectGame` class:

```
void DrawJumpingSpritesTransition(float delta, float alpha,
    RenderTarget2D renderTarget)
{
    // Instance a new random object for generating random
    //values to change the rotation, scale and position
    //values of each sub divided images
    Random random = new Random();

    // Divide the image into designated pieces,
    //here 8 * 8 =    64
    // ones.
    for (int x = 0; x < 8; x++)
    {
        for (int y = 0; y < 8; y++)
        {
            // Define the size of each piece
            Rectangle rect = new Rectangle(xfactor * x,
                yfactor * y, xfactor, yfactor);
```

```
        // Define the origin center for rotation and
        //scale of the current subimage
        Vector2 origin =
        new Vector2(rect.Width, rect.Height) / 2;

        float rotation =
            (float)(random.NextDouble() - 0.5f) *
            delta * 20;

        float scale = 1 +
            (float)(random.NextDouble() - 0.5f) *
            delta * 20;

        // Randomly change the position of current
        //divided subimage
        Vector2 pos =
            new Vector2(rect.Center.X, rect.Center.Y);

        pos.X += (float)(random.NextDouble()) ;
        pos.Y += (float)(random.NextDouble()) ;

        // Draw the current sub image
        spriteBatch.Draw(renderTarget, pos, rect,
          Color.White * alpha, rotation, origin,
          scale, 0, 0);
    }
  }
}
```

5. Get the render target of the forefront image and draw the jumping sprites transition effect by calling the `DrawJumpingSpritesTransition()` method. Insert the following code to the `Draw()` method:

```
// Render the forefront image to render target texture
GraphicsDevice.SetRenderTarget(transitionRenderTarget);

spriteBatch.Begin();
spriteBatch.Draw(textureForeFront, new Vector2(0, 0),
    Color.White);
spriteBatch.End();

GraphicsDevice.SetRenderTarget(null);

// Get the total elapsed game time
timer += (float)(gameTime.ElapsedGameTime.TotalSeconds);
```

```
// Compute the delta value in every frame
float delta = timer / TransitionSpeed * 0.01f;

// Minus the alpha to change the image from opaque to
//transparent using the delta value
alpha -= delta;

// Draw the jumping sprites transition effect
spriteBatch.Begin();
spriteBatch.Draw(textureBackground, Vector2.Zero,
    Color.White);
DrawJumpingSpritesTransition(delta, alpha,
    transitionRenderTarget);
spriteBatch.End();
```

6. Build and run the application. It should run similar to the following screenshots:

How it works...

In step 2, the `textureForeFront` and `textureBackground` will load the forefront and background images prepared for the jumping sprites transition effect. The `xfactor` and `yfactor` define the size of each subdivided image used in the transition effect. `transitionRenderTarget` is the `RenderTarget2D` object that will render the foreground image into render target texture for the jumping sprites transition effect. The `alpha` variable will control the transparency of each subimage and `timer` will accumulate the total elapsed game time. The `TransitionSpeed` is a constant value that defines the transition speed.

In step 4, we define the core method `DrawJumpingSpritesTransition()` for drawing the jumping sprites effect. First of all, we instantiate a `Random` object, and the random value generated from the object will be used to randomly change the rotation, scale, and position values of the divided subimages in the transition effect. In the following loop, we iterate every subimage row by row and column by column. When it is located at one of the subimages, we create a `Rectangle` object with the pre-defined size. Then, we change the origin point to the image center; this will make the image rotate and scale in place. After that, we randomly change the rotation, scale, and the position values. Finally, we draw the current subimage on the Windows Phone 7 screen.

In step 5, we draw the forefront image first, because we want the transition effect on the forefront image. Then using the render target, transform the current view to the render target texture by putting the drawing code between the `GraphicsDevice.SetRenderTarget(tr ansitionRenderTarget)` and `GraphicsDevice.SetRenderTarget(null)` methods. Next, we use the accumulated elapsed game time to compute the `delta` value to minus the `alpha` value. The alpha will be used in the `SpriteBatch.Draw()` method to make the subimages of the jumping sprites change from opaque to transparent. The last part in the `Draw()` method is to draw the background image first, then draw the transition effect. This drawing order is important. The texture that has the transition effect must be drawn after the images without the transition effect. Otherwise, you will not see the effect you want.

10
Performance Optimization— Fast! Faster!

In this chapter, we will cover:

- ▸ Optimizing your game's performance
- ▸ Using the EQATEC Profiler to profile your game's running time
- ▸ Reducing the game contents' loading time
- ▸ Improving game performance with garbage collection (GC)

Introduction

Performance and efficiency are like the Sword of Democritus hanging over the head of programmers. We should know how to make our applications run faster. We should choose a proper algorithm that executes quicker and consumes less memory; we should know the positive and negative aspects of using different compilers. Actually, every game has a certain fixed amount of available computing resources. Due to market forces, programmers must make sure that their games provide a good playing experience. Optimization should always be done holistically. Having a big picture first and then drilling down until you find the specific problem reduces your game performance. The difference between a novice and master chess player is not how quickly they move their pieces. The difference is that the master chess player immediately identifies the key details of the situation. Both players try to look several moves ahead, but the master only thinks about the moves that will likely lead to victory.

In optimization, there are a million different things you can do to speed up your code. A beginner will struggle because he has to try many approaches, and may not hit the nail on the head of things most likely to give big performance wins. On the other hand, good optimizers are able to quickly identify the three or four things that will make the biggest difference, measure their effects, and choose the best. For the Windows Phone 7 XNA game optimization, there is no assembly code to speed up the running code from a low level; you cannot write the custom graphics shader code to offload the special effect rendering. All computing is run on the CPU of the phone, the challenge is that the computation capacity is limited. We need to pay attention and focus on making the core computation and rendering the code to have enough time to drive the entire application. In this chapter, you will learn the techniques of how to design and analyze your code to get a good performance, how to use the EQATEC profiling tool to profile the running time of every method of Windows Phone 7 game XAP file, and look at how you can improve game performance with Garbage Collector.

Optimizing your game's performance

Games belong to a class of real-time software. This means that they are not only expected to produce the correct result, but they must also complete this within a fixed time window. In general, game developers shoot for a minimum of displaying 30 frames per second in order to produce smooth, glitch-free animations; and most prefer 60 frames per second. This means that all of the game calculations getting the player input, implementing enemy AI, moving objects, collision detection and handling, and drawing each frame must be completed within 16.7 milliseconds! When you consider that most modern video games have hundreds, or even thousands, of objects that have to be updated and drawn within that time period, it is no wonder that programmers feel they have to optimize every line of code.

However, many XNA programmers are not familiar with the tools and methods for determining when, where, how, or even if, they should optimize their code. The point of this recipe is to help you answer these questions.

Getting ready

The following section will help you to optimize your game's performances

Design versus implementation

A common response by those who question, or even outright disagree, with the idea that optimizing the code early is a bad idea, is to point out that it is far easier to change software early in its lifecycle than after it has been written. That is, of course, very true. That is why it is important to understand the difference between the design optimization and implementation optimization.

While designing a game (or any software), you must take into account the size and complexity of your game, and select the correct data structures and algorithms that can support it. A simple 2D shooter or a platformer with no more than a hundred objects interacting at any given time can probably get away with a brute force approach for handling movements and collisions. Maintaining a simple list or an array of objects and iterating through it each frame will most likely work fine, and will be very simple to implement and debug.

However, a more complex game world, with perhaps thousands of active objects, will need an efficient method of partitioning the game space to minimize the number of object interaction tests in each frame. Similarly, games requiring detailed enemy AI will need to rely on algorithms that can produce "intelligent" actions as quickly as possible.

There are many resources available that discuss game programming algorithms. Some of them are as follows:

- The use of **quadtrees** and **octrees** for partitioning the game world to minimize collision detection tests
- The **minimax algorithm** with alpha-beta pruning for efficiently finding the "best" move in two player strategy games (please check the wiki link for more information at `http://en.wikipedia.org/wiki/Alpha-beta_pruning`)
- The **A* algorithm** for efficient path finding (for more detail about the A* algorithm, please check the wiki link at `http://en.wikipedia.org/wiki/A*_search_algorithm`)

The selection of appropriate data structures and algorithms during the design phase has a far greater impact on the eventual performance of your game than any implementation optimization you will make, as your algorithms determine the maximum number of operations your game will have to perform during each frame.

In order to demonstrate this point, imagine that for your first game you write a simple 2D shooter that relies on a brute force approach to collision detection. In every frame, you simply test every active object against every other active object to see if they intersect. As you decide to have only a limited number of enemies active at a time, it works well and easily runs at 60 frames per second.

With that experience under your belt, you now want to write a second game that is far more ambitious. This time you decide to write a Zelda-like adventure game with a large scrolling game board and hundreds of objects moving around it simultaneously. (*The Legend of Zelda*, an NDS game from Nintendo. You can find out more about this game at: `http://en.wikipedia.org/wiki/The_Legend_of_Zelda`.) Using your existing code as a starting point, you get well into the game's implementation before you discover that the brute force approach that worked very well in your simple game does not work so well in this new game. In fact, you may be measuring screen draws in seconds per frame instead of frames per second!

The reason is that, comparing every object against every other object is what is known as an O(n2) algorithm (for more information on estimating the algorithm time complexity, please see the classic book *Introduction to Algorithm* second edition, `http://www.amazon.com/Introduction-Algorithms-Thomas-H-Cormen/dp/0262033844`). That is, the number of operations that have to be performed is related to the square of the number of objects on which you are operating. If you have 10 objects in your game, you only have to perform a hundred tests to see if there are any collisions. If you have a hundred objects, you have to perform ten thousand tests, which may still be possible on a modern PC if each test can be done quickly enough. However, if you have five hundred just five times as many as the last example you will have to perform 250,000 collision tests. Even if each test took only 67 microseconds, you would still be using the entire 16.7 milliseconds frame time (usually at 60 frames per second) just for collision detection. The point is that it does not matter how efficiently you implement that algorithm in a code, its performance will still devolve exponentially with the number of objects in your game, and will therefore be the single greatest limiting factor to the size of your game.

Game runs slow?

Ok, so your game is playable with most of the features you want to be implemented. However, when you test the application, you find that the animation runs like a robot, the character should run, but it is crawling. What is wrong there? You might say, it is about the compiler features, such as the `foreach` keyword, or ask whether you need to pass the matrices by reference, not by values.

You have two choices: stop there and take a step back or fix it, and start going into each method trying to figure out how to find your way around the problem on a case-by-case basis. Maybe you will even succeed and get the game back into the runnable state that you had it in hours earlier. Maybe you are even lucky enough to have not introduced yet more bugs into the process. However, in all likelihood, you have not fixed the problem and now you have code that does not run any better than when you started, but is harder to understand, harder to debug, and has kludges in it to get around problems that you introduced trying to fix the wrong problem. Your time will be much better spent finding out where your problems are before you try to fix them.

Measuring the running time

A prototype is just a simplified version of software (in this case, your game), that focuses on one particular aspect of it. Prototypes are often used as proofs of concept to show that the software will be able to work as expected. As prototypes don't have to deal with all of the details that the final software will, they can be written quickly so that, if necessary, different approaches can be evaluated.

Prototypes are frequently used to evaluate user interfaces, so that customers can provide early feedback. This can be useful for game programming too, as if you can implement a working display and control scheme, you may be able to find out what works and doesn't work before you get too far along in the actual implementation of the game. However, the use of prototypes that we are concerned with here is to determine whether an algorithm is fast enough for the game we want to write. To do that, we will want to benchmark it. Benchmarking is just the process of timing how long an algorithm takes to run.

How to do it...

Fortunately, the .NET framework makes benchmarking very easy by providing the `System.Debug.Stopwatch` class. The `Stopwatch` class provides a `Start` and a `Stop` method. It keeps track of the total number of clock ticks that occur between calls to `Start` and `Stop`. Even better, like a real stopwatch, it keeps a running count of ticks between successive calls to `Start` and `Stop`. You can find out how much time has passed by querying its `ElapsedTicks` or `ElapsedMilliseconds` properties. A `Reset()` method lets us reset `Stopwatch` back to zero.

Now, follow the steps to take advantage of the `Stopwatch` class:

1. As a showcase, the following code gives you a general picture on how to use the `Stopwatch` class for time measuring:

```
public abstract class Sprite
{
    public Vector2 Position { get; set; }
    public Color Color { get; set; }

    // Sprite's collision rectangle in screen coordinates.

    public BoundingRectangle BoundingBox { get; }

    public Sprite(
        string imageName,
        BoundingRectangle boundingBox);

    public virtual void Initialize();

    public virtual void LoadGraphicsContent(
        ContentManager content);

    public virtual void Update(GameTime time);

    public virtual void Draw(SpriteBatch spriteBatch);

    // Tests for collision with another Sprite. If a
    // collision occurs, it calls the Collide method for
    // both Sprites. Returns true if images collide.
    public bool TestCollision(Sprite item);
```

```
        // Called when the TestCollision method detects a
        // collision with another Sprite.
        //
        protected virtual void Collide(
            BoundingRectangle overlap,
            Sprite item);
    }
```

2. As it is an abstract, it is intended to be used as a parent to other `Sprite` classes that will implement its behavior, so we will create our own `TestSprite` class. `TestSprite` will generate a random starting position, directional movement vector, and speed (in pixels per second), as shown here:

```
public override void Initialize()
{
    // Set starting position.
    Position =
        new Vector2(
            random.Next(screenWidth),
            random.Next(screenHeight));

    // Create a random movement vector.
    direction.X = (float)random.NextDouble() * 2 - 1;
    direction.Y = (float)random.NextDouble() * 2 - 1;
    direction.Normalize();

    // Determine random speed in pixels per second.
    speed = (float)random.NextDouble() * 300 + 150;
}
```

3. In each frame, the following code will update its position based on its movement direction, speed, and the amount of time that has elapsed. It will also test to see if it has hit the edge of the screen, and deflect away from it:

```
public override void Update(GameTime time)
{
    // Reset color back to white.
    Color = Microsoft.Xna.Framework.Graphics.Color.White;

    // Calculate movement vector.
    Vector2 move =
        (float)time.ElapsedGameTime.TotalSeconds *
        speed * direction;

    // Determine new position.
```

```
        UpdatePosition(move);
    }

    private void UpdatePosition(Vector2 move)
    {
        Position += move;

        if ((BoundingBox.Left < 0) ||
            (BoundingBox.Right > screenWidth))
        {
            direction.X = -direction.X;
            Position -= new Vector2(move.X, 0);
        }

        if ((BoundingBox.Top < 0) ||
            (BoundingBox.Bottom > screenHeight))
        {
            direction.Y = -direction.Y;
            Position -= new Vector2(0, move.Y);
        }
    }
```

4. We will talk more about collision testing next. For now, we will see what it takes to time just moving our `TestSprite` around the screen. Inside our game, we will create a `TestSprite` object and call its `Initialize()` and `LoadGraphicsContent()` methods at appropriate places. And we will create `SpriteBatch` for our game and pass it to `Draw()`. Now all we need is to use `Stopwatch` to time it in the `Update()` method. In order to do this, we will create a couple of helper methods that start and stop `Stopwatch`, and print the amount of time it takes for each update:

```
    private Stopwatch updateTimer;
    private int updates = 0;
    private int framesPerSecond;

    private void StartTimer()
    {
        updateTimer.Start();
    }

    private void StopTimer()
    {
        updateTimer.Stop();
        updates++;

        // Show the results every five seconds.
```

```
            if (updates == 5 * framesPerSecond)
            {
                Debug.WriteLine(
                    updates + " updates took " +
                    updateTimer.ElapsedTicks + " ticks (" +
                    updateTimer.ElapsedMilliseconds +
                    " milliseconds).");

                int msPerUpdate =
                    (int)updateTimer.ElapsedMilliseconds / updates;

                Debug.WriteLine(
                    "Each update took " +
                    msPerUpdate + " milliseconds.");

                // Reset stopwatch.
                updates = 0;
                updateTimer.Reset();
            }
        }
```

5. By putting calls to `StartTimer` and `StopTimer` around the calls to our sprite's `Update()` method, we will get a report of the average time each call takes:

```
300 updates took 34931 ticks (9 milliseconds).
Each update took 0.03 milliseconds.
300 updates took 24445 ticks (6 milliseconds).
Each update took 0.02 milliseconds.
300 updates took 23541 ticks (6 milliseconds).
Each update took 0.02 milliseconds.
300 updates took 23583 ticks (6 milliseconds).
Each update took 0.02 milliseconds.
300 updates took 23963 ticks (6 milliseconds).
Each update took 0.02 milliseconds.
```

How it works...

In step 1, the `Initialize()`, `LoadGraphicsContent()`, `Update()`, and `Draw()` methods are the standard methods for Windows Phone 7 XNA Game Programming. Additionally, it provides properties for getting and setting the position and color. For collision detection, the `Collide()` method called by `TestCollision()` tests for collision with another Sprite BoundingBox values intersect.

In step 3, an actual game may want to determine the actual point of intersection so it could deflect away from that point more realistically. If you need that level of realism, you would probably want to go ahead and implement your strategy here, so you could time it. However, all we are trying to prototype here is a basic update time, so that this version is fine for our needs.

Note that the `Update()` method does not test for collisions. We don't want individual sprite testing for collisions because to do so, our `Sprite` class would have to know about other game objects and we would be severely limiting our design options for collision testing. Any change to our collision-testing algorithm could, and likely would, affect our `Sprite` class. We want to avoid anything that limits future design changes, so we will give our `Sprite` class the ability to test for collisions, but require another part of our code to determine what objects should be tested.

In step 6, each call took on average of 20 microseconds (on my development laptop your results will vary). However, notice that the very first set of updates took almost one and a half times as long to run as the others. That is because the first time these methods are called, the **JIT** compiler compiles the code and our `Stopwatch` is timing that as well. It is also possible, as this is a fairly small amount of code that is being called repeatedly, that some or all of it may be fitting in the cache, which will increase the speed of later calls.

These show some of the problems with benchmarking code. Another problem is that we are adding some time by using `Stopwatch` itself. Thus, benchmark times for prototype code can be used as a general guide, but cannot be relied upon for exact values. In fact, exact values of the time it takes for functions to run are very hard to determine. Although intended only to describe quantum phenomena, a variation of the Heisenberg Uncertainty Principle is at play here: the act of measuring something affects the thing being measured.

There's more...

Now let's expand our prototype to help us determine whether we can get away with a brute force approach to collision detection.

First, let's look at the collision handling code that I have already placed in the `Collide` method. Remember that this gets called, for both sprites, whenever the `TestCollision()` method determines a collision between two sprites. All it does is set the Sprite's color to red:

```
protected override void Collide(
    BoundingRectangle overlap,
    Sprite item)
{
    // Turn the sprite red to indicate collision.
    Color = Color.Red;
}
```

Let's give this a test by replacing our single TestSprite with an array of TestSprites. Every place we referenced TestSprite in the original code, we now have to loop through the array to handle all of our TestSprites. In order to make this a little easier to manage, we will refactor our original sprite.Update() call in the Update() method into a new UpdateSprites() method that updates every sprite. We will add a new HandleCollisions() method to our game to test for collisions. Finally, we will change the Update() method, so that it only calls StartTimer and StopTimer around the call to HandleCollisions(). The relevant sections look like the following code:

```
private TestSprite[] sprites = new TestSprite[10];

protected override void Update(GameTime gameTime)
{
    if (Keyboard.GetState().IsKeyDown(Keys.Escape))
    {
        this.Exit();
    }

    UpdateSprites(gameTime);

    StartTimer();
    HandleCollisions();
    StopTimer();

    base.Update(gameTime);
}

private void UpdateSprites(GameTime gameTime)
{
    foreach (Sprite sprite in sprites)
    {
        sprite.Update(gameTime);
    }
}

private void HandleCollisions()
{
    // This is brute force approach
    for (int i = 0; i < sprites.Length; i++)
    {
        for (int j = i + 1; j < sprites.Length; j++)
        {
            sprites[i].TestCollision(sprites[j]);
        }
    }
}
```

Looking at that, you may wonder why I am not using `foreach` for the `HandleCollisions` call. It is simply because with `foreach`, we have no way of knowing what sprites we already tested. This algorithm tests every sprite against every other sprite exactly once.

What are the results? On my machine, with 10 sprites, I get the following:

```
300 updates took 48827 ticks (13 milliseconds).
Each update took 0.04333333 milliseconds.
300 updates took 42466 ticks (11 milliseconds).
Each update took 0.03666667 milliseconds.
300 updates took 42371 ticks (11 milliseconds).
Each update took 0.03666667 milliseconds.
300 updates took 43086 ticks (12 milliseconds).
Each update took 0.04 milliseconds.
300 updates took 43449 ticks (12 milliseconds).
Each update took 0.04 milliseconds.
```

Wow! Handling collisions for 10 sprites takes only twice as long as it did just to move one sprite. How could that be? It is partly due to the overhead of using the `Stopwatch` class and making method calls, and partly due to the fact that we are measuring very fast operations. Obviously, the closer you get to the resolution of the underlying timer, the more error you get in trying to time things.

Before we go on, notice also that the impact of the JIT compiler during our first set of updates is significantly less. This shows how effective the JIT compilation is and why we don't need to worry about it affecting the performance of our game. We may take a performance hit the first time a section of code is running, but it is relatively miniscule to our overall performance.

Now let's see what happens when we increase the number of sprites to 100:

```
300 updates took 2079460 ticks (580 milliseconds).
Each update took 1.933333 milliseconds.
300 updates took 2156954 ticks (602 milliseconds).
Each update took 2.006667 milliseconds.
300 updates took 2138909 ticks (597 milliseconds).
Each update took 1.99 milliseconds.
300 updates took 2150696 ticks (600 milliseconds).
Each update took 2 milliseconds.
300 updates took 2169919 ticks (606 milliseconds).
Each update took 2.02 milliseconds.
```

Whether you should be impressed or dismayed depends on how you want to use this collision-handling algorithm. On one hand, averaging 2 milliseconds per frame is still a miniscule part of our 16.7 millisecond frame timing. If you are not planning to have more than a hundred sprites or so, this algorithm will suit your needs perfectly. However, looking at the relative time difference per sprite gives a completely different perspective. It takes us 50 times as long to handle 10 times the number of sprites.

How about when the number is increased to 500? I urge you to run this code, so that you can see the results for yourself!

```
300 updates took 28266113 ticks (7896 milliseconds).
Each update took 26.32 milliseconds.
300 updates took 28179606 ticks (7872 milliseconds).
Each update took 26.24 milliseconds.
300 updates took 28291296 ticks (7903 milliseconds).
Each update took 26.34333 milliseconds.
300 updates took 28199114 ticks (7877 milliseconds).
Each update took 26.25667 milliseconds.
300 updates took 28182787 ticks (7873 milliseconds).
Each update took 26.24333 milliseconds.
```

At this time there is no way to hide the dismay. The movement is clearly getting far less than our desired 60 frames per second! In fact, just the `HandleCollisions()` call alone is taking almost twice our allotted 16.7 milliseconds per frame. Multiplying the number of objects by 5 increased our time by 13! The times are not increasing exactly in quadric, due to overhead, but the rate of increase is clear.

Does this mean we should never consider this algorithm? Hopefully, at this point the answer is obvious. Many games can easily get away with only having an order of a hundred or so objects active at a time, which we have clearly shown can be handled easily. The fact that the algorithm is trivial to implement and maintain makes it a no-brainer for a large number of games.

On the other hand, if you know you will need to have hundreds of objects, you will need another solution. You have two options: optimize this algorithm, or find a new one. Anyone who is experienced with code optimization will see several obvious ways to make both the algorithm and its implementation more efficient.

For starters, most games don't actually need to test every object against every other object. Taking the **Space Invasion** game as an example, I don't need to test invaders for collision with other invaders. In fact, it is almost crazy to do so.

Another obvious optimization is that the `Sprite` class's `BoundingBox` property is adding the sprite's current screen position to its internal `BoundingRectangle` every time `TestCollision` is called, this despite the fact that the position changes only once or twice per frame. `TestCollision`, on the other hand, is called once for every other sprite in the game.

Note that I did optimize this in my actual Space Invasion game by updating BoundingBox in the `Position` property's setter. As we can see from these numbers, however, I would have gotten equally satisfactory results if I had used the less efficient approach shown here.

In addition, the Sprite's `TestCollision` code is computing the actual intersection rectangle even though we are not using it here. We could easily save some time by not computing it. However, we give ourselves more flexibility by going ahead and doing it. Remember that this is supposed to be a generic `Sprite` class that can be used for many games.

These suggestions don't even get into implementation optimizations, such as always passing our BoundingBoxes by reference instead of value; and providing direct access to member variables instead of accessing them through properties. These are exactly the types of optimizations suggested by many efficiency proponents in the XNA forums. However, these also make the code less readable, harder to debug, and harder to maintain.

As Space Invasion never has more than around 60 objects on the screen at a time, the unoptimized brute force approach works just fine. In addition, that is undoubtedly true for many other games as well. However, what if your game does need more than 100 collidable objects? Should you not make those optimizations so you can handle them?

The answer is... maybe. By making some of these optimizations, we can get this same brute force algorithm to handle 500 objects at a far more reasonable 6.4 milliseconds per frame.

```
300 updates took 6682522 ticks (1866 milliseconds).
Each update took 6.22 milliseconds.
300 updates took 7038462 ticks (1966 milliseconds).
Each update took 6.553333 milliseconds.
300 updates took 7023610 ticks (1962 milliseconds).
Each update took 6.54 milliseconds.
300 updates took 6718281 ticks (1876 milliseconds).
Each update took 6.253334 milliseconds.
300 updates took 7136208 ticks (1993 milliseconds).
Each update took 6.643333 milliseconds.
```

That is an impressive improvement and shows how significantly performance can be optimized through these techniques. However, the disadvantages mentioned earlier less maintainable and less flexible code should not be ignored. In addition, even if you do these sorts of implementation optimizations, keep in mind that this algorithm will still degrade exponentially as you add more objects. You may be able to move up from 100 to 500 objects, but it won't get you to 1000. At some point, you need to recognize that you need a different algorithm to efficiently handle more objects, such as the one that partitions your game space, like quad trees.

Finally, remember that 6.4 milliseconds is still 40 percent of your entire frame time. If you are maintaining on the order of a thousand or more objects at a time, other parts of your code are almost certainly also going to be difficult to manage at a reasonable frame rate. Is optimizing your collision detection the best use of your time? How do you know in advance which ones to optimize? Optimizing all of them as you go will surely take you longer to write, not to mention make your code more difficult to debug and maintain.

If benchmarking shows your algorithm has problems without implementation optimizations, you are probably better off with a different algorithm.

Using the EQATEC Profiler to profile your game's running time

Profiling your game performance is a significant part of the whole game development process. No matter how efficient the used algorithms are, or how powerful the hardware is, you still need to get sufficiently accurate CPU running time charts for different functions calling in different hardware conditions. Choosing a good profiling tool will help you to find the hot spots which consume most CPU game resources, and lead you to create the most efficient optimization. For Windows Phone, EQATEC is a good choice and in this recipe, you will learn how to use the EQATEC Profiler to profile your Window Phone game.

Getting ready

You can download the EQATEC Profiler from the official company website located at the following URL:

```
http://www.eqatec.com/Profiler/
```

The following screenshot shows what website looks like:

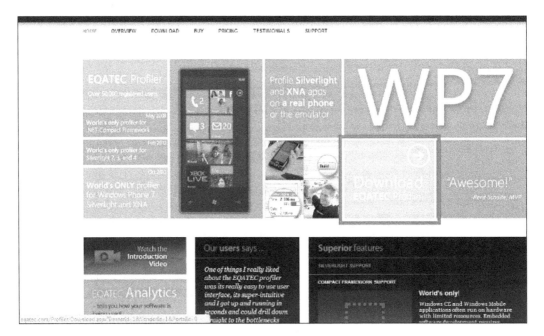

After clicking on the **Download EQATEC Profiler**, a new page will let you choose the profiler version; the free version is fine for our needs. After filling out some basic information, the website will send a URL for downloading the profiler to your e-mail address. When you have installed the downloaded profiler, you are ready for profiling your Windows Phone 7 game.

How to do it...

Carry out the following steps:

1. Run the EQATEC Profiler through the **Start** menu or through the root directory where the profiler binary application is located. If the profiler runs correctly, you should get the following screen:

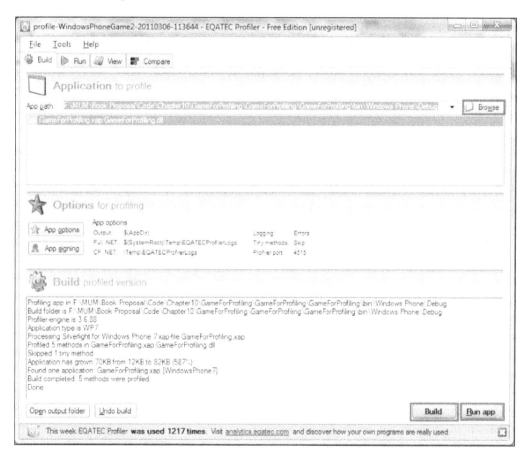

2. The **Browse** button lets you locate the root directory of your Windows Phone 7 XAP file for profiling. When the directory is set, you will choose the XAP file which will be listed in the list box under the **App path** textbox. The testing XAP file and source code can be found in the bundle file of this chapter. After that, you should click on the **Browse** button for building the profile description file that processed the number of methods in the designated application and some application metadata.

3. Then, after selecting the application you want to profile, click on the **Run** button to start the profiling. When the **Run** button is clicked, a prompt will pop up asking you about the device to be used for profiling, **Windows Phone 7 Device** or **Windows Phone 7 Emulator**. In the example, we chose the emulator as shown in the following screenshot:

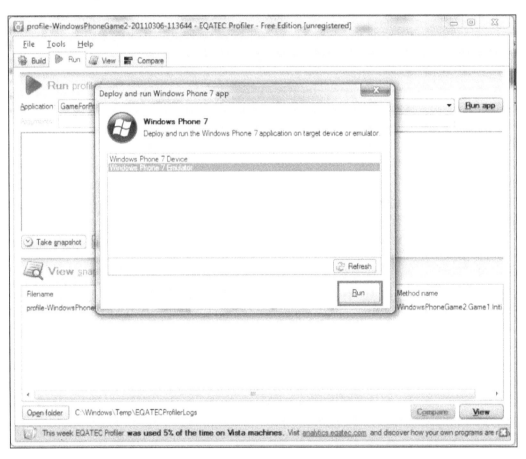

4. Under the **Run** tab, if you are sure the Windows Phone 7 application is ready, it is time for profiling. The window should look similar to the following screenshot:

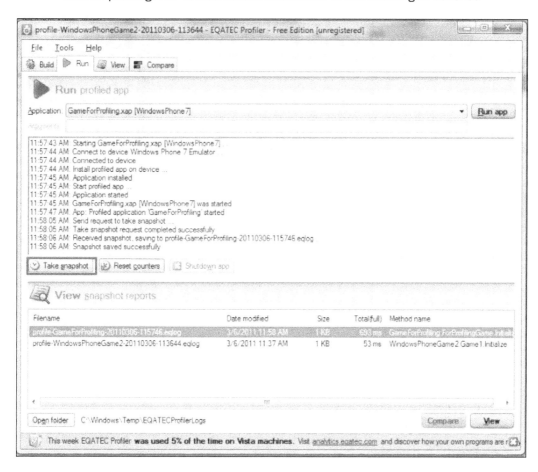

5. Now, click on the yellow **Run app** button. The profiler will automatically start a Windows Phone 7 emulator and connect to the emulator. Next, it will install the profiled Windows Phone 7 XAP file on the emulator. When this step is done, profiler will start to track and profile the designated application. At this moment, if you want to know the actual time of every method in your application costs, you need to click on the **Take snapshot** button with a timer symbol under the information list box, and a new snapshot report which includes the running time of every method will be generated. Then, click on the yellow **View** button once you have chosen the report you want to review.

6. In the snapshot view window, you will find how many milliseconds every method takes. The windows will look similar to the following screenshot:

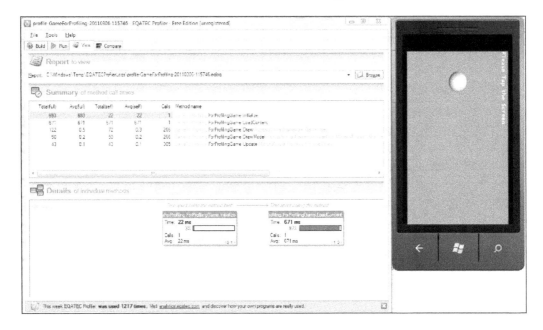

How it works...

The time of every method is listed in the list box:

- **Initialize()** method: 693 MS

- **LoadContent()** method: 671 MS

- **Draw()** method: 122 MS

- **DrawModel()** method: 50 MS

- **Update()** method: 43 MS

You can find more details in the **Details of Individual methods** panel. This panel will tell you the percentage of called method costs on time of the caller. In this example, the **LoadContent()** method consumes 671 MS which occupies 97 percent of the **Initialize()** method total time.

Reducing the game contents' loading time

As you know, most of the time, before playing a game, a screen for loading game contents will show up with a running progress bar. Without this, you may feel the game is stuck and not responding. If you know that the game is loading and can see its progress, you know that all you have to do is wait. Usually, no one wants to wait too long for playing games, however. It is wasting time and can cause frustration to the user. For better user experiences, the following sections will tell you how to reduce the loading time of game contents.

Making good loading decisions

Often, the first step in reducing loading times is to understand where the current greatest expenses are. Highlighting the frequency and timing of content loading is an effective way to evaluate and adjust loading times, as well as validate that the right content (no more and no less) is being loaded in a given scenario. Consider instrumenting the following:

- The time required to load an asset; the `System.Diagnostics.Stopwatch` object can be used for this

- The frequency with which each asset has been loaded over multiple game levels, across sessions, and so on

- The frequency with which each asset is freed

- The average lifetime

Using the XNA content pipeline to reduce file size

Compressing the game contents into an XNB file will make a great file size reduction in building time.

For the XNA framework, assets are shared between PC, Xbox, and Windows Phone 7 platforms, and you can reuse the textures, models, and so on. If a texture is consistently scaled down for display on a Windows Phone 7, consider performing that scaling offline, rather than taking the processing penalty bandwidth and memory overhead when loading the content.

Developers may also want to exploit other texture types, such as PNG, where doing so would not contribute to already compressed assets. For sparse textures, PNG on Windows Phone will typically demonstrate superior compression to a DXT-compressed content that is brought through the XNA content pipeline. In order to use other texture types, the source files must be copied to the output directory and not compiled in the content pipeline.

Note that, while DXT-compressed assets can be used natively by Windows Phone 7 GPUs, many formats including PNG need to be expanded at runtime to a raw format of 32 bits per pixel. This expansion can lead to increased memory overhead compared to DXT compression.

In order to balance the runtime memory footprint of DXT with the loading time footprint of more aggressive compression formats, developers may choose to apply custom compression and runtime decompression to the DXT content (as built by the XNA pipeline into .xnb files), which can lead to a significant reduction in loading times. Developers should balance the loading time considerations with CPU requirements to decode their custom-encoded content, as well as with memory requirements to handle and manipulate the decompressed data. The offline custom compression and runtime title-managed decompression of the DXT content can offer a good balance of reduced size (and thus, reduced loading time) without large runtime memory costs.

Developers can also pack multiple images into a single texture, as demonstrated by the content processor in the spritesheet. We have already discussed in *Chapter 4, Heads Up Display (HUD)—Your Phone Game User Interface*, that spritesheets avoid DXT power-of-two restrictions imposed by the XNA content processor, and optimize the file loading (replacing many small files with one larger one).

In the realm of sound, if native audio assets from a console title are 48 kHz, consider down sampling them to 44.1 kHz (prior to applying the XNA pipeline's own compression) for use on the phone. This will realize an immediate 8 percent savings (approximately) on storage and reading bandwidth, as well as mild CPU savings for running at the native sampling rate of the Windows Phone device (44.1 kHz).

Beyond compression, decreasing loading times can focus on data organization that focuses on the efforts of loading the content that is needed to drive to an initial interactive state, rather than preparing all possible loaded data. This is particularly important in avoiding the watchdog timer; a title that loads data for too long prior to drawing to the screen risks being terminated by the system. Developers should also give similar attention to the in-game content loading. Remember that returning to gameplay from interruptions (SMS, phone, app purchase, and so on) invalidates all the previously loaded content.

Evaluating the asynchronous background loading

Even if the game takes a substantial set-up time, there are numerous techniques to getting the user into some kind of interactive state sooner. Anything from a simplified arcade-style loading screen to cut-scenes, trivia, "did you know" facts, and other low-CPU-impact techniques can be leveraged to help smooth the setup and transition from loading to gameplay.

Loading to an initial menu state or a cut-scene, and then continuing to load additional assets in the background would seem to be appropriate strategies for masking loading times from the consumer. However, LoadContent() performs byte copies of each loaded texture asset that uses the XNA content pipeline, generating garbage. Moreover, LoadContent(), overall, will trigger the garbage collection at each megabyte of loaded data. Depending on the actual interactivity of foreground scenes, the potential CPU cost taken by garbage collection may be acceptable; playback of pre-rendered video cut-scenes takes advantage of purpose-built hardware, so the CPU utilization is typically negligible. Similarly, static or intermittently animated menu systems would likely have more success here than attempting to generate the CPU-intensive content rendered in-engine during the background loading.

Considering the custom serialization

Microsoft's .NET framework provides an easy to use method for serializing data onto disks, using types present in the `System.Xml.Serialization` namespace. Simplicity always comes with tradeoffs, however; in this case, the tradeoff is the file size. The default serialization schema is verbose. The behavior of the `XmlSerializer` is trivially easy to change, however, and can result in significant savings in file sizes.

As an example, let's consider the following class definition:

```
public class TestClass
{
    public int count;
    public float size;
    public bool enabled;
    public string
        LongNameOfAMinorFieldThatDoesntNeedALongNameInTheFile = "test";
}
```

The preceding class definition, when serialized with the default `XmlSerializer`, produces the following XML:

```
<?xml version="1.0"?>
<TestClass xmlns:xsi=http://www.w3.org/2001/XMLSchema-instance
    xmlns:xsd="http://www.w3.org/2001/XMLSchema">
    <count>0</count>
    <size>0</size>
    <enabled>false</enabled>
    <LongNameOfAMinorFieldThatDoesntNeedALongNameInTheFile>test
    </LongNameOfAMinorFieldThatDoesntNeedALongNameInTheFile>
</TestClass>
```

The default behavior of `XmlSerializer` is to treat each public field or property as an XML element. This generates quite a bit of extra data in the file; this XML file uses 332 bytes on the disk to serialize four fields. With a few simple changes, we can get significantly smaller files from `XmlSerializer`. Consider the following class declaration:

```
public class TestClass2
{
    [XmlAttribute(AttributeName="count")]
```

```
   public int count;
[XmlAttribute(AttributeName="size")]
   public float size;
   [XmlAttribute(AttributeName="enable")]
   public bool enabled;
   [XmlAttribute(AttributeName = "longName")]
   public string
      LongNameOfAMinorFieldThatDoesntNeedALongNameInTheFile = "test";
}
```

With `XmlAttribute` added to properties, the `XmlSerializer` treats the field as attributes rather than elements, and gives the attributes alternative names. The resulting XML is the following:

```
<?xml version="1.0"?>
<TestClass2 xmlns:xsi="http://www.w3.org/2001/XMLSchema-instance"
    xmlns:xsd="http://www.w3.org/2001/XMLSchema" count ="0" size ="0"
    enable ="false" longName ="test" />
```

The serialized file has significantly less wasted text. The file size also shrank to 167 bytes. This is a saving of roughly 50 percent, and a more reasonable file size to serialize four fields. Modifying your serialization code to prefer the XML attributes to XML elements will often result in similar savings. Even if you don't perform renaming, as we did in this example, you will generally get close to a 50 percent reduction, as every `XmlElement` has to have a closing tag, while attributes don't.

Avoid using `XmlAttribute` for complex types, or for collections of types. The space savings are minimal in these cases, and the resulting file is considerably more difficult to read. For larger amounts of data, consider writing a custom binary serialization code. In all cases, ensure that you time any new code to confirm any realized performance gains over the default Serializer settings.

Improving game performance with garbage collection

Discussing the garbage collector (GC) that runs on Windows Phone 7 devices is helpful for the Windows Phone 7 game developer. Anyone who has programmed in XNA for Windows or Xbox 360 before knows the GC well.

Value types versus reference types

One of the first things you must understand is the difference between value types and reference types. Value types such as `int`, `float`, `Vector3`, `Matrix`, and `struct` (this includes nullable types; a nullable type such as BOOL is just a special `struct`) live on the stack. The GC does not care about the stack. Well, technically, it cares slightly, but only to the extent that the system begins to run low on memory, and you would have to be trying very hard to get enough items on the stack to cause the system to run low on memory. So don't worry about calling "new Vector3()" or "Matrix.CreateTranslation()" in your methods that run regularly (such as `Update` and `Draw`) it is just a stack allocation and it won't anger the GC.

Classes are an entirely different matter. Classes, arrays (including arrays of value types, for example, `int [ ]`), collections (`List<>`, `Dictionary<>`, and so on.), and strings (yes, strings) are all reference types and they live on the heap. The heap is the GC's caring. It pays attention to everything that shows up on the heap and to everything that no longer has any business there, but is still hanging around.

Defining a true value checking method

Take a look at the following code listing:

```
void CheckForTrue(bool value)
{
    string trueText = "The value is true.";
    string falseText = "The value is false.";

    if (value == true)
    {
        Console.WriteLine(trueText);
    }
    else
    {
        Console.WriteLine(falseText);
    }

    return;
}
```

Every time this method runs, `trueText` and `falseText` will both be allocated on the heap and will "go out of scope" when the the method is run. In other words, "gone out of scope" simply means that there are no more references to an object. A string declared with `const` never goes out of scope, and thus does not matter to GC for all practical purposes. This is also true for any object declared as `static readonly`, as once it is created it exists forever. However, the same is not true for a normal `static`, though many might mistakenly assume so. A `static` object without the `readonly` keyword applied to it will generally exist for the life of a program. However, if it is ever set to `null`, then unless there is some other reference to it, it goes out of scope and is subject to garbage collection.

Technically, the GC runs for every 1 MB of heap allocation. Whenever the GC is running, it takes time to comb through the heap and destroy any objects that are no longer in scope. Depending on how many references you have and how complex nesting of objects is, this can take a bit of time. In XNA, the clock is on a fixed time-step by default and in Windows Phone 7, the default frame rate is 30 FPS. This means that there are 33.3333333 milliseconds available for `Update()` and `Draw()` methods to finish their CPU-side tasks. Draw prepares things on the CPU-side, then hands over the actual drawing to the GPU which, being a separate processor, does not usually affect the Update/Draw side of things, except for stalls, but those are beyond the scope of this book and most people will never run into them anyway. If they finish ahead of time, the CPU hangs out and waits until it is time to run `Update()` again. If not, then the system takes notice that it is running behind and will skip as many draws as necessary to catch back up.

This is where the GC comes in. Normally, your code will complete just fine within 33.33 milliseconds, thereby maintaining a nice even 30 FPS (if your code does not normally complete within that time, you will see serious constant performance problems that may even cause your game to crash after a little while if XNA gets so far behind that it throws up its hands and surrenders). However, when the GC runs, it eats into that time. If you have kept the heap nice and simple, the GC will run nice and fast and this likely won't matter. However, keeping a simple heap that the GC can run through quickly is a difficult programming task that requires a lot of planning and/or rewriting, and even then is not fool proof (sometimes, you just have a lot of stuff on the heap in a complex game with many assets). A much simpler option assuming you can do it is to limit or even eliminate all allocations during gameplay. You will obviously be allocating heap memory when you first start the game (for example, when loading assets in the `LoadContent()` method), and you will be allocating memory when loading levels, if you have a game with levels and decide to load each one in an interstitial screen. You will also be allocating memory when changing game screens. However, a small stutter from a couple of dropped frames in between levels or while switching screens is not a big concern the player is not going to accidentally fall off a cliff or get hit by an enemy projectile or anything when those things are happening. In fact, sometimes it makes a lot of sense to intentionally trigger the GC right before the game is going to (re)start. Triggering the GC resets the 1 MB counter and can prevent situations where the counter is at .94 MB when the level begins, such that even a small number of minimal allocations that would otherwise be perfectly acceptable, can cause problems.

Therefore, the goal is to minimize heap allocations. How do we do that? Well, the biggest contributors are needlessly creating new objects in your Update or Draw cycle and boxing value types. First, a quick note on boxing; the simplest example of boxing is casting a value type like `int` or `enum` to `object` in order to pass it as a state. Boxing is a great feature of .NET, but not recommended for game programming because of the heap allocations that can trigger the GC. So keep an eye out for it and try not to do it.

Another big contributor is creating new reference types. Every new instance of an object causes a heap allocation and increases that counter ever so slightly. There are several coding practices that will help you to eliminate needless heap allocation and increase performance for your game.

Using StringBuilder for string operations

Make any strings that never change into const strings.

Where you need strings that change, consider using `System.Text.StringBuilder` (visit `http://msdn.microsoft.com/en-us/library/system.text.stringbuilder.aspx` for more information on `StringBuilder`). All XNA methods that take a string (for example, `SpriteBatch.DrawString`) will also take a `StringBuilder` object. Make sure to use one of the constructors which take a default capacity and set it to a value high enough to hold as many characters as you plan, plus a few extra for good measure. If the internal array is large, it will never have to resize itself, and thus will never generate any heap allocations after it is created!

Drawing integer in string without garbage

If you need to draw an `int` value, such as a score or the number of lives a player has, consider using the following block of code (thanks to *Stephen Styrchak*):

```
public static class SpriteBatchExtensions
{
    private static string[] digits = { "0", "1", "2", "3", "4", "5",
                                       "6", "7", "8", "9" };
    private static string[] charBuffer = new string[10];
    private static float[] xposBuffer = new float[10];
    private static readonly string minValue =
      Int32.MinValue.ToString(CultureInfo.InvariantCulture);


    // Extension method for SpriteBatch that draws an integer
    // without allocating any memory. This function avoids garbage
    // collections that are normally caused by calling
    // Int32.ToString or String.Format. the equivalent of calling
    // spriteFont.MeasureString on
    // value.ToString(CultureInfo.InvariantCulture).
    public static Vector2 DrawInt32(this SpriteBatch spriteBatch,
                                    SpriteFont spriteFont, int value,
                                    Vector2 position, Color color)
    {
        Vector2 nextPosition = position;

        if (value == Int32.MinValue)
        {
            nextPosition.X = nextPosition.X +
                spriteFont.MeasureString(minValue).X;
            spriteBatch.DrawString(spriteFont, minValue, position,
```

```
                    color);
                position = nextPosition;
        }
        else
        {
            if (value < 0)
            {
                nextPosition.X = nextPosition.X +
                spriteFont.MeasureString("-").X;
                spriteBatch.DrawString(spriteFont, "-", position,
                    color);
                value = -value;
                position = nextPosition;
            }

            int index = 0;
            do
            {
                int modulus = value % 10;
                value = value / 10;

                charBuffer[index] = digits[modulus];
                xposBuffer[index] = spriteFont.MeasureString
                    (digits[modulus]).X;
                index += 1;
            }
            while (value > 0);

            for (int i = index - 1; i >= 0; --i)
            {
                nextPosition.X = nextPosition.X + xposBuffer[i];
                spriteBatch.DrawString(spriteFont, charBuffer[i],
                                position, color);
                position = nextPosition;
            }
        }
        return position;
    }
}
```

Taking advantage of the list for sprites

If you have a `Sprites class`, for example, create an object pool to reuse it rather than letting it fall out of scope and creating a new one each time one ceases to exist in the game and each time you need a new one. As an example, create a `generic List<>` of your `Sprites` class (refer `http://msdn.microsoft.com/en-us/library/6sh2ey19.aspx` for more information on lists). Use the `List<>` constructor overload that takes a default capacity and make sure to set it to a value high enough to contain all the objects of that sort and will exist at one time in your game (for example, 300). Then, use a `for` loop to go through and create all of the objects in the list up to the capacity. Add a `public bool IsAlive { get; set; }` property to your class to keep track of which ones are being used at any particular time. When you need a new one, loop through the list until you find one, where `IsAlive` is false. Take that one, set `IsAlive` to true, set the other properties (such as its `position`, `direction`, and so on.) to their appropriate values, and continue. When doing collision detection, loop through using a `for` or a `foreach` loop and process only the objects for which `IsAlive` is true. The same approach should be followed for updating and drawing them. Whenever one is no longer needed (for example, when it collides with something or it goes off screen), simply set its `IsAlive` to false and it will now be available for reuse without any memory allocation. If you want to be creative, you can expand on this further in several different ways. You could keep a count of the number of live objects, so that once you have processed that number in your `update` and `draw` methods, you can use the `break` keyword to get out of the loop early, rather than go all the way to the end. Alternatively, you could keep two lists: one for storing live objects and one for dead objects, and move objects between the two lists as appropriate.

Preferring struct rather than class when just an instance is needed

If you do want to create something, you can just create a new "instance" of each `Update()` or `Draw()` method. Try creating a `struct` instead of a `class`. Structures can perform most of the things that classes can (the major limitation being that they cannot inherit from another structure, a class, or anything else, but they can implement interfaces). Moreover, structures live on the stack and not on the heap, so unless you have a reference type, like a string or a class, as a field or property of the structure, you will not generate any trash using a structure. Remember, though, that an array of structures is a reference type (as are all arrays), and thus lives on the heap and counts towards the GC trigger limit whenever created.

Avoiding use of LINQ in game developing

Don't use LINQ. It looks cool. It makes your code shorter, simpler, and perhaps even easier to read. However, LINQ queries can easily become a big source of trash. They are fine in your startup code, as you are going to generate trash there anyway, just by loading assets and preparing game resources. However, don't use it in `Update()`, `Draw()`, or any other method that gets called during the gameplay.

Minimizing the use of ToString()

Minimize use of `ToString()`. At a minimum, it creates a string, which lives on the heap (refer to the *Drawing integer in string without garbage* section discussed earlier in this chapter). If you do need to use `ToString()`, try to limit how often it is called. If the string only changes every level, then generate it only once at the beginning of the level. If it only changes when a certain value changes, then generate it only when that value changes. Any limits you can set are worth it. The amount of time it takes to check a Boolean condition is so small as to be almost non-existent. You could probably fit tens and even hundreds of thousands of true/false checks for the time it takes the GC to run on a complex heap.

11
Launching to the Marketplace

In this chapter, we will cover:

- ▶ Preparing to submit your application to the marketplace
- ▶ Application submission checklist
- ▶ Submitting your application to the marketplace

Introduction

Congratulations, you have gained all of the indispensable knowledge and learned the techniques to make your own Windows Phone 7 XNA games so far. These are your achievements. Now, you really would like to have your game available to entertain people around the world. In the early days, only the game companies had this right. Your chance is coming; Microsoft Windows Phone 7 Marketplace offers you the opportunity to market your own work on Windows Phone 7 to the world, amazing! In this chapter, you will learn how to prepare the required material for submitting your application to the Windows Phone 7 Marketplace.

Preparing to submit your application to the Marketplace

When you finish your Windows Phone 7 game, the desire to let everybody around the world know about your game will drive you to submit your application to the Windows Phone Marketplace. The entire process of submitting is straightforward. Besides your original application package, there will be some necessary points to highlight. Basically, you should have the release candidate package include different sizes of application icons, the background panorama which is for regular Windows Phone applications built from XAML in Microsoft Expression Blend, and the page screenshots of your application. In this chapter, you will discover what you should prepare in detail.

Marketplace images

In order to publish your application on the Windows Phone Marketplace, you will need several images. These images are important because they represent the first impression of your application, so you should spend some time making sure that they look good. You can find royalty free artwork on the Internet or you can have artwork created by a designer. You will need the following images for your application page in the marketplace:

Image	Size (pixels)	File type
Small phone application tile icon	99 x 99	PNG
Large phone application tile icon	173 x 173	PNG
Large PC application tile icon	200 x 200	PNG
Background panorama (optional)	1000 x 800	PNG
Page screenshots (at least 1, up to 8)	480 x 800	PNG

Testing your application

You will want to test your application at several points during development, and in particular, before you submit it to the marketplace. You can test your application using the emulator. However, before you publish your application, you should test your application on an actual Windows Phone device through the following steps:

- ▶ Make sure you have an active **App Hub** membership and that your phone is unlocked
- ▶ Make sure that you have a device connected to your computer, and the Zune software is installed and running on the computer

▶ In Visual Studio, select the target device to Windows Phone 7 Emulator

▶ Press *F5* to start debugging or choose **Start Debugging** from the **Debug** menu

Certification requirements

The **Windows Phone 7 Application Certification Requirements** provide the policies and technical requirements that a Windows Phone 7 game must meet in order to pass the certification and to be eligible for listing in the Windows Phone Marketplace. The following table is a summary of the key certification requirements; however, it is recommended that you review the certification requirements in detail before submitting your application:

Category	Certification requirements
Back button	Pressing the Back button from the first screen of an application must exit the application.
	Pressing the Back button must return the application to the previous page. If the current page displays a context menu or a dialog box, pressing the Back button must close the menu or dialog box and cancel the backward navigation to the previous page.
Application Policies	If you use Location Services or Push Notification Services, review the various policies around their use.
	You must obtain "opt-in" consent if you publish a user's personal information.
Content Policies	You must ensure that the content is your own or you have approval to use the content.
Phone Capabilities Detection	You must ensure that the phone capabilities listed in the application manifest are accurate.
Application Reliability	Your application must handle exceptions raised by the .NET Framework and should not terminate unexpectedly.
	Your application must not become unresponsive to user input because of an operation within the application.
	Your application must render the first screen within 5 seconds after launch.
	Within 20 seconds after launch, your application must be responsive to the user input.
Performance and Resource Management	If your application does not complete the action taken in the Activated or Deactivated event handlers within 10 seconds, it will be terminated by the operating system.
	In order to maintain a consistent user experience, the Back button should only be used for backward navigations in the application.

Category	Certification requirements
Phone Functionality	Your application must not delay or prevent the user from initiating a call, answering an incoming call, or ending a call.
Technical Support Information	Your application must include the application name, version information, and technical support contact information and this information must be easily discoverable.
Applications Running under a Locked Screen	If your application runs under a locked screen, it must stop any UI updates, active timers, and other non-critical processing when notified that the screen is locked.

 For a complete listing of the requirements, you can visit the following URL: `http://msdn.microsoft.com/en-us/library/hh184843%28v=VS.92%29.aspx`.

Application submission checklist

As a quick review before submitting your amazing Windows Phone 7 game to the Windows Phone Marketplace, the checklist will smooth the entire submission process. The items in the list are required for marketing your Windows Phone 7 application, and the information is easy to fill out on your Windows Phone 7 dashboard. The following are the points that you need to keep in mind before going ahead with the submission:

- **Account**: You must be registered as a developer in App Hub. For registration, you need the following items to start:
    - A Windows Live ID: If you don't have a Windows Live ID, you will be directed to a link to create one
    - Your contact information
    - Credit card information: If you are a student who has a valid **DreamSpark** registration, then you don't need credit card information; currently, a credit card is the only option available for membership payment

- **Contact information**: A website address and e-mail address will allow users to contact you.

- **App title**: Apps and games are represented by titles and icons within the Windows Phone Marketplace. It is recommended that you consider the marketability of the title of your app or game. The app titles should:
    - Accurately represent the function of the app or game: Does the title accurately represent the app or game? Can a user quickly identify the purpose of the app from the title?
    - Be appealing and easy to remember: Is the title catchy? Does it stand out

from other titles with similar apps and games in the catalog?

❑ Be of the right length: Is the title too long? Will it fit in one line on the phone screen or will it be truncated? The suggested title length is between 11–15 characters. Titles that are longer than 15 characters may be truncated.

▶ **App description**: App and game descriptions are displayed on the App Details pages of the Windows Phone Marketplace, and may also be used for outbound marketing activities. The following are some best practices for writing descriptions:

❑ Keep the description brief

❑ Use simple, plainspoken language; write as if you were describing your application to a friend sitting next to you

❑ Highlight features that are exclusive to Windows Phone 7, if they are present

❑ Use bullet points to highlight features of the app and keep the bullet points brief; don't include more than six bullet points

❑ Proofread the description for spelling and grammar errors prior to submission

❑ If you are releasing an update to an application, don't reference the update at the top of the product description, unless you are highlighting a compelling new feature

❑ The language in which you write the description should match the language version of the application that you are submitting

▶ **Art**: The following is a list of some of the tiles and background artwork that can be extracted from your application to represent it in the Windows Phone Marketplace. It is not intended to be a definitive guide for creating merchandising assets such as marketing copy, logos, or screenshots, nor does it outline any specifications or requirements.

There are at least three pieces of artwork that represent your application or game. The following is a more detailed description of the artwork components of your application:

❑ **App tiles**: App tiles will be displayed as tiles in the main app tile screen for your app or game on the phone or on the marketplace.

❑ **App screenshots**: App screenshots convey the real look of your app or game in the Windows Phone Marketplace, so select scenes to demonstrate the best features and most attractive points of your app. At least one scene is required; you may use up to eight scene screenshots for previewing your app or game.

❑ **Background art**: This artwork will be used as the background panorama for your application if it is selected to be a featured app on the Windows Phone Marketplace.

▸ **XAP file**: The `xap` file created in Visual Studio 2010, or later, is the file that you submit on the App Hub. It contains the executable file plus all the resources needed by the application. Make sure that you are submitting the **release** version of the app.

▸ **App price**: Specific pricing strategies are recommended for various apps. For more information about app or game pricing, see the Windows Phone 7 App Hub FAQ at the following URL:

```
http://create.msdn.com/en-US/home/faq
```

▸ **App category**: A marketplace provides a choice of categories and top levels. The typical top-level categories are Games, Travel, Navigation, Finance, and Social. For more information, please take a look at the Application, at the following URL:

```
http://msdn.microsoft.com/en-us/library/hh202922(v=VS.92).aspx
```

 For detailed information, please refer to App Hub website at the following URL:
```
http://create.msdn.com/en-US/home/about/app_
submission_walkthrough#AppSubmissionChecklist
```

Submitting your application to the Marketplace

To make your application accessible to the whole world sounds exciting. At this stage, you have done all the development work and your application is ready to rock! From now, you only need to fill out some information in the App Hub website for submitting your application. In this chapter, you will know how to submit your application to the App Hub Marketplace step-by-step, hope you find all this interesting.

Getting ready

When you are ready to begin your submission, select the **Windows Phone** option from the **My Dashboard** menu. Click on the **Submit new app** link to start the application submission process.

Submitting your application consists of the following five steps:

1. Uploading the application
2. Providing the application description
3. Uploading the artwork
4. Setting the application pricing
5. Submitting the application

How to do it...

First, you will upload your `.XAP` package. The uploading of an application to the App Hub is a two-part process. First, you enter the basic app information and upload the `.XAP` file. After the `.XAP` file has been uploaded successfully, you can then add notes or instructions for the teams that test and certify the application.

1. Enter the following initial information for your application:

    -   **App name for App Hub**: In this field, you provide a name that uniquely identifies your app or game in the App Hub. The Application Title that will appear on the Windows Phone Marketplace will be entered during the second step: Provide the application Description.

    -   **Distribute to**: Select **Public Marketplace** for normal marketplace distribution, or **Private Beta Test** to have your application reviewed by people you select.

    -   **Browse to upload a file**: Click on **Browse** to locate your app on your computer and upload it as an XAP package. The upload process may take several minutes, depending on the size of the file and your Internet connection speed. Please make sure that your application is less than 225 MB and you have already set the language preference in **Project Properties | Application**, by clicking on the **Assembly Information** button in the window that pops up and selecting **Neutral Language** from a drop-down box control at the bottom.

    -   **App version number**: In this field, you need to select the version number of your app. Windows Phone Marketplace does not require any specific version numbering. However, a general guideline is to assign the version number in an increasing order, so that they correspond to major developments and minor upgrades in the application.

    -   **Requires technical exception?**: Select this option if your application requires an exception to the certification approval process for technical reasons. Submitting a technical exception will add several days to the certification approval process. Exception requests are not guaranteed to be approved, and should only be used in extenuating circumstances. This is an optional field. Click on the **Next** button to continue.

These options are depicted in the following screenshot:

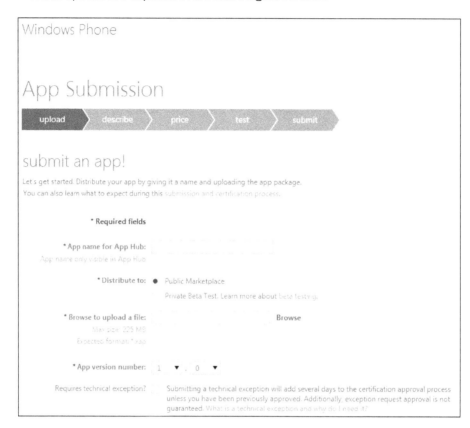

Next, you will provide details about your application that will appear on the Windows Phone Marketplace. If you are submitting a game, you can also provide ratings information for the game:

2. Provide the following information to submit your application. You will repeat these steps for each language that your .XAP package supports:

   ❑ **Category**: Use the drop-down boxes to select a category and subcategory for the type of application that you are submitting. The category that you select for your application may have tax implications that are associated with sales and royalties. Categories and subcategories are independent of the language or languages in your XAP file. Some categories don't have subcategories. For more information about categories, see the Windows Phone 7 App Hub FAQ.

   ❑ **(Language) app name**: This is filled in for you from the Title that you specified in the XAP file.

- **Short description**: You can provide a brief description that can be used to merchandise your app on the Windows Phone Marketplace and featured app listings. There is a 25-character limit to this description.

- **Detailed description**: You can provide a detailed description of the application and its functionality in this field. There is a 2,000-character limit to this description.

- **Keywords**: In this field, you can provide keywords that can be used to assist users in finding your application on the Windows Phone Marketplace. A maximum of five keywords can be used, separated by commas.

- **Legal URL**: A URL that links to legal terms, copyrights, or trademarks associated with your application. This field is optional.

- **Email address**: An e-mail address that consumers can use to contact you or your company with queries about this application. This field is optional.

- Click on the **Next** button to continue.

These are depicted in the following screenshot:

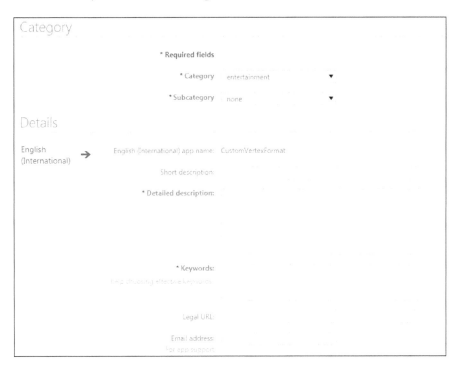

3. Next, you will upload the artwork associated with your application. All artwork must be in the .PNG format. Any artwork not customized to the resolutions specified on the following screen will not upload successfully:

- **Large mobile app tile**: This tile image is displayed when the consumer pins the tile to Start on the phone.

- **Small mobile app tile**: This tile image is displayed in the app list on the phone.

- **Large PC app tile**: This tile image is displayed in the Windows Phone Marketplace in the Zune PC client software.

- **Background art**: This panorama artwork becomes the background for your application if it is a featured app on the marketplace.

- **In app screenshots (8)**: These images provide a preview of your app or game to users who are browsing your app details page on Windows Phone Marketplace.

- Click on the **Next** button to continue.

These are depicted in the following screenshot:

4. Next, you will price your application and determine the markets in which it will be sold. You may want to consider tax implications when setting the price. The following are the things to keep in mind when setting the price and corresponding options:

    ❑ **Enable trials to be downloaded**: Select this check box if there is a trial edition of your application. Please refer to the following URL on how to create a trial application:

    ❑ `http://msdn.microsoft.com/en-us/library/ff967554(VS.92).aspx`

    ❑ **Select Price tier**: Select the price for your app in the currency of your developer account. Pricing in other countries/regions will be based on this price. In order to distribute your game or app for free, select a value of "0.00".

    ❑ **Worldwide distribution**: By default, your application will be distributed to all supported markets. When unchecked, you can manually select the countries or regions in which your application will be published.

    ❑ Click on the **Next** button to continue.

The options are shown in the following screenshot:

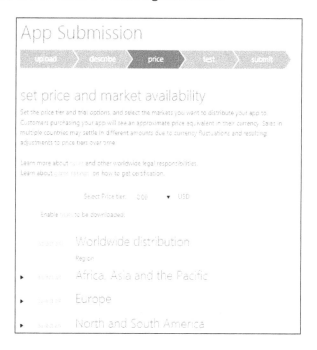

5. The final step is to submit your application. It allows you to review the details of your application before submitting it to Microsoft for getting the certification. The following information shows you the most important entries you should know to finalize the entire submission process:

- **Test notes or instructions**: Use this optional field to enter information that you want the certification testers to see. For example, if your app has unusual features or navigation, make note of those features or navigation in this field.

- **Publish options**: You can select how and when to publish your app. The following table shows the available options:

none	This is the default option. Your application cannot be submitted if you choose this option, but you can select Save and Quit and come back later to complete your submission.
As soon as it's certified	Your app will be published in the marketplace catalog as soon as it passes the certification.
As soon as it's certified, but make it hidden	This option can be used to make an application available for targeted distribution. Only people who have a deep link will be able to find your app in the Marketplace catalog; users who search for your app will not find it.
I will publish it manually after it has been certified	This option submits your application for certification, but after the certification is complete, the application will not appear in the Marketplace catalog until you manually submit it later. You can manually publish a certified but unpublished app by using a link inside your developer dashboard.

 For more details and the latest information, please refer to the following URL:

`http://create.msdn.com/en-US/home/about/app_submission_walkthrough_submit`

- ❑ When you are ready to submit your app, click on the **Submit** button. The submission will then be complete, and you can review your submissions at anytime in the dashboard.

The following screenshot shows the page that comes up when you click on the **Submit** button:

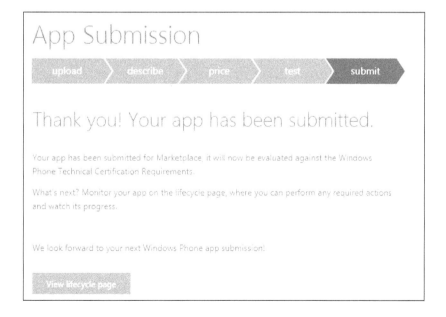

How it works...

You don't need to complete the submission process all at once; as soon as you begin, the information is stored in your account. If you decide to leave and return later, you can pick up where you left off by navigating to your app list, and then clicking on the **Edit details** link for any application with a status of **Submission in progress**. You can also select the application to see detailed information and additional action options, such as deleting the application.

After you submit your application, it will be tested for conformance to the certification requirements. If it fails the test, you will be e-mailed a report of the issues discovered, so that you can fix the problems and resubmit the application. If it passes the test, it will be published automatically if you select that option in the last step of the submission process. Otherwise, you can publish it from your app list at any time.

You can track downloads on your reports page in the dashboard, although see the **reporting FAQ** for detailed information at the following URL:

```
http://msdn.microsoft.com/library/hh202930(VS.92).
aspx#wp7faq480
```

Please follow the App Hub Marketplace regularly to get the latest information on application submitting, processing, and pricing.

Index

X

XAP file 412
XmlArray attribute 114
XML files
  processing 190
XMLImporter class 191
XMLReader object 194
XmlSerializer.Deserialize() method 115
XMLSerializer object 115, 194
XNA
  content processing flow 181

XNA content loading
  advantages 179
XNA content pipeline
  using, to reduce file size 397, 398

Y

yaw variable 87

Z

Zune software
  URL, for downloading 14

About Packt Publishing

Packt, pronounced 'packed', published its first book "*Mastering phpMyAdmin for Effective MySQL Management*" in April 2004 and subsequently continued to specialize in publishing highly focused books on specific technologies and solutions.

Our books and publications share the experiences of your fellow IT professionals in adapting and customizing today's systems, applications, and frameworks. Our solution based books give you the knowledge and power to customize the software and technologies you're using to get the job done. Packt books are more specific and less general than the IT books you have seen in the past. Our unique business model allows us to bring you more focused information, giving you more of what you need to know, and less of what you don't.

Packt is a modern, yet unique publishing company, which focuses on producing quality, cutting-edge books for communities of developers, administrators, and newbies alike. For more information, please visit our website: www.packtpub.com.

Writing for Packt

We welcome all inquiries from people who are interested in authoring. Book proposals should be sent to author@packtpub.com. If your book idea is still at an early stage and you would like to discuss it first before writing a formal book proposal, contact us; one of our commissioning editors will get in touch with you.

We're not just looking for published authors; if you have strong technical skills but no writing experience, our experienced editors can help you develop a writing career, or simply get some additional reward for your expertise.

XNA 4.0 Game Development by Example: Beginner's Guide – Visual Basic Edition

ISBN: 978-1-84969-240-3   Paperback: 424 pages

Create your own exciting games with Visual Basic and Microsoft XNA 4.0

1. Visual Basic edition of Kurt Jaegers' XNA 4.0 Game Development by Example. The first book to target Visual Basic developers who want to develop games with the XNA framework

2. Dive headfirst into game creation with Visual Basic and the XNA Framework

3. Four different styles of games comprising a puzzler, space shooter, multi-axis shoot 'em up, and a jump-and-run platformer

3D Graphics with XNA Game Studio 4.0

ISBN: 978-1-84969-004-1   Paperback: 292 pages

A step-by-step guide to adding the 3D graphics effects used by professionals to your XNA games

1. Improve the appearance of your games by implementing the same techniques used by professionals in the game industry

2. Learn the fundamentals of 3D graphics, including common 3D math and the graphics pipeline

3. Create an extensible system to draw 3D models and other effects, and learn the skills to create your own effects and animate them

Please check **www.PacktPub.com** for information on our titles

XNA 4.0 Game Development by Example

Create exciting games with Microsoft XNA 4.0

Beginner's Guide

Kurt Jaegers

XNA 4.0 Game Development by Example: Beginner's Guide

ISBN: 978-1-84969-066-9   Paperback: 428 pages

Create exciting games with Microsoft XNA 4.0

1. Dive headfirst into game creation with XNA

2. Four different styles of games comprising a puzzler, a space shooter, a multi-axis shoot 'em up, and a jump-and-run platformer

3. Games that gradually increase in complexity to cover a wide variety of game development techniques

4. Focuses entirely on developing games with the free version of XNA

Windows Phone 7.5 Data Cookbook

Over 30 recipes for storing, managing, and manipulating data in Windows Phone 7.5 Mango applications

Ramesh Thalli

Windows Phone 7.5 Data Cookbook

ISBN: 978-1-84969-122-2   Paperback: 224 pages

Over 30 recipes for storing, managing, and manipulating data in Windows Phone 7.5 Mango applications

1. Simple data binding recipes to advanced recipes for building scalable applications

2. Techniques for managing application data in Windows Phone mango apps

3. On-device data storage, cloud storage and API interaction.

Please check **www.PacktPub.com** for information on our titles